Small Cities,
Big Issues

SMALL CITIES, BIG ISSUES

Reconceiving Community
in a Neoliberal Era

Edited by Christopher Walmsley and Terry Kading

AU PRESS

Published by AU Press, Athabasca University
1200, 10011 – 109 Street, Edmonton, AB T5J 3S8
ISBN 978-1-77199-163-6 (pbk.)   ISBN 978-1-77199-164-3 (PDF)
ISBN 978-1-77199-165-0 (epub)   doi: 10.15215/aupress/9781771991636.01

Cover design by Martyn Schmoll
Interior design by Sergiy Kozakov
Printed and bound in Canada by Friesens

Library and Archives Canada Cataloguing in Publication

Small cities, big issues: reconceiving community in a neoliberal era / edited by
Christopher Walmsley and Terry Kading.

Includes bibliographical references.
Issued in print and electronic formats.

1. Small cities—Canada—Case studies. 2. Sociology, Urban—Canada—Case
studies. 3. Canada—Social conditions—Case studies. I. Walmsley, Christopher,
author, editor II. Kading, Terrance William, 1962-, author, editor

HT127.S63 2018   307.76'20971   C2016-907220-7
                                               C2016-907221-5

This book has been published with the help of a grant from the Federation for the
Humanities and Social Sciences, through the Awards to Scholarly Publications
Program, using funds provided by the Social Sciences and Humanities Research
Council of Canada.

We acknowledge the financial support of the Government of Canada for our
publishing activities and the assistance provided by the Government of Alberta
through the Alberta Media Fund.

Canada   Alberta
                Government

To Kico (2004–2017), homeless in Kamloops when we met him but whose presence in our lives made such a difference in all the years thereafter, and to all those individuals and community organizations whose collaborative efforts to improve our communities so often go unrecognized.

Contents

Part II Building Community

Acknowledgements

The authors gratefully acknowledge funding support from the Social Sciences and Humanities Research Council of Canada, through the Mapping Quality of Life and the Culture of Small Cities Community-University Research Alliance at Thompson Rivers University. We are grateful for the ongoing support provided by Will Garrett-Petts, associate vice-president, Research and Graduate Studies, and former project director of the Small Cities CURA. We also wish to thank Pamela Holway, senior acquisitions editor at Athabasca University Press, for her numerous editorial suggestions and her dedication to this book. Thanks to Ross Nelson for the maps found in this collection. And last but far from least, we extend our deepest appreciation to our partners, Lise Tessier and Keely McKibben, whose advice, support, and love made an immeasurable contribution to the book's completion.

SMALL CITIES, BIG ISSUES

Introduction

Small cities in Canada today confront serious social issues resulting from the neoliberal economic restructuring that began in the early 1980s. Drastic cutbacks in social programs, income supports, and the provision of affordable housing, combined with the offloading of social responsibilities onto the municipal level, have contributed to the generalization of social issues—most visibly, homelessness—once associated chiefly with our largest urban centres. Early acknowledgement of this trend came in 1999, with the introduction of the federal government's National Homelessness Initiative, the largest component of which was a program known as the Supporting Communities Partnership Initiative. Although most of the $305 million originally invested in this program was intended for Canada's ten largest urban centres, 20 percent was reserved for fifty-one smaller communities, all of which "had a demonstrable need to address homelessness" (Canada, HRDC 2003, 8).

The stubborn prevalence of both visible and hidden homelessness in all urban centres, irrespective of size, attests to the inadequacy of provincial and federal responses to issues such as drug and alcohol addiction, ineffective or absent mental health care, and the economic insecurity produced by precarious employment, all of which contribute to poverty and homelessness. Social and economic inequities are, moreover, exacerbated by the persistence of racist attitudes, directed not only against Indigenous peoples but also against racialized immigrants. In 2010, a federal report on immigration identified "a need for programming to address issues of racism and discrimination in Canada, given the increasing diversity of the population; the continued existence of racism and discrimination against newcomers and (visible) minorities; and the distribution of immigrants to rural areas and small cities, which have traditionally been comprised of fairly homogenous populations" (Canada, CIC 2010, ii).

In this collection, we reveal the broader forms of discrimination and social exclusion evident in local attitudes, policies, and actions directed towards individuals who are perceived as threats to mainstream values. We call into question the myth of Canada as a fair and just society, guided by principles of compassion, by exploring the social realities facing small cities in Canada. We aim to understand how citizens, community organizations, and local governments respond to the social challenges of urban life beyond the metropolis. We discuss community responses to social issues in small cities—whether they be exclusionary and reactionary or inclusionary and progressive and whether they take their shape from "big city" solutions or arise independently from local community action. We also uncover some of the distinctive attributes of the small city as it struggles to confront increasingly complex social issues arising from federal and provincial financial restraint and the effects of global economic restructuring.

Neoliberal Governance and the Small City

In Canada, as elsewhere, lower taxes, balanced budgets, an entrepreneurial environment, reduced government regulation, and the philosophy of small government have become the defining themes of governance. Following the federal lead, provincial governments have endorsed these themes and have oriented their policies towards increasing private sector investment and creating joint private-public sector initiatives. At its core, neoliberal policy aims to restore the profitability of the private sector—banks, corporations, local business initiatives—in response to the global economic problems that emerged in the 1970s and 1980s: high inflation and high unemployment, low or negative rates of growth, and rapidly accumulating government deficits. Neoliberalism seeks to address these problems by opening up new investment and consumption possibilities that are less constrained by government regulations and the limits of national markets (see Shutt 2005, 34–44).

Although the embrace of neoliberal policy has not necessarily reduced government spending, it has served to link the degree of government financial support for specific social initiatives to the fortunes of the broader economy. This has resulted in a "feast or famine" approach to government spending that entrenches a short horizon with respect to planning (Howlett, Netherton, and

Ramesh 1999, 271, 289). Under this approach, few areas of government activity are exempt from continuous adjustments or spending cuts in a period of economic uncertainty or decline. Although a wide range of government services continue to exist, they are prioritized such that when shifting economic conditions lead to the reduction of resources or increased costs in areas deemed essential, the result is spending reductions in areas considered expendable. In such circumstances, funding horizons become short and unpredictable, rendering long-term planning impossible. This reactive approach to policy making has a significant impact on local governments, which are always subject to precarious revenue transfers from higher levels of government and are generally able to raise additional revenues only through property taxes and user fees (Tindal and Tindal 2009, 207–16).

In this neoliberal environment, federal and provincial contributions as a percentage of municipal government revenues have drastically declined since the 1980s. As of 1990, federal and provincial funding accounted for 45.7 percent of local government revenues in Canada; by 1994, the figure had dropped to 25.4 percent, and by 2000, it stood at only 17.9 percent—a decline of over 60 percent in the space of a single decade (Tindal and Tindal 2009, 215). Referring to cities and communities as "collateral damage in the deficit war," the Federation of Canadian Municipalities (FCM) noted in 2013 that "like many successful campaigns, the 1990s' victory over the federal deficit came at a cost, and much of that cost was borne by Canada's cities and communities. By 2000 and the dawn of a new millennium, years of deficit fighting and downloading had left them weakened and struggling to meet their responsibilities" (FCM 2013, 8).

More than a decade into the new century, the FCM could identify only marginal improvements in government efforts to address the needs of cities and communities. It pointed instead to a "broken system" comprising "unfunded mandates" in the area of public safety, "inefficient policy and program design" in relation to investments in infrastructure, and "systemic ad-hockery" in the area of housing policy, with the last resulting in "growing cracks in Canada's housing market" that were "hurting communities, taxpayers, and the national economy" (FCM 2013, 24–25). As Robert Duffy, Gaetan Royer, and Charley Beresford (2014, 21–22) point out, the National Housing Act of 1944 stipulated that "the costs of land acquisition, public housing construction, operating costs and rental subsidies were to be shared on a 75 per cent federal / 25 per cent provincial basis." Today, not only do the federal and provincial governments fund fewer housing initiatives, but "projects that do get some support tend to require matching funds with each level of government contributing one third of the funding" (22). They go on to observe that "by itself, the transition from 75/25/0 per cent to 33/33/33 per cent would be a significant downloading if the same amount of money was being spent by the federal and provincial governments. But their funding cutbacks have left a gaping hole in our communities" (22–23).

Duffy, Royer, and Beresford (2014, 4) also note the steady decline in the federal government's share in capital investment, down from 34 percent in 1955 to only 13 percent in 2003, and the concomitant rise in the municipal share, from 27 percent to 48 percent. As they argue,

> Since the 1950s, Canada's infrastructure responsibilities have shifted from the level of government with the largest and most growth-responsive revenue base—the federal government—to the level of government with the smallest and least growth-responsive revenue base—local government. . . . Local governments are finding themselves picking up the slack on housing, mental health, addiction, social services, wastewater treatment, diking and flood management, drinking water and recreation infrastructure. (4)

The withdrawal of federal investment places an unfair burden on local governments, which must now rely on property taxes as their main source of income (McAllister 2004, 121, 126; Tindal and Tindal 2009, 215–16). Property taxes, by their nature, are highly visible and highly regressive in application, in contrast to tax rates based on income level. Moreover, the uses made of this income are subject to close critical examination by local taxpayers, and a broad local consensus is required if these taxes are to be committed to large and costly ventures. In order to be entertained, proposals for major projects presuppose a strong local confidence in the continued growth of both the population and the economic prosperity of the community. When such confidence exists, local governments may enjoy greater discretion in determining priorities and directing revenues towards a more aggressive social agenda. However, the caveat is that municipal governments must continue to rely heavily on property taxes to finance an increasingly broad social agenda.

At the same time, local governments are now compelled to play a much greater role in addressing their own infrastructure needs and fostering their own economic development by attracting investors, new residents, and tourists. Pressures for healthier and more sustainable environmental practices in planning infrastructure, as well as the need to contend with diverse social issues in the wake of federal and provincial offloading, add to the complexity of the municipal agenda. Whereas the residents of Canada's largest urban centres have long accepted that municipal governments have a responsibility to respond to local social issues, such as poverty, residents of small cities have looked to local government primarily to regulate land use, promote growth and development through bylaws, and provide a core set of services such as roads, sewage, snow removal, recreation, and so on. Small cities have only recently recognized the reality of local social needs, and this recognition has often arrived only because higher levels of government have provided some limited funding (through, for example, the National Homelessness Initiative or the Homelessness Partnering Strategy) as an incentive to address these needs. The extent to which small-city governments should be expected to fulfill social responsibilities is unclear and contested, particularly in the areas of health, social services, and housing. The reluctance to assume such responsibilities can be traced to the cost of developing and implementing social programs, to inadequate local capacities, and to the strongly held view that social programs are more properly the responsibility of the provincial government.

What Is a "Small" City?

Like all human communities, small cities are neither static nor uniform, a fact that complicates efforts at definition. Small cities are therefore often defined, at least initially, by population size. "Small" is, however, a relative term, and, with respect to cities, its meaning can vary depending on the size and distribution of the population in the country or region under study. For example, in a study of demographic change in small cities in the United States (Brennan, Hackler, and Hoene 2005), a "small" city is defined as one with a population of under 50,000; at the other end of the spectrum, a study titled "Creative Small Cities" (Waitt and Gibson 2009) focuses on the Australian city of Wollongong, which has a population of about 280,000. In short, no consensus exists as to the size of "small."

In the present work, we define a small city as an urban centre with a population in the range of 10,000 to 100,000—although we view these figures, particularly the upper one, with some degree of elasticity. This definition reflects categories originally adopted by the Federation of Canadian

Municipalities. Historically, the FCM's Rural Forum was composed of communities with fewer than 10,000 residents, while the FCM's Big Cities Mayors' Caucus represented urban areas with at least 100,000 residents, which were subdivided into medium-sized cities (those with a population of 100,000 to 450,000) and large cities (those with a population over 450,000) (Viaud 2008, 7–8). By default, then, communities of between 10,000 and 100,000 residents must be small cities.[1] And yet the upper limit is necessarily fluid. As the 2016 census revealed, not only is Canada's population growing, but it is also becoming more urban (Press 2017). Given that "small" is defined in relation to "large," as cities as a whole grow larger, what qualifies as "small" will likewise grow larger. Thus, a city whose population exceeds 100,000 may nonetheless remain a (relatively) small city. With a population (in 2016) of 127,380, for example, Kelowna is small in relation to metropolitan Victoria (population 367,770), which is itself small in relation to metropolitan Vancouver (2,463,461) (see figure i.1).[2]

The drawback of defining a small city by population alone is, of course, that such an approach misses important qualitative dimensions. As David Bell and Mark Jayne (2006a, 4–5) point out, "smallness is as much about reach and influence as it is about population size." Smallness, they argue, can also be understood as "a state of mind, an attitude, a disposition" (3): it is about "ways of acting, self-image, the sedimented structures of feeling, sense of place and aspiration" (5). A small city thus possesses a habitus distinct from that of a large city, one that may reflect an element of defensiveness, given the common conviction that "cities should be big things, either amazing or terrifying in their bigness, but big nonetheless" (5). Small cities thus constitute "a strange in-between category, neither one thing (rural) nor the other (properly urban)" (5). Similarly, W. F. Garrett-Petts and Lon Dubinsky (2005, 2) see small cities as occupying a third space "in the shadow of large cosmopolitan cities but still bound by rural history and traditions." As they point out, with respect

---

1 This definition parallels Statistics Canada's definition of a "census agglomeration," which must have a core population of at least 10,000—while a community of 100,000 or more is deemed to be a "census metropolitan area." Since a community clearly need not have a population as large as 100,000 in order to constitute a city, one could argue that what Statistics Canada calls a census agglomeration is, in fact, a small city.

2 Population figures are available at "Census Profile, 2016 Census," *Statistics Canada*, http://www12.statcan.gc.ca/census-recensement/2016/dp-pd/prof/index.cfm?Lang=E (last updated 30 November 2017).

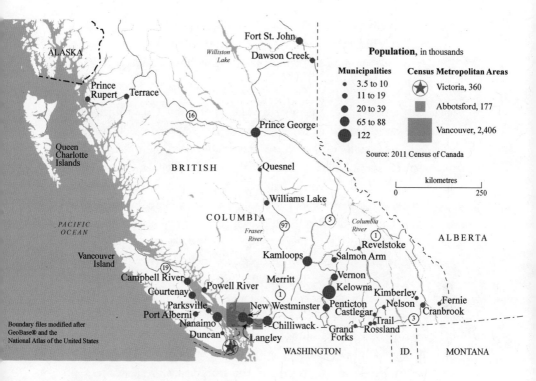

Figure i.1. Small cities in British Columbia

to culture, the small city tends to lose out in this comparison: "Big cities are commonly equated with 'big culture'; small cities with something less" (1). Whereas concert halls, museums, and major art galleries are standard features of a big city, in a small city the main cultural venue might be a local church, a high school auditorium, a university classroom, a main street pub, or donated space in a warehouse.

Descriptive comparisons of large and small cities have also been undertaken in an effort to capture the distinctive qualities of the small city. For example, Kent Robertson (2001, 11–12) suggests that, in comparison to the downtown core of large cities, small-city downtowns

- are more human scale, less busy, more walkable
- do not exhibit the problems of big cities—congestion, crime, etc.
- aren't dominated by corporate presence
- lack large-scale flagship or signature projects
- have retailing distinguished by independents

- aren't subdivided into monofunctional districts
- are closely linked to nearby residential neighbourhoods
- possess higher numbers of intact historic buildings. (Summarized in Bell and Jayne 2006a, 8)

Such a list clearly aims to paint an appealing portrait of the small city. It is useful, however, because it suggests some of the sources of small-city problems. No doubt small-city downtowns are less congested, more compact, and thus relatively easy to navigate on foot. At the same time, public transportation options may be limited, which significantly reduces the mobility of poorer residents as well as many senior citizens. In addition, while commercial areas and residential neighbourhoods are indeed often contiguous, this proximity can generate intense competition for control over physical space, pitting local business interests and homeowners against homeless people, panhandlers, addicts, or those involved in the sex trade. Such conflicts over space aggravate the NIMBY ("not in my backyard") reaction and thus intensify resistance to efforts to establish local support services and low-income housing. The lack of buffer zones is a distinguishing feature of small cities, and their spatial configuration not only exacerbates underlying social tensions but also affects how local government, community groups, and marginalized residents respond to these tensions.

Today's small city is often emerging from a history as a small town or village, a transition characterized by a growing population, an increase in the pace of development, and the gradual diversification of the local economy. With the construction of new neighbourhoods and suburbs and the addition of a larger range of retail, education, health, and social services, what was formerly a small town is transformed into a small city. It now boasts a level of occupational diversity and social stratification that clearly distinguishes it from a town, and yet it retains a "small town" feel and a sense of community that is often missing in large urban centres. Although it is far from being a metropolis, it finds itself faced with urban challenges not uncommon to big cities.

At this point in its history, the small city can be viewed as having many, although not necessarily all, of the following characteristics:

- It relies on a mixed economy (rather than on a single industry).
- Its retail sector includes "big box" and chain stores that serve a surrounding region of small towns, villages, and rural areas.

- It functions as a regional centre for health, education, social, cultural, and entertainment services.
- It provides provincial and federal government services to the surrounding area.
- It is home to a university or college.
- It has a public transit system.
- Its city council, community organizations, and local media recognize that there are social problems such as homelessness, street addictions, and visible poverty and that these require a civic response.

Owing in part to the impact of neoliberal policies, many small cities are presently in the throes of both demographic change and economic transition, shifts that have contributed to a sense of social disruption, as new forces impinge on familiar patterns of interaction. And yet research exploring the quality of life in small cities has been slow to emerge. Through its Quality of Life Reporting System, the FCM collects data regarding a series of variables, but its member communities, which currently number twenty-four, generally have populations of at least 200,000.[3] Data are therefore not collected concerning the quality of life in smaller cities. Although Gilles Viaud, of Thompson Rivers University, has developed a "quality of place" reporting system for small cities (Viaud 2011), detailed analyses are not yet available.

Indeed, a comment made more than three decades ago by Jorge Hardoy and David Satterthwaite—namely, that small cities are among "the least studied and perhaps the least understood elements within national and regional urban systems" (1986, 6)—remains largely true today. Relatively recent research on small cities (see, for example, Bell and Jayne 2006b; Bonifacio and Drolet 2016; Garrett-Petts 2005; Knox and Mayer 2009; Ofori-Amoah 2007) has examined a wide array of issues, including community identity, lifestyle, cultural development, cultural symbols, urban geography, immigration and demographic change, the political and cultural economy, downtown

3 "Member Communities," *Federation of Canadian Municipalities*, 2017, https://fcm. ca/home/programs/quality-of-life-reporting-system/member-communities.htm. The variables are demographics, affordable and appropriate housing, civic engagement, community and social infrastructure, education, employment and local economy, natural environment, personal and community health, personal financial security, and personal safety. "FCM QOLRS Indicators," *Federation of Canadian Municipalities*, 2017, https://fcm.ca/Documents/reports/FCM/QORLS_Indicators_EN.pdf.

revitalization, and sustainability. Although this research has, to some extent, recognized a specifically social dimension to small-city life, discussions of social issues still tend to take place in the context of a primary focus on the economic, environmental, and cultural dimensions of small cities. A comprehensive consideration of the variety of social issues that beset small cities has been lacking, particularly with respect to homelessness, poverty, racism, and social exclusion.

Interrogating Community

Historically, life in smaller urban centres has been approached from the vantage point of community rather than of local government, marginalized groups, or social issues. Between the late 1930s and the early 1970s, social surveyors, social anthropologists, social geographers, sociologists, and political scientists, chiefly in Britain and United States, produced scores of studies that explored community as a central concept (Day 2006, 26). Building upon the foundational work of Ferdinand Tönnies, Émile Durkheim, Max Weber, and Karl Marx, this research was set against the backdrop of a rapidly disappearing European rural peasantry and its replacement by an urban industrial workforce. Within the framework of this transformation, rural and urban, traditional and modern, interdependent and individualistic became dichotomous categories within which to understand and evaluate social life. Rural, traditional, and interdependent were clearly regarded as positive—the hallmarks of genuine community (or what Tönnies and Weber called *Gemeinschaft*)—whereas urban, modern, and individualistic were seen as negative and associated with emerging forms of social life characterized by instrumentality, alienation, and anomie.

These studies generally focused on rural or village communities, small towns, or working-class communities embedded in large industrial cities (although not on these cities as a whole). As Day (2006, 26) points out, these studies were "a holistic enterprise," one that "aimed at a total understanding of a community's nature" and provided "standards of desirable social relations." Implied in these studies was the idea of a "good life" that was in danger of vanishing and thus needed to be preserved. Robert Lynd and Helen Lynd's classic study of Muncie, Indiana, published as *Middletown* (1929), was the first to turn an anthropological lens on life in a "typical" American town. In a similar study (Warner and Lunt 1941), Newburyport, Massachusetts, was rechristened "Yankee City" and was presented as a microcosm of American community life. In both cases, however, researchers chose to study homogeneous communities, ones that lacked racial and ethnic divisions (Day 2006, 34). In Canada, research was conducted during the early 1950s in an affluent suburban Toronto community (given the pseudonym "Crestwood Heights"), whose 17,000 residents were partly Christian (60%) and partly Jewish (40%). The suburb was deemed to be a community on the strength of local relationships forged within schools, churches, community centres, clubs, and associations (Seeley, Sim, and Loosly 1956).[4]

Among these early community studies, two were particularly significant. One was Floyd Hunter's *Community Power Structure: A Study of Decision Makers* (1953), which was based on research conducted in "Regional City" (that is, Atlanta, Georgia). Hunter found that those who exercised power over community policy were for the most part not the formal leaders of local institutions and organizations; rather, control lay in the hands of a small, closely knit group, consisting primarily of businessmen, whose decision making was dominated by economic interests. A decade later, Roland Warren's *The Community in America* (first published in 1963) recognized the power of external influences—not only economic but political or cultural as well—on local communities. Warren (1978, 52) observed an "increasing orientation of local community units towards extracommunity systems of which they are a part, with a corresponding decline in community cohesion and autonomy."

In short, as Graham Day (2006, 33) notes, the village, town, or small city was no longer "a self-sufficient, inward-looking milieu, capable of commanding the commitment and loyalty of its inhabitants and meeting the majority of their needs," which is how small towns often present themselves. It was now a

---

4 Subsequent decades saw the appearance of few additional Canadian studies, among them *Little Communities and Big Industries* (Bowles 1982), a volume devoted to a familiar Canadian setting, the single-industry town. The essays in the collection explored the fabric of social life in communities—often located in northern or remote areas— that were economically dependent upon a single-resource extraction industry such as forestry, mining, or oil. In 2004, James Giffen's research from the 1940s was published as *Rural Life: Portraits of the Prairie Town, 1946* (Giffen 2004). Giffen studied three Manitoba communities, one primarily British, one primarily Ukrainian, and the third a mixture of citizens whose origins were British, Mennonite, French Métis, and Polish. Undertaken on behalf of the Manitoba Royal Commission on Adult Education, his research provided a perspective on how rural social structures affected literacy in the dominant culture.

unit enmeshed within the social structures and systems of the larger society, in which a sense of community was in steady decline. The loss of the option to remain "self-sufficient" and "inward-looking" suggests one of the challenges confronting small cities today: their circumstances are increasingly influenced by external forces—the powers of other levels of government, trends within larger cities, and the global economy—all of which not only exacerbate local social problems but also limit the autonomy that small cities can exercise in addressing these problems.

Starting in the 1970s, intellectual interest in community went into a period of relative dormancy, but, by the 1990s, social and political developments—including the collapse of the welfare state, globalization, and the growth of an ethic of competition and self-interest—had brought it back into prominence (Luloff and Krannich 2002, 1–2). In *The Third Way: The Renewal of Social Democracy* (1998), Anthony Giddens urges a stronger focus on personal responsibility and active citizenship, with communities as the cornerstone of a new progressivism. Writing in a somewhat more conservative vein, the Israeli-American sociologist Amitai Etzioni continues to expound a communitarian philosophy that seeks to reconcile liberal individualism with a commitment to community and emphasizes the link between rights and responsibilities and the need to revitalize traditional values (see, for example, Etzioni 2014). It is the work of Lena Dominelli, however, that holds particular relevance for our understanding of community responses to today's social challenges.

As Dominelli (2007, 7) observes, communities form around a shared interest or objective, a particular identity, a shared physical space, or some combination of these, and they are defined by including those who possess the shared trait and excluding those who do not, thereby creating insiders and outsiders. This leads to the exclusionary process of othering, which Dominelli defines as "an active process of interaction that relies on the (re) creation of dyadic social relations where one group is socially dominant and the others subordinate" (8). In the process of othering, "physical, social and cultural attributes are treated as signifiers of inferiority in social relations where social encounters perpetuate the domination of one group by another. During this interaction, the dominant group is constructed as 'subject,' the oppressed group as 'object'" (8–9). Stated otherwise, implicit in the division between insiders and outsiders on which communities depend for meaning is a hierarchy, in which the dominance of one community rests on its ability to consign nonmembers (the Other) to a position of inferiority. The mechanism of othering is particularly useful in understanding the lines of fracture in small cities.

In the context of Canada, this more critical perspective on community was evident as early as 1991, in David Rayside's study of Alexandria, a small industrial town of 3,500 at the far eastern tip of Ontario, not far from the Québec border. In *A Small Town in Modern Times*, Rayside set out to analyze social dynamics and power relationships, with a view to evaluating the town's image of itself as a caring, mutually supportive community. While acknowledging that the town was "in many ways a warm and humane place to live and work," Rayside found Alexandria to be a "highly fragmented society," its population "generally passive in the face of inequality" and its municipal politics "particularly resistant to new ideas" (1991, 299). Status and influence in the community were shaped by one's position in the world of production and tended to be hereditary, feminism had made little impact on traditional gender roles, and tensions existed between English- and French-speaking residents, who remained largely segregated. "Alexandria cannot become a fundamentally egalitarian society," Rayside concluded, "when the structural patterns of the larger society in which it is lodged entrench inequality between classes, between men and women, and between regions" (299). The same might be said of contemporary small cities, many of which evolved from communities such as Alexandria.

Less insular than earlier studies, newer analyses of community have adopted a more critical stance and take into account the effects of globalization, as well as of national, provincial, and local politics. No longer is community regarded as a feature of the past that simply needs to be resurrected and recaptured; instead, it is understood as something that must be created anew, within the framework of contemporary conditions. Divisions, inequities, and discrimination are now well recognized as challenges that citizens and local governments have no choice but to confront if they hope to build a more inclusive, more fundamentally egalitarian social environment.

Assessing the Collateral Damage

The term *community* has become part of the standard rhetoric of contemporary governments. The word conveys positive feelings and images and suggests aspirations to inclusivity and the willingness to address the needs of the whole.

At a more concrete level, however, the definition of community is highly contested. In the context of a small city, who constitutes "the community" at any given time is expressed both through the local government policies or initiatives already in place and through a corresponding silence (that is, the lack of policies or initiatives) regarding the needs of certain groups. Local government thus plays a critical role in inclusionary or exclusionary policies and practices implicit in which is a vision of who is genuinely part of the community. For example, the mandates of municipal committees or sub-committees send messages about which civic issues—and which groups of people—are deemed worthy of concern, as does the presence (or absence) of social development programs with staff already in place. Similarly, the annual allocation of resources to various local initiatives reveals much about a municipality's priorities and guiding values. In addition, the visible engagement of the mayor and members of city council with the city's social agenda speaks not merely to the relative strength of local advocacy but also to its potential for success in soliciting funding from higher levels of government.

As this collection reveals, through participation in nonprofit organizations and local government committees, many individuals and community groups have worked hard to resolve local social issues and advocate for more inclusive policies and programs. Their ongoing efforts open the door to new methods of community engagement and challenge local governments to acknowledge and respond to a broader set of voices. Despite significant efforts and planning, however, the broader fiscal environment within which small cities must operate places substantial constraints—both financial and jurisdictional—on success. Even though higher levels of government trumpet the virtues of community initiatives and local leadership, neither Ottawa nor the provinces have historically shown themselves willing to commit the necessary resources and thus to contribute to the creation of the healthy communities they extol.

The social realities now confronting small cities—homelessness, the impacts of deinstitutionalization, street addictions, the need for parolee integration, the sex trade, homophobia, systemic racism and discrimination, Indigenous–non-Indigenous relations, growing poverty—have received too little attention in the scholarly literature. In this collection, we highlight not merely the extent to which small cities have had to contend with these issues but, more importantly, how qualities peculiar to the small city influence the development of these social issues and alter or limit the possible solutions. We approach our examination of these issues from a number of scholarly perspectives—social work, political science, history, and sociology—to provide an integrated picture of the small-city experience in the twenty-first century. The chapters in the first part, "Displacement, Isolation, and the Other," examine the social consequences of neoliberal restructuring. As the federal government has sought to cut costs by reducing or eliminating support for social programs, and as provincial governments have followed suit, social tensions and inequities have been heightened. In the context of small cities, the result has been a process of social fragmentation, which is visible in the emergence of displaced and isolated sectors of the community. Ironically, this process is often aggravated by municipal efforts to solve the problem, especially those that rest on criminalizing behaviour deemed to be disruptive. The chapters in the second part, "Building Community," thus explore more constructive ways in which small cities might respond to growing social and economic disparities. In this respect, the very smallness of small cities is an advantage, since it opens the possibility of grassroots citizen participation of the sort associated with direct democracy. Policies that foster exclusion simply reinforce the lack of understanding on which xenophobia and othering thrive. Small-city governments are in a position to develop approaches to problem solving that would reduce fear and promote compassion.

In the end, what emerges from this overview is the degree to which government in Canada has, in recent decades, chosen to abandon the country's traditional aspirations to compassion, fairness, and social justice and instead to emulate the policies of our neighbour to the south, thereby rendering our nation ever more indistinguishable from the United States. We have witnessed the offloading of social responsibilities onto the local level, with higher levels of government evincing little commitment to long-term solutions to the social problems now besetting our cities, small and large. Although government rhetoric constantly affirms the importance of "healthy communities" and "sustainable solutions," the visible evidence points to the hollowness of such language. In the face of homelessness, growing poverty, and mounting social tensions, we are increasingly unable to deny the destructive consequences of several decades of neoliberal rule, as well as the limited capacity of local governments to solve these problems on their own.

In its second annual report on the state of our country's cities and communities, the Federation of Canadian Municipalities (FCM 2013, 23) rightly concluded that "Canada can no longer afford to have its governments continue working at cross-purposes, or in isolation, or toward short-term political fixes." The results had become all too obvious. "The time has come," the report declared, "for new and innovative thinking and political courage. It's no longer enough to say that the system is broken, the time has come to fix it" (23). Five years later, with the Liberals in power and a new National Housing Strategy officially released, there may be some cause for optimism—but it is too early to celebrate the demise of neoliberalism, a philosophy that has little use for empathy. We in Canada take considerable pride in our reputation as a country guided by compassion, a respect for difference, and a sense of fairness. We believe these qualities set us apart from other nations. Yet we face a widening gap between the convictions and the reality. As the future of the affluent continues to be secured at the expense of those less fortunate, perhaps we need to revisit our self-image and ask how far our present policies have undermined our ideals.

References

Bell, David, and Mark Jayne. 2006a. "Conceptualizing Small Cities." In Bell and Jayne 2006b, 1–18.

———, eds. 2006b. *Small Cities: Urban Experience Beyond the Metropolis*. London and New York: Routledge.

Bonifacio, Glenda Tibe, and Julie L. Drolet, eds. 2016. *Canadian Perspectives on Immigration in Small Cities*. Cham, Switzerland: Springer International.

Bowles, Roy T., ed. 1982. *Little Communities and Big Industries: Studies in the Social Impact of Canadian Resource Extraction*. Toronto: Butterworths.

Brennan, Christiana, Darrene Hackler, and Christopher Hoene. 2005. "Demographic Change in Small Cities, 1990 to 2000." *Urban Affairs Review* 40 (3): 342–61.

Canada. CIC (Citizenship and Immigration Canada). 2010. *Evaluation of the Welcoming Communities Initiative*. August. Ottawa: Citizenship and Immigration Canada. http://www.cic.gc.ca/english/pdf/research-stats/ER201103_05E_WCI.pdf.

Canada. HRDC (Human Resources Development Canada). 2003. *Evaluation of the National Homelessness Initiative: Implementation and Early Outcomes of the HRDC-Based Components*. May. Ottawa: Human Resources Development Canada. http://publications.gc.ca/collections/Collection/RH63-2-203-03-03E.pdf.

Day, Graham. 2006. *Community and Everyday Life*. London and New York: Routledge.

Dominelli, Lena. 2007. "Globalising Communities: Players and Non-players." In
    Revitalising Communities in a Globalising World, edited by Lena Dominelli, 7–16.
    Aldershot, UK: Ashgate.

Duffy, Robert, Gaetan Royer, and Charley Beresford. 2014. *Who's Picking Up the*
    Tab? Federal and Provincial Downloading onto Local Governments. Vancouver:
    Columbia Institute, Centre for Civic Governance.

Etzioni, Amitai. 2014. *The New Normal: Finding a Balance Between Individual Rights*
    and the Common Good. New Brunswick, NJ: Transaction.

FCM (Federation of Canadian Municipalities). 2007. *Losing Ground: Canada's*
    Cities and Communities at the Tipping Point. Ottawa: Federation of Canadian
    Municipalities.

———. 2013. *The State of Canada's Cities and Communities 2013: Opening a New*
    Chapter. Ottawa: Federation of Canadian Municipalities.

Garrett-Petts, W. F., ed. 2005. *The Small Cities Book: On the Cultural Future of Small*
    Cities. Vancouver: New Star Books.

Garrett-Petts, W. F., and Lon Dubinsky. 2005. "'Working Well, Together': An
    Introduction to the Cultural Future of Small Cities." In Garrett-Petts, *Small Cities*
    Book, 1–14.

Giddens, Anthony. 1998. *The Third Way: The Renewal of Social Democracy*.
    Cambridge, UK: Polity Press.

Giffen, P. James. 2004. *Rural Life: Portraits of the Prairie Town, 1946*. Edited by
    Gerald Friesen. Winnipeg: University of Manitoba Press.

Hardoy, Jorge E., and David Satterthwaite. 1986. "Why Small and Intermediate
    Urban Centres?" In *Small and Intermediate Urban Centres: Their Role in Regional*
    and National Development in the Third World, edited by Jorge E. Hardoy and
    David Satterthwaite, 1–17. London: Hodder and Stoughton.

Howlett, Michael, Alex Netherton, and M. Ramesh. 1999. *The Political Economy of*
    Canada. 2nd ed. Don Mills, ON: Oxford University Press.

Hunter, Floyd. 1953. *Community Power Structure: A Study of Decision Makers*.
    Chapel Hill, NC: University of North Carolina Press.

Knox, Paul, and Heike Mayer. 2009. *Small Town Sustainabililty: Economic, Social,*
    and Environmental Innovation. Basel, Switzerland: Birkhauser.

Luloff, A. E., and R. S. Krannich. 2002. "Introduction." In *Persistence and Change in*
    Rural Communities: A 50-Year Follow-up Study to Six Classic Studies, edited by A.
    E. Luloff and R. S. Krannich, 1–8. New York: CABI.

Lynd, Robert S., and Helen M. Lynd. 1929. *Middletown: A Study of American*
    Culture. New York: Harcourt Brace.

McAllister, Mary Louise. 2004. *Governing Ourselves? The Politics of Canadian*
    Communities. Vancouver: University of British Columbia Press.

Ofori-Amoah, Benjamin, ed. 2007. *Beyond the Metropolis: Urban Geography As If Small Cities Mattered*. Lanham, MD: University Press of America.

Press, Jordan. 2017. "Canada 2016 Census Data: Canada Is the Fastest Growing Country in G7." *Huffington Post*, 8 February. http://www.huffingtonpost. ca/2017/02/08/canada-census-growth_n_14638052.html.

Rayside, David M. 1991. *A Small Town in Modern Times: Alexandria, Ontario*. Montréal and Kingston: McGill-Queen's University Press.

Robertson, Kent. 2001. "Downtown Development Principles for Small Cities." In *Downtowns: Revitalizing the Centers of Small Urban Communities*, edited by Michael A. Burayidi, 9–22. London and New York: Routledge.

Seeley, John R., R. Alexander Sim, and Elizabeth W. Loosley. 1956. *Crestwood Heights: A Study of the Culture of Suburban Life*. Toronto: University of Toronto Press.

Shutt, Harry. 2005. *The Decline of Capitalism*. London: Zed Books.

Tindal, C. Richard, and Susan Nobes Tindal. 2009. *Local Government in Canada*. 7th ed. Toronto: Nelson Education.

Viaud, Gilles. 2008. "The Challenge of Defining a National Urban Strategy in the Context of Divergent Demographic Trends in Small and Large Canadian Cities." Paper presented at the annual meeting of the Western Division of the Canadian Association of Geographers, Bellingham, WA, 6–8 March 2008. http://content. wwu.edu/cdm/compoundobject/collection/wdcag/id/152.

———. 2011. "The Small City Quality of Place Reporting System Project: Guiding Principles and Implementation Guidelines." *Small Cities Imprint* 3 (1): 52–58.

Waitt, Gordon, and Chris Gibson. 2009. "Creative Small Cities: Rethinking the Creative Economy in Place." *Urban Studies* 46 (5–6): 1223–46.

Warner, W. Lloyd, and Paul S. Lunt. 1941. *The Social Life of a Modern Community*. New Haven, CT: Yale University Press.

Warren, Roland L. 1978. *The Community in America*. 3rd ed. Lanham, MD: University Press of America.

Part I
Displacement, Isolation, and the Other

1 Homelessness in Small Cities

The Abdication of Federal Responsibility

Terry Kading and Christopher Walmsley

Homelessness. We see it in our parks, on our streets, and in our alleys. But these are just the public faces of the issue. Homelessness also hides in tents and beneath bridges; it sleeps in shelters and eats in soup kitchens. Sometimes it moves from couch to couch, bouncing between friends and family members. Sometimes homelessness is born in the middle of the night as a woman flees from violence, or on a cold afternoon after the EI runs out and the rent is late. (HAP Steering Committee 2010, 3)

Homelessness has become a standard feature of Canada's urban landscape. That people should be obliged to live on the streets is inexcusable in a wealthy country, one capable of providing housing for the entire population. In a country of long and extremely frigid winters, continuing to tolerate homelessness is fundamentally inhumane. Although, over roughly the past two decades, measures have been undertaken by both the federal and provincial governments to address homelessness, these have so far proved inadequate to solve the problem, particularly in the face of other trends in government that work to exacerbate it. From the standpoint of public policy, homelessness is one result of the triumph of a neoliberal market ideology, with its fixation on minimizing public expenditures, in part through the privatization of social services. As has long been recognized, however, in the absence of public subsidies, no incentive exists for the private sector to build low-cost housing, which is precisely why the federal government originally intervened in the housing market. Simply put, the private sector typically shows little interest in manufacturing products (including houses) or providing services for people who cannot afford to purchase them at standard market rates.

It is also well established that the costs of homelessness far outweigh the costs of providing adequate shelter to individuals in need. In testimony provided in June 2007 to the Standing Senate Committee on Social Affairs, Science, and Technology, Kim Kerr, then the executive director of Vancouver's Downtown Eastside Residents' Association, commented: "People should be pushed to do something simply out of humanity, but if you want to talk about money, it costs $48,000 a year to leave someone on the street. It costs $28,000 a year to house them. That argument has been around for a long time. It does not seem to make any difference" (Canada, Parliament, Senate 2009, 107). Estimates of the cost differential vary, of course, depending on time and place. In 2008, for example, researchers at Simon Fraser University concluded that it costs BC taxpayers at least $55,000 per year to allow an adult with severe addictions and/or mental illness to remain on the streets, as opposed to $37,000 to provide such an individual with adequate housing and support services (Patterson et al. 2008, 10–11). Among the costs of homelessness are increased demands on health care services (often emergency ones), expenses related to the construction and operation of temporary shelters, and additional burdens on police forces and the legal system, many consequent on local bylaws that attempt to criminalize the homeless. But these are merely the quantifiable costs: the human costs are incalculable.

Yet, despite these realities, federal funding for national homelessness initiatives has steadily dwindled over the years, a trend reversed only in the March 2017 budget, with its announcement of a new National Housing Strategy. In addition, in order to access funding, individual municipalities have been expected to develop and then implement a local "homelessness plan." Communities have, in other words, been compelled to enter directly into the complexities of social planning and health policy—areas in which higher levels of government have historically assumed leadership. Small cities have limited financial resources, however, and they often lack the planning expertise required to formulate and implement effective strategies. Moreover, their jurisdictional authority is limited.

In comparison to small cities, major urban centres, some of which boast long-established social planning departments, generally have considerable experience with housing policy, as well as a greater array of options for generating new streams of revenue. They are thus in a somewhat better position to undertake homelessness initiatives—although even they have been unable to reverse the situation.[1] Quite apart from their relatively limited capacities and resources, however, local municipalities also have less flexibility and autonomy than larger cities: they are obliged to rely more heavily on the largesse and the good will of federal and provincial governments in order to make substantive inroads in addressing homelessness. This dependence introduces a highly unpredictable variable into the planning process in small cities, no matter how committed the local government may be to addressing the long-term needs of the homeless population. As a result of this contingency, whether one is attempting to evaluate a small city in contrast to larger urban centres or simply in terms of the effectiveness of its own initiatives, it is difficult to draw firm conclusions simply by looking at statistical outcomes, such as the degree of decline observed in the rate of homelessness over a given period.

In other words, to be meaningful, evaluations of relative success or failure must take into account the context within which specific responses are situated. The immediate sources of homelessness, the magnitude and demographics of the homeless population, and the local political, social, and economic forces that influence attempts at solutions—all these play a role in outcomes. In addition to estimating numbers, homeless counts, which now occur on a fairly regular basis, provide profiles of the homeless population in specific small cities. Municipal reports and planning documents, media coverage, and interviews with city planners also offer insights into local circumstances and constraints, as well as into the scale of gains. At the same time, one must recognize that neither large cities nor small ones can be expected to resolve the underlying causes of homelessness, responsibility for which resides elsewhere. In the words of one recent study, "Municipalities require a strategic federal response that addresses the underlying structural causes of

---

1 A recent study of homelessness initiatives in four major Canadian cities—Ottawa, Toronto, Calgary, and Vancouver—found, for example, that these cities had failed to achieve "sustained reductions in the number of individuals and families experiencing homelessness every year." Indeed, evidence suggests that, in some cities, "homelessness is growing among certain sub-populations, including families, youth and seniors" (Adamo et al. 2016, 3).

poverty, precarious housing and homelessness" (Adamo et al. 2016, 4). The reason that local governments now find themselves on the front line of the homelessness issue is, in short, rooted in policies devised and pursued by higher levels of government.

In what follows, we examine the origins of the homelessness crisis in Canada and its impact on small cities. We focus, in particular, on four small cities in British Columbia—Kamloops, Kelowna, Nanaimo, and Prince George—all of which have been obliged to embark on social planning initiatives in the face of growing homeless populations. By reflecting on these local responses, we hope to shed light on the consequences of the broader devolution of responsibility onto municipal governments, which are now held accountable for developing solutions to social problems not ultimately of their own creation.

Homelessness Policy in Canada: From National Programs to Local Initiatives

The increasingly visible presence of homeless individuals on the streets of cities and towns across Canada is not something over which we as a nation have had no control. Rather, the rising rates of homelessness are a result of deliberate policy changes instituted over the past several decades by the federal government, as well as by provincial administrations. Writing at the turn of the millennium, Barbara Murphy (2000, 19) succinctly summed up the main determinants of homelessness:

> At the root of homelessness is poverty and the shocking reality that we are now tolerating a level of poverty that leaves so many without a roof over their head. Beyond the root cause of poverty we also tolerate a housing situation in our cities that provides little or no accommodation the poor can afford. The formula is simple—combine a growing number of poor and a growing number of expensive housing units and we have people on the streets. Add to this a failure to recognize that the mentally ill cannot manage on their own, economically or with even the simplest of life's demands, and we have even more people on the streets.

As Murphy implies, without a shift both in public attitudes and in housing policy, the problem of homelessness will continue to grow, as indeed it has. Social and economic forces have cooperated to generate what Richard Florida (2017) calls "a crisis of gentrification, rising inequality and increasingly unaffordable urban housing," with rising prices far outstripping income growth (see Demographia 2017, 19–22). This situation has been exacerbated by efforts to reduce spending at both the federal and provincial levels, consequent on the entrenchment of neoliberal principles of fiscal management. As we will see, in government circles, the result has been broad disagreement, underscored by attitudes of intransigence, regarding who should be held responsible for the provision of adequate housing, let alone for the growing homeless population.

With respect to housing, this lack of consensus in part reflects the division of power laid out in Canada's constitution. The Constitution Act, 1867 (Canada, Department of Justice 2012), established the basic jurisdictional domains of the federal government and the provinces. Section 92 granted provincial legislatures the exclusive right to make laws concerning the "property and civil rights" of those residing within the province. Houses qualify as "property," and, in a broad interpretation of "civil rights," the provision of social services that provide support to individuals and households in dire need was originally assumed to fall within provincial jurisdiction. At the same time, as was clear from section 91, the federal government was responsible for the regulation of commerce, banking, and credit—that is, for matters relevant to the purchase of homes through mortgages as well as to financing for their construction. In addition, the federal government has always retained the constitutional power to take action on issues of national concern.

The passage, in 1937, of the Home Improvement Loans Guarantee Act, followed, in 1938, by the first National Housing Act, signalled the entry of the federal government into the realm of housing policy. This role was further solidified immediately after World War II, with the creation of the Canada Mortgage and Housing Corporation (CMHC).[2] In the early postwar period, federal policies favoured the middle class, in hopes of fostering a dynamic that would indirectly address the housing needs of low-income earners.

2 Officially founded on 1 January 1946 and originally named the Central Mortgage and Housing Corporation, the CMHC was created to administer the National Housing Act, as well as the earlier Home Improvement Loans Guarantee Act. The National Housing Act of 1938, which had been redrafted in 1944, was further amended in 1948 and 1949, partly with the goal of encouraging the construction of low-income housing. For additional discussion, see Layton (2008, 242–47).

Describing the period as "a time of federal leadership," Barbara Carroll (2002, 73) notes that "primary emphasis was placed on the provision of single-family detached owner-occupied housing for middle-income families, under the assumption that low-income problems could be solved through filtering. That is, the middle-income groups who moved to the suburbs would vacate smaller, older, cheaper housing closer to the urban core, making it available for low-income groups."

During the 1950s and 1960s, the federal and provincial governments also pushed an aggressive urban renewal strategy, targeting Canada's largest urban centres. Urban renewal programs entailed the construction of high-density housing to compensate for the dislocations associated with so-called slum clearance. The resulting public housing projects served to stigmatize the poor, however, by relegating them to cheaply constructed apartment blocks located in areas where their occupants were unlikely to intrude on the lives of middle-to upper-income home owners or undermine property values. Even with that, these large public housing initiatives generated numerous complaints and would lose support by the late 1960s. Despite their evident failings, however, such projects, which significantly expanded the role of federal and provincial governments in the provision of low-income housing, established a stock of publicly owned land, especially in larger cities, while they also created a base of housing expertise at both levels of government (Murphy 2000, 96–98; Layton 2008, 263–65).

The 1969 *Report of the Federal Task Force on Housing and Urban Development* (Hellyer 1969) is generally credited with ending the practice of "slum clearance" and redirecting efforts towards alternative approaches to the provision of affordable housing. One such approach was "mixed-income" housing. As Murphy (2000, 98–99) explains,

> Rather than ghettos of low-income residents, small-scale projects that housed residents with a range of incomes were to receive federal funding in the form of 100 percent mortgage assistance. These mixed-income projects were provided by non-profit or cooperative housing corporations which assigned a quarter of the project units to low-income tenants in exchange for the 100 percent loans. The federal government subsidized the rents of low-income tenants and, in effect, subsidized the rents of all income groups in these projects by paying the difference between what tenants paid and actual costs. Not only were projects smaller and better designed to accommodate their

predominantly middle-class residents, but mixed-income housing also got around the problem of neighbourhood resistance.

As Murphy (2000, 99) notes, such housing projects became very popular in the mid-1970s, with the total number of units rising from 1,500 in 1973 to 22,000 in 1978, even if only a fraction of these units were intended for low-income residents. Under the leadership of Pierre Trudeau, the Liberal government also followed through on a promise made in 1974 to fund a million new housing starts within the next four years, with an emphasis on the creation of low-income housing (Coutts 2000, 190, 234). While no explicit commitment existed to providing shelter for all, federal-provincial cost-sharing arrangements were making progress in addressing multiple shortcomings in both housing and social assistance.

This momentum was, however, short-lived in the face of broader economic and budgetary problems that started to emerge in the late 1970s and persisted throughout the 1980s. The multiplicity of programs, as well as the heavy subsidies required to achieve results for low-income earners, made housing an area particularly vulnerable to death by a thousand cuts, cuts that were gradually introduced by the federal government over a period of roughly a decade. Cuts to housing programs began in November 1984, not long after the election of Brian Mulroney's Conservative government, with a $217.8 million reduction in federal funding for housing development and rehabilitation (Layton 2008, 233). In 1985, federal policies changed so that financial assistance was available only for residents of low-income housing, thereby ending subsidies to low-income residents of mixed-income projects. Although social housing projects funded through cost-sharing arrangements had benefited low-income residents, the late 1980s brought cutbacks to these programs, with the number of new units falling from more than 20,000 in 1987 to under 7,000 in 1993 (Murphy 2000, 99–100). In 1993, the Mulroney government cancelled funding for new nonprofit or cooperative housing projects and capped federal expenditures on social housing at $2 billion annually. Jack Layton (2008, 233) calculates that, during the decade of Conservative rule, from 1984 to 1993, federal cuts to housing programs totalled some $1.8 billion.

The trend towards federal withdrawal from housing initiatives continued after the Liberals came to power in November 1993, under the leadership of Jean Chrétien. The 1996 federal budget, prepared by finance minister Paul Martin, announced a thirty-year plan to end federal funding for housing by gradually downloading existing federal housing programs onto the provinces and territories, with the intention of reducing the federal contribution from its current level of $1.7 billion to zero by the end of the period (Shapcott 2007, 9–10). Although this process of downloading entailed extensive negotiations between the federal government and the provinces, "the architects of this withdrawal turned their backs on towns and cities, none of which were represented in any of the inter-governmental discussions that led to the devolution of Canada's housing projects" (Duffy, Royer, and Beresford 2014, 22). During the 1990s, provincial governments replicated the federal retreat from public and subsidized housing—but, in this case, there was no "organized devolution," no process of provincial-municipal negotiation (22). Once again, cities were basically not consulted.

By the end of the decade, only a very small number of new public housing units were being built in Canada, given that the subsidies needed to promote the construction of low-income rental or housing units had largely been whittled away in the drive to rein in federal and provincial spending and balance budgets. Indeed, after 1993, when the Mulroney government terminated funding for new social housing, until the early 2000s, only British Columbia and Québec continued to provide such housing (Irwin 2004, 7), albeit on the basis of substantially reduced financial resources. Thus, by the late 1990s, neither the federal government nor provincial administrations were addressing the housing needs of low-income citizens in any significant way. In 2014, it was estimated that, over the previous two decades, some 100,000 units of affordable housing had *not* been built owing to the cancellation of programs (Gaetz, Gulliver, and Richter 2014, 5).

During the 1990s, the numbers of homeless swiftly grew in Canada's largest urban centres, as did public concern, especially given the risk of death from exposure to subzero temperatures. In late 1999, Chrétien's government announced the creation of the National Homelessness Initiative (NHI). Recognizing that "no one level of government or sector of Canadian society can, alone, solve the problem of homelessness," the NHI initially invested $753 million over a period of three years in "a strategy designed to facilitate collaborative approaches—among governments, the voluntary and private sectors—to address the challenges posed by the homeless throughout Canada" (Canada, HRDC 2001, 2). As its core objectives, the NHI aimed to:

- Facilitate community capacity by coordinating Government of Canada efforts and enhancing the diversity of tools and resources;

- Foster effective partnerships and investment that contribute to addressing the immediate and multifaceted needs of the homeless and reducing homelessness in Canada; and
- Increase awareness and understanding of homelessness in Canada. (Canada, HRDC 2003, 7)

In addition to a research component, the NHI comprised initiatives in the areas of Aboriginal homelessness and youth homelessness. Its main component, however, was the Supporting Communities Partnership Initiative, which provided funds directly to communities that had demonstrated the existence of a significant homeless population. Founded on a basic "premise," namely, that "communities are best placed to devise effective strategies to both prevent and reduced homelessness locally" (HRDC 2003, 8), the initiative sought to allow communities "to allocate funds according to their particular needs," while also encouraging "the establishment of a 'continuum of supports' (i.e., prevention, emergency shelter, outreach, support services, transitional, supportive and permanent housing)" (i). In addition to drawing up a community plan to address homelessness, participating communities were required to secure funding commitments from other sources, which the federal government would then match up to the maximum amount allocated for each community (Canada, HRDC 2001, 4). Although 80 percent of this NHI funding stream was earmarked for ten major urban centres, the remaining 20 percent was reserved for smaller municipalities that were "able to demonstrate a homelessness problem," with the federal and the provincial or territorial government jointly responsible for choosing the eligible communities (3). Fifty-one such municipalities were identified (among them the four small cities examined in this chapter), so evidently quite a few communities had no trouble demonstrating that homelessness had become problem.

A second phase of the NHI, announced in November 2005, extended these partnerships until 2007 and renewed federal funding (Canada, HRSDC 2008, i). Although one of the long-term goals of the NHI was "to develop a comprehensive continuum of supports to help homeless Canadians move out of the cycle of homelessness and prevent those at-risk from falling into homelessness" (i), the problem remained that the federal government had made no similarly long-term commitment to funding—a situation not lost on community partners. As the authors of *Home for Good: Kelowna's Ten Year Plan to End Homelessness* observed in 2009, the "duration of funding for these programs has been limited to only two to three years at a time," adding that the "lack of predictability and sustainability has led to uncertainty and inefficiency in delivering an adequate response to the homelessness crisis" (Sundberg et al. 2009, 7). In addition, according to a summative evaluation of the NHI, even though community partners reported a number of positive outcomes, they also pointed to an important area in which the program fell short:

> Despite the progress that has been made as a result of the NHI, most communities identified gaps in their continuum of supports and services, particularly in the area of affordable housing. Although not within the mandate of the NHI, the continued gap in availability of independent, affordable housing at the final stage of the continuum was identified by evaluation respondents as having a detrimental impact on establishing the overall continuum of supports and services. (Canada, HRSDC 2008, v)

In other words, many of the individuals who otherwise benefited from NHI funding probably ended up back on the streets.

Following the election of the Conservatives to power in 2006, the NHI was replaced by the Homelessness Partnering Strategy (HPS). Announced in December 2006, the HPS went into effect in April 2007 and was initially funded for two years, at $134.8 million per year (Canada, HRSDC 2009, vii)—a substantial decrease from the NHI's original budget of $251 million per year. Funding was subsequently extended until 2014 and then renewed again from 2014 to 2019, although at a decreased level of $119 million annually (Canada 2013, 10). Like the NHI, the HPS comprises a number of different components. In one funding stream, it continues to target the same sixty-one "designated communities," while another is devoted to Aboriginal communities. Originally described as a "community-based program that relies on communities to determine their own needs and develop appropriate projects," the HPS is in many respects a reworked version of the NHI.[3] Designated communities continue to be required to draw up a community plan, developed by a

---

3 "Canada—National Strategies to Address Homelessness," *The Homeless Hub*, 2017, http://homelesshub.ca/solutions/national-strategies/canada. This was the federal government's original description. For current information, see "Homelessness Partnering Strategy," *Employment and Social Development Canada*, 28 November 2016, https://www.canada.ca/en/employment-social-development/programs/communities/homelessness.html.

Community Advisory Board, and federal funding remains contingent on the provision of matching funds by the community partner.

Perhaps the chief difference between the NHI and the HPS lies in the latter's emphasis on sustainable solutions—no doubt a response, in part, to criticisms of the NHI. In the words of Employment and Social Development Canada, the HPS "works to enhance partnerships to find longer-term solutions to homelessness, strengthen community capacity and build sustainability."[4] Similarly, according to the program's Terms and Conditions, the HPS has, from the start, "been encouraging communities to adopt a more mature approach to homelessness and has supported them in shifting away from emergency responses and focussing instead on longer-term solutions."[5] These priorities are reflected in the criteria for a successful community plan, which must:

- identify gaps for addressing homelessness issues in a particular region;
- identify long-term solutions to address homelessness and how the community intends to continue these activities; and
- demonstrate that other partners will provide at least $1 for every dollar of Homelessness Partnering Strategy funding.[6]

In short, despite its own preference for short-term commitments to funding (and in ever dwindling amounts), in developing the HPS, the federal government was still looking to municipalities to take the lead in devising long-term solutions.

On the whole, the provinces—with the possible exception of Alberta, which, in October 2008, unveiled an ambitious ten-year plan to end homelessness in

---

4 "Understanding Homelessness and the Strategy," *Employment and Social Development Canada,* 23 August 2016, https://www.canada.ca/en/employment-social-development/programs/communities/homelessness/understanding.html (see "About the Homelessness Partnering Strategy").

5 "Terms and Conditions of the Homelessness Partnering Strategy," *Employment and Social Development Canada,* 12 September 2016, https://www.canada.ca/en/employment-social-development/services/funding/homeless/homeless-terms-conditions.htm (see "Introduction").

6 "Funding: Regional Projects—Designated Communities," *Employment and Social Development Canada,* 22 September 2016, https://www.canada.ca/en/employment-social-development/services/funding/homeless/homeless-designated-communities.html.

the province by 2019, at a projected cost of roughly $3.3 billion—have seemed content to collaborate in this shift of responsibility onto local governments.[7] In the fall of 2006, shortly before the HPS was announced, the BC government launched its own housing strategy, Housing Matters BC, which provoked some consternation at the local level. In a 2008 policy paper, the Union of British Columbia Municipalities (UBCM) captured the sense of ambiguity and lack of clear direction: "There appears in British Columbia the expectation at the provincial level that local governments should take on greater responsibility for affordable housing and homelessness, although there have been no discussions with local government on the nature of these new responsibilities or the tacit meaning of this shift in duties in the future" (UBCM 2008, 3).

Adding to this atmosphere of confusion was the uncertain status of federal funding for affordable housing. In 2001, Chrétien's government had introduced the Affordable Housing Initiative, a collaborative arrangement between Ottawa and the provinces and territories implemented through the Framework for Bilateral Agreements Aimed at Affordable Housing. In 2008, the federal government, now under the leadership of Conservative Stephen Harper, announced a five-year investment of more than $1.9 billion ($387.9 million annually) in housing and homelessness initiatives. This included a two-year renewal of the Affordable Housing Initiative, through to the end of March 2011, with the recipients required to match the federal funds allocated to them (CMHC 2009, 1). As the period drew to a close, disagreements arose about the framework under which funding would continue, and only in mid-2011 was the situation resolved. Under the new Investment in Affordable Housing program, Ottawa would maintain its existing transfers to provinces ($238.7 million annually), who would be responsible for matching the amount of their allocation. In doing so, however, provinces were not obliged to draw directly on their own treasuries but were free to turn for help to private-sector donors, such as charities—and/or to local municipalities (Scoffield 2011). As

---

7 See Alberta, Alberta Secretariat for Action on Homelessness (2008). With regard to the projected cost, the plan rightly emphasized that creating permanent housing for the homeless is ultimately far less expensive than continuing to "manage" the problem (9). At the same time, Alberta is fundamentally a wealthy province (despite its current budget shortfall), and it is probably no coincidence that, at the time the plan was announced, oil prices were reaching record highs. Inevitably, prices fell, as did spending on social housing (see CBC News 2015), and, as 2019 swiftly approaches, it has become clear that the original goal will not be met.

Michael Shapcott, director of research on affordable housing at Toronto's Wellesley Institute, observed, the agreement was "full of general statements" and failed to set any specific goals or targets (quoted in Scoffield 2011). It also invited provinces to further offload financial burdens onto local communities.

As this history of housing policy in Canada indicates, the ambiguities surrounding jurisdictional authority in matters of housing have conspired to allow the federal government first to step into a more active role in housing policy and then to step away from that role as money tightened. In the face of declining federal support, cash-strapped provinces chose to follow suit, cutting their own funding for housing initiatives and other social programs and looking both to the private sector and to local municipalities to make up the difference. The fight against homelessness thus increasingly became a local responsibility, with the federal and provincial governments retreating into a supporting role, declining to assume any serious responsibility for confronting the complex economic issues that give rise to homelessness or the equally complex social and moral issues that surround it. Within this context of political disengagement, small cities have been charged with finding their own solutions.

Homelessness in Context: The Small-City Predicament

The evident federal-provincial consensus that municipalities should take the lead in addressing homelessness brings to the fore numerous disparities in resources and capacities, both from province to province and among municipalities within provinces. As we have seen, in comparison to larger urban centres, small cities must already contend with more limited financial resources, as well as with a relative lack of experience in social planning. Small cities also tend to have a smaller supply of existing housing stock, and, simply by virtue of their scale, their neighbourhoods tend to abut one another, with little by way of buffer zones. Moreover, the very economic forces that have produced homelessness have taken an especially heavy toll on the ability of small cities to respond to the crisis.

Throughout the 1990s and into this century, small cities have had to grapple with escalating costs and the decay of traditional industries that once provided an economic base, coupled with budget cuts at the provincial level. Not only have small cities struggled to maintain core municipal services and meet basic infrastructure needs, but, in response to both global economic restructuring and declining provincial support, municipalities have had to focus more aggressively on local economic growth. The need to develop new revenues streams has required small cities to direct scarce resources into marketing efforts, such as branding, that aim at self-promotion, in hopes of attracting new businesses and residents (especially relatively affluent professionals) and gaining a stronger foothold in tourism and convention markets. This, in turn, has entailed building or enhancing local recreational, cultural, and sporting venues and revitalizing downtown cores, in an attempt to compete with other municipalities that are pursuing much the same strategies.

Given that, in a municipal context, annual budgets and proposed property tax increases are subject to far broader public consultation and scrutiny than is the case at higher levels of government, large expenditures associated with the need to address social issues can be hard to justify or sustain (Haddow 2002, 102). This is particularly true if such expenditures come at the expense of other public services or improvements to infrastructure. Whereas spending on measures designed to promote economic growth can be justified in terms of benefits to the community as whole, social spending serves a "powerless minority" (102). Thus, as Barbara Carroll (2002, 85) argues, "the inertia of the federal and provincial governments and the passing of responsibility for housing to municipalities leaves this area in the hands of the level of government least able to withstand the private pressures against social intervention and with a tax base which cannot be expanded in the event of economic downturn." In addition, whatever benefits might accrue from the development of innovative social programs tailored to serve local needs, such efforts could easily be thwarted by broader economic pressures and public resistance.

The reluctance of local governments to pursue homelessness initiatives also reflects the jurisdictional scope and power of such governments. Municipalities can take steps to address the most urgent needs of the homeless, for food, medical attention, and shelter from the elements, but solutions to the problem of homelessness ultimately rest on broader policies pertaining to housing and income assistance over which municipal governments have little or no control. While the existing framework of legal, health, and social services may be costly and ineffective in reducing homelessness, from a municipal perspective, the principal responsibility for creating and implementing that framework falls on the federal and provincial governments. It is not surprising, then, that in a UBCM survey conducted in 2008, municipal governments identified the "need for financial assistance from the federal and provincial governments" as one of the foremost barriers to local action, along with a lack of local capacity ("staffing resources and expertise") and inadequate leadership from higher levels of government—the fact that municipalities require "federal and provincial direction to make major changes in the local community" (UBCM 2008, 13). It is unrealistic to imagine that municipalities can address pervasive and deeply embedded social problems on their own.

With regard to housing and local demographics, small cities tend to differ in certain respects from larger urban centres. As Carroll (1990, 100) points out,

> Large cities have higher housing costs and a relatively larger rental stock. At the same time, they act as a magnet for single individuals who require short-term low-cost housing. Smaller centres, on the other hand, have a relatively greater proportion of senior citizens and families who require affordable housing in markets where rental accommodation is less common and home ownership the norm.

The 2016 census revealed the largest increase in the proportion of Canadians aged sixty-five or over in the country's history, with the figure now standing at 16.9 percent of the total population. At the same time, fewer Canadians now live in single-family dwellings—"the result of declining affordability and older people moving into smaller living spaces" (Grant and Agius 2017). As the population continues to age, the pressure on smaller cities is likely to grow, as older Canadians seek affordable housing in their retirement years. Perhaps this is all the more so in British Columbia, a province attractive to retirees.

With respect to the provision of housing, small cities are again at a disadvantage in comparison to relatively large urban centres. The small cities of today were only towns in the early postwar years, when the federal government financed the construction of public housing on publicly owned land. Because these projects generally focused on low-income populations in Canada's largest urban areas, small cities now find themselves without an equivalent stock of public lands and housing. In addition, during the postwar boom, these towns never attracted the private investment that enabled the construction of downtown office buildings, rooming houses, and hotels, which today can be purchased by city governments and renovated (or torn down and rebuilt) in order to provide housing for the homeless and others in need. Of course, smaller cities do have older neighbourhoods, but their original downtown core is often relatively compact, with retail areas dispersed in response to the construction of residential housing developments towards the outskirts of the city.

Indeed, over the past thirty years or so, the housing dynamic in small cities has tended to replicate the pattern seen in Canada's largest centres during the postwar period. New suburban housing for middle- and upper-income families continues to be built, with low-income owners and renters generally forced to rely on an older stock of housing located in and around the downtown core. However, as has also occurred in larger cities, a process of gentrification, or so-called urban renewal, has set in, with this older stock of housing undergoing redevelopment into commercial and professional establishments, as well as high-end condominiums and other upscale housing. Indeed, local governments often encourage such redevelopment by offering certain incentives, in an effort to alter the demographics of downtown areas and to revive the economic prospects of local businesses, whose customers have been lured away by big-box retailers located on the fringes of town (MacKinnon and Nelson 2005, 40–42; Sailor 2010, 123–28).

This growth and redevelopment began at a time when federal or provincial support for the construction of low-income housing had all but evaporated. As a result, affordable housing quickly grew scarce, causing rents to spiral upwards and vacancy rates to plummet. In addition, competition for what rental accommodation existed became fierce. In Kamloops, for example, the vacancy rate for rental units dropped from 7.8% in 2000 to a mere 0.4% in 2008, climbing slightly to 1.5% in 2009 and then 2.6% in 2010.[8] Such a tight rental market is especially unfriendly to low-income earners and those on social assistance, many of whom are also members of ethnic minorities. For one thing, it allows landlords to favour those they regard (for whatever reason) as the more desirable tenants. Moreover, as of 2017, the maximum allowance for shelter for a single individual living on social assistance was $375 per month, whereas the average rent for a bachelor unit, in all four cities, was over $600 per month, with rates in Kelowna rising to $859 by 2017 (SPARC BC 2011, 45; CMHC 2017, 8; see also HAP Steering Committee 2010, 15). Needless to say, such circumstances are a recipe for homelessness.

As homeless populations grew, community organizations began to undertake homeless counts, in an effort not merely to provide rough estimates of numbers but also to gather basic demographic information. A research report released in 2011 by the Social Planning and Research Council of British

8 Jeremy Deutsch, "Vacancy Rate Rises Slightly in Kamloops in 2010 Compared to 2009" (blog), *Kamloops Real Estate Blog*, 15 December 2010, http://www.kamloopsreal-estateblog.com/vacancy-rate-rises-slightly-kamloops-2010-compared-2009/.

Columbia (SPARC BC) included information gathered from the most recent counts of the visible homeless (that is, people on the streets and in shelters) in our four cities. These data indicated that the majority of the visible homeless were men—anywhere from 61% (in Kelowna) to 77% (in Kamloops). As the counts also revealed, Indigenous individuals made up a highly disproportionate share of the homeless population, accounting for 24% of the homeless in Kelowna (versus 3.8% of the total municipal population), 29% in Kamloops (versus 6.4%), 36% in Nanaimo (versus 5.2%), and 66% in Prince George (versus 11.3%) (SPARC BC 2011, 20). All in all, the total counts ranged from 103 (in Kamloops) to 361 (in Prince George). While these numbers are significant, they might not seem the stuff of crisis, at least in terms of the need for housing and support services. Once we factor in the hidden homeless, however—that is, people who have no home but are temporarily residing in some other form of accommodation—we are better able to grasp the magnitude of the problem (see table 1.1).

Table 1.1 Estimates of total homeless population

City	Counts of visibly homeless	Estimated hidden homeless population (2010–11)	Estimated total
Kamloops	103 (2010)[a]	1,167 [808 to 1,631][b]	1,270
Kelowna	279 (2007)	1,489 [1,019 to 2,103]	1,768
Nanaimo	115 / 302 (both 2008)[c]	796 [510 to 1,185]	911 / 1,098
Prince George	361 (2010)	718 [450 to 1,087]	1,079

[a] Counts were taken in October 2010 in Nanaimo, in May 2010 in Prince George, in September 2008 in Nanaimo, and April 2007 in Kelowna. While these counts generally took place within a brief period (such as a day), the precise methods varied. For details, see SPARC BC (2011, 11–15).

[b] Estimates of the hidden homeless derive from telephone surveys of 1,000 households in each of the communities: see SPARC BC (2011, 3–6). Ranges represent a 95% confidence interval (64). In other words, if surveys were taken repeatedly, the results would fall within this range 95% of the time.

[c] The total of 302, which was obtained in another count, may be the more accurate, as this count was conducted over a period of three months (June to August 2008). See SPARC BC (2011, 14).

Source: SPARC BC (2011, 19, 23).

In an effort to develop a clearer understanding of the dynamics of home-lessness, the SPARC BC researchers conducted a survey of households presently providing shelter to homeless individuals, supplemented by inter-views with local service providers and with individuals who were currently among the hidden homeless or had recently been so.[9] Most of the homeless (80%) reported staying in the house or apartment of friends or acquaintances, rather than with relatives, usually sleeping on a couch in the living room or sometimes in a spare bedroom or a garage. The length of the stay was gener-ally somewhere between one to three months, but a quarter (26%) reported stays of less than a week (SPARC BC 2011, 45). Indeed, 70% indicated that they had spent "less time at their temporary home than they had anticipated" and "either chose or were forced to leave before they were ready to go" (49). In addition to "couch surfing," other living arrangements included camping, short-term rentals, and/or sleeping in the streets. Nearly two-thirds (64%) had stayed in emergency shelters or transition housing within the past year (45).

A majority of those interviewed (56%) were somewhere in the range of twenty-five to forty-five years of age (SPARC BC 2011, 46). More than 65% reported having mental health challenges, a figure that stands in stark contrast to the Canadian population overall, in which the rate of serious mental health problems is estimated to be about 20%.[10] In addition, roughly 52% indicated that they struggled with substance use, while 48% had physical disabilities of some sort—and close to a quarter (22%) reporting facing all three challenges (56). Most were unemployed, and nearly three-quarters (74%) were receiving social assistance and/or provincial disability benefits—so these individuals were not entirely outside the system. Moreover, 82% reported having made use of community or government services over the past year in an effort to find their own place (45). As the SPARC BC researchers noted, roughly a third (34%) of those providing temporary accommodation to homeless individuals

---

9 A total of fifty hidden homeless were interviewed, ten from each of the five partici-pating communities (Kamloops, Kelowna, Nanaimo, Nelson, and Prince George). The household survey and interviews with service providers were conducted via tele-phone; the interviews with the hidden homeless took place face-to-face. For details on methodology, see SPARC BC (2011, 4–10). Among the hidden homeless interviewed, women slightly outnumbered men, although, as the report notes, the gender distribu-tion reflects the fact that the ten interviewees from Nanaimo were all women (iii, 46).

10 "Facts About Mental Illness," *Canadian Mental Health Association,* 2017, http://www.cmha.ca/media/fast-facts-about-mental-illness/. This figure was also reported by the SPARC BC researchers (2011, 56).

were in precarious financial circumstances themselves, spending upwards of 30% of their income on housing, and, notably in Kelowna and Prince George, a significant proportion of hosts were senior citizens.

Not surprisingly, the vast majority of the hidden homeless identified low income and the lack of affordable housing as the most significant barriers preventing them securing a permanent address (51). These two factors were also identified by the service providers interviewed, who further pointed to "inadequate services and/or strict criteria for government support" as major obstacles among the hidden homeless (56). It also became clear that a very permeable boundary exists between the hidden homeless and the visible homeless. To remain "hidden," the homeless rely largely on people they know, whose ability and willingness to provide temporary accommodation are often limited: at some point, their guests must move on—possibly into the street.

Shouldering the Burden: Municipal Responses to Homelessness

During the early 2000s, the need to cope with growing numbers of homeless swiftly became the dominant social planning issue in many small cities, including the four we studied, in some cases constituting the main reason that city councils chose to fund the creation of a permanent social planning position. In the face of what was perceived as a mounting crisis, initial municipal responses generally focused on relatively short-term measures, such as emergency shelters, that aimed at getting people off the streets (if only temporarily). Eventually, though, all four cities developed homelessness plans that adopted a more comprehensive perspective, one that viewed homelessness as a symptom of underlying problems.[11] As these plans recognized, sustainable solutions to homelessness would require an ongoing municipal commitment to increasing the supply of affordable housing, notably through the development of new low-income rental suites and the construction of mixed-income housing. In

---

11 Nanaimo and Kelowna engaged consultants to conduct research and draw up plans for action: for Nanaimo, see the two reports prepared by City Spaces Consulting (CSC 2008a, 2008b), and, for Kelowna, *Home for Good: Kelowna's Ten Year Plan to End Homelessness* (Sundberg et al. 2009). In Kamloops, the Homelessness Action Plan Steering Committee produced *Kamloops Homelessness Action Plan 2010* (HAP Steering Committee 2010), while the City of Prince George developed *My PG: An Integrated Community Sustainability Plan for Prince George* (Prince George 2010).

addition to the centralization of housing information and referral services, concrete initiatives included offering financial incentives to developers for building affordable housing and to homeowners willing to create secondary suites, as well as meetings with landlords to encourage rent reductions for low-income tenants. Local governments also coordinated with community organizations to advocate at the provincial and/or federal levels for the funding needed to carry out specific projects.

Plans for actions are, of course, one thing; implementation is another. Perhaps the most valuable insights into the dynamics of municipal efforts to address homelessness were provided by the social planners we interviewed.[12] As was apparent from these interviews, local initiatives had met with some success, at least in meeting the most immediate needs of the homeless. Planners pointed to increases in the number of shelter beds and spaces in transitional housing, as well as to improvements in support services. In addition, one had noted a growing willingness to "assist and support" panhandlers, which had contributed to a striking decrease in their numbers over the course of one summer. "Part of that," she said, "was just the people around the table acknowledging that there's a human aspect to the issues that someone is facing." At the same time, it was clear that measures to address homelessness had to contend with local anxieties and tensions. "We tend to get more concern for people who perceive their safety to be compromised by the homeless people downtown," another planner remarked. He went on to say that visible homelessness is "also an issue for downtown businesses," given the prevailing perception that the presence of the homeless is "jeopardizing our ability to market the downtown core to potential businesses."

Concerns voiced by local residents were by no means the only obstacles that social planners had to confront in attempting to implement specific initiatives. City councils were often reluctant to fund measures to address homelessness, interpreting them as yet another example of the shift of federal and provincial responsibilities onto municipalities. Arguments about downloading could, at times, serve as an excuse for inaction on the part of city council, even though the larger community might be in favour of moving forward on the homelessness front. As one planner put it,

---

12 Semi-structured interviews were conducted in 2010 and 2011 with social planners from Kamloops, Kelowna, Prince George, and Nanaimo, as well as Vancouver and Victoria. These interviews are the source of the quotations that follow.

We know that if we have homelessness and it's an issue in our community, and local government wants to do something, how you do that is you support housing. And in every other municipality that has been successful with the provincial government in terms of acquiring funding, they've brought something to the table, and I think it's the way it's happening right now. . . . So I find it very frustrating when I hear that argument at council, because to me, that's more of an argument for not wanting to do anything.

He went on to point out that the reluctance of city council to take action often stood "in opposition to what the community told us [about] how they view their community," with the result that council members seemed to be "out of step with the electorate." As another planner observed, however, municipal concerns over downloading were far from unjustified:

We have a council now that's much more forward thinking and receptive to what they can do to make a difference, but they've always been sensitive to the downloading, and BC is particularly bad for pointing at local government and saying, "You should be doing X," but not providing any further resources so that you can actually do X. That's been a problem.

In short, small-city councils grappling with limited revenues have good reason to be cautious, and yet even when a city council has the best of intentions, this wariness can itself become an obstacle, serving to put a brake on progress.

Quite apart from the possible need to convince city councils to move into action, social planners must overcome other hurdles in order to implement homelessness action plans. Perhaps the most common problem is the NIMBY ("not in my backyard") reaction, which tends to rear its head as proposals—for the provision of support services in a particular neighbourhood, for example, or for the construction of transitional or affordable housing—become more concrete. In the face of opposition from local residents or business associations, city council may be inclined to retreat from implementation, which often requires planners to keep revisiting previously agreed-upon plans. One social planner explained that, when city council shows signs of getting cold feet, he tells them:

"Well this is where it's led us to. You know you're going to have to accept that this is the outcome. If you didn't want to get us here, then

you shouldn't have adopted the document." So that's sort of the way I do it, I get them to agree to the broad principles, and then when it gets uncomfortable, I say, "You know we agreed on the principles. You knew it was going to get uncomfortable when it got to the particulars." . . . And most of the time they'll choose to stick to their principles.

While such tactics are part and parcel of local politics, the need to engage in them is perhaps an underappreciated aspect of the downloading phenomenon. The provincial or federal authorities who formulate policies that municipalities are called upon to implement are spared the trouble of figuring out how to overcome local resistance—which tends to arise especially when these communities are also obliged to cover much of the cost.

In addition, even when detailed plans are in place, changes in council membership as the result of local elections can easily shift priorities and bring about delays. Such changes can, in turn, have a substantial impact on the extent to which civic officials are prepared to lobby the provincial government regarding funding for homelessness initiatives. Recalling a meeting of the Union of British Columbia Municipalities, one social planner commented:

Our senior management staff sat down with the premier and with BC Housing people . . . and said, "Look, we have a huge problem with homelessness and very little resources to deal with it. We need it to be a priority." And shortly after that, they announced the Premier's Task Force on Homelessness and Mental Health. And, in fact, we did get significant results.

As another planner put it, "I can't open doors the way the mayor can." Having a supportive mayor who is both able and willing to foster local-provincial links thus appears to be a crucial factor in leveraging action from above.

In all four cities studied, social planners, often working in concert with community groups and service providers, have played a critical role in advocating for and advancing measures aimed at reducing homelessness. At the same time, a number of constraints operate at the local level that can hinder the smooth progression from initial plans to completed projects. These constraints are not fixed: rather, they vary from one place to another, in terms of their nature as well as their severity. As a result, significant inequities exist among municipalities with respect to the implementation of strategies to end homelessness—inequities that directly affect the fortunes of local homeless populations. In 2002, for example, a review of the Supporting Communities Partnership Initiative noted that "not every community has the depth of corporate or other support to fund homelessness initiatives," while some communities "simply do not have adequate local resources to match funds" (Public Policy Forum 2002, 17). In short, some communities are better equipped than others to respond to demands on the part of higher levels of government for local solutions—devised, implemented, and to a significant extent funded by community "partners." Such demands are already well entrenched, but, in the face of renewed policies of federal and/ or provincial restraint, inequities among communities could become even more pronounced.

Conclusion

As we saw earlier, in 2013, the federal government renewed funding for the Homelessness Partnering Strategy for an additional five years, from 2014 to 2019. In its renewed form, the HPS placed an especially firm emphasis on Housing First strategies, mandating that, by the beginning of April 2016, designated communities (exclusive of the ten major cities) receiving allocations of $200,000 or more must be spending at least 40 percent of that allocation on Housing First initiatives (Foran and Guibert 2013, 7). The HPS currently aims for "a balanced approach," one that "ensures that communities adopt Housing First as a cornerstone of their plan to address homelessness, yet retain some flexibility to invest in other proven approaches that complement Housing First and reduce homelessness at the local level."[13]

As a philosophy, Housing First recognizes that little can be accomplished by way of addressing the physical and psychological needs of the homeless unless they are first securely housed, at which point they can be provided with the necessary health and support services. The government's commitment to Housing First approaches is founded in large measure on the findings from a federally funded multi-year study of mental health and homelessness

---

13 "Terms and Conditions of the Homelessness Partnering Strategy," *Employment and Social Development Canada,* 12 September 2016, https://www. canada.ca/en/employment-social-development/services/funding/homeless/ homeless-terms-conditions.html (see "Introduction").

conducted by the Mental Health Commission of Canada.[14] The study, At Home/Chez Soi—carried out from 2009 to 2013 in five major cities—sought to evaluate the effectiveness, in terms of both costs and benefits, of a Housing First strategy employed among people with mental illness. The final report, released in April 2014, concluded that the Housing First approach "rapidly ends homelessness" and "can be effectively implemented in Canadian cities of different size and different ethnoracial and cultural composition" (Goering et al. 2014, 5). It also provided evidence that Housing First is a "sound investment," noting that "every $10 invested in HF services resulted in an average savings of $21.72" over the two-year period immediately following the entry of participants into the program (5).[15]

The strong endorsement of a Housing First strategy by the federal government represents a significant advance towards a long-term solution to homelessness—although, given the relatively recent embrace of this strategy, it is a little too early to judge its cumulative impact. At the same time, the effectiveness of the "partnership" model in which this strategy is currently embedded is open to question. As we have seen, the level of government that is called upon to take the lead in the struggle to end homelessness is also the most impoverished level of government, not only from the standpoint of financial resources but also in terms of human capacity. Moreover, while an emphasis on local needs and circumstances rightly acknowledges that no two communities are alike, for that very reason individual community efforts are bound to be uneven. They are also unlikely to add up to a coordinated plan. As a recent study of ten-year homelessness plans concluded, "the existing patchwork of federal and provincial programs and modest, short-term funding envelopes needs to be replaced with a comprehensive and well-integrated national plan," one that "dedicates new, long-term public funding at the levels required to reduce, and ultimately end, homelessness in Canada" (Adamo et al. 2016, 10).

14 "Understanding Homelessness and the Strategy," *Employment and Social Development Canada,* 23 August 2016, https://www.canada.ca/en/employment-social-development/programs/communities/homelessness/understanding.html#s1 (see "Housing First").

15 The savings were especially significant for individuals deemed to have high needs: an average of $9.60 for every $10 invested. Among those with moderate needs, the savings were $3.42 per $10 invested. For more information, see "Initiatives: At Home," *Mental Health Commission of Canada,* 2017, http://img.mhcc.ca/English/initiatives-and-projects/home?page=2&terminitial=39.

As we write, it might seem that a significant step has been taken in this direction. In its March 2017 budget, the Liberal government of Justin Trudeau committed $11.2 billion over eleven years to the implementation of a new National Housing Strategy. Included in this figure is a total of $2.1 billion for the HPS, which represents an increase in its annual budget from $118 million to an average of $191 million. In addition, the strategy invests a total of $5 billion over the next eleven years in a newly established National Housing Fund, intended to address critical housing needs, especially among the country's most vulnerable populations (see Canada 2017a, 132–37). Significantly, this fund, which will be administered through the CMHC, includes an Affordable Rental Housing Financing Initiative designed to provide municipalities and other housing partners with "sustained and improved access to low-cost loans for the repair and renewal of housing units, as well as for the construction of new affordable housing" (134). The government also reiterated its commitment to working with provincial and territorial governments, announcing its intention to provide a total of $3.2 billion through "a new, expanded, multilateral investment framework that will replace the existing Investment in Affordable Housing initiative" (133).

After decades of federal withdrawal from the housing arena, the new National Housing Strategy (Canada 2017b) signals a welcome shift in the overall direction of federal policy. As Greg Suttor (2017), an analyst at Toronto's Wellesley Institute, was quick to note, the National Housing Fund, with its restoration of loan financing, will be the first major housing program since the 1970s to be run by the federal government. At the same time, concerns have been raised about whether the investment is truly adequate. Suttor (2017) deemed the figure of roughly $1 billion a year for current initiatives a "modest rise" over annual funding levels of the past fifteen years. Indeed, the figure of $11.2 billion over eleven years falls considerably short of the $43.788 billion over ten years that the authors of *The State of Homelessness in Canada 2016* estimated would be necessary to end homelessness in Canada (Gaetz et al. 2016, 7). Nor does the new National Housing Strategy incorporate another of the key recommendations of this report—a National Housing Benefit, intended to prevent low-income households from losing their housing (Gaetz et al. 2016, 72–73; see also Canadian Observatory on Homelessness 2017). It is, moreover, impossible to say at this point whether the National Housing Fund, the increase in funding to the HPS, and the "expanded, multilateral investment framework" will significantly lessen the financial burden on local governments.

The fact remains that, despite the best efforts of social planners, community organizations, and local service providers, municipal homelessness initiatives will continue to be derailed by NIMBYism and other forms of civic complaint. City council members, easily swayed by the prospect of lost votes, can also be stubbornly resistant to what they perceive (often quite accurately) as federal or provincial attempts to download social and fiscal responsibility onto the local level. In addition, substantive progress on the homelessness front can all too easily be sidetracked or even stalled by election outcomes and other shifts in local political alignments. Small cities do not lack for hard-working, committed individuals who have considerable experience with social issues. But these individuals necessarily operate in a complex and highly dynamic, even volatile, context, and they often have limited power. If ending homelessness truly is a priority in Canada, the federal government must provide local officials with a clear mandate, and federal and provincial administrations must assume responsibility for ensuring that municipalities have the resources—both human and financial—necessary to achieve these goals.

Perhaps above all, both the federal and provincial governments must come to recognize that the problem of homelessness did not arise out of thin air. In Canada, as elsewhere, homelessness is a consequence of broader economic policies, policies that have dramatically heightened income disparities and rendered employment precarious. Arguably, in the absence of a shift in our underlying philosophy of governance, we will have little choice but to spend billions of dollars in an effort to remedy problems produced, at least in part, by a faltering of our collective commitment to social and economic justice. Unless we are willing to call our current priorities into question, the homeless will continue to be visible "in our parks, on our streets, and in our alleys," while the hidden homeless remain out of sight, together with those who are, through no fault of their own, living on the edge.

References

Adamo, Abra, Fran Klodawsky, Tim Aubry, and Stephen Hwang. 2016. *Ending Homelessness in Canada: A Study of 10-Year Plans in Four Canadian Cities.* Toronto: Centre for Urban Health Solutions, St. Michael's Hospital.

Alberta. Alberta Secretariat for Action on Homelessness. 2008. *A Plan for Alberta: Ending Homelessness in Ten Years.* Edmonton: Alberta Human Services. http://humanservices.alberta.ca/documents/PlanForAB_Secretariat_final.pdf.

Canada. 2013. *Economic Action Plan 2013.* Ottawa: Government of Canada. http://www.budget.gc.ca/2013/doc/plan/budget2013-eng.pdf.

———. 2017a. *Budget 2017: Building a Strong Middle Class.* Ottawa: Government of Canada. https://www.budget.gc.ca/2017/docs/plan/budget-2017-en.pdf.

———. 2017b. *Canada's National Housing Strategy: A Place to Call Home.* Ottawa: Government of Canada. https://www.placetocallhome.ca/pdfs/Canada-National-Housing-Strategy.pdf.

———. Department of Justice. 2012. *A Consolidation of the Constitution Acts, 1867 to 1982.* Ottawa: Public Works and Government Services Canada. http://laws-lois.justice.gc.ca/PDF/CONST_E.pdf.

———. HRDC (Human Resources Development Canada). 2001. *National Homelessness Initiative: A Guide to the Supporting Communities Partnership Initiative.* Ottawa: Human Resources Development Canada. http://publications.gc.ca/collections/Collection/RH4-8-2001E.pdf.

———. HRDC (Human Resources Development Canada). 2003. *Evaluation of the National Homelessness Initiative: Implementation and Early Outcomes of the HRDC-Based Components.* Ottawa: Human Resources Development Canada. http://www.urbancentre.utoronto.ca/pdfs/elibrary/Canada_Evaluation-HLN-Initi.pdf.

———. HRSDC (Human Resources and Skills Development Canada). 2008. *Summative Evaluation of the National Homelessness Initiative: Final Report.* Ottawa: Human Resources and Social Development Canada, Strategic Policy and Research Branch. http://publications.gc.ca/collections/collection_2013/rhdcc-hrsdc/HS28-149-2008-eng.pdf.

———. HRSDC (Human Resources and Skills Development Canada). 2009. *Evaluation of the Homelessness Partnering Strategy: Final Report.* Ottawa: Human Resources and Social Development Canada. http://publications.gc.ca/collections/collection_2010/rhdcc-hrsdc/HS28-160-2009-eng.pdf.

———. Parliament. Senate. 2009. *In from the Margins: A Call to Action on Poverty, Housing and Homelessness.* Report of the Subcommittee on Cities. Ottawa: Standing Senate Committee on Social Affairs, Science, and Technology. http://www.parl.gc.ca/Content/SEN/Committee/402/citi/rep/rep02dec09-e.pdf.

Canadian Observatory on Homelessness. 2017. "Canadian Observatory on Homelessness Welcomes the 2017 Federal Budget." *Homeless Hub.* 23 March. http://homelesshub.ca/blog/canadian-observatory-homelessness-welcomes-2017-federal-budget.

Carroll, Barbara Wake. 1990. "Housing." In *Urban Policy Issues: Canadian Perspectives,* edited by Richard A. Loreto and Trevor Price, 86–106. Toronto: McClelland and Stewart.

———. 2002. "Housing Policy in the New Millennium: The Uncompassionate Landscape." In *Urban Policy Issues: Canadian Perspectives,* 2nd ed., edited by Edmund P. Fowler and David Siegel, 69–89. Don Mills, ON: Oxford University Press.

CBC News. 2015. "10-Year Plan to End Homelessness in Alberta Falls Short." *CBC News, Edmonton.* 11 September 2015. http://www.cbc.ca/news/canada/edmonton/10-year-plan-to-end-homelessness-in-alberta-falls-short-1.3223712.

CMHC (Canada Mortgage and Housing Corporation). 2009. *Affordable Housing Initiative: Evaluation Report.* Ottawa: Canada Mortgage and Housing Corporation. https://www.cmhc-schl.gc.ca/en/corp/about/core/prev/upload/AHI-2009-evaluation-final.pdf.

———. 2017. *Rental Market Report: British Columbia Highlights.* Ottawa: Canada Mortgage and Housing Corporation.

Coutts, Jim. 2000. "Expansion, Retrenchment and Protecting the Future: Social Policy in the Trudeau Years." In *Towards a Just Society: The Trudeau Years,* edited by Thomas S. Axworthy and Pierre Elliott Trudeau, 221–45. Toronto: Penguin.

CSC (City Spaces Consulting). 2008a. *A Response to Homelessness in Nanaimo: A Housing First Approach—Situational Analysis.* Nanaimo: City of Nanaimo. https://www.nanaimo.ca/assets/Departments/Community~Planning/Social~Planning/Nanaimos~Response~to~Homelessness~Action~Plan/080507_Nanaimo_Situational.pdf.

———. 2008b. *Nanaimo's Response to Homelessness: Action Plan.* Prepared for the City of Nanaimo. Victoria, BC: City Spaces Consulting. http://www.nanaimo.ca/assets/Departments/Community~Planning/Social~Planning/Nanaimos~Response~to~Homelessness~Action~Plan/080707_Nan_Strategy.pdf.

Demographia. 2017. *13th Annual Demographia International Housing Affordability Survey: Rating Middle-Income Housing Affordability.* Belleville, IL: Demographia and Christchurch, NZ: Performance Urban Planning. http://www.demographia.com/dhi.pdf.

Duffy, Robert, Gaetan Royer, and Charley Beresford. 2014. *Who's Picking Up the Tab? Federal and Provincial Downloading onto Local Governments.* Vancouver: Centre for Civic Governance, Columbia Institute.

FCM (Federation of Canadian Municipalities). 2013. *The State of Canada's Cities and Communities 2013: Opening a New Chapter.* Ottawa: Federation of Canadian Municipalities. https://fcm.ca/Documents/reports/The_State_of_Canadas_Cities_and_Communities_2013_EN_web.pdf.

Florida, Richard. 2017. "Lost in Housing Hysteria, Middle-Class Neighbourhoods Have Gone Extinct." *Globe and Mail,* 24 April.

Foran, Tim, and Sylvie Guibert. 2013. *2014–2019 Renewed Homelessness Partnership Strategy.* Slide presentation. Ottawa: Employment and Social Development Canada. http://www.caeh.ca/wp-content/uploads/2013/11/LandP-IIIb-Renewed-HPS-CAEH-with-speaking-points-revised-November-12-2013-3-2.pdf.

Gaetz, Stephen, Erin Dej, Tim Richter, and Melanie Redman. 2016. *The State of Homelessness in Canada 2016.* Toronto: Canadian Observatory on Homelessness Press. http://homelesshub.ca/sites/default/files/SOHC16_final_20Oct2016.pdf.

Gaetz, Stephen, Tanya Gulliver, and Tim Richter. 2014. *The State of Homelessness in Canada 2014.* Toronto: Homeless Hub Press. http://www.homelesshub.ca/sites/default/files/SOHC2014.pdf.

Goering, Paula, Scott Veldhuizen, Aimee Watson, Carol Adair, Brianna Kopp, Eric Latimer, Geoff Nelson, Eric MacNaughton, David Streiner, and Tim Aubry. 2014. *National Final Report: Cross-Site At Home/Chez Soi Project.* Calgary: Mental Health Commission of Canada. https://www.mentalhealthcommission.ca/sites/default/files/mhcc_at_home_report_national_cross-site_eng_2_0.pdf.

Grant, Tavia, and Jeremy Agius. 2017. "Census 2016: The Growing Age Gap, Gender Ratios and Other Key Takeaways." *Globe and Mail,* 3 May (updated 12 November 2017).

Haddow, Rodney. 2002. "Municipal Social Security in Canada." In *Urban Policy Issues: Canadian Perspectives,* 2nd ed., edited by Edmund P. Fowler and David Siegel, 90–107. Don Mills, ON: Oxford University Press.

HAP Steering Committee. 2010. *Kamloops Homelessness Action Plan 2010.* Kamloops, BC: Changing the Face of Poverty, HAP Steering Committee. http://www.accesskamloops.org/docs/kamloops-homelessness-action-plan-2010.pdf.

Hellyer, Paul T. 1969. *Report of the Federal Task Force on Housing and Urban Development.* Ottawa: Queen's Printer.

Irwin, John. 2004. *Home Insecurity: The State of Social Housing Funding in BC.* Vancouver: Canadian Centre for Policy Alternatives, BC Office, and Tenants Rights Action Coalition.

Layton, Jack, with Michael Shapcott. 2008. *Homelessness: How to End the National Crisis.* 2nd ed. Toronto: Penguin.

MacKinnon, Robert, and Ross Nelson. 2005. "Urban and Economic Change in Kamloops: Postindustrial Adjustments in a Staples Economy." In *The Small Cities Book: On the Cultural Future of Small Cities,* edited by W. F. Garrett-Petts, 23–48. Vancouver: New Star Books.

Murphy, Barbara. 2000. *On the Street: How We Created the Homeless.* Winnipeg: J. Gordon Shillingford.

Patterson, Michelle, Julian M. Somers, Karen McIntosh, Alan Shiell, and Charles James Frankish. 2008. *Housing and Support for Adults with Severe Addictions and/or Mental Illness in British Columbia*. Burnaby, BS: Simon Fraser University, Centre for Applied Research in Mental Health and Addiction. http://www.sfu.ca/content/dam/sfu/carmha/resources/hsami/Housing-SAMI-BC-FINAL-PD.pdf.

Prince George. 2010. *My PG: An Integrated Community Sustainability Plan for Prince George*. Parts 1 and 2. Prince George, BC: City of Prince George.

Public Policy Forum. 2002. *Supporting Communities Partnership Initiative: What We Heard*. Ottawa: Public Policy Forum. https://www.ppforum.ca/sites/default/files/supporting_communities_partnership_initiative_0.pdf.

Sailor, Lisa E. 2010. "Conditioning Community: Power and Decision-Making in Transitioning an Industry-Based Community." PhD diss., Department of Recreation and Leisure Studies, University of Waterloo, Waterloo, ON.

Scoffield, Heather. 2011. "Ottawa and Provinces Reach $1.4 Billion Deal on Affordable Housing." *Toronto Star*, 4 July.

Shapcott, Michael. 2007. *Ten Things You Should Know About Housing and Homelessness*. Toronto: Wellesley Institute. http://www.wellesleyinstitute.com/wp-content/uploads/2011/11/wimiloon2007_0.pdf.

SPARC BC (Social Planning and Research Council of British Columbia). 2011. *Knowledge for Action: Hidden Homelessness in Prince George, Kamloops, Kelowna, Nelson, and Nanaimo*. Burnaby, BC: Social Planning and Research Council of British Columbia. http://www.sparc.bc.ca/wp-content/uploads/2017/01/knowledge-for-action-research-report.pdf.

Sundberg, Alice, Michael Litchfield, Deborah Kraus, Michael Loewen, and Jane Ritchie. 2009. *Home for Good: Kelowna's Ten Year Plan to End Homelessness*. Draft prepared for the Poverty and Homelessness Action Team, Central Okanagan, and the Kelowna Committee to End Homelessness. http://www.castanet.net/content/1243913711AFT.pdf.

Suttor, Greg. 2017. "Housing in the 2017 Federal Budget: The Broad Picture." *Wellesley Institute*. 27 May. http://www.wellesleyinstitute.com/housing/housing-in-the-2017-federal-budget-the-broad-picture/.

UBCM (Union of British Columbia Municipalities). 2008. *Affordable Housing and Homelessness Strategy*. Policy Paper #2. 24 September. http://www.ubcm.ca/assets/Resolutions~and~Policy/Policy~Papers/2008/Policy%20Paper%20 2-Affordable%20Housing%20and%20Homelessness-2008.pdf.

2 Zoned Out

Regulating Street Sex Work in Kamloops, British Columbia

Lorry-Ann Austin

It's when it's visible on the streets and interferes with daily life that people get concerned. (Mel Rothenburger, quoted in Koopmans 2003)

Prostitution may indeed be the oldest profession, and yet, in contemporary Western societies, the visible presence of sex workers on city streets is typically perceived as a cause for alarm. The above comment, made by the mayor of Kamloops, British Columbia, from 2000 to 2005, seems to epitomize a widely shared conviction that, if sex work cannot be wholly eliminated, then sex workers should at least be rendered invisible—hidden away to protect the public from unsightly scenes of degraded morality. In fact, those involved in the sex trade are more often the ones in need of protection. In the words of the United Nations Population Fund, "Social stigma and discrimination against sex workers create an environment that perpetuates a culture of violence. Their basic human rights to protection and redress are commonly disregarded; they are more often penalised and regarded as criminals" (UNFPA 2006, 39). The criminalization of prostitution contributes to this culture of violence, encouraging a view of sex workers as members of the underworld.

In the media, sex work has generated what John Lowman (2000) terms a "discourse of disposal," that is, a focus, in reportage, on efforts to banish sex workers from relatively affluent residential areas and associated business districts and to consign them instead to a city's lower-class neighbourhoods and criminal ghettoes. Lowman argues that this discourse played a role in the steep rise in the murder rate among Vancouver sex workers beginning in 1980. Many of the more than sixty-five women who disappeared from Vancouver's Downtown Eastside between 1997 and 2002 are known to have been involved in the street sex trade (Oppal 2012, 1:32–33, and see also 1:98–111). Given the association between some of these disappearances and the work of serial killers, most notably Robert Pickton, the case of the Vancouver missing women acquired a sensational element, attracting much attention in the media both before and after Pickton's arrest in 2002. The discourse that Lowman identifies, however, which implicitly equates sex workers with social garbage, not only remains prevalent but continues to exert an influence on social policy, contributing to exclusionary approaches that aim to "get rid of" sex workers by banishing them from public view.

A diverse body of academic research (see, for example, Francis 2006; Hubbard 1998; Lowman 2000; O'Neill et al. 2008) centres on the potential for public responses to the sex trade to provoke policies intended to conceal the existence of sex workers. Criminologist John Lowman asserts that the dangers associated with sex work increase when sex work is hidden from public view (Keller 2011). At the municipal level, we encounter a wide range of regulatory approaches to sex work, from law enforcement by local police and community surveillance in the form of neighbourhood patrols to the relaxed regulation of brothels and the enhancement of support services that assist sex workers in exiting the trade. Yet we need a more complete understanding of how the perceptions and interests of community members influence local policy with respect to the sex trade.

With a focus on the period from 2002 to 2009, this chapter examines the reaction of residents and business owners in Kamloops's North Shore area to the growth of the street sex trade in their community, in an effort to analyze the impact of local responses on the evolution of policy in the context of municipal governance. As John Minnery (2007) argues, in contrast to the notion of government, which places the emphasis on a single actor (the state), the term *governance* is more inclusive, extending beyond the interests of the state to encompass those of the market, as articulated by members of the business community, and of civil society at large. Local governance includes all forms of collective action directed at the development of social policy, from the decisions of municipal government to the activities of business lobby groups and community activists (Healey 2006, 302). At the same time, the formulation of social policy at the municipal level is influenced by political and economic ideologies that prevail at higher levels of government.

In 2001, the BC provincial election moved governing philosophy sharply to the right, with the landslide defeat of the New Democratic government and the election of the BC Liberal Party by an overwhelming majority. Premier Gordon Campbell's 2002 provincial budget reflected a firmly neoliberal orientation, evident in major tax cuts, reduced expenditures, and the elimination of thousands of civil service jobs (Laanela 2009). The provincial government cut funding for women's centres and legal aid, froze health care and education budgets, increased medical services plan premiums, and lifted the freeze on postsecondary tuition, actions that translated into an increase in social needs and a decrease in social resources. In the small city of Kamloops, marginalized populations became increasingly visible, while city administrators struggled to find ways to manage the problems associated with their presence. The street sex trade in Kamloops generated considerable controversy and debate among citizens and in the local media. Rather than attempt to develop a consensus-based approach to the issue, however, Kamloops pursued two discrete strategies, consisting of heightened law enforcement and efforts to suppress the sex trade, on the one hand, and, on the other, programs intended to provide social and health support to sex workers, with the goal of both encouraging and enabling them to exit the trade.

The Regulation of Sex Work: Contextual Considerations

Cities in Canada are bound by provincial and federal laws, which constrain their scope of governance. With respect to sex work, cities must abide by the provisions of the federal Criminal Code (Canada 1985), which outlaws activities integral to the sex trade. During the period under study here, it was, for example, illegal under section 213(1)(c) of the Criminal Code to communicate with someone in a public place "for the purpose of engaging in prostitution or of obtaining the sexual services of a prostitute." In 2007, however, a former sex worker, Sheryl Kiselbach, and an organization of street-based sex workers in Vancouver's Downtown Eastside challenged the federal legislation, arguing that existing prostitution laws violated the Charter of Rights and Freedoms by impeding what their legal counsel described as the right of sex workers "to work safely and live in safety, to be free from arrest and to be free from the inequalities they currently experience as a result of the laws" (Katrina Pacey, quoted in "Supreme Court" 2011; see also Pacey 2012). Two years later, in Ontario, a group of sex workers mounted a similar challenge, and, in 2010, an Ontario Superior Court judge struck down three sections of Canada's prostitution laws, observing that "provisions meant to protect women and residential neighbourhoods are endangering sex workers' lives" (Tyler 2010).

Although the Supreme Court of Canada ultimately dismissed the first case, in December 2013, the Court upheld the Ontario ruling, declaring that the three sections in question infringed upon the rights of prostitutes under section 7 of the Charter "by depriving them of security of the person in a manner that is not in accordance with the principles of fundamental justice" (Canada 2013, 1104). Sex workers celebrated this victory, although it proved to be a brief one. The Protection of Communities and Exploited Persons Act, which became law in November 2014, effectively reinstated laws against prostitution (see Canada 2014, "Summary"). Whether these new provisions will be successfully challenged remains to be seen, but the focus in litigation has clearly fallen on the potential for policy responses to endanger sex workers' lives and violate their civil rights.

Even though provincial governments have no direct jurisdiction over the legal status of prostitution, as this is the domain of the federal Criminal Code, they do, of course, have some control over the interpretation and enforcement of federal laws. Provincial officials may regulate sex work in a variety of ways, using their jurisdiction over highways and traffic, community safety, and child protection. While city governments must similarly operate within the provincial framework, they retain some independent power to respond to the sex trade via municipal bylaws that regulate the use of streets, business licensing, and the zoning of off-street sex services (Barnett 2014).

In addition, approaches to regulation surrounding the street sex trade are informed by the sociopolitical context in which the work takes place; thus, regulation will look different in different localities (see, for example, Francis 2006; Kohm and Selwood 2004; Larsen 1992). Community dialogue about the street sex trade influences this local context, producing specific city-level responses. These responses include unofficial policies that tolerate the street trade in specific areas of a city, gentrification of other areas in an effort to push out sex workers, local campaigns aimed at shaming the purchasers of sexual services, and increased funding for enforcement. Within the limits of federal and provincial legal frameworks, municipal governments are free to pursue their own policies, placing both the sex worker and neighbourhoods in which the trade takes place at the mercy of local social and political interests and dynamics.

As research on the street sex trade reveals, the discourses produced or repeated by local government, business owners, and community members interact to produce specific policy responses (see, for example, Hubbard 1998; Lowman 2000; O'Neill et al. 2008; Tani 2002). A study of the discourses surrounding sex work in Victoria, British Columbia, from 1980 to 2005 noted the prevalence of themes of contagion, which conceptualize the sellers of sex as diseased or otherwise amoral and hence as a threat to the community. As the authors point out, "Solutions are aimed at containment in order to protect the innocent, as well as business owners, from the unsightliness of outdoor sex industry work and the supposed attendant crime and disease" (Hallgrimsdottir, Phillips, and Benoit 2008, 271). In the realm of policy, such solutions typically entail efforts to restrict the street sex trade to certain spaces within a city in order to protect other spaces from its socially disruptive potential (see Hubbard and Sanders 2003). In contrast, a number of cities in Britain and Europe have experimented with formally delimited "tolerance zones," where sex workers can operate free of police harassment (see Jones et al. 2005). In June 2012, the mayor and council of the Montréal borough of Mercier–Hochelaga-Maisonneuve proposed the creation of such a zone within the borough, but Montréal's city council was swift to reject the idea, on the grounds that prostitution is illegal ("Montreal Borough Wants a 'Zone of Tolerance' for Prostitution" 2012).

The existing research also demonstrates that policy responses to the sex trade are highly sensitive to spatial configurations. Yet, to date, studies of sex work have tended to focus on major metropolitan areas: the regulation of the street sex trade in smaller cities remains largely unexplored. Not only does the sex trade occur outside of large metropolises, however, but it is, in fact, more difficult to conceal in a small city. In large cities, street sex work is usually confined to a specific "red-light" district (or districts), and buffer zones exist between these spaces and other areas in the city. As a result, most residents are insulated from the sight of sex workers plying their trade. Within the relatively concentrated space of a small city, however, the street trade may be witnessed daily by residents as they go about their routine business. This visibility generates hot debates, fuelled by emotional reactions, that escalate quickly and that demand a response from small-city governments.

As our social attitudes and political programs continue to align with right-of-centre, neoliberal orientations, sex workers and other marginalized individuals seem to face intensified scrutiny, all the more so within the small city. The conditions of modern society have produced growing numbers of people perceived as a threat to a shrinking sense of neighbourhood and community (Deutschmann 2005; Hubbard 2004; Hubbard, Matthews, and Scoular 2008). Within the small city, vocal citizens assert opinions about what they feel is missing from their community and what values they believe are in need of protection. They may also adopt a revanchist stance, exerting their collective will in an attempt to reclaim spaces perceived to have been lost to groups of marginalized individuals (MacLeod 2002).

A Visible Presence: The Sex Trade in Kamloops

Situated in the southern interior of British Columbia, at the junction of the north and south branches of the Thompson River, Kamloops is the service hub for the municipalities and rural populations within the Thompson-Nicola Regional District. The region's main hospital is located in Kamloops, as is Thompson Rivers University. The central downtown area lies on the south side of the Thompson River, near the confluence of its two branches. Across the river is another downtown business area known as the North Shore, located on the west side of the north-south flowing North Thompson River, while on the river's east side is the Tk'emlúps te Secwepemc Reserve (also known as the Kamloops Indian Reserve). Billing itself as the "Tournament Capital of Canada," Kamloops is the frequent host of sporting events and is also home to a vibrant arts and culture scene. Upscale restaurants and shops, as well as a range of business and corporate headquarters, create the impression that this small city has all the amenities found within larger metropolises. Yet, like all small cities, Kamloops is relatively self-contained, rather than forming part of a sprawling metropolitan region containing many satellite communities.

As of 2011, the population of Kamloops stood at 85,678 (British Columbia, BC Stats 2011). As is typically the case in small cities, Kamloops's administrative infrastructure is not as well developed as that of larger urban centres, and the city had relatively little experience to draw on when forced to confront the range of social issues thrust upon it in a neoliberal political climate. Sociologist Linda Bell Deutschmann, who taught at Thompson Rivers University during the early 2000s, observed that the province's cuts to social services, decreased access to legal aid, and a freeze in social assistance rates resulted in a sharp increase in visible homelessness and other social ills in Kamloops (Deutschmann 2005, 335–36). Faced with the need to attract new investments to expand its revenue base, in part to support a growing population, city administrators tended to view the visible presence of sex trade workers and other marginalized individuals as threats to economic growth. In this, the city was often joined by members of the business community, while local citizens voiced concerns about violence and safety, as well as about the impact of the sex trade on specific neighbourhoods. Together, these concerns gave rise to a discourse of exclusion, one that demanded strategies that would remove sex workers from sight. At the same time, other members of the community, and to some degree the city itself, adopted a more inclusive position, regarding sex workers as victims in need of rescue and looking to social programs for solutions.

At the time Gordon Campbell's Liberals came to power in BC, Kamloops already had one program in place designed to address the needs of sex workers: Social and Health Options for Persons in the Sex Trade, locally known as SHOP. Launched in 1997, SHOP aims to provide support to street sex workers, with a view to assisting them in abandoning the trade and becoming integrated into the social mainstream. In pursuit of this goal of inclusion, the program also offers education to the broader community about the nature of the street sex trade and the exploitation entailed in the commodification of sex. Using tax dollars and revenue generated from licensing fees levied on the city's massage parlours and escort agencies, Kamloops initially provided SHOP with an annual operating budget of $5,000. Some years after the program was implemented, an article in the *Kamloops Daily News* proclaimed that Kamloops was the only city in Canada to be the sole provider of taxpayer funds for a local program aimed at getting sex trade workers off the street (Young 2005).

As the existence of SHOP demonstrates, the street sex trade was a source of concern in Kamloops well before Campbell's victory. Perhaps unsurprisingly, for a small city, Kamloops contained no spaces, such as those so often found in larger metropolises, within which the existence of the sex trade is informally tolerated—the sex strolls in Vancouver's Downtown Eastside, for example, or the *tippelzones* in Dutch cities. It appears from newspaper reports that, during the late 1990s, the street sex trade became a source of concern in the city's downtown core, on the south side of the Thompson River, but that, early in the 2000s, the trade moved to the North Shore, apparently shifting its location in response to law enforcement efforts in the downtown. It was not long before North Shore community members began to react. In 2003, a delegation of North Shore residents and business owners visited City Hall to demand that the mayor, Mel Rothenburger, address their concerns about the influx of sex workers by banning the trade from certain public spaces. In response, Kamloops City Council considered enacting a bylaw, similar to one drafted by the City of Surrey, that would fine sex workers caught in areas near schools, parks, and residential homes, only to discover that the proposed bylaw would be unenforceable owing to constitutional issues (Hewlett 2003). The city's first attempt at "people zoning" thus ended in defeat. But the war was only beginning.

The Struggle for Territory

As a review of articles in the city's two main newspapers reveals, concerns about the street sex trade began to escalate in 2004, with community members generally adopting a revanchist stance, implicitly staking a claim to the ownership of public space on the North Shore and demanding help from the city in their efforts to defend "their" territory. Following the demise of the bylaw idea, the mayor had convened a task force charged with developing local solutions to the street sex trade, and Kamloops City Council then sponsored a series of community meetings at which North Shore residents were encouraged to take their own action to protect local neighbourhoods (Hewlett 2004a; 2004b). Various suggestions emerged from these meetings, including efforts at gentrification—cleaning up streets and local properties with a view to discouraging sex workers—as well as the formation of a block watch to patrol neighbourhoods ("Creating Safe Places Meeting Dates" 2004).

A community meeting held in July 2004 resulted in the formation of the North Shore Community Working Committee, made up of representatives from community groups and local service providers. The committee aimed to develop what *Kamloops This Week* described as a "made-in-Kamloops" solution to the related problems of drug use and the street sex trade, a process that would involve trying out various strategies to find a combination that worked. The committee sought to develop action plans and form neighbourhood associations that could represent the issues of the neighbourhood with the city ("Team Tackles Crime" 2004). Although the chair of the newly constituted committee remarked on the compassion for sex workers shown by many of those present at the July meeting, he also acknowledged that local residents did not want the sex trade in their own neighbourhoods ("Team Tackles Crime" 2004). In other words, despite an apparent recognition that sex workers were not simply criminals, the prevailing discourse remained one of exclusion: the overriding goal was to rid the area of sex workers.

As the growth of a visible sex trade continued unabated into 2005, revanchist sentiments intensified, with North Shore residents and business owners complaining loudly about sex workers lining the lower section of Tranquille Road, the area's main business corridor. Their complaints were compounded by a series of three murders, the first in 2003, in which the victims were identified as women involved with the street sex trade. The media contributed to a rising sense of peril, portraying the North Shore as dangerous and detailing residents' fears that the trade was threatening irreversible harm to the community. The owners and employees of local businesses spoke out, demanding that city staff increase the number of foot and bicycle police patrols, with the goal of moving the trade out of key business areas, while the North Shore Business Improvement Association organized meetings with city officials and the police in hopes of finding a solution ("Sex Trade Meeting" 2004; "Creating Safe Places Meeting Dates" 2004).

The idea of a neighbourhood block watch group, first proposed in 2004 during the series of community meetings hosted by the city council, became a reality in 2005 when a group of concerned citizens, men and women, joined together to create the North Shore Citizens' Safety Patrol. According to an article in *Kamloops This Week,* the patrol aimed to "step up pressure on unsavoury characters who have contributed to the problems of what some local residents describe as an area out of control" ("Taking Back the Streets" 2005). The volunteer group patrolled areas of the North Shore known to have high levels of sex trade activity, identifying and accosting possible offenders and often interacting with the police ("North Shore Patrol" 2006). Kamloops's crime prevention officer, a former member of the RCMP who strongly supported the effort, provided the volunteers with training to assist them in their activities. In groups of six, wearing brightly coloured safety vests and equipped with cellphones, flashlights, and cameras, the patrol walked the neighbourhood, trailing sex workers and snapping photographs of people seeking to purchase their services ("Crime Gets Unwelcome Shadow" 2005; "Taking Back the Streets" 2005). The patrol was accused of engaging in vigilante justice, but the group's coordinator denied this, insisting that the objective was simply to keep the neighbourhood safe ("North Shore Patrol" 2006). So did the crime prevention officer, who was quoted as saying, "This is not a vigilante group. It's a group of concerned citizens. It's prevention through presence" ("Crime Gets Unwelcome Shadow" 2005).

A few months earlier, in April, another group of concerned citizens had attended an evening presentation by an Edmonton vice squad officer and representatives from the Prostitution Awareness and Action Foundation of Edmonton. The officer painted a grim portrait of the sex worker, often little more than a child, trapped in a dangerous and abusive system. He warned against law enforcement efforts that serve only to move the trade from one location to another, usually temporarily, without getting to the root of the problem—namely, the customer. He urged the city to set up a local "john school" that would seek to rehabilitate those arrested for purchasing sex by offering them an alternative to prosecution ("Local Solution Needed" 2005). The city council and the local RCMP considered the possibility, but, in the end, the idea generated little enthusiasm. The underlying attitude seemed to be that boys will be boys—that the male sex drive was just too powerful to contain. Beneath that, one detects a familiar reluctance to hold men accountable for their actions, especially when, instead, one can blame the woman.

In addition, the SHOP program had been obliged to close down in 2005, owing to safety and liability issues resulting from a lack of adequate funding. Its closure prompted impassioned pleas from the executive director of the AIDS Society of Kamloops (ASK)—the organization under which SHOP operated—for an increase in its current annual budget of $13,500 (Young 2005). These pleas did not go unheard within the community, especially among those who were critical of tactics of exclusion and who regarded sex workers as victims of exploitation in need of protection and support. The existence of this countervailing discourse provoked considerable debate among local citizens about the merits of approaches that sought to offer help to sex workers, rather than simply remove them from sight, with Kamloops City Council coming in for criticism for its failure to provide adequate funding for the SHOP program. Especially in the wake of the three murders, however, questions also arose about the capacity of social programming such as SHOP to curb the problems associated with the sex trade. The mayor, Mel Rothenburger, expressed his skepticism on this score, arguing that, while he supported the SHOP program, harm-reduction approaches were insufficient: "We have to continue to look at enforcement, drug addiction and other areas," he said (quoted in Young 2005).

The issue of how far to tolerate the existence of the sex trade and pursue harm-reduction strategies surfaced during the November 2005 municipal election. All three mayoralty candidates (Rothenburger did not seek re-election) weighed in on a suggestion made by a progressive city councillor in Vancouver about the possible development of a city-owned, nonprofit brothel. One candidate voiced tentative support for the idea, pointing out that, if Ottawa were to legalize prostitution—brothels were, and still are, illegal under section 210 (1) of the Criminal Code—then the "controlled" environment of a licensed brothel might help to sever the link between sex work and the drug trade. The others disagreed, however, with the winning candidate, Terry Lake, declaring that "you can't solve prostitution without solving the drug problem first" ("Pondering Prostitution" 2005). As a solution to the drug problem was nowhere in sight, the question remained how best to cope with the situation on the North Shore.

In the eyes of North Shore residents, the increased visibility of the sex trade was connected to the displacement of sex workers from the city's more prosperous South Shore. This shift in location was blamed in part on the city's decision to close down low-income housing on the south side of the river and focus instead on the construction of high-density low-income housing on the North Shore. "We on the North Shore are getting fed up with the way city council keeps dumping crap on our doorstep," said one angry resident, arguing that city council had "chased all the hookers and drug dealers over to the North Shore" (Morgan 2006). Frustrated community members continued to demand that the city council increase law enforcement efforts, accusing administrators of viewing the North Shore as a lower-class area not worthy of the same quality of attention as the more upscale South Shore. Their anger reached a boiling point when they learned that the city council had approved, without prior consultation, a three-year increase in the annual budget of SHOP to $68,000 on the understanding the program would now include a drop-in centre and counselling services for street sex trade workers. These were to be housed in ASK's new headquarters, which just so happened to be located on the North Shore (Duncan 2005). In response to an outcry from North Shore business owners, the city council postponed implementation of the changes to the SHOP program, eventually signing off on a watered-down version that eliminated the drop-in component ("City to Hire Crime Officer" 2006).

As it became increasingly apparent that residents of the North Shore were simply unwilling to tolerate a visible sex trade, municipal administrators began to lean more towards exclusionary tactics, to the neglect of other options. As part of the city's initial response to citizen complaints, a subcommittee of its Social Planning Council was asked to review the sex trade policies developed in Victoria and Vancouver and to prepare a series of recommendations. The resulting report laid out a multi-pronged plan that incorporated measures aimed at prevention and harm reduction, along with treatment and healing programs, and housing and political initiatives, in addition to policing and prosecution (Hewlett 2005; Rothenburger 2005). The report met with criticism from city council members, however, with some arguing that it placed too much emphasis on social programming while failing to give adequate priority to community protection. The consensus was, moreover, that this combined strategy would have little immediate impact on the main source of complaint, namely, the visibility of the sex trade.

Faced with what was clearly a growing crisis, city administrators turned instead to the RCMP, with which the city had for many years collaborated via its Police Committee. In 2005, at the request of the city, the RCMP stepped up enforcement efforts on the North Shore with a series of undercover sting operations targeting both the purveyors and purchasers of sex services. While this crackdown did have the short-term effect of clearing prostitutes from the streets, it also provoked a debate in the community about the ethics of using undercover RCMP officers to entice marginalized sex workers into situations leading to their arrest (Bass 2007; Begley 2007; Koopmans 2007). Nor was it effective in the long term. Following their release from jail, many of the sex workers simply returned to the North Shore.

Despite the efforts of the volunteer citizens' patrol and the increased attention of the RCMP, the North Shore continued to be depicted as territory in peril. Insisting that their community was on the verge of destruction, residents and business owners relentlessly pressured Kamloops City Council, demanding definitive action. As one local resident told council members, "It's pure hell over here. I'm fed up. I want you guys to deal with it" ("Royal Pain" 2006). The city had its marching orders; what it still seemed to lack was an effective battle plan.

A Thick Red Line

In 2006, with fear and outrage escalating among North Shore business owners and residents, the RCMP worked with the city to create such a plan ("No-Go Zones Considered by Police Group" 2007; "Red Zones to Target Criminals" 2007). The new approach, which was already in use in the nearby cities of Vernon and Kelowna, involved the creation of "red zones." Borders were drawn around two areas in the city known to have a high incidence of sex trade activity and other street crime, one on the North Shore, from Tranquille Road down to the river, and a second in the South Shore downtown. The new policy aimed to prevent criminal offenders—notably, in the case of Kamloops, sex trade workers—from returning to the red zone area following an arrest. If a sex worker was apprehended within the red zone, the RCMP officer could note this fact on the criminal charge report submitted to the courts, and the courts could then prohibit the sex worker from returning to the area once released from custody ("Red Zones" 2007). People zoning had arrived in the small city of Kamloops.

With the red zones in place, the RCMP carried out a series of undercover operations in 2007 and 2008, arresting street sex workers and their customers, who were then barred from returning to the red zones after their release. In the first such operation, which took place on the North Shore in May 2007, seventeen women identified as sex workers were arrested. The action was applauded by some, especially business owners and volunteer members of the North Shore Citizens' Safety Patrol, who noted a marked improvement in the area as a result of the arrests and exclusion orders. Others, however, reacted with anger and dismay, including a writer for *Kamloops This Week*, who was incensed by the heavy-handed police action and complained of "headline-grabbing moves by the police to show they're tough on crime" (Bass 2007). As multiple critics pointed out (see, for example, Koopmans 2007), exclusion zones merely displace criminal activity from one area to another, rather than attempting to reduce crime by addressing the underlying social and economic inequities. The Chairman of the city's Social Planning Council, Ray Jolicoeur, observed that: "Enforcement just moves it around. Moving it around is not the answer. If we choose to move them, there should be a where" ("Will Gang Control Prostitutes?" 2007). Many also expressed concerns about a policy approach that appeared to drive the sex trade further underground. Following the May sweep, a local street nurse told *Kamloops This Week* that the area was "like a ghost town." This worried her. Prior to the sting, the paper reported, "most mornings, she would encounter up to a dozen women on the known strolls," but this had changed since the arrests: "I could not see a soul and that's what's scary," she commented ("Will Gang Control Prostitutes?" 2007; see also "Red Zone Forcing Prostitutes into Hiding, Councillor Claims" 2007).

Located within the red zones were social service agencies that often provided assistance to sex workers—including the ASK Wellness Centre, located on Tranquille Road. Other critics thus questioned the lack of advance consultation with local service providers. Bob Hughes, the executive director of ASK, was shocked: "The sting was ill-conceived and ill-implemented," he declared. "There was no indication they were going to do this" (quoted in Koopmans 2007). At least one city councillor agreed that the agencies offering support to sex trade workers should have been consulted about the potential effects of the new policy. The council member, Arjun Singh, sparked further public outcry by suggesting that, instead of banishing sex workers from the red zones, the city should take steps to tolerate the trade by zoning the areas as sex strolls after midnight. He also proposed that the city council actively lobby the federal government to legalize, regulate, and tax prostitution (Singh 2007; Young 2007). Amidst the heated debate that ensued, Hughes reminded the Kamloops community of its history of support for social programs such as SHOP. "We have not only acknowledged our sex trade," he wrote in the *Kamloops Daily News*. "We as a community have taken the unprecedented step of funding programming to assist those caught in its tight grasp" (Hughes 2007).

Concerns over the implications of the red zone policy for the safety of sex workers prompted Cynthia Davis, agency coordinator for the Kamloops Sexual Assault Counselling Centre, to join with other women in the community to organize a demonstration. The women, dressed in black, took to the streets in the North Shore's red zone early in July 2007. "We are very concerned that a large social action has been taken against the street workers without anyone discussing it," said Cynthia Davis, while other demonstrators spoke to reporters about the need to take action against a "flawed and discriminatory system that puts the victims at greater risk of danger and victimization." The protest provoked the wrath of one local business owner, a man who had recently been president of the North Shore Business Improvement Association. As if to illustrate the problem, he allegedly assaulted Davis during the match, twisting her arm and reportedly forcing her to her knees (Olivier and Bass 2007, quoting Davis).

The creation of the two red zones happened to coincide with the initial legal challenge to Canada's prostitution laws brought by Vancouver's Pivot Legal Society on behalf of Sheryl Kiselbach and the alliance of Downtown Eastside sex workers, and the red zone policy raised similar questions about the possible infringement of individual rights. As Cynthia Davis of the Kamloops Sexual Assault Counselling Centre pointed out with regard to sex workers, "Their civil rights are really being violated because of the red-zone tactics" (quoted in "March to Veer Through Red Zone" 2007). This was also the opinion of one of the writers for *The Galloping Beaver,* whose attention had been caught by the local newspaper report on the protest march. "The establishment of the Red Zone and the prohibitions imposed would be unlikely to survive a 'charter challenge,'" he wrote. "The implementers of the idea probably know that, but they also know the people they are banning from an area of the city are not likely to mount such a challenge and, unless they do so, the ban can be imposed at will." Indeed, the constitutionality of red zones could be called into question on a number of different grounds, depending on the circumstances—but, as one group of socio-legal commentators wryly observes, "zone restriction orders, like other similar orders issued by the courts, seem to be protected from legal and constitutional challenges" (Sylvestre, Bernier, and Bellot 2015, 290).

As a public debate over the ethics of red zones waged on in local newspapers, dissatisfaction began to emerge with exclusionary approaches to the regulation of the street sex trade. The city seemed somewhat caught off guard by the backlash against the red zone policy, which clearly required that it make some sort of accommodation to critics. The courts did recognize that the red zone exclusion orders posed a problem for sex workers trying to access social services and so allowed a temporary exception to the order for those who wanted to enter the zone in order to access such services ("Woman Gets Pass Into Red Zone" 2007). In addition, in response to public criticism over the 2007 RCMP stings targeting prostitutes, the city council unveiled a program that it had taken a year to develop. The Sex Trade Worker Diversion Program aimed to spare sex trade workers conviction and incarceration at the hands of the criminal justice system by offering them the option of enrolling in social programs and addictions treatment to assist them in exiting the trade (Hewlett 2008; Petruk 2008). Unveiled in the spring of 2008, the program was evidence of the city's commitment to longer-term solutions that would provide sex workers with an alternative to life on the street.

In short, in an effort to mediate between citizens who were demanding police action and those calling for more compassionate approaches, the municipal government tempered its reliance on law enforcement by continuing to support the SHOP program, complemented by the introduction of the Sex Trade Worker Diversion Program. Although law enforcement was effective in reducing the visibility of the sex trade in the two red zone areas, displacement—not only of the sex trade but of drug dealers as well—was an ongoing outcome of the enforcement approach, with one resident repeating a familiar complaint in March 2008: "Producing a red zone doesn't solve any problems; all it does is move them to a new location" (Phillips 2008). Indeed, the borders of the downtown red zone were eventually expanded in the wake of concerns about assaults and drug dealing in Riverside Park, located along the river immediately north of the downtown (Young 2010).

By the start of 2009, the streets in Kamloops's two red zones had been virtually cleared of sex trade workers—to the point that, early in January, the *Kamloops Daily News* ran an article titled "Seeking Sex Trade Workers," in which ASK's executive director, Bob Hughes, remarked on the dearth of visible sex trade workers. In late February, another article in the paper, "The Red Zone Effect," noted that "Tranquille Road and the nearby streets and alleys are remarkably different," citing Hughes's observation that "while it's still possible to find signs of drugs and prostitution on the North Shore's streets and alleys, the open trade in society's dysfunction isn't easily seen anymore." The article continued: "The reason? A thick red line, drawn on a map around a several-block area of the neighbourhood" (Koopmans 2008). The exclusionary tactics adopted within the small city of Kamloops had indeed resulted in a dramatic reduction in the visibility of the street sex trade and, with it, an equally marked decrease in public discussion of the issues raised by its presence. It was as if the adage "Out of sight, out of mind" had settled in Kamloops. Whereas citizens of this small city had once debated how best to safeguard the rights of marginalized individuals and ensure the safety of sex trade workers while at the same time protecting community interests, the discussion seemed to vanish into thin air as the sex workers themselves vanished into the night.

Conclusion

In the wake of the 2002 provincial election, the small city of Kamloops was obliged to cope with increased social dysfunction resulting from cuts to funding for social services in a newly neoliberal environment. Faced with the need to regulate a growing street sex trade, the city adopted two principal strategies: continued support for the SHOP program and the creation of the Sex Trade Worker Diversion Program, on the one hand, and red zone exclusion areas, on the other. In pursuing these strategies, the city was attempting to steer a path between two apparently competing bodies of community discourse, one that called for compassionate, inclusive approaches and long-term solutions and another that demanded decisive action to remove sex workers from view. Both perspectives were predicated on the conviction that, ideally, the sex trade should not exist. But whereas the former sought to assist sex workers in exiting the profession, the latter insisted only that sex work be concealed.

As the mayor of Kamloops observed early on, complaints about the sex trade arose "when it's visible on the streets and interferes with daily life." In a small city such as Kamloops, spatial proximity to a visible street sex trade challenges residents' perceptions of normalcy and their sense of community safety, as evidenced in the revanchist sentiments voiced by many North Shore residents and business owners. The implementation and enforcement of the red zone policy in 2007 and 2008 resulted in the virtual clearing of city streets, as sex workers moved to other neighbourhoods to avoid arrest during ongoing undercover police operations. Once the sex workers were (temporarily) out of sight, public debate about the sex trade—including discussions of whether red zones jeopardized the safety of sex workers and infringed on their constitutional rights—was stilled. Residents and business owners had succeeded in reclaiming ownership of the public space they once perceived as polluted by the street sex trade, and, in their eyes, that victory marked the end of the war.

In connection with funding for social programming (notably SHOP), the Kamloops city council periodically reviewed reports on program outcomes, which indicated that supportive measures did encourage sex workers to quit the trade. With regard to red zones, a similar process of assessment does not seem to have occurred. Although research indicates that policy responses that seek to conceal the sex trade, typically by means of law enforcement, place sex workers at greater risk of physical violence and expand the possibilities for exploitation, the City of Kamloops apparently made no systematic effort to evaluate the impact of its red zone policy on the safety of sex workers. No evidence exists that city administrators attempted to evaluate the effects of the policy as employed in other small cities prior to accepting the RCMP's recommendation that it be implemented in Kamloops, nor was an assessment subsequently conducted to determine whether the policy had produced any unintended outcomes.

In responding to concerns about the sex trade, city administrators tended to adopt a reactive, rather than proactive, approach, seeking to quiet citizens' complaints about the visible presence of the sex trade rather than investing time and money in developing more complex, long-term solutions. This pattern is in keeping with policy making in a neoliberal context, where tight budgets and uncertainties about future funding often frustrate efforts at long-term planning. All the same, despite its extensive reliance on exclusion zones and law enforcement, the city did continue to support social programming. What seemed missing was a framework capable of integrating these two approaches. In reporting on community opinion, local newspapers may have heightened the sense of opposition, isolating two bodies of discourse that in fact overlapped. Perhaps mirroring this division, law enforcement and social programming tended to be conceptualized as alternatives, rather than as parts of a whole.

The sex trade still exists in Kamloops, and so do the red zones. In fact, as a recent news report (Legassic 2016) indicates, the RCMP has created a third red zone, in the area of the Northills Mall ("although RCMP could not confirm when it was implemented"). As is evident from this report, the debate about the effects of the red zone policy has not subsided, with the RCMP continuing to insist that red zones do not simply displace criminal activity from one place to another and social advocates arguing that exclusion zones are not a solution. However, in the course of a public address, the superintendent of the Kamloops RCMP evidently agreed with ASK's Bob Hughes in supporting the adoption of a Four Pillars approach in Kamloops (Legassic 2016)—an approach closely similar to that discussed in 2005 by the city's Social Planning Council. Originally developed as a method for addressing street-based drug abuse, the Four Pillars model incorporates prevention, harm reduction, and treatment, in addition to law enforcement. While, in practice, the model is far from flawless (see Weaver, this volume), the implementation of such an approach in Kamloops would represent a much-needed step towards a comprehensive, long-term strategy, one that would not only integrate supportive and punitive measures but would also acknowledge the relationship between the sex trade and the drug trade.

It is probably impossible to eradicate prostitution, which has, after all, been with us since time immemorial. Moreover, no regulatory approach can overturn the poverty that gives rise to so many social ills. Programs like SHOP can, however, help us to develop the empathy needed to create caring and inclusive communities that work together to help marginalized individuals get their lives back. To the extent that we pursue approaches founded on compassion, we may slowly shift our own perceptions and come to demand that our governments do the same.

References

Barnett, Laura. 2014. *Prostitution in Canada: International Obligations, Federal Law, and Provincial and Municipal Jurisdiction.* Background Paper, Legal and Social Affairs Division, Parliamentary Information and Research Service, Library of Parliament. Publication No. 2011-119-E. Ottawa: Library of Parliament. http://www.parl.gc.ca/content/lop/researchpublications/2011-119-e.pdf.

Bass, Dale. 2007. "Is It About Public Safety? Or Public Persona?" *Kamloops This Week,* 6 July.

Begley, Jim. 2007. "Policing Isn't All Black and White." *Kamloops This Week,* 11 July.

British Columbia. BC Stats. 2011. *2011 Census Total Population Results: British Columbia Municipal and Regional District.* http://www.bcstats.gov.bc.ca/StatisticsBySubject/Census/2011Census/PopulationHousing/MunicipalitiesByReg ionalDistrict.aspx.

Canada. 2013. Canada (Attorney General) *v.* Bedford. 2013 SCC 72, [2013] 3 SCR 1101. http://www.canlii.org/en/ca/scc/doc/2013/2013scc72/2013scc72.pdf.

———. 2014. Protection of Communities and Exploited Persons Act. SC 2014, c. 25. http://laws-lois.justice.gc.ca/PDF/2014_25.pdf.

———. 1985. Criminal Code. RSC, 1985, c. C-46. http://laws-lois.justice.gc.ca/PDF/C-46.pdf.

"City to Hire Crime Officer." 2006. *Kamloops This Week,* 13 January.

"Creating Safe Places Meeting Dates." 2004. *Kamloops This Week,* 24 October.

"Crime Gets Unwelcome Shadow." 2005. *Kamloops This Week,* 17 July.

Deutschmann, Linda Bell. 2005. "Kamloops: The Risk Society Is in My Back Yard." In *The Small Cities Book: On the Cultural Future of Small Cities,* edited by W. F. Garrett-Petts, 333–48. Vancouver: New Star Books.

Duncan, Susan. 2005. "Society Must Talk SHOP with Group." *Kamloops Daily News,* 18 November.

Francis, Daniel. 2006. *Red Light Neon: A History of Vancouver's Sex Trade.* Vancouver: Subway Books.

Hallgrimsdottir, Helga Kristin, Rachel Phillips, and Cecilia Benoit. 2008. "Fallen Women and Rescued Girls: Social Stigma and Media Narratives of the Sex Industry in Victoria, BC, from 1980 to 2005." *Canadian Review of Sociology and Anthropology* 43 (3): 265–80.

Healey, Patsy. 2006. "Transforming Governance: Challenges of Institutional Adaptation and a New Politics of Space." *European Planning Studies* 14 (3): 299–320.

Hewlett, Jason. 2003. "Mayor Has Plan to Deal with Hooker Problem." *Kamloops Daily News*, 24 September.

———. 2004a. "North Shore Meet Seeks Solutions." *Kamloops Daily News*, 24 August.

———. 2004b. "Police Show How to Avoid Crime." *Kamloops Daily News*, 26 October.

———. 2005. "Group Takes Action Against Prostitution Problems." *Kamloops Daily News*, 5 May.

———. 2008. "Prostitutes to Get Help Staying Off the Streets." *Kamloops Daily News*, 23 May.

Hubbard, Phil. 1998. "Sexuality, Immorality and the City: Red-Light Districts and the Marginalization of Female Street Prostitutes." *Gender, Place and Culture* 5 (1): 55–69.

———. 2004. "Revenge and Injustice in the Neoliberal City: Uncovering Masculinist Agendas." *Antipode* 36 (4): 665–85.

Hubbard, Phil, Roger Matthews, and Jane Scoular. 2008. "Regulating Sex Work in the EU: Prostitute Women and the New Spaces of Exclusion." *Gender, Place and Culture* 15 (2): 137–52.

Hubbard, Phil, and Teel A. Sanders. 2003. "Making Space for Sex Work: Female Street Prostitution and the Production of Urban Space." *International Journal of Urban Space* 27 (1): 75–89.

Hughes, Bob. 2007. "Community Must Solve Thorny Prostitution Issue." *Kamloops Daily News*, 10 July.

Jones, Peter, David Hillier, Peter Shears, and Daphne Comfort. 2005. "Managing and Regulating Red Light Districts in British Cities." *Management Research News* 28 (8): 61–67.

Keller, James. 2011. "Police Strategy of Forcing Sex Workers Out of Sight Helped Pickton, Expert Says." *Globe and Mail*, 13 October.

Kohm, Steven A., and John Selwood. 2004. "Sex Work and City Planning: Winnipeg's Red Light District Committee and the Regulation of Prostitution."

Research and Working Paper No. 42. Winnipeg, MB: Institute of Urban Studies, University of Winnipeg.

Koopmans, Robert. 2003. "North Shore Sex Trade Raises Alarm." *Kamloops Daily News*, 23 September.

———. 2007. "Men, Women Fair Differently in Crackdown on Prostitution." *Kamloops Daily News*, 9 June.

———. 2008. "The Red Zone Effect." *Kamloops Daily News*, 21 February.

Laanela, Mike. 2009. "Gordon Campbell: Leader of the BC Liberal Party." *CBC News*, 20 March. http://www.cbc.ca/news/canada/british-columbia/gordon-campbell-leader-of-the-bc-liberal-party-1.863628.

Larsen, E. Nick. 1992. "The Politics of Prostitution Control: Interest Group Politics in Four Canadian Cities." *International Journal of Urban and Regional Research* 16 (2): 169–89.

Legassic, Ashley. 2016. "Red Zones: Pushing Offenders Across Kamloops for More Than a Decade." *InfoNews.ca*, 29 October. http://infotel.ca/newsitem/red-zones-pushing-offenders-across-kamloops-for-more-than-a-decade/it35840.

Lowman, John. 2000. "Violence and the Outlaw Status of (Street) Prostitution in Canada." *Violence Against Women* 6 (9): 987–1001.

MacLeod, Gordon. 2002. "From Urban Entrepreneurialism to a 'Revanchist City'? On the Spatial Injustices of Glasgow's Renaissance." *Antipode* 34 (3): 602–24.

"March to Veer Through Red Zone." 2007. *Kamloops Daily News*, 18 September.

Minnery, John. 2007. "Stars and Their Supporting Cast: State, Market, and Community as Actors in Urban Governance." *Urban Policy and Research* 25 (3): 325–45.

"Montreal Borough Wants a 'Zone of Tolerance' for Prostitution." 2012. *CBC News*, 17 June. http://www.cbc.ca/news/canada/montreal/montreal-borough-wants-a-zone-of-tolerance-for-prostitution-1.1131089.

Morgan, Rick. 2006. "City Council Must Stop Dumping on North Shore." *Kamloops Daily News*, 2 December.

"No-Go Zones Considered by Police Group." 2007. *Kamloops Daily News*, 12 May.

"North Shore Patrol." 2006. *Kamloops This Week*, 5 February.

Olivier, Cassidy, and Dale Bass. 2007. "Peaceful Protest Turns Ugly." *Kamloops This Week*, 15 July.

O'Neill, Maggie, Rosie Campbell, Phil Hubbard, Jane Pitcher, and Jane Scoular. 2008. "Living with the Other: Street Sex Work, Contingent Communities, and Degrees of Tolerance." *Crime, Media, Culture* 4 (1): 73–93.

Oppal, Wally T. 2012. *Forsaken: The Report of the Missing Women Commission of Inquiry*. Executive Summary and 4 vols. Vancouver: Missing Women Commission of Inquiry. http://www.missingwomeninquiry.ca/obtain-report/.

Pacey, Katrina. 2012. "Vancouver Sex Workers Win Right to Challenge Prostitution Laws." Pivot Legal Society news release, 21 September.

Petruk, Tim. 2008. "Sting Offers Social Options." *Kamloops This Week,* 25 May.

Phillips, Leslie. 2008. "Drug Dealers Simply Changed Locations." Letter to the Editor. *Kamloops Daily News,* 1 March.

"Pondering Prostitution." 2005. *Kamloops This Week,* 16 November.

"Red Zone Forcing Prostitutes into Hiding, Councillor Claims." 2007. *Kamloops Daily News,* 13 June.

"Red Zones to Target Criminals." 2007. *Kamloops This Week,* 16 May.

Rothenburger, Mel. 2005. "City Sex-Trade Group Works Hard on a Daunting Social Issue." *Kamloops Daily News,* 6 June.

"A Royal Pain That's a Crime." 2006. *Kamloops This Week,* 1 September.

"Seeking Sex Trade Workers, Society Looks for Help Delivering Outreach." 2009. *Kamloops Daily News,* 6 January.

"Sex Trade Meeting." 2004. *Kamloops This Week,* 8 August.

Singh, Arjun. 2007. "Maybe It's Time for Legal 'Stroll.'" *Kamloops Daily News,* 14 June.

Sylvestre, Marie-Eve, Dominique Bernier, and Céline Bellot. 2015. "Zone Restrictions Orders in Canadian Courts and the Reproduction of Socio-Economic Inequality." *Oñati Socio-legal Series* 5 (1): 280–97.

"Supreme Court of Canada to Weigh In on Prostitution Laws." 2011. *NEWS 1130,* 31 March. http://www.news1130.com/2011/03/31/supreme-court-of-canada-to-weigh-in-on-prostitution-laws/.

"Taking Back the Streets." 2005. *Kamloops This Week,* 22 July.

Tani, Sirpa. 2002. "Whose Place Is This Space? Life in the Street Prostitution Area of Helsinki, Finland." *International Journal of Urban and Regional Research* 26 (2): 343–59.

"Team Tackles Crime Head-On." 2004. *Kamloops This Week,* 22 August.

Tyler, Tracey. 2010. "Prostitution Laws Struck Down." *Toronto Star,* 28 September.

UNFPA (United Nations Population Fund). 2006. "HIV/AIDS, Gender, and Sex Work." Fact Sheet No. 9 in *17 Fact Sheets with Concise Information on Gender-Related Aspects of HIV/AIDS.* New York: United Nations Population Fund. http://www.unfpa.org/sites/default/files/pub-pdf/factsheets.pdf.

"Will Gang Control Prostitutes?" 2007. *Kamloops This Week,* 13 June.

"Woman Gets Pass Into Red Zone." 2007. *Kamloops Daily News.* 11 July.

Young, Michele. 2005. "SHOP Around." *Kamloops Daily News,* 13 August.

———. 2007. "Legalize Prostitution Says Singh." *Kamloops Daily News,* 14 June.

———. 2010. "Police Want Riverside Park in Red Zone." *Kamloops Daily News,* 4 December.

3 Needles in Nanaimo

Exclusionary Versus Inclusionary Approaches to Illicit Drug Users

Sydney Weaver

The best way out of addiction is overcoming dislocation by finding a secure place in a real community. (Alexander 2008, 340)

Policies designed to address illicit drug use are, on the whole, shaped less by concerns for the health and safety of drug users than by political and economic interests and mainstream community values, a pattern especially visible at the local level. At the same time, because no society is monolithic, the use of illicit drugs has spawned complex, controversial debates about the relative appropriateness and effectiveness of specific policy approaches and modes of intervention. In this chapter, I explore this debate as it unfolded over the first decade of this century in the small city of Nanaimo, British Columbia, which lies on the east side of Vancouver Island, roughly an hour's drive north of Victoria. Originally a coal mining town, Nanaimo developed an economy founded on logging and commercial fishing. As income from these industries gradually waned and rates of unemployment rose, Nanaimo was obliged to reinvent itself in an effort to diversify its economic base. Already economically depressed, the city was particularly vulnerable to the cuts in funding for social services that followed the election, in 2001, of a provincial government committed to neoliberal principles of financial management—cuts that only exacerbated existing social and economic disparities.

Nanaimo's efforts to develop a municipal policy to address illicit drug use occurred at a time when two competing approaches were available for consideration. One was the so-called war on drugs, a strategy in which drug users are implicitly viewed as enemy agents working to undermine the very moral values on which society rests. Unsurprisingly, the chief weapon in this war is law enforcement. The other was the Four Pillars approach, which combines law enforcement with three supportive measures: prevention, treatment, and harm reduction. A strategy that originated in Europe, the Four Pillars model was implemented in 2001 in Vancouver, a city located just across the Strait of Georgia from Nanaimo. The story of Nanaimo's approach to managing illicit drug use turns on the tension between these alternatives. Clearly, the Four Pillars approach strives for greater flexibility and nuance, as well as situating addiction firmly within a public health framework. And yet, as I will argue below, it falls short of ideal.

Policy Approaches to the Management of Illicit Drug Use

In North America, efforts to regulate the consumption and distribution of narcotics date back to the years prior to World War I, when both Canada and the United States enacted laws restricting access to opiates and cocaine. The "war" on drugs was officially declared in 1971, however, when US President Richard Nixon announced that drug abuse had "assumed the dimensions of national emergency," thereby requiring a "full-scale attack" to combat the problem.[1] As a management strategy, however, the war on drugs has by most accounts been a dismal failure. Propelled by the cultivation of fear and enforced through forms of state violence, this policy approach has not only failed to reduce the incidence of problematic illicit drug use but has significantly exacerbated the health and social problems of drug users (Alexander 1990, 53–93; Boyd 2004; Boyd and Faith 1999). In addition, the war-on-drugs campaign successfully diverts public attention to the "drug addict" as criminal, thereby frustrating the recognition that habitual drug use is often an adaptive response to

1 Richard Nixon, "Special Message to the Congress on Drug Abuse Prevention and Control," 17 June 1971, in *Public Papers of the Presidents of the United States,* Office of the Federal Register, National Archives and Records Service (Washington, DC: Government Printing Office, 1972). The text is available on the website of *The American Presidency Project,* http://www.presidency.ucsb.edu/ws/?pid=3048.

poverty, racism, dislocation, and trauma (Alexander 1990 and 2008; Boyd 1999, 177–182; Boyd 2004, 160–167; van Wormer and Davis 2003).

A structural analysis of the war-on-drugs policy reveals its racialized, gendered, and classist nature (Alexander 1990, 2001, 2008; Boyd 2004 and 2009; Nunn 2002). The retributive character of this approach relies on the cultivation of fear and of othering, ensuring the moral superiority of white middle-class individuals who use only licit drugs and only for legitimate medical reasons. The commitment of the public to financing the war on drugs is partially accomplished by harnessing the media in constructing marginalized people as dangerous, immoral deviants (Boyd 2004, 2009; Reinarman and Levine 2004; Taylor 2008; van Wormer and Davis 2003). As Boyd (2009, 32) observes, "Canadian and U.S. law enforcement . . . made sure that their stories and 'construction' of the illegal-drug user were supplied to journalists and politicians." With the media fuelling condemnatory public opinion, criminalization strategies flourished in both the United States and Canada throughout the twentieth century. In Nanaimo, public fear of drug users has been a prominent factor in the struggle to address illicit drug use, one that has posed substantial challenges for social rights advocates, policy makers, and users.

The Four Pillars Model

Dissatisfaction with punitive approaches to illicit drug use was officially voiced in British Columbia in 1994, with the release of a report by the Office of the Coroner (British Columbia, Ministry of the Attorney General, 1994). The report, which presented the conclusions of a task force convened to investigate an upsurge in the number of deaths in the province from drug overdoses, was highly critical of the prevailing approach to illicit drug use, with its emphasis on the punishment of drug users via the criminal justice system. Arguing that the criminalization of drug use served primarily to aggravate surrounding social problems, the report recommended that addiction be understood as a health issue. Yet, despite its urging that immediate and decisive action be taken to address the inadequacies of the present approach, little came of the report (see MacPherson, Mulla, and Richardson 2006, 127–28).

The need for a more effective strategy was especially evident in Vancouver's Downtown Eastside, which had a growing population of injection drug users. Recognizing that the war-on-drugs approach was not working, the City of Vancouver moved in 2001 to adopt a new policy, embedded in which was a more complex understanding of the nature of drug addiction and its origins. The new approach, outlined in A Framework for Action: A Four-Pillar Approach to Drug Problems in Vancouver (MacPherson 2001), called for an equal focus on the four pillars of (1) prevention, aimed primarily at youth, in an effort to head off the problem; (2) treatment, including the development of various government-funded programs for users trying to abstain from drugs; (3) the enforcement of drug laws, to enhance public safety by curbing the drug trade and associated crimes; and (4) harm reduction, which involves the promotion of health practices designed to reduce health risks for users of illicit drugs, such as the transmission of HIV and hepatitis C. Among the more controversial harm reduction measures adopted in Vancouver were a needle exchange program, which would provide users with new, sterile syringes in exchange for used ones, and a safe injection site, which would offer a secure setting in which users can inject drugs under the supervision of a health care worker. In addition to preventing overdose deaths, such sites open channels of communication between drug users and support personnel, who can educate users about the health risks associated with mainlining drugs and help them connect with social and health services, including treatment programs.

The Four Pillars framework was imported to Vancouver from Europe. The first step consisted of fact-finding trips to various European cities (among them Geneva, Zurich, Frankfurt, and Amsterdam) made by a member of Vancouver's social planning department and subsequently by local politicians, while the second entailed a similar trip by local activists, accompanied by representatives of local media. As McCann (2008, 1) points out, by adopting the Four Pillars approach, Vancouver distanced itself from the dominant ideological and legal framework that exists throughout Canada and from the entrenched American war-on-drugs perspective, ultimately earning itself a place in global discussions of drug policy. McCann (2008, 15) also describes the multi-layered complexity, fiscally and in terms of national and international contacts, that catalyzed the emergence of this policy. These are fortuitous, globalized, urban, sophisticated layers that Nanaimo, a small city off the mainland, does not possess.

Harm reduction offers substantial benefits, including significant improvements in user and community health, evident in reductions in fatal overdoses of illicit street drugs, new HIV diagnoses, and levels of street crime, as well as fewer discarded syringes (Alexander 2006, 118). Although these are noteworthy accomplishments, problems remain, chiefly in connection with the manner in which the Four Pillars framework has been implemented. Specifically, an unbalanced fiscal emphasis on enforcement has relegated the other three pillars of harm reduction, prevention, and treatment to lower-priority status. A review of Canada's Drug Strategy as reformulated in 2003 revealed that "current federal spending on harm reduction initiatives which target HIV/AIDS and other serious harms is insignificant compared to the funds devoted to treatment and, particularly, enforcement"—even though the revised strategy promised "a balanced approach to reduce both the demand for and the supply of drugs through prevention, treatment, enforcement and harm reduction initiatives" (DeBeck et al. 2006, 10). It further appeared that "while controversial interventions supported through the Drug Strategy are being held to an extraordinary standard of proof, interventions receiving the greatest proportion of funding remain under-evaluated" (10). A similar pattern was noted following the introduction, in 2007, of the new National Anti-drug Strategy (see DeBeck et al. 2009). The net result of the federal bias towards enforcement has been to mirror the war-on-drugs policy that the Four Pillars approach was intended to replace.

The relative success of a Four Pillars approach depends, of course, on the social and political context in which it is implemented. The embrace of neoliberal principles of governance, both in British Columbia and in Canada as a whole, may have thwarted balanced funding of the four pillars, given the neoliberal emphasis on "small government," which translates into an unwillingness to fund social services of the sort associated with the welfare state. In such an ideological environment, programs designed to provide support to drug users are unlikely to be high on the list of fiscal priorities. In addition, drug addiction does not accord well with the neoliberal emphasis on entrepreneurialism and productivity. As Alicia Sanderson (2011, 3) points out, the creation of North America's first safe injection site in Vancouver's Downtown Eastside met with "persistent and adamant resistance among high-level government officials in Canada and the United States." Such resistance not only imposes fiscal constraints but also generates a moral climate that discourages compassion for individuals perceived as drains on the economy. Although addiction researchers in Canada have called attention to the benefits of harm reduction (see, for example, Hathaway and Tousaw 2008), as well as to the ineffectiveness of law enforcement and its potential to increase health risks among intravenous drug users (Werb et al. 2008; Wood et al. 2004), the emphasis continues to fall on punitive measures.

Despite its vulnerability to imbalances in implementation, the Four Pillars model clearly represents a more humane and more complex response to illicit drug use than does a strategy that relies primarily or entirely on law enforcement. At the same time, a deeper analysis of the Four Pillars model reveals significant limitations on its ability to effect long-term positive changes not only in the health of individual users but in the social framing of addiction. Bruce Alexander (2006, 121) argues that "social changes of the magnitude necessary to have a substantial impact on the problem of addiction are beyond the Four-Pillar Approach." The social changes to which he refers to can be roughly summarized as the strengthening of social and community relationships, which, in his view, have eroded over time. In *The Globalisation of Addiction,* Alexander (2008, 3) points to "the growing domination of all aspects of modern life by free-market economics," which has produced a society that "subjects people to unrelenting pressures towards individualism, competition, and rapid change, dislocating them from social life." In these circumstances, community relationships that sustain the spirit are severely weakened or even destroyed, and individuals react to this sense of dislocation "by concocting the best substitutes they can for a sustaining social, cultural, and spiritual wholeness" (3). In other words, addiction is, in part, an adaptive response to an increasingly pervasive sense of loss and isolation.

This isolation of the individual from his or her social context is reinforced by the current health care framework, in which physiological good health is presumed to reflect an individual's willingness to avoid risks and cultivate a healthy lifestyle. In this view, health is in large measure a matter of personal responsibility, and individuals are assumed to be capable of free choice. This shift towards individual accountability is problematic in many respects, but it has especially damaging consequences in the context of drug addiction. As Tim Buchanan (2004, 390) points out, such a perspective "risks pathologising problem drug users by holding them solely responsible for exercising poor choices and allowing themselves to drift into drug addiction," tempting others "to embrace the view that problem drug use warrants no sympathy because it is a self-inflicted condition." At the same time, an emphasis on individual agency "tends to promote pathological notions of dependence such as the addictive personality," in an effort to account for the poor choices that culminate in this self-inflicted condition (390). What this focus on individual health neglects to acknowledge, Buchanan argues (2004), is that in many cases "problem drug use is largely a socially constructed phenomenon that has less to do with individual choice or physical dependence, and much more to do with the structural disadvantages, limited opportunities, alternatives and resources" (391).

Alexander (2008, 342) argues that, inasmuch as addiction is a response to the pain of social dislocation, drug treatment "will become more effective when it is oriented towards achieving or restoring psychosocial integration," which he defines as the "profound interdependence between individual and society that normally grows and develops throughout each person's lifespan" (58). To the extent that the Four Pillars framework fails to acknowledge the social embeddedness of addiction, its transformative power is severely curtailed. What is needed is a more inclusive and systemic approach that acknowledges the conditions that lie at the origins of drug addiction and, by fostering public understanding, can promote an attitude of compassion towards users. A social determinants of health model provides the theoretical basis for such an approach.

The Social Determinants of Health Model

Writing in *Social Determinants of Health: The Canadian Facts,* Juha Mikkonen and Dennis Raphael (2010, 7) argue that "the primary factors that shape the health of Canadians are not medical treatments or lifestyle choices but rather the living conditions they experience." This insight is fundamental to any social determinants of health framework. According to a model developed in 2002, Canadians share fourteen basic social determinants of health: Aboriginal status, disability, early life, education, employment and working conditions, food insecurity, gender, health services, housing, income and income distribution, race, social safety net, social exclusion, and unemployment and job security (Mikkonen and Raphael 2010, 9). In other words, a person's gender, race or ethnicity, and class, as well as presence or absence of a disability, determine that person's relative ease of access to food, education, housing, health and social services, social capital, and a means to earn a livelihood. In turn, a person's degree of access to these assets exerts a determining influence on the status of his or her health.

Those who become habitual users of illegal drugs could be analyzed from the standpoint of any one of these fourteen factors. I will focus here on social exclusion, however, simply because drug-addicted individuals—notably those who live in poverty and/or belong to racialized groups—tend to constitute a highly marginalized population. Social exclusion effectively denies certain citizens the opportunity to participate fully in society and thus to share equitably in its benefits. Describing the Canadian situation, Mikkonen and Raphael (2010, 32) observe that many features of our society combine to "marginalize people and limit their access to social, cultural and economic resources. Socially excluded Canadians are more likely to be unemployed and earn lower wages. They have less access to health and social services, and means of furthering their education. These groups are increasingly being segregated into specific neighborhoods."

As Robin Peace (2001, 26) notes, social exclusion is often defined in relatively narrow economic terms, as referring to "poverty, income inequality, deprivation or lack of employment." But such definitions fail to capture the psycho-social effects of exclusion. Citing reports on the European Union's Poverty Programmes, Peace emphasizes that social exclusion must be recognized both as a dynamic process, rather than a static condition, and as multidimensional. Not only does it involve "a lack of resources and/or denial of social rights," but it also frequently results "in multiple deprivations, the breaking of family ties and social relationships, and loss of identity and purpose" (26). In this respect, social exclusion contributes to the sense of dislocation that Alexander (2008) identifies.

In the case of drug users, social exclusion is often compounded by the stigma attaching to the fact of addiction, with addicts viewed as individuals lacking in self-discipline who have lost control over their lives (Room 2005). Such negative images are often compounded by other sources of stigma, such as poverty, homelessness, or a history of incarceration, which have been shown to exert an adverse impact on the health of drug users (Galea and Vlahov 2002). In addition, social processes of exclusion are fed by the media's tendency to draw connections among illicit drug use, race, and crime, thereby fuelling public fears about the "drug problem" and serving to create and sustain an atmosphere of moral panic (Altheide 1997; Boyd 2009; Eby 2009; Chiricos, Eschholz, and Gertz 1997). Somewhat ironically, efforts to exclude certain individuals from the broader public place a significant financial burden on that public—reflected, for example, in hospitalization costs for homeless persons (Hwang et al. 2011; United Kingdom, ODPM 2004, 8) as well as in the diversion of public resources, including police, into enforcement measures that often prove ineffective (Wood et al. 2004).

The potential benefits of a socially inclusive approach to problem drug use can to some extent be inferred from the positive results obtained by the adoption of a restorative justice framework in the area of corrections. Whereas incarceration isolates offenders from the society at large, restorative justice seeks to maintain social connectedness by bringing together the offender, the victim(s), and the community with a view to reparation. In this "process of coming together to restore relationships," reconciliation becomes possible between the wrongdoer and the wronged, while "the community is also provided with an opportunity to heal through the reintegration of victims and offenders" (Latimer, Dowden, and Muise 2005, 129). Research into the outcome of restorative justice programs not only reveals reduced rates of recidivism (van Wormer 2003; Latimer, Dowden, and Muise 2005, 137) but also, and perhaps more importantly, psychological benefits to all involved, deriving above all from the strengthening of relationships. As a UK government report, *Tackling Social Exclusion,* notes, a restorative justice approach implemented by Bradford's Youth Offending Team "has linked young offenders to the (often socially excluded) victims of their crimes, such as older people, in a way which has reduced some of the isolation they previously experienced" (United Kingdom, ODPM 2004, 11). Similar psychosocial benefits would almost certainly accrue from efforts to draw drug users into the community.

Situating Nanaimo

Located roughly 110 kilometres north of Victoria, Nanaimo is the second largest city on Vancouver Island. As of the 2016 census, the Nanaimo metropolitan area had a population of 104,936 people, with roughly 90,000 residents living within the city limits. By contrast, the Victoria metropolitan area was home to nearly 368,000 people, while the population of Vancouver stood at over 4 million.[2] However, population in itself does not define the small city. In setting forth an agenda for research on small cities, David Bell and Mark Jayne (2009, 689) suggest that "smallness can be more productively thought of in terms of influence and reach, rather than population size, density and growth," which points to the challenge that small cities face in developing a

2 "Census Agglomeration of Nanaimo, British Columbia," *Focus on Geography Series, 2016 Census,* Statistics Canada, 2017, https://www12.statcan.gc.ca/census-recensement/2016/as-sa/fogs-spg/Facts-cma-eng.cfm?GC=938&GK=CMA&LANG=Eng&TOPIC=1.

"competitive advantage in the global urban hierarchy." Recognizing the need to expand its economic base, Nanaimo embarked during the 1990s on efforts to extend its influence and reach, drawing on its strategic location as a port city in reasonable proximity both to the capital of British Columbia (Victoria) and to its largest metropolitan centre (Vancouver). Central to these efforts was the development of the downtown waterfront area as a tourist destination, as well as the construction of the Port of Nanaimo Centre, which houses conference facilities. As economic planners were aware, the city's task was to create "a positive image that communicates to outsiders that Nanaimo is an attractive and supportive place to live and invest" (Sailor 2010, 143).[3]

Almost inevitably, the decline of traditional industries creates a population of individuals who are not only unemployed but, in some sense, unemployable, in that their skills do not mesh with the needs of the new economy. Economic dislocation thus tends to produce not merely poverty and food insecurity but a sense of purposelessness and futility—conditions that easily give rise to social problems. In 2001, Nanaimo's unemployment rate stood at 11.6 percent, compared to the provincial average of 8.5 percent, with male participation in the labour force having declined between 1996 and 2001 from 71.5 percent to 65.9 percent (2001 census figures, cited in NWGH 2003, 9, 8). Nanaimo's struggle to carve itself a niche in a globalizing economy was thus complicated by an increase in visible homelessness, a trend noted by the BC Ministry of Health in its 1999 annual report (British Columbia, Office of the Provincial Health Officer 2000, 40). In *Reducing Homelessness: A Community Plan for Nanaimo, BC,* the Nanaimo Working Group on Homelessness (2003) argued, however, that the city's "greater concern" lay with the degree of "relative homelessness" in Nanaimo, a problem that reflected both "generational poverty and structural and transitional problems in the local and regional economy" (NWGH 2003, 8).[4]

---

3 In "Conditioning Community: Power and Decision-Making in Transitioning an Industry-Based Community" (2010), Lisa Sailor presents an insightful account of Nanaimo's quest to attract both tourists and investment (see esp. chaps. 4 and 5). She is referring here to the recommendations of the city's Economic Development Group in *Working Together to Build a Prosperous Future,* a report first presented in 1999 to the Nanaimo Chamber of Commerce.

4 A term used by the United Nations, "relative homelessness" refers to people who are at risk of becoming homeless. As defined by the Nanaimo Working Group on Homelessness, the term designates "people living in spaces that do not meet basic health

Nanaimo's difficulties were doubtless intensified by Canada's embrace of neoliberal principles of economic and social management. Neoliberalism holds that "human well-being can be best advanced by maximizing entrepreneurial and individual freedoms through the unrestricted flow of capital," a proposal that "functions best under a framework characterized by free markets, free trade, and individual liberty" (Sailor 2010, 7). Among other things, this ideology translates into a reduction in government support for social services, on the theory that these can be provided more efficiently through private-sector competition (despite considerable evidence to the contrary). At the federal level, neoliberalism entails efforts to "shrink" government by offloading fiscal responsibilities onto provinces and municipalities. Lacking adequate sources of local revenue, smaller municipalities (such as Nanaimo) often have little choice but to pursue private-sector business investments and corporate partnerships and/or to attract tourist dollars.

Nanaimo's response to the growing visibility of homelessness and drug addiction developed within this rather unforgiving neoliberal framework. Local social service providers and advocacy groups were, of course, well aware of the negative effect of funding cuts on both clients and workers. The 2003 report issued by the Nanaimo Working Group on Homelessness noted that agencies responding to the needs of drug users were under tremendous strain, with substantial waitlists for services (NWGH 2003, 19). Nor did a homeless population of drug users dovetail well with Nanaimo's plans to gentrify its waterfront.

A Shift in Discourse: The Evolution of City Policy

Between 2003 and 2008, the City of Nanaimo commissioned a series of reports relating to social development, homelessness, and illicit drug use. These reports, which provide insight into Nanaimo's struggle to address the social problem of drug use, were supplemented by two action plans drawn up by the Nanaimo Working Group on Homelessness. Also included in this analysis is the only report that focused specifically on developing an alcohol and drug strategy (NADAC Strategy Working Group 2006). I analyze these

---

and safety standards, including protection from the elements, access to safe water and sanitation, security of tenure, personal safety and affordability" (NWGH 2003, 6).

reports through a social determinants of health lens, with specific reference to social exclusion.

In 2003, Nanaimo's Social Development Strategy Steering Committee commissioned a social status report for the city, as a first phase in the creation of a social development strategy. The resulting report (John Talbot and Associates 2003) describes the situation in Nanaimo at that time in terms of its economy and key social determinants such as education, health, housing, and participation. Also produced in 2003 was *Reducing Homelessness: A Community Plan for Nanaimo, BC* (NWGH 2003). This report, prepared by the Nanaimo Working Group on Homelessness, identifies population groups at risk of homelessness, among them "people suffering from addiction"—a population that overlaps with virtually all of the other target groups, which include "people living with or at risk of HIV/AIDS, Hepatitis C, or other communicable diseases" and "people living with mental illness" (4). Poverty and social exclusion are significant themes throughout this report, reflecting a structural analysis of homelessness, and housing is appropriately described as an important social determinant of health. The report recommends a continuum of services and a communication strategy that aims to inform the public of the social and fiscal costs of homelessness. This latter recommendation is crucial to garnering public investment; the report notes that in the past, communication strategies were recommended but "not fully implemented" (28).

In 2004, by way of a follow-up to the 2003 social status report, the city released a report that proposed a social development strategy for Nanaimo (John Talbot and Associates 2004). Intended as a response to "high rates of income assistance, increasing homelessness and poverty, persistently high unemployment levels and substance misuse issues" (ii), the report was based on consultation with approximately five hundred people, including a focus group with lone and young parents and "an alcohol and drug focus group" (4). The report calls for an "inclusive" community that facilitates "social and intergenerational interaction" and "optimizes community and family support systems" (8). These proposals reflect a social inclusion model; indeed, one of the report's five main themes is inclusiveness. Also noted in this report is the public's lack of understanding of illicit drug use and how this contributes to sparse funding for relevant services (23). However, this concern with public ignorance is not reflected in the report's recommendations. Although the report emphasizes the importance of viewing illicit drug use as a health, not a criminal, issue, recommendations focus on enforcement rather than on public education and strategies to achieve social inclusion.

In 2005, the City of Nanaimo, under pressure from service providers, commissioned a study of the impact of recent zoning changes on the provision of social services (NWCI 2005). The new zoning bylaw, which had been provisionally adopted in February 2005, prohibited "social service resource centres," such as food banks, facilities that offer free meals or used clothing, and drop-in centres, from operating within the city limits. (The one exception was a Salvation Army facility.) An equally hostile spatial exclusion effort was reflected in the outright ban on any "drug addiction treatment facilities," such as "methadone clinics, needle exchanges, safe injection sites (of which there are none at present in Nanaimo) and any other centre that treats persons with substance abuse problems" (4). Although service providers had expressed concerns to city council prior to the passing of the new zoning bylaw, city council temporarily overrode these concerns. The bylaw was, however, adopted on the understanding that the City of Nanaimo would commission a report to evaluate whether the service providers' concerns were legitimate.

In the resulting report, Neilson-Welch Consulting provides a window onto the highly contested issue of illicit drug use in Nanaimo. The report describes a web of fear, experienced by all stakeholders, as both prominent and problematic: "In NWCI's view, the environment in which the zoning changes affecting service providers were conceived and adopted can be characterized as one of fear. Each of the key players in Downtown Nanaimo—business, the City, residents, social service providers—sees the signs of stress in VCAND and experiences a sense of fear" (NWCI 2005, 7–8).[5] The report describes how this pervasive fear fostered mistrust, negatively affected relationships among key players, and perpetuated a divisive "us and them" dynamic among stakeholders (9). The consultants argue that the zoning changes "divide rather than strengthen the community" (13) and that "proponents of the zoning changes are attempting to control a factor that they will be unable to control" (12)—namely, the physical location of people in need of social services. The insights revealed in this report highlight the importance—to city council, to

5 "VCAND" is an acronym, formed from street names, used in the report to designate an area of downtown Nanaimo deemed to be "at risk": it refers to "properties along Victoria Road, Victoria Crescent, Cavan, Dunsmuir (up to City Hall), Abbott and Nicol (including the New Hope Centre and the area behind it)" (NWCI 2005, 6).

the public, and to business interests—of the control and ownership of public space. These territorial efforts to spatially exclude service providers signify the intensity of fear and hostility related to illicit drug use.

The NWCI report goes on to argue that supporters of the zoning bylaw overlook two important considerations. The first concerns the capacity of service providers to manage their operations in a way that minimizes any negative impact on the area in which they are located (NWCI 2005, 12). The report thus redirects the gaze from *where* service providers are located to *how* they deliver services. As the authors further observe, "the other issue that is lost under zoning is the importance of collective action in dealing with the signs of stress" (12). The report then calls on social service providers in the area to "initiate a process of building community acceptance," to "educate clients," and to "support and hold each other accountable" (22–23). While the authors recognize the strain on service providers' already scarce resources, they argue that "providers that are unable or unwilling to commit such resources should not expect to operate in Nanaimo" (23). In addition, the report encourages client groups to recognize the need for a "balance of rights and responsibilities," with the former defined as "the rights of clients to access important services" and the latter as "respecting the needs and recognizing the concerns of the neighbourhood in which the services are located" (31).

The rights and responsibilities framework was taken up by the city, if perhaps in a somewhat lopsided fashion. As a local government official commented in an interview: "We think that there's dignity in reciprocity. In other words, if you're going to provide someone with those services, then what we ask you to do is be clear with them that when they go into the public realm, there's certain expectations about how they conduct themselves. So it's not a free lunch." If it were applied across the board, a rights and responsibility framework might have potential to guide policy founded on principles of social inclusion, but, as conceived in the report, it extends only to service users and providers. The NWCI report does discourage the city from adopting an enforcement approach to the new requirements for service providers, noting that enforcement is not "consistent with the cooperative approach being promoted" (NWCI 2005, 26). At the same time, "targeted enforcement" and an increased police presence focused on illicit drug users form part of the report's recommended strategy (29).

In naming fear and divisive sentiments among stakeholders, emphasizing a spirit of cooperation, providing some strategies to facilitate cooperation, and including a few service users in planning decisions, the NWCI report differs to some extent from others. However, while the report recommends dialogue and cooperation, urging both businesses and residents to communicate with service providers, the bulk of the responsibility is assigned to service providers. Instead, the report might also have proposed increased responsibility for the city government, including recommendations that the city address the public fear that seemed to drive city council's decision to adopt the new zoning bylaw prior to its review and that it also identify and attempt to overcome obstacles to communication among *all* stakeholders.

In 2006, the NADAC Strategy Working Group, in collaboration with various local agencies, prepared a report titled *Process for Developing an Alcohol and Drug Strategy for Nanaimo*. Describing itself as a "coalition of community, government and non-government agencies concerned with the alcohol and drug problem in Nanaimo and committed to action that will reduce the harm within our community," NADAC—the Nanaimo Alcohol and Drug Action Committee—resided within the Nanaimo Youth Services Association and was chaired by the association's director.[6] As would be expected, this resulted in the strategy's emphasis on youth, an emphasis also visible in NADAC's source of funding, the Nanaimo Addiction Foundation. Although young people are the standard target of measures aimed at prevention, an analysis of the homeless population in Nanaimo revealed that, at the time, middle-aged men formed the majority of the homeless, drug-using population: "Males outnumbered females by a wide margin: 59 males (61%) to 38 females (39%)" (Tubbs 2008, 5). The median age of Nanaimo's homeless rose from 35.6 years in 2005 to 41.39 years in 2008; of 302 homeless counted in Nanaimo in 2008, "only ten clients report that they do not use alcohol or drugs" (4). Thus, the majority of Nanaimo's homeless, illicit-drug-using population, adult men, were excluded from the city's only official alcohol and drug strategy.

Evidently, "action that will reduce the harm within our community" did not extend to reducing harm to drug users—perhaps on the unspoken assumption that they are not part of "our community." Indeed, the NADAC report (2006, 7) cites numerous American government resources that promote a punitive war-on-drugs discourse, resources that have already been

---

6 "NADAC," *Prevention Hub*, 2016, http://preventionhub.org/en/who-is-who/nadac-nanaimo-alcohol-and-drug-action-committee. This description originally appeared on NADAC's own web page (http://www.nysa.bc.ca/NADAC.html).

demonstrated to be marked by racism, classism, and sexism (Boyd and Faith 1999; Nunn 2002; Reinarman and Levine 2004). Rather than emphasizing how certain social determinants negatively affect health, the NADAC report simply notes that marginalization on the basis of "race, Aboriginal status, class background, disability, homelessness and addiction or fetal alcohol effects" has been shown to correlate with the risk of being "involved in crime" (7).

Had a structural analysis been undertaken in this report, the discussion could have been moved towards a social determinants of health model, one in which the vulnerabilities of marginalized youth would be addressed through social inclusion measures such as family counselling, employment opportunities, and supported housing (see March, Oviedo-Joekes, and Romero 2006). Although the report calls for a "paradigm shift in political will and public acknowledgment" and underscores the need "for all citizens to become healthy and productive" (NADAC Strategy Working Group 2006, 18), the strategy itself reflects a less than inclusive approach. The report recommends a "community consultation process," but the homeless and/or users of illicit drug users are not listed as target groups for consultation (27). Consultation with these citizens could have helped NADAC's working group better understand the impact of social exclusion on health and thus develop a more comprehensive and effective strategy. Given that no follow-up reports were issued, it is unclear how far city policy was influenced by NADAC's recommendations.

In 2008, the City of Nanaimo commissioned CitySpaces Consulting to develop a Harm Reduction and Housing Action Plan that would address "the increasing problems of homelessness and the related challenges of mental illness and drug addiction" (CSC 2008b, 1). The result was a series of three reports. The first, *A Response to Homelessness in Nanaimo: A Housing First Approach—Relevant Best Practices,* documents the need for low-barrier housing in Nanaimo and describes a series of best practices illustrated by initiatives in other cities that have proved effective. The Housing First model is based on the premise that "stable housing enables individuals to better address their barriers to employment, addictions, and poor health" (3) and stipulates that the provision of housing should not be contingent upon certain preconditions, such as abstinence from illicit drug use. Noting that municipalities have often been reluctant to take the lead in initiatives to address homelessness, the report significantly assigns a number of key roles to municipal government, including advocacy, problem solving, and the building of partnerships (CSC

2008a, 9). As the authors point out, "While many communities have made strides towards adopting housing first approaches and introducing significant initiatives to respond to homelessness, there continues to be opposition. Community leadership is essential to raise awareness and foster cooperation among major stakeholders" (9–10).

The second report builds on the first, detailing the need for harm reduction and Housing First services in Nanaimo (CSC 2008b). Two focus groups informed this second document, one made up of business owners and the other of service providers. Also consulted were health authority representatives, the RCMP, and presidents of neighbourhood associations—and, perhaps most important, five homeless persons were interviewed. The report identifies "balancing enforcement and service delivery" as one of the challenges faced by the city (17). CitySpaces also noted continuing problematic public attitudes, apparent in "community reluctance to *reward bad behaviour*" and a belief that "addicts choose their lifestyle and therefore are not deserving of help until they *clean themselves up*" (18; emphasis in the original).

As the report notes at the outset, harm reduction aims to "ensure that the most vulnerable and the most street-entrenched individuals have access to a range of services that will minimize harm and enable them to pursue their goals towards recovery and stability" (CSC 2008b, ES-2). This approach is an improvement on the war-on-drugs approach, but strategies are still needed to counter public opposition to harm reduction practices and to incorporate these practices into a broader framework that promotes social inclusion. As noted above, public preconceptions, which give rise to a process of othering, present an obstacle for current and former drug users who are attempting to achieve social integration. Julian Buchanan (2004, 395) explains: "For many problem drug users relapse is not simply the result of physical craving or a lack in motivation, but it is a direct consequence of a frustration and inability to secure a position in normal community life and establish everyday routines." In other words, the spatial and moral exclusion of drug users only makes it that much more difficult for them to work towards recovery. Although Housing First initiatives are a step towards social inclusion, disparaging attitudes on the part of the public may compromise the benefits of such initiatives, effectively sabotaging positive outcomes.

The final report by CitySpaces Consulting lays out an eight-point action plan to reduce homelessness in Nanaimo and improve the quality of life for the city's most vulnerable citizens (CSC 2008c). Noting that earlier efforts to tackle homelessness have tended to be "disjointed and under-resourced," the report emphasizes the need to mobilize broad support for a "comprehensive and cohesive response" to a continuing problem (13). Indeed, noteworthy among the eight points is "Facilitate community acceptance." The plan described in the report focuses on harm reduction strategies under the broader umbrella of a Housing First approach, which was to be implemented in Nanaimo through collaboration with the Vancouver Island Health Authority and BC Housing. The Action Plan developed by City-Spaces was adopted by Nanaimo City Council in 2008. According to one city official, approval of the plan "led to the signing of a Memorandum of Understanding with BC Housing in November of 2008 and funding commitments in 2009 and 2010 to construct 160 units of low-barrier housing on five sites throughout the City" (pers. comm., 2011).[7]

As is evident from these three reports, a shift towards a discourse of inclusion—however clumsy and piecemeal, and however contested by the business community and the public—did occur. This important shift could be sustained and enhanced if Nanaimo were to adopt a social determinants of health framework. This framework would support the public education needed to foster social inclusion. For instance, the city could provide information distributed by the Vancouver Island Health Authority (VIHA) about the social factors that contribute to illicit drug use. In 2006, VIHA released a discussion paper on the social determinants of health, which describes Nanaimo as "among the worst-performing areas in the province," as measured by a composite socioeconomic index based on "economic hardship, crime, health, education, children-at-risk and youth-at-risk" (VIHA 2006, 3). Nanaimo was also identified as one of the three areas with the highest level of income inequality (17). Greater public awareness of this situation could precipitate a shift in public perceptions of drug users and increased support for Housing First initiatives.

The VIHA report (2006, 23) notes the existence in BC of high levels of social exclusion among people who are unable to work or are unemployed, as well as among recipients of social assistance (23). In addition, people with physical or mental disabilities often struggle with social exclusion, and the

---

7 See "Memorandum of Understanding Between BC Housing Management Commission (BC Housing) and the City of Nanaimo Regarding the Development of Sites for Supportive Housing," 12 November 2008, http://www.bchousing.org/resources/Housing_Initiatives/MOU/MOU_Nanaimo.pdf.

report further recommends that action be taken to enable such people to "participate more fully in the opportunities afforded by their communities" (26). Nanaimo's challenge lies in translating observations about the importance of social inclusion into policy. Harm reduction services, such as those offered in Nanaimo by NARSF Programs Ltd., make a significant contribution towards social inclusion and health promotion for citizens struggling with addiction.[8] But shifts in the direction of policy and the allocation of resources must be accompanied by educational initiatives that emphasize the social context of illicit drug use and the costs of social exclusion to taxpayers, the individual, and the economy.[9] Such educational efforts would help to foster public support for harm reduction practices and for programs designed to promote social inclusion measures, which would increase the likelihood of improved funding of such initiatives.

Analysis of the Nanaimo Strategy

Spatial Exclusion

Nanaimo's attempts to resuscitate its economy by attracting both business investments and a tourist trade gave rise to a range of legal sanctions and bylaws that aimed to "disappear" the already marginalized from potentially revenue-generating public spaces. In 2005, the RCMP introduced a "multi-pronged approach" to the management of Nanaimo's growing street population (see CSC 2008b, 6–7). This approach combined surveillance and law enforcement with modifications to the built environment (in accordance with a strategy known as Crime Prevention Through Environmental Design) and with the spatial exclusion of the homeless in the form of two red zones. Although the creation of red zones led to a "marked reduction in visible homelessness and open drug use" in the red-zoned areas, it did so with the predictable result: "Many of the visible homeless and street-entrenched

---

8 Created in 1990 under the name Nanaimo and Area Resource Services for Families, NARSF Programs Ltd. offers a number of programs oriented towards harm reduction, including a needle exchange available through its Mobile Health Outreach program, as well as the Linked to Treatment (L2T) Program and the Harris House Health Clinic. For more information, see "Philosophy of Harm Reduction Programs," NARSF Programs Ltd., 2012–14, http://www.narsf.org/harm-reduction-programs/philosophy/.

9 On these costs, see United Kingdom, ODPM (2004, 7–8).

population were pushed out of downtown and into neighbouring areas" (7). As is well recognized, such tactics of dispersal merely move a problem around: as the report noted, no evidence existed to suggest any actual reduction in the number of homeless. In fact, as service providers pointed out, the use of red zoning increased health and safety risks for the homeless, in part by preventing access to crucial social services located in the downtown, and also contributed to "further *criminalization* of problems like addiction and mental illness" (7; emphasis in the original).[10]

The red zones were intended to support the revitalization of Nanaimo's downtown by sparing the relatively affluent the sight of citizens deemed undesirable. Ultimately, the goal was to remove unsightly bodies and replace them with more "sightly" ones symbolic of health and prosperity. As the city official I interviewed put it, "You need young, talented, ambitious people from outside to come here," adding that this is "the thing that appeals" to members of city council. The same official also spoke approvingly of the role of the RCMP ("God bless 'em") in "busting up" groups of homeless drug users: "They'll drag them around, so to speak, in small subgroups around the city, not allowing them to roost anywhere and to claim possession of a territory." The metaphor is one of warfare, with society's marginalized citizens cast in the role of enemy invaders who have no right to a home—not even on the street.

Public Perceptions of Drug Users

As we have seen, the report prepared in 2005 by Neilson-Welch Consulting called attention to the fears that fed into discussions of Nanaimo's population of homeless drug users (see NWCI 2005, 7–9). Research has explored how fear can propel policy (see, for example, Allen 2000; Brinegar 2000; and Kingfisher 2007), a mechanism perhaps visible in the decision of Nanaimo City Council to implement its zoning bylaw prior to undertaking a review of the possible consequences (NWCI 2005, 1). Fears about the visible presence of "derelicts"—panhandlers, drug addicts, hookers, and so on—are often driven in part by concerns about property values or business investments, but they also reflect an equation of such individuals with potentially violent criminals,

---

10 See Austin (this volume) for an analysis of the RCMP's use of red zones in Kamloops. Drawing on a case study of homeless shelters in Columbus, Ohio, Andrew Mair (1986) argues that the homeless threaten systems of meaning essential to production and consumption in the postindustrial city.

with the result that the marginalized are assumed to pose a threat to personal security. "They might choose your business next to do their crack in front of, " the city official I interviewed remarked of drug users, "and you're not safe—no one is safe in this community from these people."

Punitive public attitudes towards illicit drug users continue to plague Nanaimo (see, for example, Sterritt 2018). Although Nanaimo has taken concrete, visible action towards supporting a harm reduction, Housing First approach to drug addiction, these initiatives must be sustained by community education directed towards transforming public views of drug users, which is a critical first step in fostering social inclusion. As Room (2005, 152) points out, "psychoactive substance use occurs in a highly charged field of moral forces," within which the processes of marginalization and stigmatization operate. Educating the public about such processes and the moral judgments that underlie them might help to shift community perceptions of drug users. If, for example, community members were informed about life events common to many users of illicit drugs—including domestic violence and abuse, trauma, and the experience of racism (see, for example, Bungay et al. 2010; Maté 2008; Shannon, Spittal, and Thomas 2007)—their fears might give way to a more sympathetic perspective. Advocacy groups and progressive city officials have a crucial part to play in promoting an understanding of addiction as a public health issue, in educating the public about the effects of social exclusion, and in evolving and supporting policies aimed at incorporating drug users into the community.

In particular, efforts must be made to offset the negative images that abound in the popular media, which in turn shape public perceptions. With regard to addiction, Alexander (2008, 367) emphasizes the need to pro-duce and circulate information that can counter the existing "propaganda apparatus," with the goal of "replacing the indoctrination system with com-munications media that foster psychosocial integration" (367). The Nanaimo Working Group on Homelessness was well aware of the need for an effective communications strategy. As the group noted in its *Nanaimo Homelessness Partnering Strategy Action Plan* (2007, 15), "past efforts, such as the Homeless-ness Action Week that broadened participation and public relations efforts, provided opportunities for improved sharing of information on activities, and strengthened relationships with policy makers and the media."

Social Inclusion: A Way Forward

Drug users have historically experienced all four of the key components of social exclusion described by Mikkonen and Raphael (2010, 32): *denial of participation in civil affairs,* as a result of various legal and institutional mechanisms; access to *social goods,* such as housing, health care, and education; *exclusion from social production,* that is, from opportunities to participate in and contribute to social and cultural activities; and *economic exclusion,* in the form of the inability to access a means to livelihood. In Nanaimo, as elsewhere, these processes of exclusion have been reinforced by openly condemnatory public attitudes, against which advocates of harm reduction strategies must struggle. The efforts of advocacy groups and service providers such as the Nanaimo Working Group on Homelessness and Nanaimo and Area Resource Services for Families, combined with a commitment by social planners and city council members to effect change, have resulted in substantive movement towards social inclusion. These foundational steps are commendable, but Nanaimo needs to build on them.

As Alexander (2008, 58) argues, psychosocial integration—the antithesis of social dislocation—"reconciles people's vital needs for social belonging with their equally vital needs for autonomy and achievement." Efforts that aim at the social inclusion of drug users must attend to both sets of needs. In this connection, Alexander proposes that ways be found "to draw land out of the control of the market" (371)—in other words, to reclaim public space. Other steps towards achieving social integration include a revival of the local arts, which, as Alexander points out, are "a necessary part of the imagery that holds communities together, contributing to people's sense of identity and shared meaning" (372), as well as activities that create a sense of community solidarity based not on uniformity but on "cultural fusion" (376–77). Municipalities can foster social integration by organizing and funding inclusive community events held in public spaces, by linking Housing First sites to community social and recreational activities, and by supporting creative, artistic initiatives that showcase the talents of marginalized citizens (such as Vancouver's Hope in Shadows project, which highlights the photographic skills of residents of the city's Downtown Eastside).

Buchanan (2004, 394) also recommends services for drug users that focus on "reorientation and reintegration," including "befriending schemes, buddying programmes, mentoring schemes, structured day programmes, sheltered work programmes, voluntary work, and basic adult education." As he points out, initiatives focused on the drugs themselves and/or on the individual user are doomed to fail; these must be accompanied by fundamental changes in both social conditions and public attitudes towards those trapped in addiction. Drug users, whether active or abstinent, require support in their endeavours to engage in active citizenship, whether through employment readiness programs, life skills training, or other opportunities to invest in meaningful lives. Nanaimo could bolster Housing First initiatives with additional strategies aimed at social inclusion, such as providing incentives to businesses to hire recovering addicts who are attempting to join the workforce, ensuring that low-income citizens can afford access to public recreational facilities, and creating opportunities for socially marginalized groups to participate in community events.

As Mikkonen and Raphael (2010, 32) remind us, socially excluded citizens are frequently denied access to participation in civic affairs. This mechanism of exclusion is visible in the formulation of social policy, which often occurs in the absence of any input from those at whom the policy is directed. Instead, drug users must be given a voice in the creation and shaping of policies and services that directly affect their lives. Not only must their contributions be actively sought, but their ability to contribute must be practically supported by the removal of obstacles that prevent them from participating in consultations and attending meetings. Research indicates that face-to-face personal contact between members of ostracized groups and dominant, nonstigmatized groups reduces prejudicial attitudes towards the homeless (Lee, Farrell, and Link 2004), towards persons with AIDS (Herek and Capitanio 1997), and towards persons living with mental illness (Reinke et al. 2004). In community and policy-making settings, face-to-face contact between users, former users, and other members of the community could prove extremely valuable in reshaping public attitudes and in revising drug users' own self-image.

Efforts to undo social exclusion perhaps focus overmuch on fostering a sense of social belonging, at the expense of strengthening personal autonomy and the capacity for accomplishment—two qualities that are essential to our sense of self-worth and that addiction almost inevitably undermines. In developing future strategies, Nanaimo would do well to look for ways not only to help drug users become part of the community but also to grant them their right to autonomy and to present them with opportunities to achieve.

Conclusion

This review of Nanaimo's efforts to manage illicit drug use reveals a lengthy and complex debate, one that speaks to both the challenges and the importance of reconciling a multiplicity of conflicting perspectives through a process of education and collaboration. I have argued that adopting a social determinants of health framework, in support of the goal of social inclusion, would allow for a more sustainable solution to the coexisting problems of homelessness and drug addiction in this small city. Central to achieving both spatial and social inclusion is education, a priority identified by the Nanaimo Working Group on Homelessness. Images of the "dangerous homeless drug addict" that have historically permeated public and political discourse must continue to be challenged and subverted. Writing about resistance to Vancouver's safe injection site, Andrew Hathaway and Kirk Tousaw (2008, 13) emphasize the power of arguments founded on human rights. While acknowledging that "popular perceptions of addiction and drug use have slowly been destabilised by evidence-based knowledge," they go on to point out that, in Vancouver, "social activists bridged chasms that research evidence could not in forcing recognition that 'addicts' are sons and daughters, brothers, sisters, parents" (13).

Efforts aimed at reducing fear and positioning drug addiction as a health issue forms the basis for increased public tolerance, paving the way for the introduction of socially inclusive policies and practice. Fostering public understanding of drug addiction could take a variety of innovative forms, including posters in public places, community "town hall" events featuring speakers and short plays, radio spots, and interviews with drug users focusing on life circumstances—such as poverty, domestic violence, sexual abuse, or systemic discrimination—that contributed to their addiction. With this foundation of education aimed at engendering public acceptance, subsequent efforts to develop "user-friendly" public spaces, to encourage drug users to participate in community activities, and to provide these marginalized citizens with opportunities for work or education would be better supported.

More than a decade ago, in the discussion paper in which it recommended the adoption of a social determinants of health framework, the Vancouver Island Health Authority observed: "The kind of communities that we develop is a more important determinant of the health status of the population than the kind of health care system we construct" (VIHA 2006, 27). It added that whether "we are willing to act on this knowledge" is something that "remains to be seen" (27). By taking such action, Nanaimo could position itself as an innovative leader in managing drug addiction and provide an example of hope to other small cities struggling with poverty, homelessness, and drug use in a political and economic climate hostile to those disadvantaged by neoliberal policies. Enlightened health leadership and progressive civic leadership can certainly contribute to building more compassionate and inclusive communities. Ultimately, however, the impetus to change must come from the people who live in those communities.

References

Alexander, Bruce K. 1990. *Peaceful Measures: Canada's Way Out of the "War on Drugs."* Toronto: University of Toronto Press.

———. 2001. *The Roots of Addiction in Free Market Society.* Vancouver, BC: Canadian Centre for Policy Alternatives.

———. 2006. "Beyond Vancouver's 'Four Pillars.'" *International Journal of Drug Policy* 17 (2): 118–23.

———. 2008. *The Globalisation of Addiction: A Study in Poverty of the Spirit.* Oxford: Oxford University Press.

Allen, Tom C. 2000. *Someone to Talk to: Care and Control of the Homeless.* Halifax: Fernwood Publishing.

Altheide, David L. 1997. "The News Media, the Problem Frame, and the Production of Fear." *Sociological Quarterly* 38 (4): 647–68.

Bell, David, and Mark Jayne. 2009. "Small Cities? Towards a Research Agenda." *International Journal of Urban and Regional Research* 33 (3): 683–99.

Boyd, Susan C. 1999. *Mothers and Illicit Drugs: Transcending the Myths.* Toronto: University of Toronto Press.

———. 2004. *From Witches to Crack Moms: Women, Drug Law, and Policy.* Durham, NC: Carolina Academic Press.

———. 2009. *Hooked: Drug War Films in Britain, Canada, and the United States.* Toronto: University of Toronto Press.

Boyd, Susan C., and Karlene Faith. 1999. "Women, Illegal Drugs, and Prison: Views from Canada." *International Journal of Drug Policy* 10 (3): 195–207.

Brinegar, Sarah J. 2000. "Response to Homelessness in Tempe, Arizona: Public Opinion and Government Policy." *Urban Geography* 21 (6): 497–513.

British Columbia. Ministry of the Attorney General. 1994. *Report on the Task Force into Illicit Narcotic Overdose Deaths in British Columbia.* Burnaby, BC: Office of the Coroner, Ministry of the Attorney General.

British Columbia. Office of the Provincial Health Officer. 2000. *A Report on the Health of British Columbians: Provincial Health Officer's Annual Report, 1999.* Victoria, BC: Ministry of Health and Ministry Responsible for Seniors.

Buchanan, Julian. 2004. "Missing Links? Problem Drug Use and Social Exclusion." *Probation Journal* 51 (4): 387–97.

Bungay, Vicky, Joy L. Johnson, Colleen Varcoe, and Susan C. Boyd. 2010. "Women's Health and Use of Crack Cocaine in Context: Structural and 'Everyday' Violence." *International Journal of Drug Policy* 21 (4): 321–29.

Chiricos, Ted, Sarah Eschholz, and Marc Gertz. 1997. "Crime, News and Fear of Crime: Toward an Indentification of Audience Effects." *Social Problems* 44 (3): 342–57.

CSC (CitySpaces Consulting). 2008a (January). *A Response to Homelessness in Nanaimo: A Housing First Approach—Relevant Best Practices.* Prepared for the City of Nanaimo. Victoria, BC: CitySpaces Consulting. https://www.nanaimo.ca/assets/Departments/Community~Planning/Social~Planning/Nanaimos~Response~to~Homelessness~Action~Plan/080107_Nanaimo_BP_Research_MG.pdf.

——. 2008b (May). *A Response to Homelessness in Nanaimo: A Housing First Approach—Situational Analysis.* Prepared for the City of Nanaimo. Victoria, BC: CitySpaces Consulting. https://www.nanaimo.ca/assets/Departments/Community~Planning/Social~Planning/Nanaimos~Response~to~Homelessness~Action~Plan/080507_Nanaimo_Situational.pdf.

——. 2008c (July). *Nanaimo's Response to Homelessness: Action Plan.* Prepared for the City of Nanaimo. Victoria, BC: CitySpaces Consulting. http://www.nanaimo.ca/assets/Departments/Community~Planning/Social~Planning/Nanaimos~Response~to~Homelessness~Action~Plan/080707_Nan_Strategy.pdf.

DeBeck, Kora, Evan Wood, Julio Montaner, and Thomas Kerr. 2006. "Canada's 2003 Renewed Drug Strategy: An Evidence-Based Review." *HIV/AIDS Policy and Law Review* 11 (2): 1, 5–12.

——. 2009. "Canada's New Federal 'National Anti-drug Strategy': An Informal Audit of Reported Funding Allocation." *International Journal of Drug Policy* 20 (2): 188–91.

Eby, David. 2009. "Closing Ceremonies: How Law, Policy and the Winter Olympics are Displacing an Inconveniently Located Low-Income Community in Vancouver." *Planning Theory and Practice* 10 (3): 395–418.

Galea, Sandro, and David Vlahov. 2002. "Social Determinants and the Health of Drug Users: Socioeconomic Status, Homelessness, and Incarceration." *Public Health Reports* 117 (Suppl. 1): S135–45.

Hathaway, Andrew D., and Kirk I. Tousaw. 2008. "Harm Reduction Headway and Continuing Resistance: Insights from Safe Injection in the City of Vancouver." *International Journal of Drug Policy* 19 (1): 11–16.

Herek, Gregory M., and John P. Capitanio. 1997. "AIDS Stigma and Contact with Persons with AIDS: Effects of Direct and Vicarious Contact." *Journal of Applied Social Psychology* 27 (1): 1–36.

Hwang, Stephen Wesley, James Weaver, Tim Aubry, and Jeffrey S. Hoch. 2011. "Hospital Costs and Length of Stay Among Homeless Patients Admitted to Medical, Surgical, and Psychiatric Services." *Medical Care* 49 (4): 350–54.

John Talbot and Associates. 2003. *Social Development Strategy for Nanaimo—Phase 1: Social Status Report*. Prepared for the Social Development Strategy Steering Committee, City of Nanaimo. Burnaby, BC: John Talbot and Associates. https://www.nanaimo.ca/assets/Departments/Community~Planning/Social~Planning/Social~Development~Strategy/Soc_Status_Rpt.pdf.

———. 2004. *Social Development Strategy for Nanaimo*. Prepared for the Social Development Strategy Steering Committee, City of Nanaimo. Burnaby, BC: John Talbot and Associates. https://www.nanaimo.ca/assets/Departments/Community~Planning/Social~Planning/Social~Development~Strategy/Soc_Dev_Strategy.pdf.

Kingfisher, Catherine. 2007. "Discursive Constructions of Homelessness in a Small City in the Canadian Prairies: Notes on Destructuration, Individualization, and the Production of (Raced and Gendered) Unmarked Categories." *American Ethnologist* 34 (1): 91–107.

Latimer, Jeff, Craig Dowden, and Danielle Muise. 2005. "The Effectiveness of Restorative Justice Practices: A Meta-analysis." *Prison Journal* 85 (2): 127–44.

Lee, Barrett A., Chad R. Farrell, and Bruce G. Link. 2004. "Revisiting the Contact Hypothesis: The Case of Public Exposure to Homelessness." *American Sociological Reivew* 69 (1): 40–63.

MacPherson, Donald. 2001. *A Framework for Action: A Four-Pillar Approach to Drug Problems in Vancouver*. Vancouver: City of Vancouver. http://www.communityinsite.ca/pdf/frameworkforaction.pdf.

MacPherson, Donald, Zarina Mulla, and Lindsey Richardson. 2006. "The Evolution of Drug Policy in Vancouver, Canada: Strategies for Preventing Harm from Psychoactive Substance Use." *International Journal of Drug Policy* 17 (2): 127–32.

Mair, Andrew. 1986. "The Homeless and the Post-industrial City." *Political Geography Quarterly* 5 (4): 351–68.

March, Joan Carles, Eugenia Oviedo-Joekes, and Manuel Romero. 2006. "Drugs and Social Exclusion in Ten European Cities." *European Addiction Research* 12 (1): 33–41.

Maté, Gabor. 2008. *In the Realm of Hungry Ghosts: Close Encounters with Addiction*. Toronto: Vintage Canada.

McCann, Eugene J. 2008. "Expertise, Truth, and Urban Policy Mobilities: Global Circuits of Knowledge in the Development of Vancouver, Canada's 'Four Pillar' Drug Strategy." *Environment and Planning A* 40 (4): 885–904.

Mikkonen, Juha, and Dennis Raphael. 2010. *Social Determinants of Health: The Canadian Facts.* Toronto: School of Health Policy and Management, York University.

NADAC Strategy Working Group. 2006. *Process for Developing an Alcohol and Drug Strategy for Nanaimo.* Nanaimo, BC: Nanaimo Alcohol and Drug Action Committee.

Nunn, Kenneth B. 2002. "Race, Crime and the Pool of Surplus Criminality: Or Why the 'War on Drugs' Was a 'War on Blacks.'" *Journal of Gender, Race, and Justice* 6: 381–445.

NWCI (Neilson-Welch Consulting Inc.). 2005. *City of Nanaimo Social Services Study: Report.* Prepared for the City of Nanaimo. Kelowna, BC: Neilson-Welch Consulting Inc. https://www.nanaimo.ca/assets/Departments/Community~Planning/Publications~and~Forms/Soc_Serv_Study.pdf.

NWGH (Nanaimo Working Group on Homelessness). 2003. *Reducing Homelessness: A Community Plan for Nanaimo, BC.* Nanaimo: City of Nanaimo.

———. 2007. *Nanaimo Homelessness Partnering Strategy Action Plan, 2007–2009.* Nanaimo: City of Nanaimo.

Peace, Robin. 2001. "Social Exclusion: A Concept in Need of Definition?" *Social Policy Journal of New Zealand* 16: 17–35.

Reinarman, Craig, and Harry G. Levine. 2004. "Crack in the Rearview Mirror: Deconstructing Drug War Mythology." *Social Justice* 31 (1–2): 182–199.

Reinke, Rebecca R., Patrick W. Corrigan, Christoph Leonhard, Robert K. Lundin, and Mary Anne Kubiak. 2004. "Examining Two Aspects of Contact on the Stigma of Mental Illness." *Journal of Social and Clinical Psychology* 23 (3): 377–89.

Room, Robin. 2005. "Stigma, Social Inequality, and Alcohol and Drug Use." *Drug and Alcohol Review* 24 (2): 143–55.

Sailor, Lisa E. 2010. "Conditioning Community: Power and Decision-Making in Transitioning an Industry-Based Community." PhD diss., Department of Recreation and Leisure Studies, University of Waterloo, Waterloo, Ontario.

Sanderson, Alicia. 2011. "Insite as Representation and Regulation: A Discursively-Informed Analysis of the Implementation and Implications of Canada's First Safe Injection Site." Master's thesis, Department of Criminology, University of Ottawa, Ottawa.

Shannon, Kate, Patricia Spittal, and Vicky Thomas. 2007. "Intersections of Trauma, Substance Use, and HIV Vulnerability Among Aboriginal Girls and Young Women Who Use Drugs." In *Highs and Lows: Canadian Perspectives on Women* and Substance Use, edited by Nancy Poole and Lorraine Greaves, 169–75. Toronto: Centre for Addiction and Mental Health.

Sterritt, Spencer. 2018. "City of Nanaimo Rejects Chase River Location for $7 Million Supportive Housing Project." Nanaimo News NOW, 19 February. http:// nanaimonewsnow.com/article/569426/city-nanaimo-rejects-chase-river-location-7-million-supportive-housing-initiative.

Taylor, Stuart. 2008. "Outside the Outsiders: Media Representations of Drug Use." Probation Journal 55 (4): 369–87.

Tubbs, Rebecca. 2008. Continuing and Shifting Patterns in Nanaimo's Homeless Population: Based on the September 2008 Homeless Count. Nanaimo, BC: Nanaimo Working Group on Homelessness. http://www.nanaimo.ca/assets/ Departments/Community~Planning/Social~Planning/Social~Geography/ Census08ReportHomeless.pdf.

United Kingdom. ODPM (Office of the Deputy Prime Minister). 2004. Tackling Social Exclusion: Taking Stock and Looking to the Future—Emerging Findings. London: Office of the Deputy Prime Minister, Social Exclusion Unit.

van Wormer, Katherine. 2003. "Restorative Justice: A Model for Social Work Practice with Families." Families in Society 84 (3): 441–48.

van Wormer, Katherine, and Diane Rae Davis. 2003. Addiction Treatment: A Strengths Perspective. Pacific Grove, CA: Brooks/Cole-Thomson Learning.

VIHA (Vancouver Island Health Authority). 2006. Understanding the Social Determinants of Health: A Discussion Paper from the Office of the Chief Medical Health Officer. Victoria: Vancouver Island Health Authority.

Werb, Daniel, Evan Wood, Will Small, Steffanie Strathdee, Kathy Li, Julio Montaner, and Thomas Kerr. 2008. "Effects of Police Confiscation of Illicit Drugs and Syringes Among Injection Drug Users in Vancouver." International Journal of Drug Policy 19 (4): 332–38.

Wood, Evan, Patricia M. Spittal, Will Small, Thomas Kerr, Kathy Li, Robert S. Hogg, Mark W. Tyndall, Julio Montaner, and Martin T. Schechter. 2004. "Displacement of Canada's Largest Public Illicit Drug Market in Response to a Police Crackdown." Canadian Medical Association Journal / Journal de l'Association médicale canadienne 170 (10): 1551–56.

4 Being Queer in the Small City

Wendy Hulko

Administrator: *How was your trip to Puerto Vallarta?*
Me: *Great—it was all gay, all the time. I'm experiencing culture shock being back in Kamloops.*
Administrator [tone of surprise]: *Are you gay?*
Me [tone of incredulity]: *Yeah!*
Administrator: *I didn't know. Well, why would I know though? It shouldn't matter in this day and age. Does it matter anymore?*
Me: *Yes, it does. That's why I took a break from teaching sexual diversity last fall—I'm identified more as a queer faculty member than as a gerontologist and health researcher. I'm surprised you didn't know, as I'm one of the only queers on campus.*
Administrator: *But what about [faculty member X] and [faculty member Y]?*
Me: *They left, and so did [faculty member Z].*[1]

In Canada, as elsewhere, research on sexual orientation and gender identity/ expression has generally focused on large urban centres, where the proportion of LGBTQ people is estimated to be higher than it is for the population

---

1 This conversation took place in 2010. The campus climate has improved since then, owing in large part to a greater number of openly queer faculty members in the School of Social Work and Human Service and in other professional programs such as law. There has also been an increase in the administration's recognition of the importance of celebrating various forms of diversity, demonstrated, for example, by its willingness to speak at the annual campus Pride Parade.

as a whole (Fredriksen-Goldsen and Muraco 2010; MetLife MMI 2010).² This concentration no doubt reflects what Mary Gray (2009, 3) calls "narratives of escape to urban oases," which encourage LGBTQ youth to migrate to cities that already have sizable queer communities, where resources and opportunities for support and acceptance are more available than in a rural setting (Poon and Saewyc 2009, 121). There is, however, a growing literature related to queer people who live in rural areas, including a special issue of the *Journal of Lesbian Studies* titled "Rural Lesbian Life: Narratives of Community, Commitment, and Coping" (see Cohn and Hastings 2011). While many of these studies centre on gay, lesbian, and bisexual youth (see, for example, Gray 2009; Palmer, Kosciw, and Bartkiewicz 2012; Poon and Saewyc 2009; Saewyc et al. 2007, 42), attention has also been focused on older lesbian women and gay men (see, for example, Comerford et al. 2004; Fenge, Jones, and Read 2010; McCarthy 2000). Despite this, a twenty-five-year review of the literature on aging and sexual orientation found that, out of a total fifty-eight studies published from 1984 to 2008, only three (5%) focused exclusively on older gays and lesbians living in rural areas (Fredriksen-Golden and Muraco 2010, 396).

In general, small cities have not been the site of much research to date, and, in the research that does exist, they are often lumped together with rural and remote communities under the umbrella of nonurban settings. Yet geographic location clearly plays a role in identity formation and community building—as Gray (2009, 5) puts it, "without question, rural youth negotiate queer desires and embodiments under different logistical realities"—and small cities are distinct not only from large urban centres but also from rural towns. While larger sociocultural transformations with respect to LGBTQ rights, such as the removal of homosexuality from the Diagnostic and Statistical Manual of Mental Disorders (DSM) in 1973 and the legalization of same-sex marriage, undoubtedly have an impact on small cities, the speed and manner by which prescriptive or legislated change plays out may differ, and innovations that occur in small cities may not migrate to the same extent as those that originate in large urban centres.

---

2 In this chapter, I use LGBTQ as an acronym inclusive of lesbian, gay, bisexual, transgender, transsexual, two-spirit, intersex, queer, and questioning individuals and communities.

In this chapter, I discuss identifying as queer and finding community from the perspectives of lesbian and bisexual women and transgender persons living in small cities and rural towns in the interior of British Columbia. I use the word *queer* to refer to people who identify outside the rigid sex/gender system (Butler 1990) that presumes heterosexuality and prescribes gender conformity and to indicate that I view sex and gender, along with other identity categories, as socially constructed. I agree with Nagoshi and Brzuzy (2010, 434): "'Queer' is an identity, a theory about nonheteronormative sexuality, and a theoretical orientation for how identity is to be understood."[3] At the same time, I acknowledge that not all LGBTQ people are comfortable being identified as queer, particularly older ones who remember this word being used to harm and have no desire to reclaim it, and that the word *queer* may hold different meanings for those who identify as such (see Peters 2005).

LGBTQ Research to Date: Age, Geography, and Intersectionality

Studies related to rurality and sexual and/or gender identity have addressed the implications for service providers of having nonheterosexual clients (Oswald and Culton 2003) and the ways in which community influences sexual identity development and expression, depending on several factors: an individual's location, whether urban or rural (Comerford et al. 2004; Poon and Saewyc 2009; Oswald and Culton 2003); access to gay spaces such as clubs, coffee shops, and areas of town (Pritchard, Morgan, and Sedgley 2002; Valentine and Skelton 2003); and the ability to access queer-oriented formal (such as health care) and informal (friendship-based) networks and communities (Comerford et al. 2004; Heaphy 2007; Heaphy, Yip, and Thompson 2004; McCarthy 2000; Oswald and Culton 2003). The availability of "gay space" has been found to positively influence the expression of sexual identity in both rural and urban settings (Comerford et al. 2004; Valentine and Skelton 2003), and the absence of gay space to have a direct negative effect (Oswald and Culton 2003). For example, in their exploratory, naturalistic study of the experiences of fifteen self-defined lesbians in rural Vermont, Comerford and colleagues (2004, 428) found that in rural environments,

---

3 For a primer on queer theory, see Wilchins (2004).

where few, if any, public, gay-positive physical spaces exist, their participants "felt a great deal of comfort" in the existence of a lesbian community.
Likewise, on the basis of their observational study of the Manchester gay
village (a large urban centre), Pritchard and colleagues (2002, 118) note that
"gay and lesbian spaces have emotional and psychological importance as
empowering places in a 'straight' world." In their analysis of rural and urban
differences related to sexual orientation in the 2003 BC Adolescent Health
Survey, Poon and Saewyc (2009) argue that "lesbian, gay, and bisexual adolescents in rural communities may need additional support and services as
they navigate adolescence" (118) and recommend "informal help networks,
which could link LGB adolescents with peers and LGB adults" (122), as well
as interventions focused specifically on mental health, substance abuse, and
sexual education.

Although LGBTQ people in small cities and rural towns have not been
well researched, the general concept of "community" figures strongly in
research on the identity development and/or maintenance of LGBTQ people.
A frequent theme in this research is the impact of formal and informal social
networks on the lives of LGBTQ people, including the roles that family and
friends play in supporting the health and well-being of the LGBTQ person.
For example, in a qualitative study of older LGBTQ people in Britain, Brian
Heaphy (2007) found that both sexuality and (normative) gender expression
have an impact on experiences and interactions within the nonheterosexual community, as well as outside of it.[4] In a study using grounded theory,
Tracey Rickards and Judith Wuest (2006) discovered that women who come
out at mid-life lost credibility within their social and health care networks;
they argue that the health care system must re-evaluate taken-for-granted
assumptions about patients.[5] Susan Comerford and colleagues (2004)
identified social isolation and community building as major themes in
their qualitative study of the lives of older lesbians in rural Vermont. The
aforementioned research indicates that older LGBTQ people rely more on
personal support networks based on family (including chosen family) and

---

4 For early research on sexual orientation and the experience of aging, see also
Gabbay and Wahler (2002); Heaphy, Yip, and Thompson (2004); and Shankle et al.
(2003).

5 For more on women coming out as lesbian in mid-life, see Larson (2006). On sexual
identity formation among youth, see Hollander (2000); Rosario et al. (2001); Saewyc
(2011); and Swann and Spivey (2004).

friends, while younger ones rely more for personal support on public networks such as gay-straight alliances (GSAs) and clubs (Taylor and Peter 2011). These public networks are not always available in small cities and rural towns, where virtual communities may be one of the only source of peer support and information about identity development and services (Gray 2009; Hulko 2015).

Significant gaps exist in the research about the life course of LGBTQ people (Fredriksen-Goldsen et al. 2017) and comparisons between older and younger generations in terms of how these groups relate to one another socially and experientially.[6] Furthermore, there is a conspicuous lack of research on LGBTQ communities in Canada, especially in small cities and rural and remote areas of the country. The research reported below attempted to address these gaps and limitations through interviews and focus groups with two separate demographic groups (described as younger and older), both being made up of women who identified as sexual and/or gender minorities. The research team explored their perspectives on identity and community through an intersectional lens. Intersectionality refers to ways in which identity categories such as race, class, gender, sexual orientation, and age are inextricably linked and interact with one another to shape an individual's relationship to oppression and privilege (Hulko 2009). Researchers and theorists using an intersectional lens do not attempt to isolate a particular aspect of a person's identity nor to prioritize one form of oppression over another; rather, they consider various facets of a person's social location and treat oppressions as interactive and mutually reinforcing. Most intersectionality scholars who address geographic location do so in a dichotomous way: a researcher, for example, might explore urban and rural locations, with rural women being the focus of inquiry.[7]

---

6 For notable exceptions, see Floyd and Bakeman (2006) and Grov et al. (2006). For more on the historical and environmental contexts of older LGBTQ adults' lives see the special issue of *The Gerontologist* reporting on Fredriksen-Goldsen and colleagues' landmark study, Aging with Pride: National Health, Aging, and Sexuality/Gender Study, conducted in 2014 and involving 2,450 LGBTQ Americans aged 50 and older (Fredriksen-Goldsen and Kim 2017).

7 For more on intersectionality as it relates to research on women, see Hankivsky et al. (2010) and Simpson (2009).

Exploring Queer Women's Identity in Interior British Columbia

This chapter arose out of a research project that I conducted in 2008–9 in collaboration with Natalie Clark, one of my colleagues at Thompson Rivers University. Drawing on insights from critical, feminist, anti-oppressive research (see Brown and Strega 2005; DeVault 1999; Kirby, Greaves, and Reid 2006; Reid, Brief, and LeDrew 2009), we set out to explore the impact of age on the experience of identifying as a sexual and/or gender minority in a small city or rural town. Focus groups and individual interviews (in person and by email) were conducted with fourteen female and seven transgender persons. The twenty-one participants represented two demographic groups, younger (n = 14) and older (n = 7), with those in the former group ranging in age from 15 to 30 years (average 20.5 years) and those in the latter from 52 to 61 years (average 56 years).[8] Sixteen of the participants were living in small cities, while the other five were from rural towns; three were Indigenous, and the remainder were white, one of whom was an ethnic minority. With regard to sexual orientation, thirteen identified as lesbian, five as bisexual or pansexual, and three as straight.[9]

Five themes were identified through the thematic and comparative data analysis process—identity, intersectionality, aging, geography, and community. This chapter focuses on the latter two in relation to being queer in the small city, starting with geography or the extent to which size matters.

---

8 Through purposive sampling (snowball and convenience), we initially aimed to recruit women under the age of 25 and over the age of 60. When we had difficulty locating women over the age of 60, and after several women in their fifties asked to participate, we dropped the age to 50 for the older group. Of the original fourteen participants who self-identified as younger, one disclosed her age to be 30 during data collection; we thus eliminated her from our analysis of the youth data (see Hulko 2015; Hulko and Hovanes 2018). I have included her in this chapter, however, as her age skewed the results only with respect to the original purpose of our study.

9 The three participants who identified as "straight" were transgender individuals, one of whom identified himself as formerly bisexual and lesbian. We included both male-to-female and female-to-male transgender persons because we did not wish to conflate either gender or sexual orientation with biological sex. Rather, we left it up to potential research participants to exclude or include themselves on the basis of their understanding of the purpose of the study.

Size Matters: Population Size and Queer Community

Most of the older research participants and several of the younger ones had lived in cities and towns of varying sizes over the course of their lives. These participants spoke at length about the influence of specific places on their identity development and their connection to community, mainly in relation to the small BC city where they were now living. For example, one of the older lesbian participants—who, like many women of her generation, had given into the pressure to marry—had come out after her husband announced that "I'm not really going to be able to satisfy you, and I think we should break up, get a divorce." Having found no "gay scene at all" in the small BC city where she had been living, she had decided to move back to Winnipeg, figuring that "Winnipeg's gotta be a good place to come out." The impact of population size was also highlighted by a younger lesbian woman from a rural town who, on more than one occasion, had hitchhiked to the closest small city in order to participate in a support group for queer youth:

> For me, living in a small town where everyone knows everybody, it's like, "hey you're [name], you're the lesbian." . . . I live in a population of about forty. Everybody knows everybody . . . obviously I have some other issues going on at the moment, though—like, I know I am a lesbian, but not a lot of people know that I think I might be transgendered.

A young lesbian couple spoke of their experiences in two small cities in BC as related not only to population size but also to the degree of religiosity and the strength of faith communities. The small city where they both grew up is located in what is known as the "bible belt" and one of them explained that, "it was definitely worse there, by far. . . . We didn't know anyone else who was gay at all growing up. Well, I had one gay friend, but that was it." Still, the small city where they now resided was, one of them said, "hard in different ways, I think, than where we grew up. . . . It takes a while to realize where to go [and] where not to go."

One younger transgender individual (who formerly identified as a lesbian) went to high school in two places—first in a small rural town in Alberta and then in Edmonton. In contrasting these experiences, he identified population size as the significant factor. He described having had "a huge problem coming out" in the high school in the rural town, the only choice of school in what he called "a small hick town." In the Edmonton high school, however, "I could fully be a lesbian and they were fine. But, see, Edmonton is bigger." Another younger transgender participant moved from a small city in Alberta to a much smaller city in British Columbia and felt that the former was more supportive of her gender fluidity. This acceptance was linked to the existence of a pride group on campus, which "helped make me connect the dots a little bit," and to her involvement in social work, as well as to the difference in population size. Describing the small BC city in which she was now living, she said, "It's very redneck: people screaming at you, swearing, cussing, giving me the finger— that's normal." She went on to describe the small Alberta city from which she had moved as "a lot more accepting," attributing this greater flexibility largely to the "greater population" while noting there still was "definitely a segment of red neck." Similarly, an older lesbian woman identified the presence or absence of like-minded people as related to the size of a city. Prior to settling in a small city in British Columbia, she had lived in Vancouver, Montréal, and Los Angeles, where she was active in the women's movement. Living in a small city had, she said, "narrowed my opportunities." She paused and then added, "It has made me socialize with people that I really wouldn't be caught dead with, but there they are, and there I am, and from their perspective, I probably look just as much [like them] they wouldn't be caught dead with me either."

One of the older lesbian women, who was originally from a country in northern Europe, had immigrated to Canada as an adult and had subsequently come out as a lesbian; in the country from which she had emigrated, she said, "it would be, 'Shhhh!' It would not be as easy to be a lesbian as in Canada." She was one of three participants who referred to their experiences in countries outside North America. Another was a younger lesbian woman who said she had a "tendency to go to really Roman Catholic countries," including a Latin American country, where she lived with Catholic families for a year, and Spain, where she spent some time in "a really queer-friendly city." The third was a younger lesbian woman who had spent a few months living in a Spanish-speaking country. The size of the cities in which they resided was not highlighted by any of these participants; rather, it was the difference in the country that was the focus.

Another younger participant, who identified as transgender and had moved from a small town to the small BC city in which she now lived, noted the threat of violence from a family member in addition to the lack of acceptance within her community, both due to her gender expression. She described her home town as "really small—you could just walk around town in one hour." In her home community, she said, "they don't accept us at all. . . . My dad, every time he sees me, he wants to beat me up." Although she did not speak of violence or abuse growing up in a small town, one of the older lesbian women described how she discovered the rules of who to love and who not to love after falling in love with another young woman (whom I will call Anne) in eastern Canada, where she lived:

> I grew up in a very isolated area—very, very isolated . . . and I didn't know 'til I was fourteen that there were rules about who you could love and couldn't love. I didn't even know, I couldn't even have cared less, it didn't register, that's not how we lived at that time anyway. . . . When I was fourteen, I found out there were laws and rules that said I could not be in love with Anne, but the simple fact was that I was.

An older transgender and bisexual woman spoke of the challenges of living in a small city but said that this can become easier over time, depending on the fortitude of the individual:

> I find that living in a smaller community, being transgendered, living as a female with a male ID and all that stuff, that has a harsh impact on somebody that's different. . . . Wherever you go people judge you, people disrespect you, people harass you and call you derogatory names. But you know, if one has the courage and the strength to endure all that and to become fully committed to the community, that all changes over time, you know, it gets easier.

The reality of living in a small city, where there is not as much anonymity and, as two older participants described, "everybody knows everybody else's business" and "you run into your doctor, your lawyer, your shoemaker . . . your hairdresser," was mostly seen as a negative by the younger participants and as positive by the older ones. "If you've got an issue," said one older lesbian woman, "you either have to learn to deal with it like a grown up, or you have to talk to your neighbour. You can't sit back in a small town in the same way and go 'Bloody fags!' because in a small town [your neighbour] could very well be the one you're talking about."

All of the younger participants who had only lived in small cities or rural towns expressed a desire to move to a larger city like Vancouver— that is, to "escape to urban oases" (Gray 2009, 3). "I despise small towns," a young participant wrote in her emailed response to the interview questions. "They've never been anything but a negative impact on my life and my identity, and as soon as I have the money, I am out of here." A younger lesbian woman who grew up in a small city, moved to Vancouver after high school, and returned to her hometown for a few months each summer confirmed the suspicions of all the youth who wanted to move to the big city. "I have definitely, since I've moved to Vancouver, found more of an open and understanding community. So . . . that's where you're going to find it—in a larger centre." Vancouver was identified by another young lesbian woman as the "most comfortable place I know" and the place where she found "role models." She was clearly impacted by experiencing the Vancouver Pride parade in the company of her girlfriend:

> The first time we went down there to the Pride parade was three years ago, and that was just so much fun, just seeing everyone on the streets, holding hands and clearly gay. . . . One day, I'd like to live there. It's just too damn expensive, but I think that's where [we] usually go, you know, to feel that sense of community.

These sentiments about an open and understanding community and identifiable role models being more common in a large city were echoed by another younger lesbian woman, who moved to Calgary after graduating from high school in a small city in northern BC. In Calgary, she said, she put "theory into practice" and "hung out with lesbians all the time." This enchantment with the big city was absent among the older women, who instead focused on the positive aspects of the sense of community one finds in small cities or rural towns—the ties among neighbours or fellow citizens. Many of the older lesbian women spoke of community size as being more important for younger people than for those at their age in terms of accepting oneself and finding women with whom to form friendships and/or intimate relationships, although they surmised that their own experience may have been different had they been single. Thus, the responses of participants indicate that age and stage of life relates to the degree of comfort to be found in cities of different sizes when one is queer.

Accessing Community: The Search for Safe Spaces

While the participants defined community in different ways, most referred to the presence or absence of an LGBTQ community in small cities and rural towns. "Community can mean so many things," said one younger participant who lived in a small city. "It can mean your family, it can mean the LGBT community itself, it can be the physical area." She added: "I think, for the most part, here, sense of [LGBTQ] community is, like, nada."

Unsurprisingly, the LGBTQ community was seen to play an important role in normalizing and validating same-sex relationships through creating spaces where people can feel comfortable expressing their same-sex attraction—at dances put on by the local LGBTQ group, for example. An older participant described the importance to her of such spaces and the gay and lesbian community in the small BC city where she lived:

> I can go there with my partner and can show my affection to her in public. I can hug her and I can kiss her, I can dance with her, which I can't do in the street here. I could, but—I'd feel uncomfortable—don't feel safe doing it. But in that community, I can do it, and that's what was important to me about that community.

Another older lesbian woman had lived in a number of large North American cities when she was younger and credited these experiences with helping her to develop a positive self-identity as a lesbian feminist. "Community is very important for younger people, [for] knowing who they are, absolutely . . . I don't think that will ever change," she said. But she lamented, for younger women in particular, the lack of community in the small city where she was living now. "There aren't enough women here. We used to have dances alone and dances with [the local LGBTQ group] and . . . it's not enough really, it doesn't make a community." She described community as "people you feel comfortable with, that you share common values with, that you can be around casually, drop in easily," but in her small city, she said, "it's dying of thirst and starvation. . . . I don't feel community here at all." Despite that absence of community, however, attempts were being made to create it, to organize informal gatherings centred on games and conversation. "We want to be with people where it doesn't have to be dancing and loud noise and drinking, or loud music and drinking," she said. "We've got that going, we've started that, but it's only about twelve people."

Accessing "the community" was raised as an issue by younger participants, including a bisexual woman who told us in her emailed response, "I can't really say that I have found a sense of community at this point, but I hope to in the future." A younger lesbian woman who wasn't sure of the meaning of community knew that she needed to find the access key if she wanted to connect with other lesbian and bisexual women in the small city where she was living: "It almost feels like you need some sort of special key to access this strange community." This need for a "special key" was linked to the absence of a physical space for LGBTQ community members to gather, be it a café, bar, or community centre.[10] As one younger lesbian woman said, "I think that community is dependent on space." This was echoed by an older lesbian woman, who felt that until societal barriers to freedom of expression are removed, artificial meeting places are required: "If you cannot walk down the street holding hands, what that says to me is that there is still a barrier for people with a certain quality about them for meeting others, so you have to create, for lack of a better description, an artificial place, meeting place, which is a form of community." That is, until heternormativity—the presumption and privileging of heterosexuality—is recognized and addressed, designated and identifiably gay space is needed; in this space, members of the queer community can gather and provide emotional support to one another.

The loss of the local women's resource centre in one small city was keenly felt by the older lesbian women in that community, who spoke of this meeting place as one where they provided one another with emotional support and engaged in social activities that were not connected to music and alcohol. "We had a really good group going," said one older participant. "We got it together, we did camping, we did picnics, we did this, that, and the other thing, and sat and had weekly good discussions. We helped people in their relationships; we let them, you know, spill their guts, whatever they needed to do."

In addition to sharing their thoughts on the degree to which their current, former, and ideal places of residence (rural towns, small cities, large urban centres) could be considered safe for and accepting of queer people, the participants identified specific places that they choose to frequent and those that they try to avoid (see table 4.1). Generally, the unsafe spaces were public spaces

---

10 For more on the importance of gay space, see Comerford et al. (2004) and Valentine and Skelton (2003).

and the safe ones were more private, and the younger participants identified more specific places than the older ones did. For example, while anyone can attend a LGBTQ dance, these events are put on for and by members of the queer community and attendees are unlikely to encounter LGBTQ-phobia.

Table 4.1 Safe and unsafe spaces

Safe	Unsafe
Younger women and trans-persons	
Support groups for queer youth (mixed and trans) run by community agency	Transit exchange
	Downtown core in general
Dances put on by the local LGBTQ group	The town or city's main street
Youth centre run by community agency	Parks late at night
Friend's house	Buses
In bed	Going out at night alone
Campus LGBTQ student club	Bars
"Pink mafia" places (businesses owned by LGBTQ people)	Shopping mall and its surroundings
	Church
Internet	
This place (the meeting room where the interview was conducted and where a queer youth group convenes)	
Older women and trans-persons	
Specific live music venue	Specific nightclub with exotic dancers
This place (the restaurant where the interview took place)	Classroom in a high school
	Particular nightclub on a Friday or Saturday night
Women's dances	
Neighbour's house	Shopping mall
Dances put on by local LGBTQ group	Park downtown
Social service agencies	
United Church	

It is surprising that the younger women and transgender persons did not identify schools as being unsafe spaces, while the older women did. The results of a recent Canadian survey of high school students indicate that homophobia, biphobia, and transphobia exist "in every class in every school" in this country, with 64 percent of LGBTQ students and 61 percent of students with LGBTQ parents reporting feeling unsafe at school (Taylor and Peter 2011, 8; see also Haskell and Burtch 2010). Further, it is well known that sexual minority youth are more likely to be suicidal than their heterosexual peers (Saewyc, Konishi, Chiaki, and Homma 2014, 90, 97, 100). It is also generally accepted that schools have a role to play in addressing this health disparity. In their analysis of data from the BC Adolescent Health Survey, Saewyc and colleagues (2014) found that school-based GSAs and anti-homophobic bullying policies can reduce LGB students' odds of discrimination, suicidal thoughts, and suicide attempts (97–98) and stress the need for more research on the protective impact of peer groups and anti-bullying policies (101).

Conclusion: "The World Is Slowly Changing"

In spite of the considerable challenges associated with living in a small city or rural town where one is defined as deviant on the basis of one's gender expression and/or sexual orientation, the older participants in this research expressed the view that life was better or easier for younger queer people than it had been for their generation. One older woman said, "There's so much more tolerance now," adding, "This generation's society is a little more accepting now." Another older participant emphasized the significance of those who came before, speaking of the pioneers who had paved the way, to some extent, for the youth of today. Her comments received a lot of support from the other focus group participants, all older lesbian women, who nodded and murmured in agreement as she spoke:

> I even consider ourselves lucky at our age group, the ladies that went before us and the ground they broke. They were in a very intense time and living really on the edge—dangerous lives, really dangerous lives. The police really took a fancy to roughing up the women as well as the men. So . . . even though the kids today are even that much more lucky, I still count myself very fortunate that I didn't come out until I was thirty.

This was not enough for the younger participants, though, who were craving celebration of their queerness and the myriad ways in which their sexual and gender identities affected their lives rather than acceptance of them as "absolutely normal and like everybody else." They wanted easily identifiable role models and mentors, as well as the freedom to express themselves in all their queerness.

A clear continuum presented itself in this research, with rural towns identified as the least desirable and supportive and the least likely to have a sense of community and large urban centres as the most desirable and supportive and the most likely to fulfill "the dream." Small cities, where most of the participants were living, were identified as a middle ground between these two extremes: they generally had an LGBTQ community, albeit very small and difficult to access, and were clearly more supportive than the rural towns in which many of the participants originated or grew up. Still, small cities fell short of the dream of the big city for many of the participants, particularly the youth.

In my opinion, though, the answer is not to encourage youth to move to larger centres. As Lesley Marple (2005, 74) argues in her reflection on queer-community organizing in Nova Scotia, "queer oppression is not unique within rural communities, and removal of queers from the rural sphere is not going to remedy this social flaw for either the queers or the community in question." I argue that we should work to create more affirming communities within small cities and rural towns by building on the positive aspects of knowing your neighbours and running into your doctor, lawyer, or hairdresser at social events. At the same time, we should reject the ideal of community that Iris Young (1990, 227) describes, one that "expresses a desire for the fusion of subjects with one another which in practice operates to exclude those with whom the group does not identify" and that "denies and suppresses social difference"; rather, we need to promote an alternative "ideal of city life as a vision of social relations affirming group differences" and "as an openness to unassimilated otherness" (227). A city—small or large—that embraces diversity and demonstrates openness and tolerance of immigrants, LGBTQ people, and artists is a city that is destined to grow and be economically successful, as is shown in the research of Florida, Mellander, and Stolarick (2010). Through an analysis of forty-six census metropolitan areas and census agglomerations in Canada, they found a strong relationship between higher regional incomes and expressed openness and tolerance towards gay people, bohemians, immigrants, and visible minorities (310). Thus, making the small city more inclusive and affirmative of sexual and gender diversity (and discouraging LGBTQ people from moving to the big city) could have a positive impact on small cities both economically and socially.

A practical implication of the research reported in this chapter is the need to focus more attention on community building and to create opportunities for lesbian, bisexual, and transgender women (and other queer people) to connect with one another, and for LGBTQ youth to connect with older mentors (see Bohan, Russell, and Montgomery 2002), in the context of their small cities or rural towns. At the same time, formal support should be increased in small cities and rural towns through enhancement and/or creation of programs like Safe Spaces (see Hulko et al. 2010) and GSAs (see Saewyc et al. 2014; Taylor and Peter 2011). This would go a long way towards enticing LGBTQ people to live and remain in small cities and increasing the vibrancy of smaller communities for all of their inhabitants.

In terms of future research, it will be important to address the extent to which characteristics of individual cities or towns, other than their size, make a difference in the development of identity and formation of community for LGBTQ people. Another area of research that is lacking is the investigation of whether or how the experiences of gay and bisexual men in small cities and rural towns differ from those of lesbian and bisexual women and transgender persons in such places. Finally, evaluative research on the impact of formal support services such as safe spaces and/or informal support networks would assist in both building community and developing social services that are affirmative towards LGBTQ people.

Acknowledgements

The research on which this chapter is based was funded by two Aid to Small Universities grants from the Social Sciences and Humanities Research Council of Canada and grants from two research networks funded by the Michael Smith Foundation for Health Research (Women's Health Research Network and BC Rural and Remote Research Network). I would like to thank my research team, including co-investigator Natalie Clark, research assistants Jessica Hovanes, Erica Bouffioux, and Megan Stevenson, and community partners Kari Bepple and Dr. Maijo Heimo for their contributions; and all the lesbian, bisexual, and transgender participants for their willingness to share their views.

References

Bohan, Janis S., Glenda M. Russell, and Suki Montgomery. 2002. "Gay Youth and Gay Adults: Bridging the Generation Gap." *Journal of Homosexuality* 44 (1): 15–41.

Brown, Leslie, and Susan Strega, eds. 2005. *Research as Resistance: Critical, Indigenous, and Anti-oppressive Approaches.* Toronto: Canadian Scholars' Press.

Butler, Judith. 1990. *Gender Trouble: Feminism and the Subversion of Identity.* London and New York: Routledge.

Cohn, Tracy J., and Sarah L. Hastings. 2011. "Special Issue: Rural Lesbian Life: Narratives of Community, Commitment, and Coping." *Journal of Lesbian Studies* 15 (2): 141–47.

Comerford, Susan A., M. Maxwell Henson-Stroud, Corbett Sionainn, and Elizabeth Wheeler. 2004. "Crone Songs: Voices of Lesbian Elders on Aging in a Rural Environment." *Affilia: Journal of Women and Social Work* 9 (4): 418–36.

DeVault, Marjorie L. 1999. *Liberating Method: Feminism and Social Research.* Philadelphia: Temple University Press.

Fenge, Lee-Ann, Kip Jones, and Rosie Read. 2010. "Connecting Participatory Methods in a Study of Older Lesbian and Gay Citizens in Rural Areas." *International Journal of Qualitative Methods* 9 (4): 320–33.

Florida, Richard, Charlotta P. A. Mellander, and Kevin M. Stolarick. 2010. "Talent, Technology and Tolerance in Canadian Regional Development." *The Canadian Geographer* 54 (3): 277–304.

Floyd, Frank J., and Roger Bakeman. 2006. "Coming-Out Across the Life Course: Implications of Age and Historical Context." *Archives of Sexual Behavior* 35 (3): 287–96.

Fredriksen-Goldsen, Karen I., and Hyun-Jun Kim. 2017. "The Science of Conducting Research with LGBT Older Adults—An Introduction to Aging with Pride: National Health, Aging, and Sexuality/Gender Study (NHAS)." *The Gerontologist* 57 (S1): 1–14. doi:10.1093/geront/gnw212

Fredriksen-Goldsen, Karen I., Amanda E. B. Bryan, Sarah Jen, Jayn Goldsen, Hyun-Jun Kim, and Anna Muraco. 2017. "The Unfolding of LGBT Lives: Key Events Associated with Health and Well-being in Later Life." *The Gerontologist* 57 (S1): 15–29. doi:10.1093/geront/gnw185

Fredriksen-Goldsen, Karen I., and Anna Muraco. 2010. "Aging and Sexual Orientation: A 25-Year Review of the Literature." *Research on Aging* 32 (3): 372–413.

Gabbay, Sarah G., and James J. Wahler. 2002. "Lesbian Aging." *Journal of Gay and Lesbian Social Services* 14 (3): 1–21.

Gray, Mary L. 2009. *Out in the Country: Youth, Media and Queer Visibility in Rural America.* New York: New York University Press.

Grov, Christian, David S. Bimbi, José E. Nanin, and Jeffrey T. Parsons. 2006. "Race, Ethnicity, Gender, and Generational Factors Associated with the Coming-Out Process Among Gay, Lesbian, and Bisexual Individuals." *Journal of Sex Research* 43 (2): 115–21.

Hankivsky, Olena, Colleen Reid, Renee Cormier, Colleen Varcoe, Natalie Clark, Cecilia Benoit, and Shari Brotman. 2010. "Exploring the Promises of Intersectionality for Advancing Women's Health Research." *International Journal for Equity in Health* 9 (5): 1–15.

Haskell, Rebecca, and Brian Burtch. 2010. *Get That Freak: Homophobia and Transphobia in High Schools*. Halifax: Fernwood Publishing.

Heaphy, Brian. 2007. "Sexualities, Gender, and Ageing: Resources and Social Change." *Current Sociology* 55 (2): 193–210.

Heaphy, Brian, Andrew K. T. Yip, and Debbie Thompson. 2004. "Ageing in a Non-heterosexual Context." *Ageing and Society* 24: 881–902.

Hollander, Gary. 2000. "Questioning Youth: Challenges to Working with Youth Forming Identities." *School Psychology Review* 29 (2): 173–79.

Hulko, Wendy. 2009. "The Time- and Context-Contingent Nature of Intersectionality and Interlocking Oppressions." *Affilia: Journal of Women and Social Work* 24 (1): 44–55.

———. 2015. "Collaboration and Affirmation: Supporting Younger Lesbian and Bisexual Women and Transgender Youth in Small Cities and Rural Communities." In *LGBTQ People and Social Work: Intersectional Perspectives*, edited by Brian J. O'Neill, Tracy A. Swan, and Nick J. Mulé. Toronto: Canadian Scholars' Press, 193–212.

Hulko, Wendy, Kari Bepple, Jenny Turco, and Natalie Clark. 2010. "Safe Spaces in BC's Interior: Working with LGBT Youth to Promote Mental Health." *Visions* 6 (2): 27–29.

Hulko, Wendy, and Jessica Hovanes. 2018. "Intersectionality in the Lives of LGBTQ Youth: Identifying as LGBTQ and Finding Community in Small Cities and Rural Towns." *Journal of Homosexuality* 65 (4): 427–55.

Kirby, Sandra L., Lorraine Greaves, and Colleen Reid. 2006. *Experience, Research, Social Change: Methods Beyond the Mainstream*. 2nd ed. Peterborough, ON: Broadview Press.

Larson, Nancy C. 2006. "Becoming 'One of the Girls': The Transition to Lesbian in Midlife." *Affilia: Journal of Women and Social Work* 21 (3): 296–305.

Marple, Lesley. 2005. "Rural Queers? The Loss of the Rural in Queer." *Canadian Woman Studies* 24 (2–3): 71–74.

McCarthy, Linda. 2000. "Poppies in a Wheat Field: Exploring the Lives of Rural Lesbians." *Journal of Homosexuality* 39 (1): 75–94.

Metlife MMI (Mature Market Institute). 2010. *Still Out, Still Aging: The MetLife Study of Lesbian, Gay, Bisexual, and Transgender Baby Boomers.* Westport, CT: Metlife MMI.

Nagoshi, Julie L., and Stephan/ie Brzuzy. 2010. "Transgender Theory: Embodying Research and Practice." *Affilia: Journal of Women and Social Work* 25 (4): 431–43.

Oswald, Ramona Faith, and Linda S. Culton. 2003. "Under the Rainbow: Rural Gay Life and Its Relevance for Family Providers." *Family Relations* 52: 72–81.

Palmer, Neal A., Joseph G. Kosciw, and Mark J. Bartkiewicz. 2012. *Strengths and Silences: The Experiences of Lesbian, Gay, Bisexual and Transgender Students in Rural and Small Town Schools.* New York: Gay, Lesbian, and Straight Education Network.

Peters, Wendy. 2005. "Queer Identities: Rupturing Identity Categories and Negotiating Meanings of Queer." *Canadian Woman Studies* 24 (2–3): 102–7.

Poon, Colleen S., and Elizabeth M. Saewyc. 2009. "Out Yonder: Sexual-Minority Adolescents in Rural Communities in British Columbia." *American Journal of Public Health* 99 (1): 118–24.

Pritchard, Annette, Nigel Morgan, and Diane Sedgley. 2002. "In Search of Lesbian Space? The Experience of Manchester's Gay Village." *Leisure Studies* 21 (2): 105–23.

Reid, Colleen J., Elana Brief, and Robin L. LeDrew. 2009. *Our Common Ground: Cultivating Women's Health Through Community Based Research.* Vancouver: Women's Health Research Network.

Rickards, Tracey, and Judith Wuest. 2006. "The Process of Losing and Regaining Credibility When Coming-Out at Midlife." *Health Care for Women International* 27: 530–47.

Rosario, Margaret, Joyce Hunter, Shira Maguen, Marya Gwadz, and Raymond Smith. 2001. "The Coming-Out Process and Its Adaptational and Health-Related Associations Among Gay, Lesbian, Bisexual Youths: Stipulation and Exploration of a Model." *American Journal of Community Psychology* 29 (1): 133–60.

Saewyc, Elizabeth M. 2011. "Research on Adolescent Sexual Orientation: Development, Health Disparities, Stigma, and Resilience." *Journal of Research on Adolescence* 21 (1): 256–72.

Saewyc, Elizabeth M., Chiaki Konishi, Hilary A. Rose, and Yuko Homma. 2014. "School-Based Strategies to Reduce Suicidal Ideation, Suicide Attempts, and Discrimination among Sexual Minority and Heterosexual Adolescents in Western Canada." *International Journal of Child, Youth and Family Studies* 5 (1): 89–112.

Saewyc, Elizabeth M., Colleen Poon, Naren Wang, Yuko Homma, Annie Smith, and the McCreary Centre Society. 2007. *Not Yet Equal: The Health of Lesbian, Gay, and Bisexual Youth in BC.* Vancouver: McCreary Centre Society.

Shankle, Michael D., Charles A. Maxwell, Esther S. Katzman, and Stewart Landers. 2003. "An Invisible Population: Older Lesbian, Gay, Bisexual, and Transgender Individuals." *Clinical Research and Regulatory Affairs* 20 (2): 159–82.

Simpson, Joanna. 2009. *Everyone Belongs: A Toolkit for Applying Intersectionality*. Ottawa: Canadian Research Institute for the Advancement of Women (CRIAW). http://www.criaw-icref.ca/sites/criaw/files/Everyone_Belongs_e.pdf.

Swann, Stephanie K., and Christina A. Spivey. 2004. "The Relationship Between Self-Esteem and Lesbian Identity During Adolescence." *Child and Adolescent Social Work Journal* 21 (6): 629–46.

Taylor, Catherine, and Tracey Peter. 2011. *Every Class in Every School: The First National Climate Survey on Homophobia, Biophobia, and Transphobia in Canadian Schools*. Toronto: Egale Canada Human Rights Trust. http://egale.ca/wp-content/uploads/2011/05/EgaleFinalReport-web.pdf.

Valentine, Gill, and Tracey Skelton. 2003. "Finding Oneself, Losing Oneself: The Lesbian and Gay 'Scene' as a Paradoxical Space." *International Journal of Urban and Regional Research* 27 (4): 849–66.

Wilchins, Riki. 2004. *Queer Theory, Gender Theory: An Instant Primer*. New York: Allyson.

Young, Iris Marion. 1990. "City Life and Difference." In *Justice and the Politics of Difference*, 226–56. Princeton, NJ: Princeton University Press.

5 "Thrown Out into the Community"

The Closure of Tranquille

Diane Purvey

Between 1958 and 1985, Tranquille Institution, located not far west of Kamloops, British Columbia, opened its doors to hundreds of developmentally and intellectually disabled individuals. Some stayed just a few years and received training that enabled them to live in the community, while others left only when the institution closed in 1985 as part of the provincial government's plan to deinstitutionalize those with mental and physical disabilities. In the years following its closure, Tranquille existed as a ghost town, unoccupied and physically closed to the outside world, although very much alive in the collective memory and imagination of many Kamloopsians. This chapter explores the reaction of the citizens of Kamloops to the closure of Tranquille and to the impending deinstitutionalization of its residents.

The closure of Tranquille had a considerable economic, political, and social impact on the city of Kamloops. As the third-largest employer in the area, the institution was an economic generator and had a stabilizing effect on local businesses, schools, and health services. The closure of Tranquille and the relocation of the institution's residents to various communities in the province meant significant job losses that had repercussions throughout the city—this at a time of nationwide recession, when the unemployment rate in British Columbia reached a staggering 15 percent (Statistics Canada, Labour Force Survey 2018). Despite a professed acceptance of the social philosophy underlying deinstitutionalization, Kamloopsians protested against the decision to close Tranquille, and many also fought the creation of neighbourhood group homes to house former residents. Although the closure went ahead as planned and many of the former residents were relocated to the city, the experience of deinstitutionalization as it unfolded in Kamloops is a potent reminder of the vital link between institutions and the communities that surround them.

A Brief History of Tranquille

In late-nineteenth-century British Columbia, people with intellectual and developmental disabilities were housed in the Public Hospital for the Insane, located in New Westminster, which opened its doors in 1878 as the Provincial Lunatic Asylum (Scott 2011, 93). It was not long before overcrowding led to the construction of other such facilities, notably the Hospital for the Mind, also known as Essondale Hospital (and eventually as Riverview Hospital), which opened in 1913 at Coquitlam. In those early days, little practical distinction was made between people with developmental disabilities and those with mental illness, although gradually this situation changed. Starting in the 1920s, the Public Hospital for the Insane began to specialize in the custodial care of the "feeble-minded" (with other patients transferred to the Essondale Hospital) and, in 1950, was renamed the Woodlands School, with its focus shifting to the institutional education of children with intellectual disabilities.[1] In 1958, overcrowding at Woodlands led to the use of Tranquille as a similar centre in the interior of British Columbia, and, in 1976, a third facility opened at Glendale Lodge, near Victoria. Tranquille was thus the only "hinterland" institution of its kind in the province.

Tranquille was not among the province's early mental institutions; rather, it began life as a tuberculosis sanatorium. In 1906, the British Columbia Anti-Tuberculosis Society, which was looking for land in the province's dry belt on which to establish a sanatorium, approached the Fortune family, owners of an extensive ranch at the mouth of the Tranquille River. In view of public concerns about the highly infectious nature of the disease, the Kamloops Board of Trade was willing to support the construction of a sanatorium

---

1 "Woodlands Institution," n.d., *Inclusion BC,* http://www.inclusionbc.org/our-priority-areas/disability-supports/institutions/woodlands-insitution; see also Erna Kurbegović and Colette Leung, "British Columbia's Provincial Hospital for the Insane Is Renamed the Woodlands School," 2013, *Eugenics Archives,* http://eugenicsarchive.ca/discover/connections/525e2883c6813a5469000000a.

"near but not in" the city (Norton 1999, 41; see also Harris 2010, 5). After some negotiation, the sale of land was inked, and the King Edward Sanatorium opened its doors in 1907, providing respite for thousands of afflicted men, women, and children. In 1921, the institution changed from private to public hands when the provincial government purchased the site and, the following year, acquired the neighbouring Cooney ranch, bringing Tranquille's size to 191 hectares.[2] Because of the economic viability and financial benefits of raising food at the site, a farm was established at Tranquille Institution, which produced fruits and vegetables, dairy products, meat, and honey for the residents. Surplus food production allowed for sales and trade with other local producers.

By the mid-1950s, however, the tuberculosis crisis had waned, owing in large measure to the development of antibiotics, and, in 1958, the sanatorium closed. Tranquille subsequently became a something of a political football, with the provincial government hesitating about the site's future and the merchants and citizens of Kamloops pushing for the institution's revitalization. After much lively debate, local Social Credit MLA and Minister of Highways Phil Gaglardi announced that Tranquille would reopen, under the Department of Mental Health, to relieve the overcrowded facility of Woodlands (Norton 1999, 173–74).

By 1958, the site consisted of just over forty buildings, four of them designated as hospitals. Among the remaining buildings were cottages for doctors' housing, a fire hall, a kitchen, laundry, farm buildings and a dairy barn, nurses' buildings, and resident dormitories. The institution had also been modernized with a power plant and central air-conditioning. The buildings were linked by underground tunnels, used for transferring food and laundry. Above ground were magnificent, lush gardens said to rival the famous Butchart Gardens in the province's capital, as well as orchards and extensive vegetable and berry gardens.[3] In 1958, in reference to the self-sufficiency of the compound, a *Vancouver Sun* reporter dubbed Tranquille "a whole little city in itself" (Norton 1999, 173). Although this is an oft-cited and fondly used descriptor, Tranquille

---

2 Harris (2010) provides a detailed account of the terms of this sale (5–6), as well as the sale of the Fortune family ranch (7). As she notes, since at least 1897, both families had been taking in tuberculosis patients as boarders, although the infected were obliged to live in tents (5).

3 Jordan Keats, "From the Inside Out: A Brief History of Tranquille," 31 March 2008, *Jordan Keats* [blog], http://blog.jordankeats.com/history-of-tranquille/.

was not an actual city—officials did not wield civic power and the residents were not granted rights of citizenship, such as the right to vote.

At its peak, Tranquille housed about seven hundred residents, or roughly a quarter of the provincial institutionalized population of those with developmental and intellectual disabilities. The age of residents ranged widely, from young children to senior citizens. Tranquille's initial mandate was twofold: to serve those living in the interior and northern reaches of the province and to limit its clientele to those then called the "educable retarded" (Norton 1999, 178), that is, those whose disabilities were relatively less severe. As John Lord and Cheryl Hearn (1987, 20) note, however, during the 1970s, "the model of care in institutions began to shift from one of primarily custodial care to one of preparing, training, and habilitating those people with 'potential' for community living." As a result, between 1971 and 1983, more than four hundred residents of Tranquille were deinstitutionalized (20), some of whom moved to group homes in nearby Kamloops. This exodus was offset by an influx of new residents, many of them transferred to Tranquille from Woodlands or other provincial institutions—people whose disabilities were more severe and who were deemed to need permanent custodial care. In 1983, the director of resident care at Tranquille, Alex McIntosh, estimated that 80 percent of the residents were "profoundly retarded" (quoted in Kettner 1983). As Lord and Hearn (1987, 20) point out, this shift in the composition of the resident population meant that staff were accustomed to caring for people who, in their estimation, could not safely transition into life in the community but instead required "segregated, protective, custodial environments."

Tranquille as a Total Institution

A *total institution* is one that creates a physically isolated, self-contained, and all-encompassing world. The concept of a total institution was developed by sociologist Erving Goffman, notably in the essays collected in *Asylums* (1961), to describe a range of institutions founded on "the bureaucratic organization of whole blocks of people" (6) who are required to sleep, work, and play within the confines of the institution and thereby physically isolated from the larger society. Prisons and mental hospitals are Goffman's key examples, but he suggests others, including orphanages, concentration camps, boarding schools, army barracks, and monasteries. As Goffman notes, total institutions differ to some degree in their overarching purpose. In contrast to prisons, which exist "to protect the community against what are felt to be intentional dangers to it" (4–5), mental hospitals, along with TB sanatoriums and leprosaria, are "places established to care for persons felt to be both incapable of looking after themselves and a threat to the community, albeit an unintended one" (4). In a total institution, the autonomy of residents is subverted: they have little, if any, control over their daily activities and are instead subject to the authority of those who operate the institution. In the case of groups of people who are already assumed to be incompetent and/or dangerous, institutionalization serves to reinforce their marginalization.

Tranquille certainly qualified as a total institution, one at which the process of marginalization operated in two directions. Not only were patients rendered peripheral to society at large but, as Lord and Hearn (1987, 23) observe, "the longer a family member lived in the institution, the more of an outsider the family became." With considerable anguish and sorrow, families entrusted the lives of their children to Tranquille, partly for lack of alternatives and partly on the basis of medical opinion to the effect that institutional care was the best, and quite possibly the only, option for their child (9–11). However, as time passed, parents came to feel like intruders at Tranquille. They were "eased out of a parental role" (25) and placed in the position of visitors, watching someone else care for their child—a child who, over time, became increasingly unfamiliar to them. Tranquille, like other institutions of the day, did not routinely inform parents about their child's progress or setbacks, as if parents were no longer in charge of—or even necessarily concerned about—the welfare of their child. In addition, the use of heavy medication for behaviour control often meant that parents were unable to communicate with their child, thereby increasing their sense of alienation (23–24). In this way, just as the residents at Tranquille were marginalized, so were their families.

An institution is defined not solely by its residents and their families but also by those who work there. In the all-encompassing setting of a total institution, workers come to identify with their place of employment—its people, policies, and physical and organizational structures—making it difficult for them to envision a life for themselves outside of the institution. This phenomenon of envelopment is illustrated by a Tranquille staff member's comments: "The way we always looked at it, there were a thousand people at Tranquille. Four hundred lived there and six hundred worked there. . . . But all our lives are based, substantially, on the institution" (quoted in Lord and Hearn 1987, 18). Many of the staff at Tranquille were firmly entrenched, having founded their careers on the institution; the unionization of most of the staff, in 1977, enhanced job security, but it also increased the workers' sense of personal investment in the institution (19).

As a physical and psychological environment, Tranquille fit the description of a total institution: it was, in many ways, its own world. Yet this does not mean that no significant interaction occurred between the residents of Tranquille and the city of Kamloops. A series of eight interviews conducted in 2009 with former employees of Tranquille provide insight into these interactions.[4] Tranquille residents frequently travelled to the city for social events and shopping; eighty-six of them regularly worked at Pleasant Industries, a worksite for the mentally ill; and younger residents attended nearby Fitzwater School, a public school for those with disabilities (interview, Barb). During the baseball season, Kamloops leagues would schedule games at the baseball field at Tranquille twice a week, and Tranquille residents would come out to see the games and cheer on the players. Former employees also talked about going to Tranquille on their days off to visit with residents and other workers, taking residents on picnics or camping, and inviting them over to their own houses for holiday dinners (interview, Charlotte; "Upset Families Battle Move" 1984). Regular Sunday outings for Kamloopsians included a visit to the sunken gardens at Tranquille, and the institution annually held open houses, when visitors could tour the facilities and grounds. Barbecues, corn roasts, and other events that drew on the bounty of Tranquille's farm and ranch were also held on site every year; in the early 1970s, upwards of seven hundred guests attended the annual barbecue (interview, Charlie).

In addition to such social events, many Kamloopsians volunteered their time with the residents. Some of the workers at Tranquille lived on site and raised their children there (interview, Charlie; McRae 1983), while some parents lived in Kamloops solely because their child was housed at Tranquille and they want to be able to visit regularly ("Ombudsman Studies Tranquille" 1984). This flow of individuals between Tranquille and Kamloops suggests an intimate link between the two communities, one that extended beyond Kamloops's reliance on Tranquille as an economic driver. Clearly, the institution occupied a central place in the lives of those who worked there. But, because so many Kamloopsians were connected in some way to Tranquille,

---

4 These interviews were conducted by the author and a research assistant. In the comments quoted, the interviewees are identified by pseudonyms.

whether directly or indirectly, the institution was also an inextricable part of the identity of Kamloops.

The Decision to Close Tranquille

Beginning in the 1960s, Canadians' attitudes towards institution-based psychiatric care began to shift, as did government policy (Sealy and Whitehead 2004, 250). Between 1965 and 1980, nearly fifty thousand beds were closed in Canadian residential psychiatric facilities.[5] Beginning in the 1960s, a similar shift away from institution-based care took place in most Western countries. According to Marijke Gijswijt-Hofstra and Harry Oosterhuis (2005, 14–15), there were numerous reasons for this trend, some practical and others ideological and ethical: "the introduction of psychotropic drugs from the 1950s; nationally designed plans to integrate psychiatry into the overall health and social care-providing system of the welfare state; the anti-psychiatric criticism of institutional and medical psychiatry; the striving for humanistic reform of the care and treatment of psychiatric patients and enhancement of their social integration and civil rights; and last but not least, financial and political considerations." The closure of Tranquille was motivated by the "last but not least": the economic and political climate, both provincial and national.

In 1981, the BC government, under the leadership of Premier William Bennett, leader of the Social Credit Party, expressed its commitment to expanding community supports and services with a view to the deinstitutionalization of people with developmental disabilities (Lord and Hearn 1987, 27). Two years later, however, in a neoconservative response to the growing recession, Bennett's government launched a severe restructuring of social services, education, and the public sector. Bennett's 1983 budget and the twenty-six bills that accompanied it eliminated whole categories of social services, abolished the Human Rights Commission and rent controls, drastically increased class size in public schools, and essentially stripped public sector employees of their power to engage in collective bargaining. In particular, Bill 3, the Public Sector Restraint Act, gave government employers the right to fire public workers without cause and severely curtailed seniority rights, while at the same time the government vowed to reduce the number of provincial employees by 25

5 "After the Asylum," n.d., *History of Madness in Canada,* http://aftertheasylum. appso1.yorku.ca/en.

percent (Poole 1987, 80–81). Negative reaction to the so-called restraint budget of 1983 swelled, culminating in the Operation Solidarity series of rotating strikes in British Columbia in the late fall of 1983.

The 1983 budget also contained plans for the almost immediate closure of Tranquille, slated for December 1984. In a press release issued on 8 July 1983, the Ministry of Human Resources announced its decision "to accelerate the thrust towards deinstitutionalization for the mentally retarded" (quoted in Lord and Hearn 1987, 27), thereby attempting to frame the closure within the context of its earlier commitment to community living. Grace McCarthy, the minister of Human Resources and the public face of deinstitutionalization in the province, subsequently argued that the closure was also a matter of fiscal responsibility, pointing to the high cost of continuing to operate Tranquille. Speaking before the Legislative Assembly on 8 March 1984, McCarthy stated: "We won't apologize for the time-frame. I will tell you why the time-frame: Tranquille needed a lot of financial investment to improve it. Some has already been done, but the physical plant needs millions of dollars invested in it." As she went on to declare, "We will look back on this year—a year of restraint—as the most aggressive year of deinstitutionalization that probably this province has ever seen or will see, and we should be proud of the fact that we can do it in this time" (British Columbia, Legislative Assembly 1984, 3719).

But pride was not the response articulated by the citizens of Kamloops. The recession of the early 1980s hit resource-based towns hard, but Kamloops was a national economic black spot: unemployment in the region was close to 20 percent, and Tranquille was the third-largest employer in the city, with close to six hundred people working at the institution (Lord and Hearn 1987, 58, 2). The response of Kamloopsians to the announced closure was one of protest—by the parents and advocates of the residents, by the Tranquille workers, and by the people of Kamloops in general.

Protests by Parents and Advocates

The responses of parents of the residents varied. Most first heard of the closure on the evening news broadcast of 7 July 1983. The first direct contact between the government and families occurred six to eight weeks after the public announcement via a form letter from the government planners to the parents of Tranquille residents. During this two-month lag, rumours abounded, and the lack of official information heightened parents' anxiety. In late July, an article in the *Sentinel* titled "Nobody Has Told Parents Anything" identified one the parents' chief concerns: "They're on edge about how receptive the community will be to having mentally handicapped living among them. 'The attitude of the community is still in the 1800s,' claimed a Kamloops mother. 'We don't want to throw them out into the wilds where anyone can take advantage of them'" (Crump 1983). Indeed, concern for the safety of their children was a reason often heard from parents who objected to the prospect of deinstitutionalization. Parents spoke enthusiastically of the freedom of residents to wander the gardens of Tranquille, juxtaposing this vision of autonomy and safety to the busy traffic of city streets and possible encounters with predatory strangers. The lack of both consultation and reliable information served to reinforce parents' long-standing sense of themselves as outsiders (Lord and Hearn 1987, 44). Years, sometimes decades, of being pushed to the periphery had done nothing to prepare them for anything like engaged decision making about their children's future.

There is no doubt that deinstitutionalization represented a significant change for families. A small number of parents wrote to their Member of Parliament, pointing out that they had moved to Kamloops to be near their child and were distressed that their child might be moved to a group home in another city (Johnson 1984b). Other parents painfully recounted how emotionally difficult it had been for them to place their child at Tranquille, noting that they had done so under medical advice that this would be best for their son or daughter (Lord and Hearn 1987, 11–12). Now they were being told that institutional care was not the best option, forcing them to revisit their original decision, which brought with it no small sense of guilt. Some were afraid to take their child back home. Parents who had grown apart from their child or had simply grown old worried that they were no longer in a position to care for their adult child ("Upset Families Battle Move" 1984). Others supported the concept of deinstitutionalization but worried about how it would be implemented ("Ombudsman Studies Tranquille" 1984). Unlike other groups that resisted the closure, however, parents as a group did not organize against it; they remained isolated and relatively passive. This reaction attests to their degree of alienation and disempowerment.

In contrast to parents, advocacy groups—notably British Columbians for Mentally Handicapped People (BCMHP, now the BC Association for Community Living)—were initially supportive of the closure and had, in fact, been advocating deinstitutionalization for several years, on humanitarian grounds.

Addressing the Legislative Assembly on 11 July, Minister McCarthy had, more-over, promised a joint planning approach to the closure of Tranquille:

> We will take into consideration the staff of Tranquille when this change is made. We will take into consideration the families of the clients of Tranquille, the community, and the union representing the staff. They will all be involved in the closing of this institution that has served British Columbia so well, with great love and care, over very many years. (British Columbia, Legislative Assembly 1983a, 210)

The BCMHP was thus anticipating a joint planning process, one in which it would be directly involved. But, as the group soon discovered, the government had no intention of engaging in a cooperative approach to planning (see Lord and Hearn 1987, 46–47). It was not long, then, before its initial optimism gave way to concern.

In response to being closed out by the government, the BCMHP shifted its focus to developing a strategy to support families by linking local societies with parents who had sons or daughters at Tranquille. For example, the Kamloops chapter of the BCMHP, the Kamloops Society for the Mentally Handicapped (now the Kamloops Association for Community Living), hosted information days for the parents and the public, letting parents know their rights and educating the community about the benefits of deinstitutionalization ("Kamloops Group Studies Tranquille Closure" 1983).

Advocacy groups felt so strongly about the rights of the mentally challenged that they engaged in civil disobedience to protect them. In July 1984, the government announced plans to transfer a number of "medically fragile" residents from Tranquille to Victoria's Glendale Lodge.[6] The transfer, of a total of fifty-five residents, was scheduled for September. Citing the government's promise that it would not shift residents from one institution to another, the BCMHP held blockades at Tranquille when the transfers were made, sponsored candlelight vigils, used the media to share poignant personal narratives about the individuals who were to be transferred, attempted to get the BC Supreme Court to block the transfers, and appealed to Karl Friedmann, BC's ombudsman (who supported them). They argued that the transfer to Glendale "betrays the promise of deinstitutionalization" ("Ombudsman Studies

---

6 For a detailed account of the rationales for and responses to these transfers, see Lord and Hearn (1987, 119–36).

Tranquille" 1984). Of particular concern were the parents who had settled in Kamloops to be close to their children in Tranquille. A transfer to Glendale would mean either relocation and a career or job change for the parents or else costly travel expenses that many parents could ill afford, particularly in light of the depressed economy. But all of this protest was to no avail; the transfers went ahead. Articulating his dismay at the situation, Al Etmanski, the executive director of the BCMHP, opined that the Ministry of Human Resources had "chickened out" and could not bring itself to achieve full deinstitutionalization: "It was sort of like building a bridge that missed the other side by five feet" (quoted in Knox 1985).

Protests by Workers

For the most part, Tranquille employees responded to the announcement of the closure in two ways: they expressed apprehension about their own job security, and they voiced a lack of confidence in the ability of residents to adapt to life outside of Tranquille. Their current contract was set to expire in October 1983, and, in view of Bill 3, their most immediate concern was that they would be fired, lose their seniority, and be unable to secure another government position. Tranquille employees were represented the British Columbia Government Employees Union (BCGEU) and by the Union of Psychiatric Nurses of BC. When, shortly after the closure was announced, union representatives learned that the government had made no plans for Tranquille's staff (Lord and Hearn 1987, 56), the workers decided to occupy the site. Beginning on 20 July, workers took over the administration buildings, successfully preventing management from accessing the site, and, in the days to come, would take over the employee cafeteria, the fire hall, and other sites until virtually the whole complex was under their control. The occupation lasted for three weeks, with the workers refusing to leave until they were assured job security.

In interviews and newspaper articles, the workers also expressed concern about the fate of the residents, worrying that some residents would not be able to make the transition to a group home in such a short time. "They are not ready or equipped to be 'thrown' out into the community," one remarked; "furthermore, the community is not ready to handle this grade of mental retardation" (quoted in Grant 1983). Some questioned whether community living was truly the better option. "For many of our residents," said one worker, "Tranquille is the only home they have ever had. They enjoy the security and attention they get from this facility. The residents here have not been given a choice as to whether they want to go or not" (quoted in Paine 1983). Granted, these expressions of concern may well have been rooted in a more fundamental fear of job loss. Yet, at least to some extent, they may also have reflected the workers' conviction that the care they provided at Tranquille was important—that the residents, most of whose disabilities were quite severe, needed their attention and protection.

On 10 August 1983, after twenty-one days of occupation, the protest was called off, but the workers, who remained without a firm assurance of job security, vowed to continue their fight. Later that same day, Tranquille workers participated in an Operation Solidarity rally in Kamloops that attracted four thousand protestors.

Protests by Kamloopsians

The reaction of Kamloops citizens was expressed primarily in terms of fears about the social and economic impact of the closure. A poll released on 7 June 1984 showed that 75 percent of those surveyed disagreed with the decision to close Tranquille, with many citing a lack of adequate facilities in the community for the mentally handicapped (33%) and a concern that the closure would increase unemployment (28%) (Johnson 1984a). Many letters to the editor in the local newspapers likewise expressed concerns about the loss of jobs and the economic impact of the closure on the city. Although Minister McCarthy assured the Kamloops community that the vacated property would be turned to another use and that "something will be done in terms of providing some kind of industry there for the municipality" (British Columbia, Legislative Assembly 1983a, 210), the worries of city residents were not assuaged.

In August 1983, an article in the *Sentinel* quoted Dave McPherson of the BCGEU as noting that Tranquille contributed $13.37 million annually to the Kamloops economy in terms of provisions purchased for the institution and the wages spent by its nearly six hundred employees. He estimated the spin-off effects of the closure as costing the city $40 million annually. And he anticipated a devastating impact on the social fabric of the community as people left the city in search of jobs elsewhere ("Tranquille Closure Carries $40 Million Tag" 1983). A storefront campaign was launched during which retailers placed posters in their windows calling on the government to take a second look at the closure of Tranquille, and Tranquille workers affixed small "Tranquille wages" stickers on their dollars to provide merchants with an indication of the spending power of Tranquille employees (McRae 1984c). Mayor Mike Latta set up a task force a month after the announcement of the closure to grapple with its impact. Noting the exodus of employers from the city in recent years, he stated that "the city just doesn't need another major out-migration and loss of jobs" (quoted in "Tranquille Workers Meet" 1983).

Some Kamloopsians expressed disquiet about the influx of former Tranquille residents into the community. The greatest immediate concern was that the city would be overrun with uncontrollable mentally handicapped people, "the ones who jump up and down and bounce off walls" ("Tranquille Closing Fuels Fear in City" 1984). Homeowners were upset about group homes being established in their neighbourhood, fearing inadequate supervision of residents, lack of safety for their own children, and declining property values (Hoff 1984b). This resistance formed along class lines, with the complaints predominantly coming from the residents of neighbourhoods higher on the socioeconomic scale (Hoff 1984a).

There is no doubt that the media inflamed a public outcry. Emotional and exaggerated responses were printed in the newspapers, variously derogating Tranquille residents as "total vegetables" or voicing fears that those released might "rape our women and children" ("Tranquille Debate Takes a Wrong Turn" 1984). The newspapers were also peppered with eyewitness accounts of observations of such things as handicapped men masturbating in public (Hanson 1984), children being attacked, and Tranquille residents "being totally destructive . . . ripping curtains off the walls" (Ferry 1984). Homeowners complained that advocacy groups were encouraging clergy to pressure them to accept group homes in their neighbourhoods. When the BCGEU launched an advertising campaign that equated deinstitutionalization with "dumping" people in the community (McRae 1984a, 1984b), others accused public workers of whipping up a campaign of hysteria and bigotry against the people they were paid to serve.

Group homes were funded by the provincial government and operated by a combination of private owners and nonprofit organizations such as the Kamloops Society for the Mentally Handicapped, with service providers chosen by the Ministry of Human Resources largely on the basis of bidding (see Lord and Hearn 1987, 99–101). The fight against group homes entered the judicial arena when a group of Kamloops citizens organized a legal challenge based on land-use contracts, claiming that community care facilities were not defined as a permitted use in some of the city's residential areas. Kamloopsians also demanded open public meetings to discuss the location of the group homes and sent petitions to city council. Kamloops already had a high concentration of group homes resulting from the gradual deinstitutionalization in the pre-1983 period, and there was a feeling that a saturation point had been reached.

In the end, the government stopped holding neighbourhood information sessions about group homes and instead set such homes up quietly so as to avoid a community ruckus. This was entirely legal, since the majority of the group homes were small, between three to seven people, and did not require community consultation. In all, about eighty former residents were placed in community care in Kamloops; the other residents were purportedly placed as close to their home communities as possible (British Columbia, Legislative Assembly 1983b, 916; 1983c, 2913). Of the fifty-nine group homes across the province that were developed for the men and women previously housed at Tranquille, only six engendered a negative community response—but three of these six were in Kamloops (Lord and Hearn 1987, 102). In all likelihood, the economic reality of the closure within an already depressed area exacerbated community tensions.

Long-Term Impacts of Closure

In the end, fewer than twenty Tranquille employees kept government jobs in Kamloops (Knox 1985). Many employees—over a hundred—accepted transfers to either Woodlands or Glendale. Others took early retirement, found jobs in local group homes, or went into another branch of employment altogether. Many still get together regularly. Fifteen to thirty former employees meet for monthly lunches, with their numbers blossoming to eighty at Christmas (interview, Charlotte). There have been two reunions, the first in 1990, which was attended by over eight hundred people, and a second in 1998 ("Hundreds Expected for Reunion" 1990; Duurtsema 1998). Former employees express considerable bitterness about the way in which deinstitutionalization was handled, and they are angry that, in the long run, Tranquille has acquired a negative reputation, in that institutionalization has come to be regarded as bad. In interviews, these former employees maintained that the residents were safe and protected. "If people could see how we dealt with the residents and how happy it was, people would think differently," said a psychiatric nurse, adding, "We were their family" (interview, Charlotte). Another former employee also invoked the metaphor of family to describe the relationship of professional staff with the residents: "We treated them well, they trusted us; we were like family to them." She also took issue with the prevailing image of Tranquille: "I never considered Tranquille an institution," she said (interview, Barb). These former employees valued their monthly reunions, which gave them an opportunity to reminisce and share pleasant memories of their days at Tranquille. "I just loved Tranquille," said the psychiatric nurse, who had worked there from the late 1960s until its closure. "The last day at Tranquille was the saddest day of my life" (interview, Charlotte).

Another group of former employees, however, criticized these gatherings as too self-focused, arguing that the constant harking back to the "good old days" at Tranquille was more about the employees themselves, who seemed to give little thought to what was best for the residents. This group seemed to be more connected to the former residents, often socializing with them. One former worker, speaking for some of the staff, stated: "The last reunion, clients weren't allowed to come. It was to be staff remembering staff. We all boycotted it. If we are not a group, then I don't want to go" (interview, Trudy). Moreover, not all former workers had rosy memories of Tranquille. "We tried our best out there, but it was all wrong," one said. "There were a lot of good people there, but it was an institution" (interview, Frank). Another commented, "People made the best of what they had out there. Staff had to survive Tranquille, just like the residents did" (interview, Joan). And, regarding the closure, one former employee recalled: "It was stressful to watch people feel like their lives were over. There were more jobs, but people didn't see it as an opportunity to grow—they didn't think of the residents' lives improving. They saw it as the end of their lives" (interview, Trudy).

Whether the residents' lives did improve is a matter of debate. Follow-up studies of the closure of Tranquille have raised doubts about the degree to which deinstitutionalization actually occurred. A study conducted by John Lord and Alison Pedlar (1991), who examined the life situation of eighteen former residents of Tranquille four years after its closure, demonstrated that "simply moving people into homes in the community does not necessarily ensure enhanced quality of life" (1). The study found that some homes were clearly still institutional in nature (15); that the majority of homes simply had no involvement with neighbours (20); that while some parents expressed great joy over the reunification of their families, less than half of the residents had some family involvement (25–26); and that "in" the community does not mean "of" the community (57). Another study compared the deinstitutionalized Tranquille residents to the institutionalized Woodlands and Glendale residents and found no significant difference in quality of life between the groups:

> That the Tranquille matched group and the Woodlands/Glendale matched group did not differ on most variables may be considered a positive finding in itself as the Tranquille subjects did not deteriorate by the move to the community. In other words, they were as well off in the community as the other subjects were remaining in the institution. On the other hand, the philosophy of proponents of deinstitutionalization has been premised on a belief that individuals in institutions are actively at risk of greater deterioration than are comparable individuals in the community. This was not substantiated in this study. (Wilcox 1988, 202–3)

As yet another researcher concluded: "Invisible walls continue to isolate people in their communities" (Le Cavalier 2005, 13)

To scholars of deinstitutionalization, this is a familiar theme. Across Canada and the United States, initial enthusiasm for deinstitutionalization waned with the growing awareness that many discharged residents were leading impoverished lives in the community, struggling with addictions, and swelling the ranks of the homeless. The new visibility of those with mental health challenges, previously hidden away in remote institutions, fuelled the perception that deinstitutionalization had failed. It also appeared that the quality of life for many of those in community care was either not appreciably different from the days of the institution or had in fact deteriorated. Many argued that the institution had not disappeared but had simply changed location—a process referred to as "trans-institutionalization" (Morrow, Dagg, and Pederson 2008, 2; see also Niles 2013, 69–78). Individuals were now housed in smaller facilities, but these were still institutional in nature. Scholars have thus argued that the tensions and challenges of long-term institutional care have been reproduced rather than resolved with deinstitutionalization (see, for example, Davies et al. 2016).

Some lessons learned from the closure of Tranquille were applied to the subsequent closure of Woodlands and Glendale, in 1996. When Tranquille closed, individuals were placed in group homes in accordance with the principle that those with similar abilities should be placed together; compatibility and existing friendships were not considered. As a result, not only did many residents lose friends through deinstitutionalization, but they also found themselves "locked-in" to a home shared with others with whom they did not get along (Lord and Pedlar 1991, 45). And these incompatible groupings created less-than-happy staff. When Glendale and Woodlands were closed, the placement of residents in group homes was centred much more on compatibility and friendships than on similar needs. The planning and process of the deinstitutionalization of Woodlands and Glendale also took place over a longer period, allowing for more preparation and care to be put into consultations with residents, family members, employees, and community. Moreover, both New Westminster and Victoria had complex and dynamic economies that could more easily weather the economic fallout of deinstitutionalization, on top of which, by the time these two facilities were closed down, the provincial economy was more robust. All of this meant that the closures of these institutions went more smoothly and enjoyed greater community support.

Conclusion

When the closure of Tranquille occurred within such an unexpectedly tight time frame, the city of Kamloops reacted. The response took the form of resistance, although this resistance assumed different forms. Predictably, some Kamloopsians focused on their own self-interests, opposing the closure out of fear that group homes and their presumably unruly residents might infiltrate their own neighbourhood. Others reacted to the economic implications of the closure, seeing in it the prospect of personal job loss and/or a further blow to an already ailing local economy. These concerns led many to question the philosophy of deinstitutionalization, as well as the abrupt imposition of provincial government policies without due consideration of their consequences. At the same time, disability rights advocates protested the government's failure to embrace a vision of community living for all. Had the closure been handled in a more gradual and consultative manner, it might not have generated such an impassioned and largely negative response. Likewise, had the closure occurred during a period of economic buoyancy rather than crisis, or had the government made concrete plans to replace Tranquille with some other economic generator, the closure might not have seemed as threatening.

And yet, in fact, the decision to close Tranquille was abrupt, hastily implemented, and poorly planned, and this, more than anything else, speaks to the government's motive: to save money. Institutions such as Tranquille were enormously expensive to maintain, not the least because they employed hundred of public sector workers, and they also tied up government capital that could be used for other purposes. This economic rationale was articulated by McCarthy on 11 July 1983, three days after the announcement that Tranquille would be closed. Defending the closure in terms of the province's draconian budget, McCarthy said: "This budget speaks to a fragile economy, but the fact is that recovery is not only possible, it's on its way. But it's on its way if we downsize government. It's on its way if we can restrain ourselves from the demands on the public purse." As she went on to say: "We can't spend ourselves and borrow ourselves into the future. It has to stop today" (British Columbia, Legislative Assembly 1983a, 209, 210).

In an analysis of the deinstitutionalization movement in North America, Chavon Niles (2013, 55–56) argues that the closure of state-run mental hospitals was motivated not "by humanitarian concerns for those deemed mentally ill" but rather by the "desire to cut costs." Citing comments made by a former medical superintendent at the Queen Street Mental Health Centre in Toronto, Niles suggests that Ontario's initial pursuit of deinstitutionalization amounted to the deliberate discharge of patients into the community "irrespective of the quality and functionality of the community support services available, rather than a carefully planned and executed policy" (68). Yet, despite this lack of adequate preparation, the state could draw on the rhetoric of humanitarianism to mask underlying economic motives: "By deinstitutionalizing patients, the government was able to save a substantial amount of money and present society with the belief that this was being done under the guise of humanitarian care for the once rejected" (68–69). These observations point to an important conclusion about deinstitutionalization: properly handled, it is actually not a cost-cutting measure. It becomes one only when the state refuses to spend the money needed to ensure that former residents of institutions are not simply "thrown out" into the community but are given the support they require in order to succeed.

In 1991, the provincial government sold the Tranquille site to a private owner, and, although it has since changed hands several times, its future remains to be seen (Fortems 2016). Institutionalization lives on in Kamloops, however, in the form of group homes nestled into local neighbourhoods. The institution is now within the city rather than next door to it. But the economic influence of these small, invisible institutions is not nearly as profound as was that of Tranquille, a total institution employing hundreds of Kamloopsians. In this way, the economic blow of deinstitutionalization to the Kamloops economy has implications for other small cities that depend to some extent on a total institution, such as a prison or a military base, for their economic stability.

As this chapter also demonstrates, Tranquille did not exist in a vacuum. Tranquille was a total institution, but it was one intimately linked to Kamloops through a web of well-travelled connections. A complex reciprocal relationship existed between Tranquille and the city of Kamloops: neither one was "a whole little city by itself." Today, more than thirty years after the institution closed down, the memory of Tranquille endures, embedded deeply in the Kamloops psyche.

References

British Columbia. Legislative Assembly. 1983a. *Legislative Debates (Hansard)*. 33rd Parl., 1st Sess. 11 July 1983. https://www.leg.bc.ca/documents-data/debate-transcripts/33rd-parliament/1st-session/33p_01s_830711p.

———. 1983b. *Legislative Debates (Hansard)*. 33rd Parl., 1st Sess. 18 August 1983. https://www.leg.bc.ca/documents-data/debate-transcripts/33rd-parliament/1st-session/33p_01s_830818p.

———. 1983c. *Legislative Debates (Hansard)*. 33rd Parl., 1st Sess. 20 October 1983. https://www.leg.bc.ca/documents-data/debate-transcripts/33rd-parliament/1st-session/33p_01s_831020p.

———. 1984. *Legislative Debates (Hansard)*. 33rd Parl., 2nd Sess. 8 March 1984. https://www.leg.bc.ca/documents-data/debate-transcripts/33rd-parliament/2nd-session/33p_02s_840308p.

Crump, Debbie. 1983. "Nobody Has Told Parents Anything." *Kamloops Daily Sentinel*, 29 July.

Davies, Megan, Erika Dyck, Leslie Baker, Lanny Beckman, Geertje Boschma, Chris Dooley, Kathleen Kendall, Eugène LeBlanc, Robert Menzies, Marina Morrow, Diane Purvey, Nérée St-Amand, Marie-Claude Thifault, Jayne Melville Whyte, and Victor Willis. 2016. "After the Asylum in Canada: Surviving Deinstitutionalisation and Revising History." In *Deinstitutionalisation and After: Post-War Psychiatry in the Western World*, edited by Despo Kritsotaki, Vicky Long, and Matthew Smith, 75–95. London: Palgrave Macmillan.

Duurtsema, Elspeth. 1998. "Tranquille Reunion Welcomes Everyone." *Kamloops This Week*, 27 May.

Ferry, Jon. 1984. "Handicapped Caught." *The Province*, 25 March.

Fortems, Cam. 2016. "Tranquille on the Market for $15.9 Million." *Kamloops This Week,* 28 January.

Gijswijt-Hofstra, Marijke, and Harry Oosterhuis. 2005. "Introduction: Comparing National Cultures of Psychiatry." In *Psychiatric Cultures Compared: Psychiatry and Mental Health Care in the Twentieth Century,* edited by Marijke Gijswijt-Hofstra, Harry Oosterhuis, Joost Vijselaar, and Hugh Freeman, 9–32. Amsterdam: Amsterdam University Press.

Goffman, Erving. 1961. *Asylums: Essays on the Social Situation of Mental Patients and Other Inmates.* New York: Anchor Books.

Grant, Sylvia. 1983. "Residents' Future Concerns Workers." *Kamloops Daily Sentinel,* 31 July.

Hanson, L. 1984. "Sex on the Street." *Kamloops News,* 19 March.

Harris, Ashlynn. 2010. "Tranquille Development: Past Influences, Present Realities." *Small Cities Imprint* 2, no. 1: 3–11.

Hoff, Janis. 1984a. "Tranquille Transfer Worries Hills Residents." *Kamloops News,* 9 March.

———. 1984b. "Aberdeen Group Rejects Handicapped Home." *Kamloops News,* 16 March.

"Hundreds Expected for Reunion." 1990. *Kamloops Daily News,* 25 July.

Johnson, John. 1984a. "Poll Shows City Against Tranquille Closure." *Kamloops News,* 7 June.

———. 1984b. "Mother Doesn't Want Handicapped Son Sent to Victoria." *Kamloops News,* 19 July.

"Kamloops Group Studies Tranquille Closure." 1983. *Kamloops Daily Sentinel,* 30 November.

Kettner, Bonni Raines. 1983. "Handicapped Become Items to be Peddled." *The Province,* 25 July.

Knox, Jack. 1985. "Tranquille Questions Unanswered." *Kamloops News,* 24 January.

Le Cavalier, Louise. 2005. "Health Services to Adults with Intellectual and Developmental Disabilities in British Columbia: Building Partnerships with Communities." *International Journal of Nursing in Intellectual and Developmental Disabilities* 2 (1).

Lord, John, and Cheryl Hearn. 1987. *Return to the Community: The Process of Closing an Institution.* Kitchener, ON: Centre for Research and Education in Human Services.

Lord, John, and Alison Pedlar. 1991. "Life in the Community: Four Years After the Closure of an Institution." *Mental Retardation* 29 (4): 213–21.

McRae, Allan. 1983. "Job Loss Rumors, Fear Rampant at Tranquille." *Kamloops News,* 15 July.

———. 1984a. "Tranquille May 'Dump': Residents Could Go to Hospitals." *Kamloops News*, 12 March.

———. 1984b. "'Deunionization' Charged by the BCGEU." *Kamloops News*, 29 May.

———. 1984c. "Workers Claim Merchants' Support." *Kamloops News*, 11 June.

Morrow, Marina, Paul K. B. Dagg, and Ann Pederson. 2008. "Is Deinstitutionalization a 'Failed Experiment'? The Ethics of Re-institutionalization." *Journal of Ethics in Mental Health* 3 (2). http://www.jemh.ca/issues/v3n2/documents/JEMH_v3n02_article_Deinstitutionalization_a_failed_Experiment.pdf.

Niles, Chavon. 2013. "Examining the Deinstitutionalization Movement in North America." *Health Tomorrow* 1: 54–83.

Norton, Wayne. 1999. *A Whole Little City by Itself: Tranquille and Tuberculosis.* Kamloops, BC: Plateau Press.

"Ombudsman Studies Tranquille." 1984. *Kamloops Daily Sentinel*, 8 August.

Paine, Leslie. 1983. "Tranquille Programs Continue." *Kamloops Daily Sentinel*, 31 July.

Poole, Peter. 1987. "Organized Labour vs. the State in British Columbia: The Political Limitations of Trade Unions." Master's thesis, Department of Sociology and Anthropology, Simon Fraser University, Burnaby, BC.

Scott, Ken. 2011. "Society, Place, Work: The BC Public Hospital for the Insane, 1872–1902." *BC Studies* 171 (Autumn): 93–110.

Sealy, Patricia, and Paul C. Whitehead. 2004. "Forty Years of Deinstitutionalization of Psychiatric Services in Canada: An Empirical Assessment." *Canadian Journal of Psychiatry* 49 (4): 249–57.

Statistics Canada. Labour Force Survey. 2018. "Annual Average Unemployment Rate, Canada and Provinces, 1976–2017." Compiled by the Newfoundland and Labrador Statistics Agency, Department of Finance. http://www.stats.gov.nl.ca/statistics/labour/pdf/unemprate.pdf.

"Tranquille Closing Fuels Fear in City: Councillor." 1984. *Kamloops Daily Sentinel*, 14 March.

"Tranquille Closure Carries $40 Million Tag Says Union." 1983. *Kamloops Daily Sentinel*, 24 August.

"Tranquille Debate Takes a Wrong Turn." 1984. *Kamloops News*, 19 March.

"Tranquille Workers Meet." 1983. *Kamloops News*, 18 August.

"Upset Families Battle Move." 1984. *The Sun*, 7 September.

Wilcox, Carol L. 1988. "A Study of Deinstitutionalization of the Moderately, Severely, and Profoundly Retarded Populations of the Three Major Institutions in British Columbia." Master's thesis, Departments of Psychology and Education, University of Victoria, Victoria, BC.

6 Fitting In

Women Parolees in the Small City

Jennifer Murphy

Despite an overall decline in the crime rate in Canada since the start of the 1990s (Allen 2016, 4–5), public concerns about crime and criminals have, if anything, escalated rather than diminished—a response, in part, to fears inculcated by the media in support of the neoliberal elaboration of the carceral state. At the same time, neoliberal policies pursued both by the federal government and by provincial ones have tended to shift responsibility for social programming onto municipalities and to emphasize the need for community-based solutions to social problems that are in many ways the product of neoliberalism itself. On the whole, however, little evidence exists to suggest that the focus on community-level responses to social problems such as homelessness, addictions, and crime has encouraged greater tolerance for difference and diversity among the residents of Canadian towns and city neighbourhoods. Rather, it appears to have encouraged increased wariness and vigilance, with those who belong to the dominant group intent on maintaining a clear distinction between those who are, and are not, worthy of inclusion in the community.

At the municipal level, plans for development often focus on building social cohesion, as well as on creating "healthy" communities of the sort that will attract investments and the promise of future growth. Rarely does the emphasis fall on the integration of marginalized groups into the community as a whole. Instead, and as a number of chapters in this volume illustrate, the presence of such groups, particularly those consisting of individuals regarded as deviant or morally corrupt, tends to provoke attempts on the part of mainstream community members to ban or isolate these unwelcome intruders, who simply have no place as "insiders" in a well-regulated community. Under any circumstances, this exclusionary reflex poses a serious obstacle for the men and women in prisons and penitentiaries across Canada, who will be expected to reintegrate into local communities following their release. Reintegration is especially difficult, however, in relatively small cities. While it may be possible to live in anonymity in large urban centres, this is seldom possible in smaller communities.

This chapter focuses on the experiences of five women in the small city of Kamloops, British Columbia, women who were attempting to return to the community following their release on parole. Drawing on a series of semi-structured interviews with these women, I seek to recover what Ken Plummer (2001, 90) aptly called "voices from below," with a view to understanding the issues that surround reintegration from the standpoint of those most directly affected.[1] The perceptions of these women and their ideas about what would help them succeed in desisting from crime provide an invaluable counterpoint to "top-down" discussions of social exclusion and correctional programming. They also shed light on the dangers of visibility for those stigmatized by a criminal record.

Women and the Canadian Penal System

The Canadian penal system recognizes two levels of responsibility for the incarceration of those convicted of a crime: provincial and federal. Provinces are responsible for offenders who have been sentenced to a jail term of less than two years; such offenders serve their sentence in a provincial correctional centre. Offenders sentenced to two years or more are the responsibility of Correctional Service Canada (CSC) and are housed in federal prisons. In addition, municipalities maintain jails, which hold those who have been arrested for a crime (whether by the RCMP or by local authorities) and are awaiting a bail

---

1 The interviews in this chapter form part of a larger study into reintegration issues experienced by both men and women parolees in two small cities in the southern interior of British Columbia, Kamloops and Kelowna. Semi-structured interviews were used to gather data; these interviews were then transcribed in their entirety and then analyzed using narrative and feminist approaches in an effort to uncover what Sandra Harding (1986, 193) described as an "oppositional consciousness" that challenges dominant social norms around crime, addictions, and the nature of belonging.

hearing. City jails are also used for overnight lock-ups in connection with misdemeanours.

According to Canada's former correctional investigator, Howard Sapers, the number of women incarcerated in federal prisons has been growing, up from 502 in 2006 to 680 in 2016—an increase of 35 percent (Sapers 2016, 62). The increase has been especially dramatic among federally sentenced Indigenous women. In his annual report for 2010, Sapers noted that Indigenous women incarcerated in federal prisons were "the fastest growing segment of the offender population," their number having grown by close to 90 percent over the preceding decade (Sapers 2010, 43). This increase continued: as by 2016, Indigenous women accounted for 36 percent of female inmates (Sapers 2016, 62), even though Indigenous people represent less than 5 percent of the Canadian population overall. As a review of their files indicated, virtually all of these women had a history of "traumatic experiences, including sexual and/or physical abuse," while more than half had either attended a residential school or had a family member who did (43). In addition, "two-thirds of their parents had a substance use issue," and nearly half (48%) had been removed from their family home (43). There is no reason to think that such patterns are anything new.

In his annual report for 2015–16, Sapers (2016, 44) also noted that Indigenous inmates remain "more likely to be classified as maximum security, spend more time in segregation and serve more of their sentence behind bars." In 2012, his office had released a special report, *Spirit Matters*, that criticized CSC for its inadequate implementation of sections 81 and 84 of the Corrections and Conditional Release Act (Canada 1992)—sections that were "intended to ameliorate over-representation of Aboriginal people in federal penitentiaries and address long-standing differential outcomes for Aboriginal offenders" (Canada, Office of the Correctional Investigator 2012, 3).[2] The report argued

---

2 In the description of the report, section 81 of the Corrections and Conditional Release Act made it possible for CSC "to enter into agreements with Aboriginal communities for the care and custody of offenders who would otherwise be held in a CSC facility," with the goal of providing for "a degree of Aboriginal control, or at least participation in, an offender's sentence" (Canada, Office of the Correctional Investigator 2012, 3). Section 84 aimed "to enhance the information provided to the Parole Board of Canada and to enable Aboriginal communities to propose conditions for offenders wanting to be released into their communities" (4)—although, as the report pointed out, in the hands of CSC, this had become a "cumbersome" and "onerous" process.

that, by neglecting these two sections, CSC had failed to abide by the intentions of the Supreme Court as outlined in the *Gladue* decision ([1999] 1 SCR 688), which mandated judges to use specific criteria in determining sentencing for Indigenous offenders. As the report indicated, healing lodges—originally envisioned as an Indigenous alternative to incarceration in a federal institution—were few and far between, and those operating under section 81 were chronically underfunded (3–4). It further noted that, "until September 2011, there were no Section 81 Healing Lodge spaces available for Aboriginal women" (3), making it especially difficult for women, in particular, to access culturally relevant programming. In addition, while CSC claims to support the principles of restorative justice, its efforts to implement these principles have been limited to programs carried out within the correctional setting.

Decisions about parole for federal offenders are made by the Parole Board of Canada, an independent body that operates under the Corrections and Conditional Release Act.[3] It appears that women are granted conditional release more readily than men: according to the parole board, in the five years from 2010–11 to 2014–15, the grant rate for full parole was 39 percent among women, as opposed to 25 percent among men (Canada, Parole Board of Canada, 2015, 31). In the same period, women also proved somewhat more likely than men to complete full parole successfully (86% versus 81%), although no significant difference was observed in relation to day parole (50, 48). For both men and women, recidivism, as signalled by the revocation of parole, more often reflects a breach of parole conditions than the commission of a new offence. In 2014–15, the rates of revocation for a breach of condition were 10 percent and 8 percent, for those on full parole and day parole, respectively, while the rates of revocation for a new offence were 3 percent and 1 percent, respectively (44).

Understanding how men and women manage to reintegrate successfully into community upon release provides a wider perspective about the efforts of parolees, correctional agencies (both government and nonprofit), and other community members. This opens the view beyond a narrow focus on recidivism rates, which are, in fact, a measure of unsuccessful reintegration. In

---

3 "Parole Board of Canada," Government of Canada, 2016, https://www.canada.ca/en/parole-board.html. The Parole Board of Canada also has jurisdiction in provinces and territories that do not have their own parole boards. See "Federal and Provincial Responsibilities," Public Safety Canada, 2015, https://www.publicsafety.gc.ca/cnt/cntrng-crm/crrctns/fdrl-prvncl-rspnsblts-en.aspx.

addition, reintegration for both men and women who have served either a significant federal sentence or several sentences over a period of years may be measured in a number of different ways and may look different at various stages of a parolee's life. According to Shadd Maruna (2001), desistance—that is, the ability to abstain from crime—is not an either/or proposition. Rather, it should be understood as a trajectory punctuated by occasional setbacks, much as recovery from addiction is generally marked by intermittent periods of relapse.

Deinstitutionalization and Incarceration: The Policy Context

Since the 1980s, when policies of deinstitutionalization were widely embraced at both the federal and provincial levels, the influx of the formerly institutionalized into local communities has provoked a dramatic increase in social conflict (Wharf 1990). After the major recession in the early 1990s, federal responsibilities for social programs were downloaded, first onto provincial governments and then onto municipalities, as a way to balance federal and provincial budgets and eliminate deficits.[4] In response, resistance developed to the reintegration into the community of ex-offenders, former psychiatric in-patients, and recovering addicts, many of whom simply joined the ranks of the homeless. The proliferation of halfway houses, group homes, and shelters to assist in reintegration only increased community anger, and the perception grew that communities had reached a saturation point in integrating "outsiders."

Even though there was a decade-long period of sustained economic growth at the end of the twentieth and beginning of the twenty-first centuries, there was no effort to restore funding for social programs to the levels that existed before the cutbacks of the 1990s. Instead, federal and provincial governments focused on tax cuts to individuals and corporations, while encouraging privatization of formerly public services, such as health care and employment programs. The election of a Conservative federal government in February 2006 was accompanied by promises of a "tough on crime" approach that would include harsher penalties for offenders. Between 2006 and 2011, the

---

4 For a useful discussion of Canadian social policy in the final decades of the twentieth century, see chapter 12, "The Welfare State Since 1980," in Alvin Finkel's *Social Policy and Practice in Canada* (2006).

costs for federal prisons rose by 87 percent, reaching $2.98 billion in the fiscal year 2010–11 (Davis 2011).

Kamloops itself has had a long history of community involvement in institutions, and some of the attitudes prevalent in the community in the late 1990s were informed by the response to the announcement, in July 1983, of the impending closure of Tranquille, an institution for developmentally delayed adults and children. As Diane Purvey notes in the previous chapter, the provincial government made the decision to close Tranquille without prior consultation with the community, and the closure took place a mere eighteen months later. Wharf (1992) describes this process as a prime example of poor planning and top-down decision making on the part of the neoconservative Social Credit provincial government of the day. The legacy of that process became apparent in Kamloops when the John Howard Society, Thompson Region proposed opening a halfway house for men on the North Shore in 1999. Resistance focused again on the idea of "saturation," exemplified by the initial sense of grievance (not borne out by city statistics) from the mainly working-class North Shore residents that this area of the city already had a disproportionate amount of social housing. Membership in the opposition group spread to include community residents from all across the city, who focused on grassroots organizing to mobilize protests at city hall. Municipal politicians who originally supported the halfway house proposal rapidly changed their minds and withdrew planning permission, and in the November 1999 municipal elections, in which a new mayor and council were elected, political opposition to halfway housing in the city solidified (executive director, John Howard Society, Thompson Region, pers. comm., 10 October 2005).

Since 1999, however, the city has become a centre in the region for psychiatric services, and two new psychiatric facilities for patients transitioning from Riverview Institution in New Westminster to the community have opened, one on the North Shore and one on the South Shore. In addition, half a dozen new social housing complexes have been built by the John Howard Society, Thompson Region, in partnership with BC Housing and other community agencies, in which parolees are housed among other low-income tenants (executive director, John Howard Society, Thompson Region, pers. comm., 20 November 2009). No major protests have ensued, and there appears to be an acceptance of these new social housing complexes as long as there is no discussion of parolee involvement. This "hidden" but contested area for local residents, as well as social service agencies and the "outsiders" themselves, has led to a focus on "invisibility" for parolees, both men and women, who reside in Kamloops and an apparently willful blindness on the part of municipal politicians and community members to recognize the Other in their midst.

Outlook and Its Residents

In 2010, when the interviews were conducted, the five women who are the focus of this chapter were all living in a three-quarters house in Kamloops, which I will call Outlook Apartments. Prior to their parole, all five had been incarcerated in the only federal women's facility in British Columbia, the Fraser Valley Institution, located in Abbotsford, about 285 kilometres south-west of Kamloops. While they are still in the prison, women who have been granted parole prepare a release plan, which specifies their preferences with regard to geographic location, type of employment, and level of support. The women have three options: Outlook, a halfway house in Vancouver, or a private home placement.

Opened in 2004 as a pilot project, Outlook provides housing for women who have been granted either day or full parole. At the time, the only other facility for federal women parolees in British Columbia was a halfway house in Vancouver. In comparison to a halfway house, a three-quarters house offers less on-site support, in an effort to encourage independent living, which is a key step in integrating into the community. Owned and operated by the John Howard Society, Thompson Region, and governed under BC's Residential Tenancy Act (2002), Outlook consists of satellite one- and two-bedroom apartments in Kamloops's North Shore area; it is a neatly kept, low-rise building in a working-class neighbourhood of older homes. Women are eligible to live at Outlook when they are granted day or full parole. CSC pays for support services and provides a living allowance for the resident women, who can stay until their warrant expires (that is, until their sentence is completed). The building is a women-only space: the parole officer and all the support workers are women. Men can visit the apartments only if they pass a criminal records check and home assessment. Even then, they are not allowed to stay overnight; however, children can visit with their mothers and stay overnight.

A counsellor is available seven days a week at Outlook to assist with life skills: shopping, budgeting, and so on. Major issues for the women include parenting skills, crisis management, poor impulse control, and coping strategies. All the women interviewed had multiple difficulties—for example, problems with substance abuse, chronic mental health conditions, emotional issues stemming from sexual, physical, and/or emotional abuse, and poor literacy and numeracy skills. The John Howard Society, Thompson Region hopes that the women will use the organization as a temporary bridge to the community so that they will learn how to access community services, which they will eventually need to do on their own (executive director, John Howard Society, Thompson Region, pers. comm., 12 November 2008). Most of the five interviewees had lengthy histories of incarceration, however, and had become accustomed to institutional life. Both the support workers and the parole officer expressed concerns about the women's sense of entitlement: having had a great deal of support within the institutional setting, the women felt challenged when they were expected to develop some degree of independence. In addition, most of the women had, at best, minimal work experience.

Outlook generally houses five women at a time, and they have a structured daily routine. They check in with a support worker by phone several times a day and keep a logbook that details their comings and goings. If they are out of the apartment for more than two hours, they must contact the support worker to notify her. There are two support workers: one works during the day and the other checks on curfew at night (9:00 p.m.). The women were all provided with psychological counselling on a weekly basis, focusing on the crime cycle, sexual and physical abuse, and reintegration into the community.

All the women had multiple diagnoses, which posed a number of obstacles to reintegration, but their expectations for successful re-entry were very high—and, according to their support workers, not realistic. The executive director of the John Howard Society, Thompson Region and the parole officer both argued that the Fraser Valley Institute "enables" women and allows them to be unrealistic in their goals; the women came to Outlook with a sense of entitlement, and "they lose the picture about serving a sentence for a crime" (parole officer, pers. comm., 30 November 2005). A number of major barriers to reintegration were identified by the executive director of the John Howard Society, Thompson Region, the support workers, and the women themselves. In particular, they were concerned about employment, since local businesses are generally unwilling to hire federal offenders regardless of the nature of their crime. Similarly, most employment agencies in the community will not recruit volunteers with criminal records let alone volunteers with histories of violent crime like those of most of the women. As a result, many of the women gained experience through volunteer work, mainly at the SPCA.

The five women interviewed for this study, whom I will call Patricia, Amanda, Jane, Danny, and Frances, ranged in age from their mid-twenties to fifty-three. One woman was Indigenous, and another identified as trans-gender. Their parole terms ranged from one year to life, and they had served various lengths of time—from two to eighteen years—in the federal prison system. One woman was serving a life sentence for second-degree murder, and two others had served several federal sentences (and numerous provincial sentences) for drug-related crimes. Two of the women had just completed their first federal sentence. They had all been living at Outlook for three to six months at the time of the interviews. While the women were a diverse group in terms of age, criminal history, and length of incarceration, they shared a number of characteristics, such as low educational levels, limited work histories, significant mental health diagnoses, and addiction problems. This combination of issues led to a multiplicity of challenges in finding (and keeping) employment, maintaining sobriety, and reintegrating into commun-ity. The narratives themselves reveal the difficulties facing the women, both as individuals and as a group, to "fit into" the Kamloops community.

The Interviews: Common Themes

In describing the barriers to reintegration that they encountered, the women identified four overlapping areas of concern: employment and education; mental health issues and addictions; membership in the community; and visibility versus invisibility. For the most part, these women had to struggle to fit into dominant patterns of female behaviour, and, in interviews, they depicted themselves as living relatively isolated lives in Kamloops, drawing their support mainly from one another. In the eyes of both the parole officer and the support workers, however, the women's tendency to stick together as a group posed a problem, one that not only complicated efforts to provide support to these women but also exacerbated the barriers that already existed for former inmates.

Education and Employment

Four of the five women interviewed had not completed Grade 12. For Danny, transgender and in her early fifties, the educational challenges were related to learning disabilities: "I failed Grade 2, 3, and 4—no one diagnosed me as dyslexic until I was an adult." She finally got the help she needed in prison to learn to read and write: "Well, I finally passed Grade 10 with the help of a tutor, but that's as far as I got." Patricia, the youngest parolee interviewed and the person with the longest work history, had also not passed Grade 12: "I'm studying for the GED exam right now so that I can go back to school to study business. Eventually, I'd like to work in the hospitality industry." Frances, a First Nations woman who had lived on a remote reserve in the North for her whole life until incarceration, had not been interested in formal schooling. "I live a traditional life," she said, "sewing, hide-skinning, and that supports my family." Only Jane had finished high school, but when she tried to upgrade her education in Kamloops, she found that she was ineligible for financial assistance because she had previously defaulted on a student loan.

The connection between education and employment was clearly articulated by several of the parolees, who were frustrated that they were not able to access the training for employment that they had expected both in prison and on the outside. Several of the interviewees also saw this issue as specifically related to women in the federal system. For example, Amanda stated that "the women are left behind," and Jane returned to the subject several times in the course of the interview, stating that "the women are forgotten" and "the John Howard Society say they have a program to help us find work, but they don't." Both Jane and Amanda wanted to work in construction, which is still regarded as a nontraditional field for women, but they had been unable to get the training they requested. Patricia, though, had a job to return to once her parole was over. "I've always worked in the service industry," she said. "I was a supervisor in a restaurant in Kelowna before I went to jail. As a matter of fact, my old boss offered me my job back when I can get back to Kelowna."

For women deemed unemployable due to physical or mental disability, the application for income assistance was described as difficult and demeaning. Jane described the humiliation of being interviewed by the local Ministry for Employment and Income Assistance office to determine eligibility for welfare benefits:

Women lose hope in the first two minutes in that office. I've complained to the manager about how they're treated, but she doesn't care. There's a thirty-day work search program required before you qualify for funding. I can't even volunteer: even churches and the thrift shops won't accept volunteers with addictions problems, plus a criminal record is the biggest barrier.

Although the women expressed interest in becoming productive members of the community, the challenges to becoming a volunteer or worker in the community were considerable. At the time of the interview, Jane and Amanda were delivering the daily newspaper at 6:00 every morning. Shortly after the interviews took place, local police contacted the parole office with their concerns that the women might use the paper route as an opportunity to look for houses to break into, and both women were advised that they could not continue with the job. Jane encapsulated the frustration of being unable to go to school, volunteer, or work: "I'm feeling trapped. I don't want to go back to jail. I'm just fading away. Right now, it's a bad day. I'm not feeding my soul, not productive."

Mental Health Issues and Addictions

A complicating factor for the women in their reintegration process was the prevalence of both mental health diagnoses and addiction problems. All the women in this study attended Alcoholics Anonymous (AA) and/or Narcotics Anonymous (NA) programs (sometimes daily), as well as counselling and psychiatric appointments. Prescription medication to treat anxiety, depression, schizophrenia, or bipolar spectrum disorder was commonly given to the parolees on a long-term basis. Several women reported long-term use of prescription medication, in some cases from childhood onwards, in addition to struggling with addiction to alcohol and illegal drugs.

Maidment (2006, 72) states that approximately half of the women in Canadian prisons admit to addiction to alcohol and/or drugs, and she suggests that the figure is actually much higher. Most of the women discussed addiction and its role in their trajectory towards incarceration, release, and then reincarceration. While current medical approaches to addiction focus on harm reduction rather than abstinence and the 12-step model, parolees routinely have a "no drugs and alcohol" clause attached to their parole conditions and can be reincarcerated if that clause is breached. For Danny, serving a life sentence and on parole for the rest of her life, a zero-tolerance policy with regard to alcohol and drug use is likely to result in repeated reincarcerations.

For the most part, however, the women supported the 12-step abstinence model rather than harm reduction. For example, Jane, who described herself as "an addictive personality" and whose siblings and nieces and nephews have all struggled with addiction problems, was vehement in her denunciation of any suggestion that drugs should be legalized:

> Eighty percent of the people in prison are there because of a drug
> addiction, but legalizing drugs isn't the answer . . . I've spent time in
> the Downtown Eastside, and I've seen what happens to women addicts.
> Harm reduction makes no sense. The Four Pillars approach just
> enables people to stay addicts—the safe injection site is just wrong.

She subscribed instead to the AA/NA model and attended meetings two or three times a week. The meetings, she said, "are helping to keep me clean but nothing else—I'm very frustrated because I need to be able to support myself and opportunities [for work] don't open up overnight." In addition, Jane had the opportunity to go to a halfway house for women in Vancouver but refused, since "it's drug-infested and there's lots of absences—I just don't want to be in the lifestyle any more." She was also critical of government-funded addiction programs. "Government hasn't broken the cycle of drug addiction," she said, partly because government officials "don't look to us as a source of information but as part of the problem." But, she added, "my fellow citizens and society and government are part of the problem."

Most of the other interviewees also had dual diagnoses of mental health problems and addiction issues. Amanda had been incarcerated several times for crimes relating to drug addiction, and at her last conviction, her parents told her that while they were supportive of her, they were relieved that she had been arrested because they knew that "I was going to die soon on the streets if I hadn't been caught." Danny, who was fifty-three at the time, had spent her childhood in the foster care system in Ontario, described herself in her twenties as "an angry adult on dope" who made poor choices. Her adulthood had been marked by addiction and periodic stays in psychiatric wards, where she was diagnosed as having a personality disorder, and she was finally given a life sentence for second-degree murder: "I've spent most of my life in institutions—I was on the outside for no more than ten years as an adult, just functioning, sometimes doing different jobs, often doing nothing."

Frances described the controls exerted by the parole system in the community. Referring to drug and alcohol abuse, she said, "I've had a couple of slips since I've been here because of the stress." The last slip was a few weeks before the interview, when she was arrested and spent the weekend in the city jail; she was under a week of house arrest at the time of the interview. The struggle with both addictions and mental health diagnoses compounded the difficulties the women faced in fitting in to the Kamloops community. It decreased their ability to look for paid employment or volunteer work and added to the difficulties most of them faced in dealing with the boredom and isolation they experienced in living in a small city that they did not know well and where most of the citizens they interacted with were support or health care workers, corrections officials, addiction counsellors, or, occasionally, fellow church-goers. Informal ways of meeting other community members seemed to be absent. As Amanda expressed it, "I get up, I go for a walk, I pass the time."

Membership in the Local Community

The women had a variety of comments about reintegration into the community, mostly predicated on their placement in a small city that was not their home. Most of the women expected to return to their home community once their parole ended, particularly if they could not find work or a supportive subcommunity in Kamloops. The difficulties they expressed focused on their need to stay occupied and involved in addiction recovery and mental health stabilization while they were in Outlook, especially in the face of isolation, loneliness, and boredom.

Jane had the longest involvement in the community; she had spent time in Kamloops in the 1980s, and it was where her serious addiction problems began. She had lived for the past eighteen years in Vancouver, however, and did not want to return there. She relied on the community for some support, particularly the Secwepemc community on the local reserve. She described being helped by Elders when she was looking for counselling on addiction issues, and she regularly attended sweats on the reserve, although she did not identify as Indigenous. She clearly articulated her sense of herself as a citizen: "[I] have a real interest in politics. I always vote. Just because I was a convicted criminal doesn't mean I'm not a citizen of Canada with the same rights as everyone else." She also wanted to form connections and relationships with people in the community who could help her set up a program to assist women with addiction problems on their release from prison. "I'm looking to the community for support," she said, "and I've made connections at TRU [Thompson Rivers University] and with community nurses at Interior Health."

In contrast, Frances, who stated that she had no connection to Kamloops and that she "was so lonely in the city," refused to be involved with the First Nations community in the area, saying, "It's not my band here." She described herself as "keeping to myself, not doing anything, I don't know anyone." She spoke sadly several times in the interview about her need to go home; she was trying to get transferred to Prince George at the time of the interview so that her family could visit her. They could not afford to travel to Kamloops to see her, and she had not seen her four children or her young grandchild for almost three years. She also said that, while she thought that the worst thing about prison was the loneliness, "it's been pretty lonely here too." This sentiment was expressed by several of the women, who described their group as supportive of one another but who were frustrated that they seemed unable to meet and form connections with other people.

Danny described herself as introverted, "not a social butterfly"; she did not want to mix with people on the outside. She had some support from the other women in the building but did not appear concerned about meeting more people in Kamloops. She attended medical appointments regularly in Vancouver, where she thought there was more understanding of the challenges she faced as a transgender person. Indeed, she felt that her status as a transgender individual was a more significant barrier to reintegration than her status as a parolee: "I realized when I got here that there's not much diversity in Kamloops."

Only Patricia seemed to feel at home in Kamloops. She attended the local church, where she "felt very welcome," and she believed that she was reintegrating quickly because the living conditions in Outlook were "closer to real life than Fraser Valley Institution." Patricia's circumstances were considerably different from the other four women, although she also shared an addiction history with them. She was the youngest of the group, had served only one federal sentence, was closely connected to family, and knew the community well even though she had not lived in Kamloops previously. Unlike the other women, she could pass as a regular member of the community, and the stigma of being an "ex-con" did not seem to attach to her in the same way that it did to the others. She fully expected to return to regular life after her parole ended and described her crime as an aberration: "I was on a seriously wrong path."

Visibility Versus Invisibility

The women also spoke of the tension between their need to reintegrate into the community and the pressure to remain invisible within a political climate that stigmatizes ex-offenders and parolees. Although Jane said that she had not personally experienced problems in the community, she spoke of community attitudes that were of concern to her, mainly gathered from reading newspaper reports. She expressed the dilemma succinctly: "The mindset in this community is once a criminal, always a criminal. You're free, but you're not—they're looking over your shoulder all the time. [But] when you're sitting in the community, but not in the community—doing nothing—it's useless."

All the women expressed concerns about being identified in the community as parolees and about the impact that would have on their ability to work, volunteer, or even remain safe in Outlook. Jane had a paradoxical approach to invisibility, sometimes disclosing her status to people she met and sometimes not. She acknowledged that "the word *halfway house* is an issue in this community," but she seemed frustrated about having to remain invisible: "People have to stay hidden—it helps the John Howard Society to remain hidden, but the community can't help us if we're hidden."

Several of the women also spoke about the need to remain hidden within the North Shore location of Outlook. Jane said that few people in the neighbourhood knew that Outlook housed federal parolees, since "it's the quietest house on the street." Indeed, before the building was bought by the John Howard Society, Thompson Region, the apartments had been rented by women most of whom were involved in the sex and drug trades. While Outlook had remained under the radar, both Jane and Amanda described it as a "very sneaky tactic" on the part of the John Howard Society. They felt that the neighbours had a right to know who was living in the apartment building, and yet Amanda also stated that "I feel safe in this house" because of the anonymity. Patricia commented on the location itself: "The neighbourhood isn't good, but there are some good people in the nearby houses." She said that she kept a low profile in the neighbourhood and that no one seemed to know that Outlook housed parolees. Her connections with the neighbourhood centred around church attendance, and she was the only woman interviewed who seemed to have made some friends in the community.

For other parolees, such as Danny and Frances, the focus was less on trying to build a community within Kamloops and more on remaining hidden in a community that is limited in terms of diversity (Danny) or attempting to move out of the community as quickly as possible to return to a familiar place (Frances). The dislocation for Frances was spatial, cultural, and temporal, and the only solution that she saw was to leave Kamloops: "I'm hoping to be in Prince George by Christmas." Until then, Frances seemed to experience her release on parole into Outlook as simply another form of incarceration that left her lonely and isolated.

Implications for the Small City

A number of key themes emerged from the data. Clearly, parolees face multiple barriers in their efforts to reintegrate successfully into the small city, some of which are related to the extensive, long-term effects of numerous incarcerations and reincarcerations. Another theme is the impact of both individual well-being (physical and mental health, addiction issues) and community tolerance (access to housing, employment, professional and personal supports) on reintegration. Sapers (2007) discusses the pervasive barriers to successful reintegration, describing the limited program capacity in prisons in the area of retraining, addictions, and mental health—for Indigenous women in particular and for both men and women generally. Both Ken Plummer (1995) and John Ralston Saul (2008) address the issues facing the dispossessed: Plummer, in negotiating an identity of "difference," and Saul, in proposing a fluid and nonlinear approach to citizenship within the "métis civilization" of Canada. These themes were woven throughout the narratives and expressed in a variety of ways: the difficulty in moving towards living independently after years of institutionalization and control by numerous authorities; the frustration around limited programming in prison that hadn't led to meaningful employment after release; and the stigmas associated with living in poverty, in poor health, and in social housing units.

In addition, the prevalence of chronic and persistent mental health conditions and addiction problems among parolees—often as concurrent disorders—further complicates and often compromises parolees' ability to remain in the community. Howard Sapers argues that because women offenders tend to have low educational levels, limited employment histories, and mental health and addiction problems, they need to be provided with a number of services to assist in reintegration upon release—for example, comprehensive mental health assessments and treatment, educational upgrading, and employment training. Currently, most employment training in federal prisons consists of food preparation, cooking, cleaning, and laundry services—that is, domestic work (Sapers 2010, 49–50). Most of the women interviewed for this study rejected this training for menial, minimum-wage jobs as useless, and they expected the John Howard Society, Thompson Region or a similar organization to provide them with training that would help them move into higher-paid and more interesting work.

The major themes emerging from the interviews focused on the adaptation of parolees to their post-prison environment in terms of living conditions (housing, employment, and income), health (physical, mental, and addiction issues) and personal identity (the stigma of the "ex-con," along with race and ethnicity). The onerous conditions of their release were challenged quite forcefully by the women in Outlook, who demanded more services from local agencies than originally planned by Correctional Service Canada and the John Howard Society, Thompson Region. These women managed their tainted identities through the development of a close-knit group within the small apartment building in which they lived, often continuing relationships that had developed during their incarceration in the Fraser Valley Institution.

The challenge of finding resources in smaller communities is also a factor in the tolerance of these cities to accommodate "outsiders" or "others" as members or citizens. The women described difficulties in finding family doctors or other health professionals to provide a continuum of care for them rather than having to rely on walk-in clinics. Both parole officers and support workers with the John Howard Society, Thompson Region had, with mixed results, asked their own family doctors to provide care for parolees when they were unable to assist them in finding medical care.

The women also considered the need for invisibility to be a hindrance in finding employment and, more generally, in reintegrating into the community. In addition, many of the women struggled to reconcile their need, as a group, to remain hidden within the community and their right to exercise personal control over their anonymity, in, for example, making decisions about whether to conceal or reveal their status to neighbours or new partners. The visibility/invisibility dilemma is, however, complicated by the manner in which an "ex-con" is marked by his or her past—what Dominique Moran (2014) calls "inscriptions of incarceration." The marks of a parolee's tainted history may be embodied, in the form of tattoos or the tough, masculine, stance of some of the women, and therefore difficult to hide. But these marks may also be internal, in the form of low self-esteem and an attitude of hopelessness and defeat. Along with the ubiquity of mental health diagnoses, coupled with low levels of education and literacy, these psychological factors contribute to a lack of employment opportunities and the relegation of former offenders to the ranks of the underclass.

Another small city in British Columbia, Prince George, has incorporated the three-quarters model into its own reintegration programs for women federal parolees (executive director, John Howard Society, Thompson Region, 18 January 2013). Prince George, which is roughly the same size as Kamloops, has a prison and a remand centre, as well as drug and alcohol treatment centres. It also has a significant Indigenous population, and there is pressure from the CSC to provide resources and services to parolees who want to return to their home communities, whether in town or on reserve.

Conclusion

Evaluating the process of reintegration requires a shift in focus from a dichotomy between rehabilitation (success) and recidivism (failure) towards an understanding of reintegration and "desistance" (Maruna 2001) as a continuum that may involve a number of reincarcerations. The rehabilitative trajectory of most of the parolees whom I interviewed included occasional breaches of parole conditions (and consequent reincarceration), addictions treatments (in detox and rehab centres), and psychiatric care (both in and out of psychiatric wards). Few new offences were committed, however, and most of the parole breaches involved drug and alcohol conditions. In the five years following the initial interviews, I received regular updates on the status of the five women, during which time several of them returned to prison for breaches of parole. At the end of the five-year period, Jane, Patricia, and Frances had achieved warrant expiry and were living in the community. Amanda and Danny had returned to prison.

Understanding reintegration also demands a recognition of the degree to which women parolees, especially, occupy transcarceral spaces in which their confinement is perpetuated by social controls embedded in the community, in the form of the stigmatization of former offenders (Moran 2014). These five parolees provided differing views on rehabilitation, but they all expressed the need for adequate housing, along with retraining and employment opportunities. Ultimately, the findings of this study indicate the need for a fundamental reframing of reintegration, from a focus on what puts parolees back in prison to a broader and more complex understanding of what keeps them out of prison. In the small city, two factors that contribute to successful reintegration are sufficient resources and services and an acceptance by the general community of difference and diversity, which would indeed allow the women to "fit in."

References

Allen, Mary. 2016. *Police-Reported Crime Statistics in Canada, 2015*. Ottawa: Minister of Industry. http://www.statcan.gc.ca/pub/85-002-x/2016001/article/14642-eng.pdf.

British Columbia. 2002. Residential Tenancy Act. SBC 2002, c. 78. http://www.housing.gov.bc.ca/rtb/bc_laws/RTA.html.

Canada. 1992. Corrections and Conditional Release Act. SC 1992, c. 20. http://laws-lois.justice.gc.ca/PDF/C-44.6.pdf.

Canada. Office of the Correctional Investigator. 2012. *Spirit Matters: Aboriginal People and the Corrections and Conditional Release Act*. Catalogue No. PS104-6/2013E-PDF. Ottawa: Office of the Correctional Investigator. http://www.oci-bec.gc.ca/cnt/rpt/pdf/oth-aut/oth-aut20121022-eng.pdf.

Canada. Parole Board of Canada. 2015. *Performance Monitoring Report, 2014–2015*. Ottawa: Parole Board of Canada. https://www.canada.ca/content/dam/canada/parole-board/migration/005/009/093/005009-3000-2015-en.pdf.

Davis, Jeff. 2011. "Penitentiary Costs Soar 87%: Conservatives' Get-Tough-on-Crime Policy Behind the Increase." *Vancouver Sun*, 19 July.

Finkel, Alvin. 2006. *Social Policy and Practice in Canada: A History*. Waterloo, ON: Wilfrid Laurier University Press.

Harding, Sandra. 1986. *The Science Question in Feminism*. Ithaca, NY: Cornell University Press.

Maidment, MaDonna R. 2006. *Doing Time on the Outside: Deconstructing the Benevolent Community*. Toronto: University of Toronto Press.

Maruna, Shadd. 2001. *Making Good: How Ex-convicts Reform and Rebuild Their Lives*. Washington, DC: American Psychological Association.

Moran, Dominique. 2014. "Leaving Behind the 'Total Institution'? Teeth, Transcarceral Spaces and (Re)inscription of the Formerly Incarcerated Body." *Gender, Place and Culture* 21 (1): 35–51.

Plummer, Ken. 2001. *Documents of Life 2: An Invitation to a Critical Humanism*. 2nd ed. London: Sage.

Sapers, Howard. 2007. *Annual Report of the Office of the Correctional Investigator, 2006–2007.* Catalogue No. PS100-2007. Ottawa: Minister of Public Works and Government Services Canada. http://www.oci-bec.gc.ca/cnt/rpt/pdf/annrpt/annrpt20062007-eng.pdf.

———. 2010. *Annual Report of the Office of the Correctional Investigator, 2009–2010.* Catalogue No. PS100-2010. Ottawa: Minister of Public Works and Government Services Canada.

———. 2016. *Annual Report of the Office of the Correctional Investigator, 2015–2016.* Catalogue No. PS100E-PDF. Ottawa: Office of the Correctional Investigator.

Saul, John Ralston. 2008. *A Fair Country: Telling Truths About Canada.* Toronto: Viking Canada.

Wharf, Brian. 1990. "Social Services." In *Urban Policy Issues: Canadian Perspectives,* edited by Richard A. Loreto and Trevor Price, 170–88. Toronto: McClelland and Stewart.

———. 1992. *Communities and Social Policy in Canada.* Toronto: McClelland and Stewart.

Young, Jock. 1999. *The Exclusive Society: Social Exclusion, Crime, and Difference in Late Modernity.* London: Sage.

7 Walking in Two Worlds
Aboriginal Peoples in the Small City

Sharnelle Matthew and Kathie McKinnon

*The Circle lives. Like the Phoenix, the Circle rises from the
ashes of near death with renewed life and vigorous strength.
(Derrick 1990, 25)*

Today, the Secwepemc communities of south-central British Columbia
are engaged in a process of decolonization and healing. The work of truth
telling and the rediscovery, reclamation, and resurgence of Secwepemc
self-determination and culture are essential to rebuilding communities and
nations in the wake of colonization and oppression, past and present. The
process of decolonization is holistic: it involves the recovery of a spiritual sense
of self, family, and community founded on balance, on interconnectedness
with nature and the Creator, and on reciprocity and the integrity of the whole.
Most importantly, as Bruyere (1999, 173) observes, it is a "re-identification,
re-affirmation and re-assertion of all things Aboriginal."

One outcome of the process of decolonization is that some of the Secwepemc communities near the small city of Kamloops, British Columbia,
now provide certain services to their own members, such as primary and
secondary education, basic health care, income assistance, child welfare, and
rural policing. However, all of these communities still depend on Kamloops
for hospital care, specialized medical services, dental care, and mental health
care, as well as for counselling, legal and financial services, postsecondary education, and access to retail outlets and entertainment venues. This means that

Secwepemc peoples and those who accompany them on the path to wholeness and healing must "walk within two worlds."

To make sense of this double reality and to help explain the lived experience of our communities, we often use the metaphors of the Circle and the Box. The Circle represents the cultural reality of Aboriginal communities; the Box symbolizes the dominant cultural world view. In what follows, in hopes of providing a deeper understanding of these metaphors, we will draw on oral histories and teachings of Elders, as well as on historical research, to describe the processes of colonization and oppression from which Aboriginal peoples in our nation and all across Canada are emerging. Although we aim to tell the story of the Secwepemc people as our Elders told it to us, we recognize that our communities are growing and changing. New economic, cultural, and social realities are emerging, and we will describe these as well. As social work practitioners, we constantly confront the effects of colonization, as well as the implementation of unreasonable and often conflicting bureaucratic policies. On a daily basis, we support our people in their own healing in an effort to help them overcome these challenges. Through examples drawn from our own practice, we hope to illustrate our approach to "walking with" our people towards wholeness in light of the differences in world view that exist between the Circle and the Box.

The Circle and the Box: Two Cultural Paradigms

Although Aboriginal reserve communities are sometimes quite remote, it is not uncommon for these communities to lie in fairly close proximity to larger non-Aboriginal cities or towns. In Kamloops, a small red wooden bridge crosses the South Thompson River, which separates the Tk'emlúps te Secwepemc Reserve from the city itself. Bridges are normally intended to create connections, but the red bridge also symbolizes the line of divide between these two communities—the gap between two distinct cultural realities, that of the Circle and that of the Box. The red bridge is the physical link to the city of Kamloops, but, in the minds of those in the Secwepemc community, it is associated with the need to access services that are not available on the reserve itself. Whether in Kamloops or in Salmon Arm or Clinton or Williams Lake or other small cities in Secwepemc territory, the services provided off reserves are founded on the values, assumptions, and types of knowledge characteristic of the dominant culture. Those who provide these services often lack even a minimal awareness of the long-term effects of colonization and generally do not even attempt to incorporate Aboriginal culture, values, or knowledge into their practice.

In our own practice, we use the metaphors of the Circle and the Box as an educational tool to identify the systemic cultural differences that exist between Aboriginal peoples and non-Aboriginal peoples. These differences, shown in figure 7.1, have been developed from the work of Jann Derrick's (1990) cultural teachings.

Circle	Box
Circular	Square
Spiritual	Hierarchical
Child based	Adult based
Native family systems	non-Native family systems
Traditionally female led	Male led
Asks "What is true?"	Asks "What is wrong?"
Focuses on harmonious relationships	Focuses on power and control
Co-creative	Superior/inferior
Person-centred practice	Expert-/professional-centred practice
Aboriginal cultural perspective	Dominant cultural perspective
Natural/traditional practice	Evidence-based practice/science
Holistic model/strength-based	Medical model/pathology-based
Indigenous construct	Western construct
Subjective	Objective

Figure 7.1. The Circle and the Box

These differences are very real. To meet the needs of the whole person and to avoid practices that are oppressive and insensitive, it is essential to recognize that the Western perspective is *not* universal and can often seem quite alien to an Aboriginal person. In this respect, the model of the Circle and the Box can be very useful. Contrasting the two world views helps our people understand that their own perspective is not "wrong," but merely different, and it can also serve to remind non-Aboriginal service providers that their own assumptions and priorities may differ from those of their clients. At the same time, it is important to recognize that these metaphors are simplified constructions. Clearly, not all Aboriginal cultures are identical, nor are all the cultures broadly categorized as Western, and a set of binary oppositions cannot adequately sum up the totality of either perspective or conceptualize the complicated relationships that exist between Aboriginal and non-Aboriginal worlds. The variances between the Circle and the Box should be understood not as absolutes but as the opposite poles of a continuum that lead to differences in emphasis. It is the points of overlap that create the potential for cross-cultural understanding and awareness.

These symbols can help us to remember and understand that profound differences in world view exist. Whereas people raised in the dominant culture are rarely required to step outside the Box, Aboriginal people are constantly expected to relinquish their own world view and adopt another. As a result, their lived reality is conflicted and complex. Both the Circle and the Box are part of their day-to-day experience in a kaleidoscopic mix that is never stable but is constantly changing with the person, the time, and the circumstances. Moreover, many Aboriginal people have been colonized to internalize the world of the Box, such that the debilitating messages it delivers have become central to their outlook. Identifying the world of the Circle and its presence in their lives and within their community, family, culture, and history is part of the process of empowerment, healing, and decolonization.

Even though some within the Box incorporate elements of the Circle in their professional practice, overall, a profound sense of disconnection and lack of understanding exists between the two. The challenge of our work is to build holistic relationships with those we walk with in order to help them navigate the space that exists between the Circle and the Box. Our understanding of the Circle begins with the wisdom of our Elders.

Our Ancestors' Stories and History

Our Elders continually speak of the importance of Secwepemc stories and history in their teachings. They have told us many stories about how our ancestors lived long before European contact, about their kind-hearted spirit and their traditional holistic perspective on the world. The Elders' stories, rich in historical, spiritual, and cultural meaning, fill in the Circle and provide a context for the complex histories and cultural realities of those we walk beside every day.

Aboriginal peoples have occupied the ecologically diverse south-central region of British Columbia's Interior Plateau for thousands of years. The Secwepemc Nation originally occupied a vast territory of roughly 180,000 square kilometres that extended from the area west of the Fraser River as far as the edge of the Rocky Mountains and from the upper Fraser River in the north to points south of the Arrow Lakes. According to our Elders, there were originally thirty-two Secwepemc communities. Although, to some extent, each community had its own ways, there were commonalities such as respect for nature, the Secwepemctsín language, and traditional Secwepemc knowledge, values, ceremonies, and stories.[1]

Prior to the arrival of Europeans, Secwepemc communities governed themselves in accordance with the principle of reciprocity and held a number of ideals in common, among them honour, equality, health, and the sharing of resources, power, and knowledge. While everyone benefited, those with the greatest need received more. All people had a role to play in the community, with the whole depending on the contribution made by each individual. As others have noted, "Many Aboriginal peoples retain notions of the person as defined by a web of relationships that includes not only extended family, kin and clan but, for hunters and other people living off the land, animals, elements of the natural world, spirits and ancestors" (Kirmayer, Simpson, and Cargo 2003, 18). People were accountable to and responsible for one another, and all community members cared for the children of the community, who were considered special gifts from the Creator.

Today, out of the original thirty-two, only seventeen Secwepemc communities remain: Xats'úll (Soda Creek), T'éxelc (Williams Lake), Esk'ét (Alkali Lake), Stswécem'c/Xgét'tem' (Canoe/Dog Creek), Tsq'éscen (Canim Lake), Llenllenéy'ten (High Bar), Stil'qw/Pelltíq't (Whispering Pines/Clinton), Tsk'wéylecw (Pavilion), St'uxwtéws (Bonaparte), Skitsesten (Skeetchestn), Tk'emlúps te Secwépemc (Kamloops), Simpcw (North Thompson), Sexqeltqín (Adams Lake), Sk'atsin (Neskonlith), Quaaout (Little Shuswap), Splatsin (Spallumcheen), and Kenpésq't (Shuswap) (see figure 7.2).

---

1 For more about Secwepemc history, language, and culture, see the websites of the Secwepemc Nation, http://www.landoftheshuswap.com/index.html, and of the Tk'emlúps te Secwépemc band, http://tkemlups.ca/. On the history of Canada's First Nations more generally, see Dickason (2002) and Dickason and Newbigging (2010).

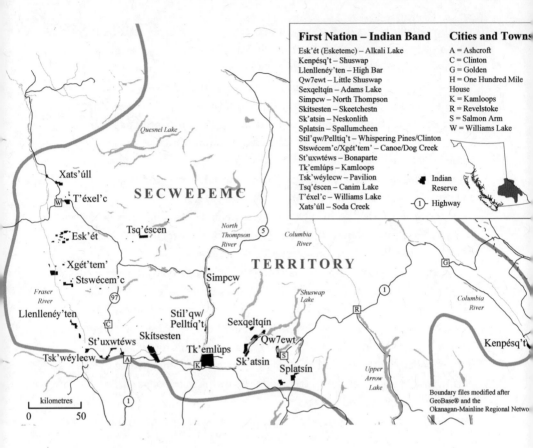

Figure 7.2. Secwepemc territory

Colonization

The first recorded contact between Aboriginal peoples and Europeans in the interior of British Columbia occurred in 1793, with the arrival of the explorer Alexander Mackenzie and his party, followed, in the first decade of the 1800s, by similar groups led by David Thompson and Simon Fraser. Small fur-trading posts were soon established, and in 1821, the Hudson's Bay Company began operations in Secwepemc territory (ALBAA Research Team 2010, 7, 18). During roughly the first half of the nineteenth century, the success of the fur trade demanded that traders rely on the knowledge and skills of Aboriginal hunters and guides, resulting in what Robin Fisher (1992, xxviii) argues was a "mutually beneficial economic system." However, what reciprocity existed ended with the onset of the Fraser River Gold Rush, in 1858, and the Cariboo Gold Rush, which began a few years later, in 1861. This invasion of newcomers marked the beginning of settlement. The Europeans who arrived to pan for gold and then to farm, build homes, and establish churches and businesses were not dependent on Aboriginal peoples for trade and saw no reason to adapt to their ways. As Fisher (1992, xxix) observes, "Gold miners, settlers, missionaries and government officials, in different ways, all required the Indians to make major cultural changes, and the whites now had the power to force change."

The shift in the economic base from the fur trade to agriculture created competition for land, bringing Aboriginal communities into potential conflict with white settlers. In the eyes of settlers, "the mere fact that Indians existed" posed a problem: they were viewed as "an obstacle to the spread of 'civilization'—that is to say, the spread of European, and later Canadian, economic, social, and political interests" (Aboriginal Healing Foundation 2002, 3). In the wake of the gold rushes, the freedom to which Secwepemc peoples had been accustomed was eroded, as they were increasingly confined to reserves and obliged to interact with missionaries, settlers, and government agents. In addition, with Europeans came diseases previously unknown in Aboriginal communities. It is estimated that a third of BC's Aboriginal peoples perished in the smallpox epidemic of 1862–63 alone (ALBAA Research Team 2010, 7), and, over time, many Secwepemc communities disappeared entirely.

In the Canadian context, colonization has been defined as "the process of taking control over and assimilating Aboriginal people through formal government policies. From an Aboriginal perspective, it refers to the theft of ancestral homelands and resources, as well as attempts to destroy Indigenous languages and cultures" (Chansonneuve 2005, A19). Central to this process was the Indian Act, introduced by the Canadian government in 1876. The Indian Act enabled the state to exert extensive legal and administrative control over Aboriginal communities. The original act and its subsequent amendments imposed a system of bands, defined the boundaries of reserves, and created the national policy of residential schools, as well as prohibiting:

- the acquisition of land or the control of land use (1876 to present)
- voting in federal elections (until 1960)
- voting in provincial elections (until 1949)
- voting in municipal elections (until 1948)
- participation in potlatches (1884–1951)

- participation in festivals and dances (1895–1951)
- the possession of alcohol on reserve or intoxication on or off reserve (1876–1970)
- the sale of agricultural products without permission (1881 to present)
- prosecuting land claims or retaining a lawyer (1927–51)[2]

The Indian Act has justly been described as "nothing less than a conspiracy. Examined as a whole, it exhibits a clear pattern founded on conscious intent to eliminate Indians and 'Indianness' from Canadian society" (Mathias and Yabsley 1991, 35).

One major impediment to the westward expansion of white settlement was the existence of Aboriginal title, as recognized in the Royal Proclamation of 1763. In 1870, the Canadian government began negotiating a series of treaties with Aboriginal peoples, with the intent of acquiring legal ownership of their lands. However, aside from Treaty 8 (1899), which covered the northeast corner of the province, these treaties did not extend into British Columbia. After the Colony of Vancouver Island was established in 1849, treaties were negotiated with Aboriginal groups on the island, but once the Colony of British Columbia was founded, in 1858, the Ottawa government terminated funding for such negotiations, placing the burden of cost on the colony itself. The solution pursued by Joseph Trutch, who became governor of British Columbia in 1864, was simply to ignore the existence of Aboriginal title (UBCIC, n.d., 2). Instead, the government of British Columbia arbitrarily created new reserves or made "cut-offs" to existing reserves, thereby reducing their size, without any meaningful consultation with Aboriginal peoples. This includes cut-offs to reserves in both Secwepemc and Okanagan territory (Smith 2009, 163).

This policy continued after British Columbia became a province, in 1871, and ultimately brought the provincial government into conflict with the federal government. The result was a Royal Commission, convened in 1912 and headed by J. A. J. McKenna, the special commissioner appointed by Ottawa, and Richard McBride, the premier of British Columbia. The McKenna-McBride Commission, as it is commonly known, set out to resolve these federal-provincial disputes by determining, once and for all, the location and size of reserves. The question of Aboriginal title was deliberately not included in the agenda, nor was the commission to involve itself in other

---

2 For a detailed overview, see "Appendix: Federal and Provincial Legislation Restricting and Denying Indian Rights," in Mathias and Yabsley (1991, 40–45).

issues of concern to the Aboriginal population. The commission was granted the authority to propose cut-offs to reserves, provided that it had obtained the consent of a majority of the adult men in the band whose lands were involved (UBCIC, n.d., 4).

Especially because south-central British Columbia boasts some of the richest agricultural lands in the province, the reserves in the Kamloops Agency were one target of attention. Prior to the arrival of the McKenna-McBride Commission in the area, the Kamloops Board of Trade prepared a resolution requesting that the Secwepemc living on the Tk'emlúps te Secwépemc Reserve be removed from the vicinity of the city. The board presented this request to the commission, setting off a series of debates. As historian Keith Smith (2009, 185) observes, "It is clear that the Secwepemc and Okanagan were already becoming increasingly restricted to the fragments of their territories that had been reconfigured as reserves. While their representatives patiently tried to explain to the commissioners the importance of retaining the pieces that remained, the commissioners were in no position to understand what they heard."

The report of the McKenna-McBride Commission, submitted in 1916, recommended cut-offs to the land of fifty-four reserves, a total of nearly 47,059 acres. At the same time, it also recommended the addition of a little over 87,290 acres. However, whereas these additions were valued at $444,838 (an average of about $5.10 per acre), the value of the cut-off land was assessed at $1,522,704 (an average of roughly $32.35 per acre). In the Kamloops Agency, nearly 3,500 acres, valued at roughly $130,815, were designated to be cut off and replaced by 1,477 new acres, the value of which was a mere $7,385. Of these 3,500 acres, 2,165 lay in the Qu7ewt (Little Shuswap) Reserve (Smith 2009, 185, 186). Further disputes ensued between the two governments, which culminated in a review of the commission's recommendations. Even though Aboriginal peoples rejected the overall authority of the commission to reduce reserve sizes, when the recommendations were finalized, in July 1924, thirty-five cut-offs were made from territory belonging to twenty-three bands (UBCIC, n.d., 8). Entire Aboriginal communities were forcibly relocated to often tiny, useless pieces of land with few resources.

In addition to these efforts at dispossession, the Canadian government sought to destroy Aboriginal culture by removing children to residential schools, where they would be suitably re-educated. Two such schools were established in Secwepemc territory, one adjacent to Kamloops and the other near Williams Lake, at the site of the St. Joseph's Mission. Founded in 1890, the Kamloops Indian Residential School operated until 1978; the St. Joseph's Mission School operated from 1891 to 1981 (Walmsley 2005, 10). At these two schools, multiple generations of Secwepemc girls and boys aged five and older were legally taken from their families and communities and forced to live in church-administered institutional settings, where they were subjected to harsh discipline and frequently terrorized by members of the staff. Separated from their families, their community, and their traditional homelands and forbidden to speak their language, these children lost their culture, their spiritual foundations, and their sense of identity. This was an act of cultural violence that left Secwepemc families and communities profoundly shattered.[3]

Today, the policies of the Canadian government towards Aboriginal peoples in the late nineteenth and first part of the twentieth centuries are regarded as nothing less than a legally sanctioned program of cultural genocide (White and Jacobs 1992, 18). Chansonneuve (2005, 5) argues that "the tools of cultural genocide are cultural shame, cultural disconnection, and trauma" and notes that "unresolved, multiple disconnections and historical trauma are directly responsible for many of the problems facing Aboriginal people today." Despite official apologies from the federal government, the impact of these many decades of personal and cultural trauma is not so easily undone. Although some would prefer to believe that the era of colonization is long over, others argue that colonizing attitudes and assumptions are as pervasive and oppressive as ever and that colonization remains "an imposing and dominating force" (Hart [Kaskitémahikan] 2009, 37). It is simply more covert now than in the past.

Secwepemc Communities Today

Like Aboriginal peoples elsewhere in the country, Secwepemc communities still grapple with the devastating effects of colonization and the legacy of intergenerational trauma resulting from the Canadian government's suppression

---

3 Survivors of these schools are now beginning to speak out about their experiences. On the Kamloops school, see the accounts collected in *Behind Closed Doors* (Jack 2000) and in *Resistance and Renewal* (Haig-Brown 1998). On St. Joseph's Mission School at Williams Lake, see *Victims of Benevolence* (Furniss 1992) and Bev Sellars's *They Called Me Number One* (2013).

of language, culture, religion, and identity. This legacy includes alcohol and drug addiction; a high rate of suicide among youth; violence in families; poverty; inadequate housing, income, and transportation; high levels of unemployment; and lower life expectancies. In spite of this, today's communities are rising from the ashes. Between 2006 and 2011, the Aboriginal population in Canada grew 20.1 percent, in comparison to 5.2 percent for the non-Aboriginal population.[4] In 2011, 46.2 percent of the country's Aboriginal population was under the age of twenty-four, in comparison to 29.5 percent of the non-Aboriginal population (Statistics Canada 2013, 8, 16).

Community members are now committed to filling specific roles in our communities themselves rather than relying on non-Aboriginal experts with little or no cultural knowledge. Some expressions of this change have been the creation of community health services on reserve and our own child welfare agency, which provides mental health services, family mediation, alternate care services (foster care), and cultural education and support services to the children and families of our nation. Cultural education and support refers to creating a greater awareness of familial cultural history, encouraging participation in culturally relative ceremonies, and developing knowledge of traditional languages. In addition, most communities now offer income-assistance services, on- and off-reserve housing services, recreational programming, and employment training opportunities. These services have become possible in part because an increasing number of our community members complete high school and pursue postsecondary education.

Community members are also returning to reserve communities to provide leadership in a range of professional, administrative, and technical roles. They are creating trusting partnerships and fostering new initiatives. One example is the Quaaout Lodge and Spa at Talking Rock Golf Course, a project undertaken by the Quaaout or Little Shuswap band. This distinctive hotel, situated beside a PGA golf course in a spectacular setting, attracts

---

4 Among First Nations, as opposed to all Aboriginal peoples, the increase stood at 22.9 percent (Statistics Canada 2013, 8). The total population of the Secwepemc Nation is difficult to determine. All Secwepemc communities include members who live off reserve, whether permanently or only for periods of time, and in several communities, more members now live off reserve than on. In addition, reserves may include residents who are not in fact members of the Secwepemc Nation. According to estimates, smaller bands may contain as few as two hundred members, while larger ones, such as the Tk'emlúps te Secwépemc, may have a thousand or more.

international, national, Aboriginal, and non-Aboriginal guests and has the capacity to host large events. It is also the number one culturally inclusive employer in the area. In addition to the standard amenities, the lodge offers cultural activities that include workshops on topics such as the seven teachings, the medicine wheel, and the talking circle. According to Chief Oliver Arnouse (pers. comm., November 2014), "Quaaout" refers to the place where the rays of the morning sun first touch the ground. Designed by the Elders, the lodge was laid out so that its four corners are located where the sun's rays first hit the earth at the beginning of each of the four seasons.

Hunting and gathering have always been communal activities in Secwepemc communities, with food shared among members of the group. Today, as part of the reclamation of traditional values and cultural practices, food is again being shared as more and more communities set up community freezers. Stocked by contributions from the community, such freezers provide food for those in need, reduce shame, and demonstrate community generosity. In addition, over the past ten years, communities have taken back the solstice through cultural ceremonies held on the longest and shortest days of the year. These are traditional feasts that unite the community. Through traditional storytelling, art making, dance, drumming, healing circles, smudging, sweat lodges, sun dance ceremonies, pipe ceremonies, naming ceremonies, traditional forms of adoption, and other traditional activities, a community awareness has developed that improves trust, respect, communication, and healing. In these ways and others, Secwepemc people continue to gain strength and focus their collective efforts on deconstructing the ways of the Box that were imposed on them, overcoming their historical dislocation, and strengthening the Circle.

Yet in spite of these many accomplishments, when community members leave the reserve to seek services across the red bridge in the small city of Kamloops, they confront a different world. For many Aboriginal people, seeking any type of service outside their own community is anxiety provoking. For some, even the thought of interacting with a small city's urban institutions or mainstream organizations is daunting. The lone Aboriginal parent of three young children, carrying a large diaper bag, knows she will be the first to be followed by store security in the grocery store. On a daily basis, we see how Aboriginal children, youth, families, and communities carry forward the pains of the past while enduring their own experiences of racism and oppression. Rarely, though, are those who live and work inside the Box able to comprehend this emotional universe, and they generally remain oblivious to its presence.

Poverty and lack of transportation often limit Aboriginal people's ability to access services off reserve. Some do not own vehicles, and it is not uncommon for even an older person who lives on one of the more isolated Secwepemc reserves to spend hours walking or hitchhiking to the nearest city for a needed service. City buses and the HandyDART shuttle for the disabled do not provide service beyond the city limits: the city bus does not cross the red bridge. Taxis are usually out of the question, as some reserves are many hours from the nearest city and the fares are unaffordable for most people. In addition, service providers generally assume that their clients are literate and reasonably fluent in English. Many Aboriginal people need both translation and explanation of medical procedures, treatment plans, and social service or legal documents. They may also need someone to explain the terms and conditions laid down by social workers, probation officers, and the police. More profoundly troubling, though, is the sense of feeling lesser—the sense that one has not been heard, the sense that one is not worthy of being heard, the sense that one's voice has been silenced by service professionals. This is a continuation of the legacy of oppression that perpetuates, in the present, feelings of powerlessness, inferiority, shame, and anger.

Double-Sided Cards: Our Stories of Practice

As professionals, we navigate on a daily basis the very distinct worlds of the Circle and the Box. At times, we feel as though we have double-sided cards. One side of the card identifies us as mental health professionals, armed with the credentials and skills required by the modern health care system. When we walk in the world of the Box, we must speak the language of health professionals in order to access the best possible care for those we walk beside when they are seeking services in Kamloops, just across the red bridge. Since the language of the Box is complex and scientific, we need a thorough understanding of it in order to become compassionate translators. Many of those we walk with do not understand this pathologizing, deficit-based language, in which both the body and the mind are regarded as if they were inanimate objects in need of repair. Terms such as *diagnosis* and *prognosis* can be alarming to some people, as can talk of test results, treatment modalities, or psychotropic medications. Even though our academic qualifications and professional experience are equivalent to—and in some cases, better than—those of our non-Aboriginal colleagues, we have both been the target of condescending verbal and nonverbal treatment that seems intended to remind us that we, too, are lesser, just like our poor, marginalized sisters across the bridge.

The Circle side of our card represents a holistic approach to wellness, in which we view ourselves as allies rather than as experts. Our work is grounded in human relationships and in the seven teachings: honesty, humility, trust, wisdom, love, respect, and bravery (Wesley-Esquimaux and Snowball 2010). These seven teachings, which emphasize holistic well-being, traditional knowledge, and empowerment, help us to navigate the particular realities of those we walk with—the multiple forms of oppression, the intergenerational trauma, and the various issues that, in consequence, these individuals face in their daily lives. As allies, we encourage the use of the seven teachings in conjunction with contemporary modes of intervention, and we also draw on the stories and ceremonies of the ancestors and on the cultural knowledge preserved by our grandmothers and grandfathers and by the traditional healers, or medicine people. We honour participation in traditional practices such as smudging, sweat lodge ceremonies, healing circles, sharing circles, pipe ceremonies, sun dance ceremonies, feasts, and other forms of healing. These seven teachings and ceremonial traditions respectfully uphold a holistic and collaborative approach to well-being based on wholeness, balance, connection, harmony, growth, and spiritual restoration. The Circle encompasses all realms, those of human beings and those of Mother Earth, and symbolizes the interconnectedness and interdependence of all the elements that contribute to the balance of the whole (Bopp et al. 1985).

When working from the circular side of our card, we sensitively and respectfully act as helping messengers who translate and transfer knowledge from the Box to the Circle in ways that will be meaningful to individuals, to families, and to the community. In so doing, we strive to create an awareness of the human strengths and the capacity for resilience that flow from the power of collective relations and traditions. As the Circle is strengthened, Secwepemc communities are gaining a greater sense of empowerment and becoming ever more self-reliant. Yet they must still depend on the non-Aboriginal community for the provision of many services.

The stories that we share below are drawn from our practice, but to protect the privacy of others, we have combined elements from different specific situations and experiences. These story collages capture a sense of the two worlds within which we walk and how they intersect. Our first story illustrates the discriminatory attitudes that we often encounter, as well as the way we use our two-sided card. Some time ago, one of us accompanied a teenage male and his family to a hospital emergency room in a small city in the local area. Five weeks earlier, this young man had been admitted to the adult psychiatric unit, assessed, and diagnosed with a psychotic disorder, and it was apparent from conversations with his family that he was experiencing another psychotic episode.

At the hospital, I shared all the young man's relevant information and history with the emergency room nurse. The nurse seemed somewhat disengaged, but she listened and documented what she needed to and then proceeded to the nursing station, which was only a few feet away. She turned to another nurse and said, with obvious condescension, "Boy, we have a smart one over there. I usually don't get this much information from them. This one really knows her stuff." Her remarks were demeaning, discriminatory, and unprofessional, and they also betrayed a complete lack of sensitivity to other Aboriginal people in the emergency room, who might have overheard them. It was as if we, as Aboriginal people, were simply not there. Ironically, the young man's hallucinations protected him from her comments, since he was not cognizant of what had just happened.

The young man's mom, dad, siblings, aunties, grandparents, and several other community members, all of whom were seated in the waiting room, were clearly very scared by what they had witnessed earlier, before the trip to the emergency room. For some of the older family members, the sterile institutional setting of the hospital compounded their fears, triggering residential school memories. I aimed to re-establish, with the family, the world of the Circle while sitting in the Box of the waiting room. This involved building respectful relations with the young man's family and with the community members in attendance. Together, we shared many stories about traditional and nontraditional approaches that the family hoped to incorporate as part of their boy's healing journey.

With some apprehension, this very traditional family decided that it was in their son's best interests to remain in the hospital, as they felt that Western medicine would best suit his healing journey at this point. When I returned to the linear side of the card, a consultation process took place with an emergency room physician, whose attitude was very different from that of the nurse. He compassionately agreed with all the family's concerns, while also understanding and respecting their cultural traditions. Walking back to the Circle, I continued to engage in more storytelling with the boy's family in the waiting room. This was a means to share, interpret, and transfer information to the family as to what they might expect and what might happen next and to create awareness of how these specific actions might contribute holistically to their child's well-being.

The young man remained on the psychiatric unit for approximately three weeks. Prior to his discharge, the boy's family requested a family meeting with the psychiatrist who was in charge of the case. This request was denied: we were told that the psychiatrist had no time for such a meeting. To us, this response exemplifies the power of the Box to control and oppress by regulating access to expertise. It conveyed a clear message that this young man and his family were not important, that their voices were not worth listening to. The harmonious, mutually respectful relationships so fundamental to the Circle were ignored. In the end, the family received no information from the hospital specific to the young man's future care after discharge.

Our second story concerns the way in which the bureaucratic processes surrounding Aboriginal health needs can actually impede essential treatment. A teenage Aboriginal girl who was involved with both the local health care system and the judicial system was diagnosed with major depression. The depression was first identified by a physician, and the clinical diagnosis was confirmed by the child and youth forensics team that supported her. The young girl came from a family strongly rooted in cultural traditions, and family members were concerned about using pharmaceuticals instead of traditional medicines and modes of healing. However, after weighing the options, her family decided that psychotropic medication was the best way to cope with her depression and ensuing suicide ideation.

The girl's doctor wrote a prescription, but the pharmacist refused to fill it. He said that special authorization was needed from Aboriginal Affairs and Northern Development Canada (AANDC, now Indigenous and Northern Affairs Canada) for the medication, since it was not one of the drugs covered under AANDC's Non-insured Health Benefits (NIHB) Program, and that it was not his responsibility to obtain this authorization. The list of medications available to Aboriginal people through the NIHB Program is constantly changing and has also been significantly reduced over the past decade—changes that most Aboriginal people are unaware of until they are in a doctor's office or at the pharmacy. As a result, Aboriginal people constantly experience difficulty in accessing adequate and appropriate medications. While a doctor is needed to prescribe appropriate medications in the first place, she must also be knowledgeable about NIHB's current list of approved medications. In this case, the need for special authorization created a life-threatening barrier for this young girl. It meant that she had to go back to her doctor, and her doctor had to write to the NIHB Program to advocate for her psychotropic medication. This appeal process took six months. Throughout this period, the girl continued to experience major depression, recurring suicide ideation, and suicide attempts. When the request was denied, the physician appealed a second time. As before, this bureaucratic process took months. At the end of this second appeal process, AANDC finally agreed to approve the drug, but only in a generic form. To government bureaucrats, the fact that this was a life or death situation for a young girl and her family was evidently of no concern. Moreover, in this case, the girl had the benefit of active collaboration and advocacy on the part of many culturally sensitive and allied supporters—the Aboriginal social worker, the physician, the forensics team, and her family. It is sad to think of what might have happened otherwise.

A third story reveals how cultural assumptions can contribute to insensitivity and lack of understanding. Many of our families have no phones; therefore, mail and home visits are the only ways to communicate. One day, we were called into the local public school to see a young boy who was exhibiting high levels of anxiety and a tendency towards disruptive behaviour. His difficulties had recently escalated to the point where he was no longer productive in the learning environment. We asked whether his parents had been contacted and were informed that there was no family phone, that many letters had gone to the house, and that administrators had attempted several home visits, to no avail. At this point, the school authorities were thinking of expelling this young boy.

When we went to the boy's home, it was immediately obvious that poverty was a major factor in his life. His mother indicated that she had no food, and she had no way to get to the food bank. When we asked about the school's letters and attempted visits, his mother became defensive. In the corner of her small, sparsely furnished apartment sat a large box of unopened mail. For some Aboriginal adults, literacy is a very sensitive subject. To ask the direct question "Can you read?" risks shaming the person. Eventually, the boy's mother confided that she could not read or write and was therefore unaware of her son's anxiety and behavioural challenges at school. It was not until this moment that we could begin to work holistically with this young boy and his mother and to begin to address his family's needs. In the world of the Box, language and literacy are taken for granted.

Situations such as those described above are by no means unusual in our practice. They illustrate some of the ways in which the legacy of the past continues to haunt the present. In 1996, the Royal Commission on Aboriginal Peoples noted that Aboriginal young people are currently "paying the price of cultural genocide, racism and poverty, suffering the effects of hundreds of years of colonialist public policies." The commission's report continues:

> The problems that most Aboriginal communities endure are of such depth and scope that they have created remarkably similar situations and responses among Aboriginal youth everywhere. It is as though an earthquake has ruptured their world from one end to another, opening a deep rift that separates them from their past, their history and their culture. They have seen parents and peers fall into this chasm, into patterns of despair, listlessness and self-destruction. They fear for themselves and their future as they stand at the edge. (RCAP 1996, 139)

One of the most urgent problems facing Aboriginal youth is the impulse to suicide. In its 1995 report on suicide among Aboriginal people, the commission reported that among "aboriginal youth aged 10 to 19 years, the suicide rate was five to six times higher than among their non-aboriginal peers" (Chenier 1995, 2).

Tragically, we encounter many suicide attempts and some completed suicides in the communities we walk with. We have received as many as eight intakes of suicide ideation typically involving youth, in a single week. Suicide intervention forces us into a survival mode in which we must neglect other people on our caseloads owing to the immediate demands of crisis management, coupled with an overall lack of service capacity. There is nothing worse than responding to a completed suicide of a child and meeting that child's parents. But an event of this magnitude devastates the entire community, and therefore the services needed are extensive. We walk with humility beside an entire community on its collective healing journey. This takes a great amount of time, and we work long hours, days, weeks, and months when we lose a young person.

This part of our practice is about being with; it is relationally responsible. We hold the community's pain deep in our chests and throats. The community's tear-soaked tissues are gathered and given to an Elder to burn in a ceremonial fire. Services and resources are also extended to community members who live off reserve and in the small city. Urban agencies, both Aboriginal and non-Aboriginal, play an integral role in addressing the grief and loss of experienced by community members. Together, they raise awareness on and off the reserve about the threat of suicide and work to create trauma informed practices. When we are called upon to respond to suicide, our double-sided card is essential. It allows us to negotiate the very distinct administrative worlds of the coroner, the police, and the school while also walking with and through the waves of grief enveloping our communities.

Interconnections

From time to time we have encountered amazing human beings, from a wide variety of cultural backgrounds, who live and work within the Box. These remarkable individuals seem to understand and have a different way of working with Aboriginal people. They include the doctor described above who relentlessly fought the bureaucratic Box to ensure that his young patient received the medication she so desperately needed. They include the empathetic doctor who, even though he knew that this action could not be justified as medically necessary, sent the teenage youth for further tests in hopes that his paranoid delusions could be dispelled for him. They include the teacher who kind-heartedly listened to an Aboriginal child who was struggling with the ugly reality of racism and cultural identity issues, who took the time to build a relationship with him, and who had enough insight to connect him with a respected Elder for guidance, learning, and nurturing. They also include the RCMP officer who caringly supported a young rape victim, putting her in contact with culturally sensitive supports and services and sharing from a place of heartfelt honesty that he would do whatever it took to catch the person who did this to her. Such "acts of solidarity," Gord Bruyere (1999, 179) writes, "require the courage to undertake the development of relationships in a manner that should have happened hundreds of years ago."

As Bruyere (1999, 179) also notes, anyone who genuinely wishes to understand Aboriginal people must be "willing to share in the emotional legacy of our shared history." A few do seem capable of actively listening to the stories of Aboriginal people. They are attuned to ask questions, to engage in courageous conversations, and, most importantly, to refrain from judging the Aboriginal people they meet. As a result, they gain a greater awareness of the historical context of Aboriginal peoples, and they increase their understanding of the Circle. These people respectfully embrace the Circle while working as allies, advocates, role models, and mentors within the systems of the Box. The voices of these individuals consciously raise awareness of the need for social justice, equality, respect, empowerment, harmony, balance, and wholeness, not only for Aboriginal people but also for society as a whole. Standing up for change awakens the gifts inside us all to build the capacity for interconnection and create stronger relationships with the Circle and the Box. These all too rare individuals understand the importance of caring unconditionally for all people and of aligning their actions with the Creator's heart. The seven teachings are inherent in their spirits regardless of the colour of their skin or their cultural identity. As Jann Derrick (1990, 5) writes, "We are each born as 'circles'—whole and perfect and intuitively wise."

Conclusion

As the realities of our practice illustrate, Aboriginal peoples walk within two contrasting systems, the Circle and the Box. We observe that, at times, the Box leaves them no room for inclusion and ignores the voices of those it claims to serve. Conversely, we see that some inside the Box do have the ability to embrace and respect the ways of the Circle. They seem to understand that being quiet enough to listen, to hear the stories of the Circle without judgment, is essential to healing. This willingness to listen respectfully, asking questions when necessary for clarity, can empower the voices of others and lead to transformative dialogues. But even the most empathetic individuals can only do so much when the institutions within which they walk are still dominated by the ways of the Box.

In our own work, we see certain signs that give us hope—signs that institutions are slowly starting to recognize the existence of the Circle. Thompson Rivers University has an Elders program that provides support to Aboriginal postsecondary students, but the Elders also give lectures to audiences that include non-Aboriginal listeners, offer opening prayers at university events and ceremonies, and welcome campus visitors to Secwepemc Territory. The local school district now employs Aboriginal support staff and an Aboriginal family counsellor, who work together to ensure the success of Aboriginal students. At the hospital, the Aboriginal Patient Navigators program provides a broad spectrum of support services to Aboriginal patients and their families and strives to alert medical staff to cultural considerations. The BC Ministry of Children and Family Development and Aboriginal child welfare agencies now make use of family group conferencing, an approach pioneered in New Zealand and founded on the traditional Maori style of decision making. These conferences allow a child's extended family and other community members to participate in resolving difficult questions and planning for a child's safety and well-being. In each case, the Box is reaching out to the Circle and is in a process of change itself.

If we hope to bring the worlds of the Circle and the Box into a closer, more balanced relationship, however, greater institutional collaboration will be needed. Health care, education, and judicial and social services still largely exist in separate worlds. Similarly, plans for economic development, transportation systems, and improvements to infrastructure proceed along parallel lines. To take only one example, the small city of Kamloops and the Tk'emlúps te Secwépemc Reserve share a river, but the idea that the two could join together in planning the development of a waterfront area that would be common to both has never been explored. This ongoing lack of coordination reflects not only the legacy of colonization but also a reality enshrined in the Canadian constitution. Municipalities are structurally part of provincial governments and must answer to them, but the affairs of Aboriginal peoples are still controlled by Indigenous and Northern Affairs Canada, a branch of the federal government. This administrative division creates tiny federal islands in the midst of provinces, which deepens the sense of separation and can also put up legal roadblocks to collaboration. Geographically side by side, the city of Kamloops and the Secwepemc community map out their respective futures in isolation, from opposite sides of the red bridge.

In *A Fair Country,* John Ralston Saul (2008, 3) reminds us that Canada is a "métis civilization," one that has been "heavily influenced and shaped by the First Nations." And yet, he writes, what is "both curious and troubling is that we cannot bring ourselves to talk about how profoundly our society has been shaped over four centuries in its non-monolithic, non-European manner by the First Nations" (6). He suggests that this silence is rooted in fear, fear above all of the Aboriginal "other." As he puts it, Euro-Canadians were frightened of those "whose place this was and in whose shadow they—and eventually we—would have to find our reality" (6). Finding this reality will require the courage to step inside the Circle and embrace Aboriginal ways of knowing and being. Political and professional leaders must come to understand that transformative change depends on the integration of the parts into the whole. As long as the country continues to deny part of itself, healing cannot occur.

Acknowledgements

We wish to acknowledge the stories of the Elders who have crossed our paths. Their wisdom, guidance, knowledge, teaching, and sharing enhances our own learning and practice, especially when we are called upon to forge connections for those we walk beside. We are indebted to Chief Oliver Arnouse, Michelle Canaday, Garlene (Jules) Dodson, Floyd Eustache, Cheryl Matthew, Geri Matthew, and Tina Matthew for reviewing the text to ensure that it accurately reflects a Secwepemc view of the history of their people.

References

Aboriginal Healing Foundation. 2002. *The Healing Has Begun: An Operational Update from the Aboriginal Healing Foundation.* Ottawa: Aboriginal Healing Foundation. http://www.ahf.ca/downloads/the-healing-has-begun.pdf.

ALBAA (A Learning Bridge for Aboriginal Adults) Research Team. 2010. *A Handbook for Educators of Aboriginal Students.* Kamloops, BC: Thompson Rivers University.

Bopp, Judie, Michael Bopp, Lee Brown, and Phil Lane, Jr. 1985. *The Sacred Tree: Reflections on Native American Spirituality.* 2nd ed. Lethbridge, AB: Four Worlds International Institute for Human and Community Development.

Bruyere, Gord. 1999. "The Decolonization Wheel: An Aboriginal Perspective on Social Work Practice with Aboriginal Peoples." In *Social Work with Rural and Northern Communities,* edited by Roger Delaney, Keith Brownlee, and Margaret McKee Sellick, 170–81. Thunder Bay, ON: Centre for Northern Studies, Lakehead University.

Chansonneuve, Deborah. 2005. *Reclaiming Connections: Understanding Residential School Trauma Among Aboriginal People.* Ottawa: Aboriginal Healing Foundation. http://www.ahf.ca/downloads/healing-trauma-web-eng.pdf.

Chenier, Nancy Miller. 1995. *Suicide Among Aboriginal People: Royal Commission Report—Mini-Review.* Ottawa: Library of Parliament, Research Branch. http://www.parl.gc.ca/Content/LOP/researchpublications/mr131-e.pdf.

Derrick, Jann. 1990. "The Box and the Circle—Two Systems of Life: A Model for Understanding Native/Non-native Issues." Paper presented at the annual meeting of the Mokakit Indian Education Research Association, Ottawa, 13 October 1990. http://files.eric.ed.gov/fulltext/ED331666.pdf.

Dickason, Olive Patricia. 2002. *Canada's First Nations: A History of Founding Peoples from Earliest Times*. Don Mills, ON: Oxford University Press.

Dickason, Olive Patricia, and William Newbigging. 2010. *A Concise History of Canada's First Nations*. 2nd ed. Don Mills, ON: Oxford University Press.

Fisher, Robin. 1992. *Contact and Conflict: Indian-European Relations in British Columbia, 1774–1890*. 2nd ed. Vancouver: University of British Columbia Press.

Furniss, Elizabeth. 1992. *Victims of Benevolence: The Dark Legacy of the Williams Lake Residential School*. Vancouver: Arsenal Pulp Press.

Haig-Brown, Celia. 1988. *Resistance and Renewal: Surviving the Indian Residential School*. Vancouver: Arsenal Pulp Press.

Hart, Michael Anthony (Kaskitémahikan). 2009. "Anti-colonial Indigenous Social Work: Reflections on an Aboriginal Approach." In *Wícihitowin: Aboriginal Social Work in Canada*, edited by Raven Sinclair (Ótiskewápíwskew), Michael Anthony Hart (Kaskitémahikan), and Gord Bruyere (Amawaajibitang), 25–41. Halifax: Fernwood Publishing.

Jack, Agnes. 2000. *Behind Closed Doors: Stories from the Kamloops Residential School*. Penticton, BC: Theytus Books.

Kirmayer, Laurence, Cori Simpson, and Margaret Cargo. 2003. "Healing Traditions: Culture, Community, and Mental Health Promotion with Canadian Aboriginal Peoples." *Australasian Psychiatry* 11: 15–23.

Mathias, Chief Joe, and Gary R. Yabsley. 1991. "Conspiracy of Legislation: The Suppression of Indian Rights in Canada." In *In Celebration of Our Survival: The First Nations of British Columbia*, edited by Doreen Jensen and Cheryl Brooks, 34–45. Vancouver: University of British Columbia Press.

RCAP (Royal Commission on Aboriginal Peoples). 1996. *Report of the Royal Commission on Aboriginal Peoples*. Vol. 4, *Perspectives and Realities*. Ottawa: Royal Commission on Aboriginal Peoples. https://qspace.library.queensu.ca/handle/1974/6874.

Saul, John Ralston. 2008. *A Fair Country: Telling Truths About Canada*. Toronto: Penguin.

Sellars, Bev. 2013. *They Called Me Number One: Secrets and Survival at an Indian Residential School*. Vancouver: Talonbooks.

Smith, Keith D. 2009. *Liberalism, Surveillance, and Resistance: Indigenous Communities in Western Canada, 1877–1927*. Edmonton: Athabasca University Press.

Statistics Canada. 2013. *Aboriginal Peoples in Canada: First Nations People, Métis and Inuit—National Household Survey, 2011*. Ottawa: Minister of Industry. http://www12.statcan.gc.ca/nhs-enm/2011/as-sa/99-011-x/99-011-x2011001-eng.pdf.

UBCIC (Union of BC Indian Chiefs). N.d. "Background to the McKenna-McBride Commission." *Our Homes Are Bleeding: Digital Collection*. http://www.ubcic. bc.ca/Resources/ourhomesare/narratives/Background_1.htm.

Walmsley, Christopher. 2005. *Protecting Aboriginal Children*. Vancouver: University of British Columbia Press.

Wesley-Esquimaux, Cynthia C., and Andrew Snowball. 2010. "Viewing Violence, Mental Illness, and Addiction Through a Wise Practices Lens." *International Journal of Mental Health and Addiction* 8: 390–407.

White, Lavina, and Eva Jacobs. 1992. *Liberating Our Children—Liberating Our Nations: Report of the Aboriginal Committee*. Victoria: Family and Children's Services Legislation Review Community Panel—Aboriginal Committee.

Part II
Building Community

8 Social Planning and the Dynamics of Small-City Government

Christopher Walmsley and Terry Kading

As a professional practice, social planning has existed for more than half a century, and many Canadian municipalities now incorporate social planning into the structures of local government. In British Columbia, the city of Vancouver has an extensive and well-established social planning department, but numerous smaller municipalities also employ social planners, with some allocating a part-time planner to handle social concerns within a larger department devoted to community planning. A local government may also have a social planning advisory committee that reports to city council. Yet, despite the growth of social planning as a function of local government, and the availability of social planning models, relatively little research has focused specifically on the practice of social planning in smaller cities. How does social planning operate at the local level? In a tight fiscal environment, how do practitioners justify what they do to city councils and other civic leaders? In what ways do social planners interact with community organizations? What obstacles do social planners encounter, whether within local government or in the community at large? Drawing in part on interviews with social planners, this chapter examines the practice of social planning at the level of local government in British Columbia, with the aim of enriching our understanding of how small cities respond to social issues.

In North America, the origins of social planning can be traced back to the work of the Community Chest (the forerunner of United Way America) and community welfare councils, which attempted to assess community needs and make rational decisions about how to allocate funds (Rothman and Zald 2001, 301). In the United States, interest in social planning blossomed in the wake of the Model Cities program, instituted in 1966 by the federal government in the face of growing concerns about urban poverty and violence. In contrast to earlier urban renewal projects, with their focus on slum clearance, the new program emphasized the need for a comprehensive approach to planning, one that aimed at the rehabilitation of existing neighbourhoods and involved the participation of the community itself (Gilbert and Specht 1977, 179). Although the Model Cities program ultimately foundered (it was terminated in 1974), it created a surge of interest in social planning that lasted from the late 1960s throughout the 1970s—a period that one planner we interviewed described as the "golden era of social planning."[1]

A pivotal early contribution to the concept of social planning was Jack Rothman's "Approaches to Community Intervention," first published in 1968. Basing his analysis on a set of twelve variables, Rothman identified three distinct approaches to community intervention: "locality development," "social action," and "social planning/policy" (2001 [1968], 29). The first two approaches both stress grassroots action but differ in their overall orientation and in the strategies they employ. In locality development, the focus falls on community capacity building. According to Rothman, "the basic change strategy involves getting a broad cross section of people involved in studying and taking action on their problems," with the professional practitioner becoming "a teacher of problem-solving skills" through "small task-oriented groups" (45). In this model, the practitioner functions above all to facilitate a process of consensus building among various segments of the community. The social action model is more attuned to hierarchies of power within a community, with the emphasis falling on disadvantaged or marginalized groups and on adversarial tactics that aim at achieving social justice. As Rothman put it, "The basic change strategy involves crystallizing issues and organizing people to take action against enemy targets," and the practitioner "seeks to create and guide mass organizations and to influence political processes" (45, 39). In contrast, Rothman envisaged the social

---

1 Comments made by social planners derive from semi-structured interviews conducted in 2010 and 2011. A total of nine planners were interviewed, from a mix of large and small cities in British Columbia. The cities are not named to protect the anonymity of those interviewed.

planning/policy model adopting a top-down approach to intervention, one that entails a "technical process of problem solving regarding substantive social problems" (31). "The style is technocratic," he wrote, "and rationality is a dominant ideal. Community participation is not a core ingredient and may vary from much to little" (30). Described as "data-driven," this approach relies on professional planners who are skilled at designing "formal plans and policy frameworks" (31), with the beneficiaries of social services primarily cast in the role of "clients" or "consumers" (41). Rothman recognized that, in practice, the three approaches overlap (35): as he noted, he was describing these models in "ideal-type form" (29).

The influence of Rothman's typology is visible in debates about the extent to which social planning is task-focused rather than process-focused (see Gilbert and Specht 1977) or "technical" as opposed to "interactional" (see Rothman and Zald 2001, 306). Arguing that social planning is properly understood "as a specialized practice area of social work," James Dudley (1978, 37) acknowledged "the tendency of social workers who are social planners to identify with economists, physical planners, organizational experts," and other specialists in fields external to social work. As a professional practice, social planning appears to have some similarities to social work, while also overlapping with the field of community development—defined in a handbook prepared for Human Resources Development Canada as "the planned evolution of all aspects of community well-being (economic, social, environmental and cultural)" founded on "a process whereby community members come together to take collective action and generate solutions to common problems" (Frank and Smith 1999, 3). Indeed, one of the planners we interviewed described social planning as "good community development work—networking, collaboration, cooperation, and communication."

In a study of the Social Planning Network of Ontario, a coalition of voluntary-sector social planning organizations in Ontario, Susan Arai and Donald Reid (2003, 68) note that, in keeping with the goals of such organizations more generally, network members aimed at achieving "citizen participation in social policy development, improvement of service delivery, and decentralization in the decision-making process through strategies . . . best described as community development, social action or social reform." In other words, the work of voluntary-sector social planning organizations (or social planning councils, as they are often called) has traditionally been oriented more in the direction of Rothman's locality development and social action models. Beginning in the late 1990s, however, the staff of several organizations within the Ontario coalition began to notice the growth of a "business mindset" within local social planning organizations, reporting that they were experiencing increased pressure to concentrate on service provision and to soften their approach to advocacy, a trend that had seriously diminished their ability to engage both in policy analysis and in public education and outreach (78, 79).[2] This shift in emphasis is, of course, perfectly consistent with the neoliberal embrace of the principles of the "new public management." The fact remains, however, that the rise of neoliberalism has undermined the freedom of voluntary-sector social planning organizations to choose their own priorities and the values to which they subscribe (see, for example, Evans, Richmond, and Shields 2005).

One might predict that, in a neoliberal era, "technocratic" approaches to social planning, with their emphasis on data-driven, task-focused approaches to problem solving, would be in the ascendant among social planners employed by local governments, which need to be able to demonstrate concrete, measureable results to funding partners. Most social planners would probably agree that social planning aims to be guided by rationality and evidence-based approaches to decision making—and yet they would also recognize social planning as a sociopolitical process that seeks some level of participation on the part of citizens. As Marie Weil (2005, 239) suggests, moreover, while social planners have always needed research and analytic skills, they must also possess the mediation and communication skills required to engage community members successfully in recursive processes of action and reflection.

Social Planning and Local Government in Canada

Historically, local governments in English Canada have operated poorhouses and provided various forms of relief, while also sharing with the provinces the costs of keeping children in orphanages (Adamoski 2005, 32, 34; Finkel 2006, 48–50). In Québec, poverty relief and the provision of other social services was the responsibility of individual Catholic parishes until the 1960s, with

---

2 As Arai and Reid (2003, 87) point out, during the 1990s, funding from both the United Way and municipal governments declined, forcing six of Ontario's social planning organizations to close and six others to merge into a single entity, while yet others closed temporarily as they cast about for the funds needed to ensure their survival.

the province and municipalities providing financial subsidies to the parishes (Vaillancourt 1988, 205–252). The situation in English Canada began to change during the Depression when municipalities struggled to provide assistance to growing numbers of unemployed, prompting the federal government to involve itself in poverty relief. The intervention of the federal government in relief culminated several decades later in the emergence of the welfare state and its elaborate federal-provincial cost sharing arrangements.

One aspect of the early twentieth century charitable sector, the community welfare councils, have survived until today. In fact, many major Canadian cities (including Toronto, Ottawa, Hamilton, Winnipeg, and Edmonton) continue to rely heavily on voluntary-sector social planning councils.[3] As Susan McGrath and Peter Clutterbuck (1998, 3) point out, the work of such councils has traditionally been driven by three central principles: "a commitment to a collective response to social need; a belief in citizen participation in public planning processes; and a reliance on research and knowledge creation to guide the processes." Today, these councils, most of which are registered as charities, conduct research, provide public education and outreach, and advise city government on matters related to social issues and social planning. In British Columbia, the Social Planning and Research Council of BC, a charitable organization founded in 1966, serves the entire province, while the Community Social Planning Council operates in the greater Victoria area (where the city government also has a Community Planning Division). In addition, several other municipalities and regional districts likewise have their own nonprofit local social planning councils (although Vancouver does not).

Largely relieved of their responsibilities in the area of social services, local governments have chiefly focused on the regulation of local land use through zoning bylaws and on the provision of core services such as roads, sewage, water, garbage, street lighting, fire and police protection, snow removal, parks, recreation, and cultural activities. Given this relatively narrow service role, and given that municipalities operate under provincial legislation and are financially accountable to the province, they have considerably less autonomy

---

3 As Québec shifted in the direction of the modern welfare state, the social planning dimensions of community services were built into the provincial system of Centres locaux de services communautaires, which employed community organizers. Since roughly the mid-1980s, however, the role of the voluntary sector in social service provision has expanded considerably: see, for example, Jetté (2011); Savard, Bourque, and Lachapelle (2015).

than other levels of government in Canada. At the same time, despite these limitations on their scope of operation, municipal governments have the most immediate and concrete presence in the lives of local residents. As one social planner commented, "It's the level of government they have the greatest access to, and so people see that as their first place of default, I guess, when they want to talk to government." As a consequence, when problems emerge, residents turn to their local government to express their concerns, regardless of the level of jurisdiction that is formally responsible for resolving the problem.

Over roughly the past four decades, local concerns have grown, partly as a result of the dismantling of the Canadian welfare state that has accompanied the rise of neoliberalism. At the same time, both the federal government and provincial administrations have backed away from their previous role in the provision of social services. (On the "downloading" pattern, see chapter 1 in this volume.) In consequence, local governments have found themselves once again responsible for responding to social issues, a task for which some are better prepared than others. Moreover, many of them have undergone a rapid and sometimes turbulent period of growth, evolving in only a few decades from small towns into regional centres for air transport, advanced education, health care, recreational and cultural activities, and government and retail services. Their populations have not only expanded but diversified, and both economic pressures and income disparities have increased. Local governments have thus become responsible for planning a broad set of services, a shift that has frequently involved a steep learning curve. With respect to social planning, small cities are often still finding their way, in contrast to the province's largest city, which has been coping with large scale poverty and other social issues for many decades.

The Benefit of Experience: Vancouver

Vancouver is most assuredly not a small city. According to the most recent census, the Vancouver metropolitan area is home to more than 2.46 million people—more than half of the province's total population of roughly 4.65 million.[4] Governed by the Vancouver Charter ([SBC 1953], c. 55), the city has long had a racially diverse population marked by significant disparities

---

4 At the time of the census, the exact figure was 2,463,431 million, with 631,486 people residing in the City of Vancouver, while the population of British Columbia stood at 4,648,055 million. "Census Profile: Vancouver [Census Metropolitan Area]," *Statistics*

in income. It also has a long history of responding to social needs within its borders. Vancouver has operated social services directly since 1915, funding a day nursery for working mothers and an old age home, in addition to providing relief payments, mothers' allowances, and old age assistance, and has been awarding significant annual grants to social agencies in the city since 1946 (Vancouver 1998, 3).[5] Its Social Planning Department, established in 1966, began operation in 1968, with the arrival of its first director.

Writing about a decade after its creation, Christiane McNiven (1979, 209) found that Vancouver's Social Planning Department had "no serious problems of basic survival." Budget reviews had not reduced the size of the department, and its community grants budget had also been maintained, suggesting not only that the department was well entrenched in the civic structure but also that its activities were recognized as valuable (209). Its legitimacy was reflected in the mission statement adopted by the City of Vancouver in 1994: "To create a great city of communities, which cares about its people, its environment, and the opportunities to live, work and prosper." As the statement went on to specify, one of the city's central objectives was "to enhance community and individual well-being—social, economic and physical" (Vancouver 1994, 1). Today, the functions once performed by the Social Planning Department are spread across several divisions of the Community Services Group, including Social Policy and Projects, Housing Policy and Projects, and Cultural Services. As one social planner we interviewed pointed out, however, the influence of the city's early involvement in social planning can be felt in many departments, from engineering and police to libraries and recreation. It is visible in the encouragement given to city departments to consider the human aspect of their policies and services, to develop mechanisms for citizen consultation and participation in decision making, and, in particular, to facilitate the inclusion of marginalized members of the community.

Vancouver's extensive community grants program supports the core operations of broad-based social agencies such as the Association of

Canada, 2016, http://www12.statcan.gc.ca/census-recensement/2016/dp-pd/prof/index.cfm?Lang=E (search "Vancouver").

5 By 1946, the City of Vancouver was contributing to the Vancouver General Hospital, the Juvenile Detention Home, and the Family and Juvenile Court. It had a charitable grants budget of $373,000 and made grants to twenty-five organizations, including the Children's Aid Society, the Salvation Army, and the Marpole Infirmary (Vancouver 1998, 4).

Neighbourhood Houses BC and Family Services of Greater Vancouver, but it also funds organizations that focus on specific needs, such as those of seniors. As one planner explained, in addition to supporting agencies that offer outreach to seniors as a whole, "we provide more than twenty grants to organizations providing services to seniors, but they are targeted at isolated seniors or seniors who belong to a particular ethnic background that require additional support, like Spanish seniors or Vietnamese seniors." In addition, the city is sometimes called upon to respond to newly emerging communities, such as inland refugees. "No one was looking into their issues, and there were thousands and thousands of them," one social planner told us. "Because of federal legislation, they were not recognized as immigrants, but they needed services." Another problem is racism, the planner added, explaining that the city was presently engaged in a multi-year "youth-led anti-racism dialogue and youth engagement strategy to address some of the racism and discrimination issues that face youth."

As was also clear from the interviews we conducted, the city had been active in the area of child care services, using its regulatory power to offer density bonuses to land developers in exchange for the construction of new facilities. Ten child care centres had been built by developers in connection with new projects in the downtown core, with the ongoing operational expenses of the centres financed through developers' contributions to a child care endowment fund. In addition, the city had contributed to the creation of three thousand new spaces in licensed group child care centres all across the city, whether by providing land or existing buildings or by working with community partners to finance the construction of new facilities. In these ways, the city is able to draw on its social planning experts to support the development of new social infrastructure, often without direct civic expenditures. Vancouver has, in short, accumulated both experience and expertise in social planning, which has given it the confidence and flexibility needed to respond effectively to existing and emergent social issues.

Relative Newcomers: Small Cities

In British Columbia, a 1994 amendment to the Municipal Act specified that city councils "may provide for social planning to be undertaken, including research, analysis and coordination relating to social needs, social well-being and social development in the municipality."[6] In the wake of this legislation, a number of smaller cities developed local social planning frameworks. A social plan—described by the City of Prince George (2002, 6) as "a long-range visioning document intended for the community to use to plan ahead"—provides the conceptual framework within which concrete actions can be initiated in support of local social development goals. In 1996, Kelowna became the first small city to create a municipal social plan (see Kelowna 1996), and others followed suit. These included three other cities in which we conducted research: Prince George, Nanaimo, and Kamloops (see, respectively, Prince George 2002; John Talbot and Associates 2004; and SPARC BC 2009). These social plans varied in length (from 44 to 196 pages) and in details of methodology, as well as in the specific outcomes that the city hoped to achieve. Prior to their approval by city council, however, each entailed a process of public consultation, the collection of qualitative and quantitative data, the identification and prioritization of key themes and concerns, and the articulation of specific strategies. Each of the plans identifies anywhere from six to ten priority areas, and all include housing, health, and safety among them. Most also list education and employment as areas of concern. Emphasis is sometimes placed on specific issues—downtown revitalization (Prince George), human rights (Kelowna), the Indigenous community (Kamloops), child care (Kelowna), youth (Kamloops), substance use (Prince George, Kamloops)—but attention also falls on broader concerns such as "community life" (Nanaimo), "accessibility"—meaning "physical access to amenities and services" (Kelowna 1996, 27)—, and "safe spaces, alternative transportation and environmental health" (Kamloops).

In addition, small cities began hiring social planners, and this century has witnessed considerable growth in social planning as a function of local government. Not all local governments use the term "social planning": some prefer "social development" or "community development" or even "community planning" (although this term is also used to describe all planning activities at the municipal level). Similarly, because local governments differ in their organizational structure, the person responsible for activities related to social

---

6 Municipal Act [RSBC 1996], c. 323, part 15, s. 530, http://www.bclaws.ca/civix/document/id/consol1/consol1/96323_00. Originally enacted in 1979, the Municipal Act has since been replaced by the Local Government Act, although the rights and duties of municipalities are laid out primarily in the BC's Community Charter [SBC 2003], c. 26, http://www.bclaws.ca/civix/document/id/complete/statreg/03026_00.

planning may work in a variety of settings—although, as our discussions with social planners revealed, in some cases the position had originally been created in response to a particular social issue, such as homelessness or juvenile prostitution, which had in turn influenced the placement of the position within the administrative structure. Nanaimo currently employs two social planners, who work in the Social Planning Division of the Department of Community Planning, while Prince George has a Social Development Division located in the Department of City Services. Kelowna has a Community Planning and Strategic Investments Division (of the office of the City Manager) that comprises several subdivisions, including Policy and Planning and Community Planning. Kamloops locates social planning in the Social and Community Development Division of the Department of Parks, Recreation, and Culture. While the location of the position and its title may vary, the emphasis of the work will fall more (or less) towards social issues depending on changing municipal priorities, issues, and concerns.

Several of the social planners we interviewed worked outside a departmental structure, reporting directly to the city manager. These planners seemed to enjoy considerable autonomy, as well as the freedom to interpret their role in accordance with social priorities and community needs. Clearly, however, regardless of their title or their structural position, social planners in small cities are fundamentally generalists. A high-priority issue may provide the current focus of their work, but they may also manage the civic grants program, provide input into plans for the development of housing or other civic facilities, coordinate social service planning, advocate for zoning changes, sit on civic advisory committees concerning social issues, and so on. As one social planner noted, "Any one day, I might be dealing with four different social planning topics." Whatever else they may be doing, however, social planners are expected to work with city councils and other civic officials to develop municipal social policy and to devise and implement strategies for addressing specific social issues.

As we will see, interactions between social planners and local city councils involve a complex mix of advocacy, education, and negotiation. City councils in small cities are composed of individuals elected not on the basis of party affiliation but on the strength of their own values and their positions on topics of local concern. As a result, depending on the composition of the electorate, city council members may represent quite a broad spectrum of ideological orientations, and social planners in small cities must learn to navigate their way through what may be a complex tangle of political sympathies and priorities. Their task is further complicated by the fact that city council members may still be struggling to define the boundaries and cost implications of the municipal role in social programs. In addition, changes in the composition of the local council as the result of city elections can have significant implications for particular social initiatives, impeding progress until newer councillors are convinced of the value of these efforts by the local social planner. To the extent that the entire concept of social planning remains somewhat novel, social planners may find themselves constantly having to prove their worth to city councils, by resolving citizen complaints, successfully prying funding loose from higher levels of government, and engaging with community groups to arrive at solutions to pressing issues.

The Practice of Social Planning in a Small-City Environment

The nine social planners whom we interviewed offered a wide array of descriptions of social planning. One said that social planning deals with "all the human aspects of someone's life," while, according to another, it aims at "building a quality of life that's attractive." Others referred to planning more broadly, suggesting that social planning concerns "the social issues related to the planning field" or that it seeks to "expand the basket of what planning is." Yet another felt that social planning was about creating "sustainable growth for cities," a goal that "includes four pillars—social, environmental, economic, and cultural." All the planners, however, placed at least some emphasis on the planner's role in ensuring the efficient coordination of community services at the local level, so as to prevent ad hoc responses, eliminate duplication, identify service gaps, and maximize the impact of available resources. The theme of efficiency was supplemented by the recognition that effective local coordination, the creation of community consensus and support, and a well-thought-out plan can attract investment from senior levels of government. Local social planners recognize that a key component of their job is to develop strategies that will induce the province or the federal government to make major investments in social infrastructure. As one social planner noted, "Pretty much all of the work we do is done on the assumption that we are part of leveraging other resources and other partners." Moreover, if a local government can demonstrate that, with a relatively small investment of staff time and tax dollars, it has multiplied external investment fifty times and created tangible community benefits, it makes a persuasive argument for its responsible stewardship of local tax dollars.

From 1968, when Vancouver's Social Planning Department began operations, through to 1996, when it became part of the city's Community Services Group, all three of its directors had a background in social work, and a similar pattern was evident among social planners in Victoria. In contrast, the social planners to whom we spoke variously had backgrounds in urban planning, content expertise in a particular area (such as homelessness, child care, or immigrant populations), or community expertise—that is, an in-depth knowledge of the local community's social services gained through active participation in its committees, projects, and actions. Regardless of their original training, those we interviewed described a wide range of facilitation skills that are essential to their position, sometimes identifying this aspect of their work as "community development." Through a variety of public consultation strategies, social planners reach out to community members to solicit their views, help to coordinate the activities of various community organizations, mediate between competing interests, and develop planning processes that aid in building consensus. Whether at the municipal or the provincial level, they also act as community advocates, pressing for needed change. Some social planners gave less emphasis to "technocratic" planning and policy skills, focusing instead on developing specific social programs or on helping to foster cooperative and constructive responses to local social needs.

Others, however, stressed the importance of creating social policy at the local level to provide an ongoing framework for action beyond the four-year life cycle of an elected council. As the four social plans reviewed earlier illustrate, affordable housing, homelessness, child care, and the sexual exploitation of youth are among the key areas in which local social policy has been developed. Some communities (such as Prince George) underscore the need for coordinated community action with local government and community partners on housing, health, and safety issues. This work is clearly based, in part, on the results of empirical research, including demographic data that allow for the identification of social trends, which can in turn provide the rationale for proceeding in a particular direction. Empirical data may also be employed in consultations with city council, municipal employees, and/ or local community groups, often in connection with processes of knowledge building. As one social planner described it, "You're helping decision makers make informed decisions, so there is an education component because you're undertaking research, you're consolidating it, and you're communicating it in such a manner that it's going to help them move forward." One planner employed recent census information to inform communities about possible neighbourhood amenities:

> There are no families at your end of town—it's all singles and couples. So why get a Costco? Couples don't buy at Costco, singles don't buy at Costco because the lines are too big. But you will get a Starbucks, because families don't go to Starbucks. With coffee at nine bucks, who can feed a family at Starbucks?

Planners might also employ health data to help communities identify their priorities. For example, if the local teenage pregnancy rate is significantly higher than the provincial average, this suggests the need for concerted community action.

Social planners who work in small cities often see themselves as a bridge between the city government and the community and thus make a conscious effort to facilitate communication in both directions. Noting that "a lot of work that we do is public consultation," one planner explained that she asks city staff members to let him know when they "have something coming up, like a public forum . . . because we can send it out to a bunch of different networks that might attract a different group of people." On the community side of the equation, social planners will advise residents about how best to pursue an issue with the civic administration:

> Some want to go to council; they feel that's the best place for their issue. I try to inform them that there's a social planning council, there are subcommittees, and council looks to those committees for opinions—so if you go straight to council on a social issue, they're likely going to tell you to go to the other committees to get some feedback.

Public consultation frequently entails some element of mediation, which is another prominent feature of the work of social planners in small cities. Planners may be called upon to mediate between factions within the community whose interests are in conflict, but they may also need to mediate between city hall and a specific community group whose stance on a issue differs from that of local government. In addition, mediation skills are essential to strategies aimed at promoting the inclusion of marginalized segments of the community.

One social planner emphasized the importance of being "at the table" with various civic departments during internal planning processes rather than at the end of a routing slip, with no opportunity to do more than write comments on a proposal. Face-to-face interaction enables social planners to represent community concerns more effectively and to respond directly to the opinions of other city staff members, with a view to working out a mutually acceptable solution to a problem.

With regard to community conflicts, one social planner described the use of "good neighbour agreements" to quell anxieties surrounding decisions to locate facilities such as homelessness shelters or free health clinics in a particular area. If local residents and business owners are to accept such facilities, they need to have a mechanism for registering their concerns, whether these pertain to personal safety or to the possibility that the presence of homeless people and others deemed socially undesirable will drive away local business customers. As the planner explained, good neighbour agreements are founded on the principle that, while basic social services "should not be denied to anybody, ever," service providers have a responsibility to the broader community. Providers are therefore asked to make it clear to their clients that "when they go into the public realm, there are certain expectations about how they conduct themselves." Such agreements, he said, give "businesses a place to voice their complaints," while also enabling the city to hold service providers accountable for the behaviour of their patrons.

In cities both large and small, efforts to provide services for those in need frequently meet with some degree of resistance on the part of relatively privileged community members, who perceive in these efforts a threat to their own interests. At the same time, the high visibility of some groups, such as sex trade workers, transient youth, and pan-handlers, in the relatively close environment of a small city, throws such resistance into high relief, and can assume the form of a crisis requiring the immediate engagement of the city's social planner. As a number of social planners observed, such crises ironically tend to distract them from the ongoing task of developing policies and procedures that might help to prevent such crises. Given the perennial possibility of reactive community input, often of the not-in-my-backyard variety and typically both vocal and negative, social planners must work to design inclusive planning processes or otherwise devise innovative solutions to conflict. In connection with the proposed construction of multi-family affordable housing, one planner described an approach that had proved to work well:

the city selected six different parcels of public land that were all potential sites for such housing and then held a single public consultation session regarding rezoning. "Then you're doing it all at once," the planner explained, "and one neighbourhood can't say, 'Well, the other neighbourhood isn't getting it.'"

Although small cities frequently employ only a single social planner, some also have a standing committee that advises the mayor and city council on matters related to social planning, with the social planner often providing staff support to that committee. Other small cities lack such a committee, but city council may strike advisory committees in connection with specific concerns, such as a lack of affordable housing or the sexual exploitation of youth. The creation of such ad hoc committees may be driven by community concern about an emerging issue, or the availability of funding from senior levels of government and the need to demonstrate a local planning process under civic leadership. Sometimes, committees are linked to high-priority issues identified in the city's social plan, with their formation constituting an initial step in the process of developing policies aimed at resolving these issues. A city may also need to convene a committee as part of a regional strategy designed to address a pervasive social issue, such as homelessness. Regardless of the rationale for the creation of such a committee, however, social planners emphasized the importance of bringing together those who are knowledgeable about an issue with those who have an interest in creating effective solutions. This broad-based approach involves a cross-section of stakeholders that includes representatives of community-based organizations and local social service agencies, local senior public officials in health, education, social services, recreation, and policing, and local political leaders.

Given that civic leaders are not necessarily convinced that local government should be held responsible for resolving social issues, social planners may find themselves having to justify the work they do. Several of the planners we interviewed recalled city council members objecting to a proposed plan on the grounds that it overstepped the bounds of what they regarded as the proper scope of municipal government. They also heard councillors complain that expecting the city to formulate a certain strategy or to provide such-and-such a service was simply another attempt on the part of the province and/or Ottawa to "download" responsibilities onto local government. Several planners noted that a major component of their job was to convince city councils that plans and recommendations did not entail large financial commitments at the local level. "I have to be clear with them that I am not dragging municipalities into places they ought not to be," one said. "You have to be careful of that," he added, "because they'll go, 'Wait a minute! We're being downloaded on again by the province.'" Indeed, another remarked that local government tends to be seen as simply "a receptacle" for the downloading of responsibilities that properly belong to other levels of government. However, if social planners advocate that the city take responsibility for areas formerly under the purview of a more senior level of government, this may cause tension in the relationship between planners and city councils. Some city councillors may even view the very creation of a social planning position as tending to encourage such downloading and may therefore adopt a somewhat suspicious (or even hostile) attitude towards proposals put forward by the planner.

Faced with possible resistance from local city council members, social planners must look for opportunities to persuade councillors of the advantages of assuming active leadership with regard to social issues. Social planners who were hired partly on the basis of their "content expertise"—that is, their familiarity with a particular social issue (or issues)—can, for example, leverage that expertise in support of proposed strategies. Doing so may simply be a matter of education, with the planner providing the mayor and council with the evidence on which a proposal is based and an explanation of why it can be expected to achieve certain concrete goals. Typically, however, getting city council on board also requires a hard-headed recognition that, as elected officials, councillors will not necessarily be moved by the humanitarian principles traditionally embraced by social workers and voluntary-sector organizations. Social planners may thus need to devise arguments that will convince council members that a particular action is in their political self-interest. Such arguments often involve considerations of cost-effectiveness, given that city councillors are held accountable by the electorate for the outcome of budgetary decisions. A planner might also argue that a certain proposal is likely to succeed in gaining funding from government programs and/or other potential partners, including private donors and voluntary-sector organizations.

This is not to suggest that social planners limit themselves to pragmatic arguments. Sometimes a planner will argue that city council should approve a particular action—funding for a homeless shelter, for example, or a zoning change needed to permit the operation of a halfway house for abused women—simply "because it is the right thing to do," as one planner said. Planners may also assume the role of the "voice of the excluded," speaking at city hall on behalf of street youth, the homeless, or others excluded from decision-making processes. Planners sometimes spoke of the need for "internal advocacy," in which they explain the perspectives of community groups to city departments and staff. Advocacy might mean negotiating with housing developers for the inclusion of certain amenities. As one planner indicated, in discussing housing proposals with developers, she asks questions such as, "Are you going to consider child care? What's your parkade looking like? Are you going to make sure it's safe for women and kids? Are you going to provide bike storage or a bike parking area? Are you going to include a gathering place for people?" Advocacy may also include working with the mayor, city councillors, and city staff to build a strong case for funding from the province to support the development of new social infrastructure. As several of the social planners we interviewed observed, however, one of their most fundamental tasks, as advocates, was to attempt to raise the consciousness of local government—to move it towards a place of greater social engagement and responsibility. "Every time I get in front of council," said one, "I see that as my job."

It would, in short, be wrong to regard the social planners who work in small cities as "technocrats," imposing government plans in top-down fashion, as Rothman's model conceived. While planners certainly have a role in formulating policy and designing strategies for its implementation, they are closely involved with the communities in which they live, serving as allies and advocates, mediating in disputes, and working to keep lines of communication open. In this respect, they remain closer to the grassroots traditions of community development and share many of the same values—compassion, altruism, cooperation, mutual support—that have long informed the voluntary sector.

Conclusion

As is well recognized, despite a discursive emphasis on the importance of innovation, the austerity regimes associated with neoliberalism tend to breed caution and conservatism. Municipal governments—which, even in the best of circumstances, operate in a tight fiscal environment—are in no way immune to this trend. As a result, they are often reluctant to spend local tax dollars on initiatives that hold no promise of generating revenue, no matter how well justified these actions are in terms of social responsibility. As became clear in the interviews we conducted, social planners often see themselves as their local government's social conscience, encouraging city councillors and other members of city staff to remember that "communities" consist of people and to think about the human aspects of policy and planning. While a social planner who has earned the respect of senior city officials is obviously at an advantage, persuading local government to adopt a more explicit social agenda is an ongoing challenge, in which social planners require the support of others.

Especially in the relatively intimate context of a small city, building alliances is therefore essential to the work of social planners, and, as always, it involves two reciprocal processes. Social planners need to enlist the active support of those in the community—service providers, members of organizations dedicated to helping those in need, concerned citizens—who are already sympathetic to their goals. In this regard, planners must work to ensure that such people are represented on advisory committees, as well as to foster participatory processes that reach out to the community and allow their voices to be heard. At the same time, social planners must engage in dialogue with their colleagues in city government, seeking to educate them about specific social issues and to explain why taking action to address them is ultimately in the city's best interests. Planners can also engage in a similar process with members of local business associations and others in the private sector who may otherwise tend to regard those who are homeless, or who work in the sex trade, or who struggle with drug addictions or mental illness, simply as threats to their commercial objectives.

Although they may yet need to act on the recognition, local governments are in a position to contribute to the creation of communities that are more inclusive and more responsive to the needs of all who live in them. They can transform the local environment through the development of social plans and policies that target specific social issues, through the establishment of advisory committees and task forces, through the provision of land and community grants, and through active efforts to build consensus among the many segments of a local population. They may also do so by participating in the development of regional strategies that constitute a collective response to pressing social issues and by advocating for greater strategic investment on the part of senior levels of government in the strengthening of social infrastructure and in programs that support the provision of social services. While social planners cannot singlehandedly prompt local government to adopt a longer-term perspective and a more progressive social agenda, they are an integral force in the process.

References

Adamoski, Robert. 2005. "Persistence and Privilege: Boarding and Single Fathers in the Practice of Child Rescue, 1901–1930." In *Child and Family Welfare in British Columbia: A History,* edited by Diane Purvey and Christopher Walmsley, 29–52. Calgary: Detselig.

Arai, Susan M., and Donald G. Reid. 2003. "Impacts of a Neo-liberal Policy Shift on Citizenship and the Voluntary Sector: A Policy Delphi with Social Planning Organizations." *Canadian Review of Social Policy* 52: 67–92.

Dudley, James R. 1978. "Is Social Planning Social Work?" *Social Work* 23 (1): 37–41.

Evans, Bryan M., Ted Richmond, and John Shields. 2005. "Structuring Neoliberal Governance: The Nonprofit Sector, Emerging New Modes of Control and the Marketisation of Service Delivery." *Policy and Society* 24 (1): 73–97.

Finkel, Alvin. 2006. *Social Policy and Practice in Canada: A History.* Waterloo, ON: Wilfrid Laurier University Press.

Frank, Flo, and Anne Smith. 1999. *The Community Development Handbook: A Tool to Build Community Capacity.* Prepared for Human Resources Development Canada. Ottawa: Minister of Public Works and Government Services.

Gilbert, Neil, and Harry Specht. 1977. "Process Versus Task in Social Planning." *Social Work* 22 (3): 178–83.

Jetté, Christian. 2011. "The Role of Community Organizations in the Transformation of the Social Development Model in Québec." *Canadian Journal of Nonprofit and Social Economy Research / Revue canadienne de recherche sur les OBSL et l'économie sociale* 2 (1): 61–74.

John Talbot and Associates. 2004. *Social Development Strategy for Nanaimo.* Nanaimo, BC: City of Nanaimo. http://www.nanaimo.ca/assets/Departments/ Community~Planning/Social~Planning/Social~Development~Strategy/Soc_ Dev_Strategy.pdf.

Kelowna. 1996. *Social Plan 1996.* Kelowna, BC: City of Kelowna, Department of Planning and Development Services.

McGrath, Susan, and Peter Clutterbuck. 1998. "Third Sector Transformation in an Emerging City State: A Case Study of the Toronto Social Planning Council." In *Working Papers from the Third International Conference, Geneva, Switzerland, July 8–11, 1998.* Geneva: International Society for Third-Sector Research. http://c. ymcdn.com/sites/www.istr.org/resource/resmgr/working_papers_geneva/ McGrath.pdf.

McNiven, Christiane. 1979. "The Vancouver Social Planning Department." In *Community Work in Canada,* edited by Brian Wharf, 197–224. Toronto: McClelland and Stewart.

Prince George. 2002. *Prince George Social Plan.* Prince George, BC: City of Prince George, Community Planning Council.

Rothman, Jack. 2001 [1968]. "Approaches to Community Intervention." In *Strategies of Community Intervention,* 6th ed., edited by Jack Rothman, John L. Erlich, and John E. Tropman, 27–64. Itasca, IL: F. E. Peacock.

Rothman, Jack, and Mayer N. Zald. 2001. "Planning and Policy Practice." In Rothman, Erlich, and Tropman, 298–311.

Savard, Sébastien, Denis Bourque, and René Lachapelle. 2015. "Third Sector Organizations in Québec and the New Public Action in Community Development." *Canadian Journal of Nonprofit and Social Economy Research / Revue canadienne de recherche sur les OBSL et l'économie sociale* 6 (2): 28–41.

SPARC BC (Social Planning and Research Council of British Columbia). 2009. *Kamloops Social Plan.* Kamloops, BC: City of Kamloops.

Vaillancourt, Yves. 1988. *L'évolution des politiques sociales au Québec, 1940–1960.* Montréal: Presses de l'Université de Montréal.

Weil, Marie. 2005. "Social Planning with Communities: Theory and Practice." In *The Handbook of Community Practice,* edited by Marie Weil, 215–43. Thousand Oaks, CA: Sage.

Vancouver. 1994. "Mission, Objectives and Values." Corporate Policy No. CG-001-01. http://vancouver.ca/policy_pdf/CG00101.pdf.

———. 1998. *Social Planning: Celebrating Thirty Years, 1968–1998.* Vancouver: City of Vancouver, Community Services.

9 The Inadequacies of Multiculturalism

Reflections on Immigrant Settlement, Identity Negotiation, and Community in a Small City

Mónica J. Sánchez-Flores

Multiculturalism is a controversial topic in the world today. In Canada, it has supporters who credit it with single-handedly reducing racism and discrimination, and detractors who blame it for Canada's lack of a clear-cut sense of national identity—or see it as a reinvention of white supremacy. Debates surrounding multiculturalism are, of course, inevitably bound up with the topic of immigration, which is the principal source of Canada's "visible minority" population. In recent decades, interest in multiculturalism has been spurred by increased population movements around the world, often cited as one of the defining features of globalization. As is well recognized (see, for example, Giménez 2005; Knox 2000), globalization is primarily an urban phenomenon, managed both economically and politically by a network of "global cities" that exert a powerful pull on migrant populations, as is evident in the influx of immigrants into Canada's major metropolitan centres (Montréal, Toronto, and Vancouver) over the past several decades. At the same time, both the federal and provincial governments have sought ways to encourage newcomers to settle in smaller cities, partly to allow for a more even distribution of population and partly to improve the country's capacity to absorb immigrants (Drolet et al. 2008, 22). Since 2000, an increase has indeed been observed in the number of newcomers settling in cities on the Prairies and, to a lesser extent, in other areas of the country (see Bonikowska, Hou, and Picot 2015, table 1). Yet scholars are only beginning to explore the immigrant experience in smaller cities.

To date, research on immigration in Canada has primarily focused on the big gateway cities to which immigrants have traditionally settled. A major objective of this chapter is thus to point towards the many areas of interest that small cities present for research into the immigrant experience. In what follows, I draw on my own experience as a racialized immigrant to Canada, one who finally settled in the small city of Kamloops, BC, with a view to critiquing the concept of multiculturalism. I briefly discuss the main criticisms directed towards multiculturalism theory and policy and consider whether these criticisms are also relevant in the context of small cities. I also explore the idea that small cities can be even more supportive of immigrant integration than large ones, as the former have enough immigrants to create a vibrant and socially diverse environment but not enough to allow for the fragmentation of immigrant populations into ethnic enclaves. The visible concentration of immigrants in ethnic neighbourhoods and business centres, so often observed in large cities, tends to encourage the perception that ethnicity is the prime (or even the sole) source of identity for immigrants. But, of course, ethnicity represents only one thread in the complex tapestry of human identity. For individual people (racialized or not), identity is never clearly defined. Rather, it is a constant inner negotiation and is entwined between self and others in intricate ways that include collective and ascribed features, as well as individual choices and characteristics. As I will argue, however, the concept of multiculturalism cannot cope with the complexities of identity.

The Challenge of Diversity

At the time that the 2011 National Household Survey was conducted, one in every five people in Canada was foreign-born (Statistics Canada 2013, 6), with new residents arriving from countries throughout the world (8). More than two hundred ethnic backgrounds were represented (13), and 19.1 percent of Canadians identified themselves as members of a visible minority (14). Canada's policy of multiculturalism is framed within a postcolonial world order that supports supremacist cultural inertias embedded in the balance of power of the world. This capitalist global order continues to privilege the global north as the seat of civilized life. The enduring legacy of colonialism and its racist ideologies remain responsible for the discrimination and exploitation to which immigrant populations are subject. Racism lies at the root of the commonplace assumption that racialized immigrants' identities are based solely on their traditional cultures, which are stereotypically seen as backward and thus as holding values and beliefs that are incompatible with the Canadian liberal and progressive ones. This perception generates problems that do not solely affect the marginalized immigrants—even when they suffer the most palpable material consequences: it does serious harm to everyone. It enables the privileged to feel superior—a kind of "moral damage," in that no benefit can accrue from "grounding one's existence on injustices" (Smith 2007, 378)—and it produces a society infested by anger, fear, and lack of trust (Sánchez-Flores 2010).

The federal blanket policy of multiculturalism is typically framed in lofty rhetoric about acceptance and the appreciation of diversity. This rhetoric is not without its purpose, but such pronouncements should be complemented by specific measures that take into account the particular circumstances in which immigrants find themselves when settling in Canada. Such measures cannot be designed and made to work for immigrants without clear knowledge of those circumstances, such as the size and social composition of immigrant-receiving communities. In the absence of an understanding of concrete realities, multiculturalism amounts to a collection of preconceptions founded on stereotypical ideas about ethnic identity, as reflected in and reinforced by the reductionist self-definitions on which census forms and other such surveys rely. Multiculturalism may be based on ideals of social inclusion, rights, and celebration of diversity, but it fails to address, much less to dislodge, the postcolonial habits and attitudes that are deeply embedded in Canadian society and that continue to feed othering and discrimination against racialized immigrants.

As mentioned above, contemporary immigration is eminently an urban phenomenon in the sense that immigrants tend to settle in cities, and immigrants to Canada prefer to settle in relatively large cities rather than in rural areas. In 1996, 73.4 percent of recent immigrants (those who had arrived in the past five years) settled in Toronto, Montréal, or Vancouver, but by 2006, the figure had dropped to 68.9 percent (Chui, Tran, and Maheux 2007, 20). Of the immigrants who arrived in Canada between 2006 and 2011, only 62.5 percent chose to live in one of those three large cities (Statistics Canada 2013, 11), and the census of 2016 revealed a further decline, to only 56.0 percent (Statistics

Canada 2017, 3). This trend has been accompanied by a significant increase in the number of new immigrants bound for somewhat smaller cities, notably on the Prairies (Calgary, Edmonton, Regina, Saskatoon, and Winnipeg), with the proportion of immigrants settling in the Prairie provinces more than doubling from 2001 to 2016 (Statistics Canada 2017, 2 and table 1). Clearly, the experiences and concrete circumstances of immigrants vary depending on whether they settle in major metropolitan areas, in smaller urban centres, or in rural communities. However, from the standpoint of the immigrant experience, the familiar dichotomy of *urban* versus *rural* is not useful in that, even as it continues to reinforce entrenched stereotypes, it masks the diversity of urban settings.

Although studies on immigration to Canada have historically focused on the country's three largest cities, some work has been done on immigration to second- and third-tier Canadian cities (see, for example, Anucha, Lovell, and Jeyapal 2010; Di Biase and Bauder 2005; Lusis and Bauder 2008), and the 2006 issue of *Our Diverse Cities* was dedicated to the topic.[1] Yet very few studies have focused on immigration to Canadian urban centres with a population of under one hundred thousand (see Drolet et al. 2008; Drolet, Robertson, and Robinson 2010; Drolet and Robertson 2011; Sethi 2010; Teixeira 2011). As is clear from the introduction to this volume, small cities cannot be adequately defined on the basis of population alone: their smallness is as much a matter of character as size. Generally speaking, however, small cities present all the advantages of urban life that immigrants seek, but at a lower cost, while allowing them to escape the alienating anonymity of big urban centres. Indeed, small cities preserve a sense of community that I argue may be conducive to immigrant integration. Despite the dearth of research pertaining to them, smaller cities thus offer an exciting context in which to explore settlement conditions, the complexities of identity, and how patterns of inequality play out for immigrants.

---

1 James Frideres was the guest editor of this issue of *Our Diverse Cities,* which is available at http://canada.metropolis.net/publications/Diversity/our_diverse_cities_vol2_en.pdf. In his opening essay, Frideres (2006) defines second- and third-tier cities in terms of population: 500,000 to a million and 100,000 to 500,000, respectively. By this definition, both Calgary and Edmonton are now first-tier cities, as their metropolitan populations now exceed a million. Yet, in terms of reputation and influence, neither city is truly comparable to Toronto, Montréal, or Vancouver, which tends to underscore the inadequacy of purely quantitative definitions.

As noted above, immigration and multiculturalism are intimately related to each other, but what is in people's minds when they speak about multiculturalism? In Canada, this concept refers to at least five interrelated phenomena: the existence of ethnic and racial diversity in the same society or community, a state policy complete with educational and public avowal strategies, a liberal political theory, an ideology that supports the status quo, and an emblem of the Canadian identity. Ethnic and racial diversity is evident in Canadian cities, both big and small, but it is especially apparent in its three major urban centres. According to the 2011 National Household Survey, foreign-born individuals accounted for 46.0 percent of Toronto's total population, 40.0 percent of Vancouver's, and 22.6 percent Montreal's (Statistics Canada 2013, 10). As a state policy, multiculturalism was formalized in legislation in the wake of Pierre E. Trudeau's announcement in 1971: this legislation includes the Immigration Act of 1976, which created a system of points that was intended to rule out decisions based on racist preferences, and the Multiculturalism Act, adopted by Parliament in 1988. As a political theory, multiculturalism draws on the egalitarian spirit of liberalism, with its emphasis on individual rights. It is further enshrined in section 27 of the Canadian Charter of Rights and Freedoms, which specifies that the rights and freedoms laid out in the Charter "shall be interpreted in a manner consistent with the preservation and enhancement of the multicultural heritage of Canadians." But multiculturalism is also an ideology—a set of ideas designed to encourage the acceptance of social diversity and make it seem the natural and right order of things. Politicians routinely rely on the public embrace of multiculturalism to attract new immigrant voters and also as a source of political legitimation. Finally, multiculturalism as the celebration of diversity has become an integral part of what it means to be Canadian. As Will Kymlicka (2010, 7) points out, "Canadians view immigrants and demographic diversity as key parts of their own Canadian identity." Kymlicka adds that, according to polling surveys, Canadians are more likely than citizens of any other liberal democracy from the global north to support multiculturalism and view it with pride (7). All of these different manifestations of multiculturalism are interrelated in complex ways that interact and overlap with structures of inequality and culturally embedded racism inherited from the colonial past.

Multiculturalism: Three Critiques

The criticisms that have been raised against multiculturalism can be grouped into three categories. The most familiar one argues that policies of multiculturalism undermine social cohesion and threaten national unity and a sense of national identity. In this view, multiculturalism is seen as supporting immigrants in preserving their traditional cultures and in Balkanizing their host societies. A second critique relates to the tendency to conceive of cultures as discrete, self-contained, identifiable "things," which is the way cultures have been mistakenly represented in the past. As Anne Phillips (2009, 8) tells us, writings on multiculturalism "have exaggerated not only the unity and solidity of cultures but the intractability of value conflict as well." In this reified vision, cultures inculcate distinct sets of norms, values, and preferences that shape people's identity and behaviour in consistent and hence predictable ways. The second objection, then, contends that, in subscribing to a view of cultures as internally coherent, multiculturalism fails to capture the complexity of individual identities, reducing them to stereotypes. The third objection builds on the second one: these stereotypical images of traditional cultures of immigrants inform public perceptions of newcomers, encouraging the view that immigrants hold traditional attitudes and beliefs that are backward and contrary to the liberal values of modern societies. In their application, then, policies of multiculturalism effectively reproduce the standard colonial dichotomy between superior (nationals of the developed world) and inferior (racialized immigrants).

So we have three criticisms, according to which multiculturalism: (1) weakens national identity in modern liberal nation-states and thus ghettoizes cities and Balkanizes populations; (2) holds a simplistic conception of human identity, one in which ethnic cultures are seen as stereotypes and as the sole source of immigrant identity; and (3) preserves colonial supremacist attitudes and even a rearticulated form of racism. How do these critiques relate to the lives of immigrants in big versus small cities?

With respect to the first objection, visibly segregated ethnic groups in the neighbourhoods and business centres of larger cities have been closely associated to the perception that multiculturalism ghettoizes urban life and undermines to national unity (see Bibby 1990; Bissoondath 1994; Gwyn 1995). As the 2006 census revealed, the reason that immigrants most often gave for choosing to settle in one of Canada's three largest cities was to join an existing social network of family and friends (Chui, Tran, and Maheux 2007, 20). The concept of social networks refers to "bonds of family relationships, friendships, mutual acquaintances, and shared regional origin" (Pandit and Holloway 2005, iv). A rich body of work now exists in North America on the way that these networks influence and support the settlement of newcomers (see, for example, Portes and Sensenbrenner 1993). The operation of these networks is closely linked to the development of territorially concentrated groupings of businesses and housing—clusters that have been called "ethnic enclaves" and that appear to exist not only in the big metropolises but also in second- and third-tier Canadian cities (Razin and Langlois 1996; Fong and Wilkes 2003). Even though ethnic communities organize themselves in associations and groups to pursue their common interests, visible ethnic enclaves in the form of neighbourhood or business areas are not evident in smaller urban centres.

In a study of immigrants to Montréal, Raymond Breton (1964) came up with the concept of the "institutional completeness" of an ethnic community, which he defined as existing "whenever the ethnic community could perform all the services required by its members" (194). This comprehensive provision of services requires that the group be formally organized and that its structure include "organizations of various sorts: religious, educational, political, recreational, national, and even professional" (194). In Montréal, Breton observed that this level of formal organization could be sustained as long as the ethnic community had a large number of members; when that number dwindled, organizations disappeared.

Subsequent studies on ethnic communities have, however, challenged the notion of spatial concentration as a condition for the identification of such communities, focusing instead on the relational dimension of networks in the construction and preservation of ethnic identity (see Goldenberg and Haines 1992). These studies examine the strategies that immigrants use to cultivate their ethnic identity and to foster a sense of an ethnic community in an era in which connectivity is sustained by advanced communication technologies, but they do not explore diversified sources of identity for immigrants who are spatially separated from one another and who therefore have little choice but to interact with the host local community.

In big cities, the spatial and organizational elements of institutional completeness, supported by a sufficiently large community of immigrants, have the effect of creating a highly cohesive interpersonal local network of members who have no need to develop ties with the host community to satisfy their needs. For example, it is common knowledge that in Richmond, BC (located within the Vancouver metropolitan area), a Chinese immigrant does not need to speak English to work, live, and fulfill basic daily needs. As Peter Blau (1977) noted in exploring the role of heterogeneity in social integration, large groups of immigrants, such as those found in major metropolitan areas, are more cohesive and tend to maintain relationships exclusively within the group, whereas members of smaller groups must look for relationships beyond the group. Although evidence indicates that ethnic social networks do exist in small cities and that immigrants seek them out and make extensive use of them (Drolet, Robertson, and Robinson 2010), ethnic groups in these cities typically lack the numbers needed to produce institutional completeness. In small urban centres, immigrants are therefore forced to interact with the surrounding community, which, in accordance with Blau's model, should mean that small cities are more conducive than large ones to social integration. More research is needed, however, into precisely how ethnic social networks operate in small cities, but a perception of social segregation in ethnic enclaves due to immigration is not evident in them.

The second objection to multiculturalism is that the concept is based on a simplistic view of human identity. Much has been written about how multiculturalism and its policies essentialize culture and fail to grasp its complexities, a phenomenon that has ramifications for the understanding of identity. Embedded both in policies of multiculturalism and in the first critique of such policies is a conception of human identity as fundamentally an expression of one's culture of origin—a conceptualization that is at odds with current knowledge about identity as complex, diversified, and constantly negotiated, the construction of which taps into a multiplicity of sources, ethnicity being but one. In this view of identity, newcomers have a choice between retaining their ethnic identity (that is, remaining "other") or becoming more "like us," although the latter can only be a matter of degree for certain ethnic minorities, given that racial markers remain in place (as signalled by the Canadian term "visible minority").[2]

---

2 According to section 3 of Canada's Employment Equity Act (Canada 1995), visible minorities are "persons, other than aboriginal peoples, who are non-Caucasian in race or non-white in colour."

One of the problems with the representation of identity as mainly stemming from ethnicity is that it characterizes people as *either* autonomous, rational, and individualistic *or* attached to an ethnic group that swallows and cancels such individuality. This conception of identity in general and of ethnic identity in particular is simplistic because it construes people as "culture peons," or slaves to their own culture, which supposedly determines immigrants' values, beliefs, and behaviour. This is also related to the politicization of cultures as coherent wholes that can be claimed as sources of rights. But this notion of cultures paints an unrealistic picture of how people live and experience their identity (ethnic or not). Today, identity in the sense of lived experience is more readily seen as fluid and constantly changing, yet a construction of ethnic identity as something solid, clear, and distinct prevails in simplistic representations and misrepresentations of immigrants (often in the form of stereotypes) in the life of cities both big and small.

My own experience as a racialized immigrant to a small city in Canada may illustrate the point that human identity is complex and diversified, rather than emanating solely from ethnicity. I am a Mexican woman of indigenous descent who now lives in the small city of Kamloops, BC. I arrived in Canada in 2005, as a family-class immigrant, having left my academic job in Mexico City to marry a Canadian man of Scottish ancestry, and first landed in the rural community of Lillooet, BC, two hours away from Kamloops by road. As a racialized woman in Canada, where I am regarded as a visible minority, I have become more aware of my indigenous heritage; in Mexico, my sense of self was shaped by a much stronger emotional attachment to the modern *mestizo* Mexican national imaginary, which is fundamentally syncretistic.[3] I grew up in the Mexican middle class, which emerged during the 1960s and 1970s (that is, during my parents' generation) largely as a result of free higher education in public institutions. I completed my BA at El Colegio de México, in Mexico City, but, with funding from scholarships, went on to earn an MSc and PhD at the University of Edinburgh. In Mexico, I have relatives or extended kin in both the working class and the middle-to-upper classes, and my education allowed me entry into political networks and into the Mexican upper classes.

3 The term *mestizo* refers to the mixture of blood between the Catholic Spanish colonizers and the native peoples, which is supposed to have produced the "race of bronze." This *mestizo* identity was the ethnic basis on which the modern Mexican nation-state was formed.

I am a mother and wife in a cross-cultural family, a world traveller, a regular practitioner of yoga, a lover of international food, an avid reader of mystic writings, as well as of fiction, and a speaker of Spanish, English, and French. I am also a faculty member at Thompson Rivers University who specializes in sociology and political theory, an active participant in the faculty association and the co-chair of its equity committee, and a distance education instructor. In Kamloops, I have strong ties to a group of Latin American friends, based in part on commonalities: we share a nostalgia for our homelands and their traditional foods and a taste for various forms of Latin American music (salsa, son, rumba, merengue, reggaeton) with Spanish lyrics (although when I lived in Mexico, I rarely listened to such music). I also have strong ties of friendship to people in the diverse cosmopolitan community of Kamloops, which includes people from all over the world as well as Canadians of all colours and backgrounds. The cultural sources of my identity have an objective, external dimension, in that they are to some extent grounded in the cultural affiliations and practices characteristic of my Mexican heritage as well as the various groups to which I am now related. But they also have a subjective dimension, which derives from my personal choices about how to position myself in relationship to these groups—my own sense of who I am and my individual agency. I expand here on my own background in order to illustrate the multiplicity of identity sources possible in a single racialized immigrant. While some are based in group identifications, many more reflect individual life experience and personal attitudes, preferences, and choices.

The problem of representing human identity in simplistic terms links to the third and most recent critical objection to multiculturalism. The assumption that culture or ethnicity defines immigrants' identity and behaviour does more than simply deny them their capacity to make choices based on individual judgment and preferences: it also allows mainstream Canadians to exalt themselves as progressive—as more enlightened and "civilized"—when they are confronted with practices and customs of racialized minorities that are unfamiliar to them or that they simply do not fully understand. Thunera Thobani (2007) argues, for example, that the policy of multiculturalism supresses both knowledge about the complexities of a diverse society such as Canada and knowledge about the complexities of identity facing people who come from diverse backgrounds. Cultural sources and identity formation interact in complex ways, but this interaction is also tied to structures of inequality created by prejudice and public perception, and, to this day, the media handle difference through the use of stereotypes.

Another example is the common perception, also reinforced by the popular media, that traditional cultures are oppressive to women and children. This perception is founded on "the idea, as Leti Volpp (2001, 1198) puts it, "that 'other' women are subjected to extreme patriarchy," whereas women in the global north are presumed to be "secular, liberated, and in total control of their lives." This simplistic dichotomy rests on the self-aggrandizing claim that gender subordination survives only in traditional cultures, as if North America were already free from patriarchal and oppressive cultural practices, but it also illustrates how racialized women's behaviour is assumed to be motivated by culture and not by personal choice. The tension between modern/traditional, individualist/collectivist, and secular/religious views of the world merely updates the colonial racist order by redefining the terms of inferiority and identifying racialized immigrant minorities as holding the inferior side of the dichotomies (traditional-collectivist-religious).

Intersecting Stereotypes in the Small City

In smaller cities and towns, the tensions generated by the stereotypical juxtaposition of the affluent, modern, liberal world to the poor, traditional, collectivist world are framed within another familiar dichotomy, that of urban/large and rural/small—two realms assumed to embody opposing world views. It is assumed, for instance, that because smaller populations tend to be more homogeneous, people in these smaller communities have a less tolerant attitude towards difference. The Citizenship and Immigration Canada report on the evaluation of the Welcoming Communities Initiative assumes that racism and discrimination are more prevalent in "rural areas and small cities, which have traditionally been comprised of fairly homogeneous populations" (Canada, CIC 2010, 17). In the United Kingdom, the national imagination construes rural life as homogeneous, formed by white middle-class British people with an idealized conflict-free life in contrast to urban life in big cities, which are rife with problems, some of which come from their diverse population, and this popular representation sustains racism against minorities in rural communities (see, for example, Garland and Chakraborti 2007; see also Day, this volume).

In a study of Kelowna, a small city in southern British Columbia, Aguiar, Tomic, and Trumper (2005) characterize the city as a hinterland that sells itself to other Canadians from bigger cities as a "white space" for outdoor fun, an ideal retirement location, and a safe haven for business. The authors claim that embedded in this vision is a type of racism that need not rely on official legal sanctions for its "powerful exclusionary practices because it is woven into the customs, norms and representations of the every day" (131). And yet they fail to clarify how this racism operates in concrete situations and has clear structural consequences. Such representations of smaller population centres as more racist and prejudiced rests on urban/rural dichotomy that may obtain at the far ends of the spectrum but that ignores the grey areas in between—the space in which small cities exist. I argue that small cities do not exhibit the same dynamics of demographic composition as the small rural areas with which they are so often grouped.

An incident that occurred in Kamloops several years ago clearly illustrates the use of stereotypes in the perception of culturally marked minorities in this small city. The incident sparked much public discussion of socially constructed cultural dichotomies, including the clash not only between an oppressive-traditional culture of racialized people and the liberation of women in white societies but also between a rural mentality comfortable with sameness and a more open urban-cosmopolitan one that can accept difference. In March 2013, a woman in a local supermarket took it upon herself to tell another woman, who wore full head and face coverings and was accompanied by her husband, that she did not have to wear such garb in Canada and that she should get a better man (Youds 2013). Her comment was, of course, based on ignorance about the meaning of veils for Muslim women, but it also cancelled out the agency of the woman herself—as if her decision to wear this garment had nothing to do with her personal capacity for decision making. As Volpp (2001, 1192) says, "Because the Western definition of what makes one human depends on the notion of agency and the ability to make rational choices, to thrust some communities into a world where their actions are determined only by culture is deeply dehumanizing."

The *Kamloops Daily News* ran a story about the incident, highlighting the fact that the article happened to appear on International Day for the Elimination of Racial Discrimination and representing the episode as a "racist incident" and a "racist confrontation" that provided an example of how not to behave in the presence of difference (Youds 2013). Two days later, an editorial in the same paper lamented the homogeneous whiteness of the Kamloops population, commenting that it was not surprising to find racist outbursts "in the depths of the white north" because "ignorance flourishes in small places" (Koopmans 2013). The editorial constructed Kamloops as a primarily white rural backwater in need of a more open outlook on difference. This provoked a letter of rebuttal from a reader who claimed that the incident had not been "racist" because "Muslim is not a race, it is a religion" and that it could be explained (although not justified, because it was rude) as an understandable reaction against "an affront to women's rights." The reader further argued that the "Islamist prejudice against women" was not acceptable in "our culture" because "we have matured beyond this" (Cruickshank 2013). And so the letter to the editor, which assumes that in North America women have been fully liberated, brings us back to the tug-of-war between the purportedly inferior values and beliefs of racialized minorities and the higher moral ground of liberal values.

My contention is that the stereotypical dichotomy between the xenophobic mentality of rural areas and small towns and the more tolerant one of larger cities needs to be further examined in the light of the specific demographic dynamics that may exist in small urban centres. In the end, the event in the Kamloops supermarket ended up with two writers on different sides of the issue each claiming a moral high ground, with the letter writer using a cultural stereotype and the editorial writer using a rural stereotype. This illustrates the need for more research on how racist exclusionary mechanisms contribute to the social construction of space, especially in smaller cities, and what the consequences are. Clearly, the experience of diversity in small cities cannot be accurately characterized by the use of stereotypes. Although the following reflections on Kamloops may not be representative of the ways in which racism and discrimination are experienced in other small cities in Canada, they seek to problematize the taken-for-granted assumption that small cities are *eo ipso* places where racism and discriminatory practices are experienced more often than in larger centres.

Kamloops as an Immigrant Destination

As noted above, immigrants are starting to find destinations such as Kamloops, a small city and local hub, attractive for settlement. With a municipal population of just over 90,000, Kamloops—located "at the junction of four major highways, two major railways and the North and South Thompson rivers" (Drolet et al. 2008, 23)—is a centre for services and transportation in the Thompson-Okanagan region. It is home to a university that serves a total of about 27,000 students, roughly 12.5 percent of whom are international students (TRU 2017). With 1,092 employees, Thompson Rivers University is the fourth-largest employer in Kamloops, after the Royal Inland Hospital, the local school district, and the Highland Valley Copper Mine (Venture Kamloops 2018). Kamloops has an emerging industry in agri-food products and services, high-tech manufacturing, and nonmetallic mineral products, and a lively economy that includes its role as a transportation and service centre, its proximity to ski resorts, and its function as host for dozens of regional, provincial, and national tournaments. The city's diverse economy creates opportunities for employment in the service sector, in the construction industry, and in local shops and businesses. The services available in Kamloops cater not only to the local population but also to residents of surrounding smaller communities and towns that cannot sustain the infrastructure of a city.

Research on settler experiences in Kamloops reveals that reasons for choosing this city include the opportunities for employment, entrepreneurship, and education; the existence of family and friends in the city; the ethnic and religious communities; language services; access to medical services; housing; and "a welcoming host population" (Drolet, Robertson, and Robinson 2010, 220). While ethnic and religious communities do exist in Kamloops, the city lacks spatial ethnic enclaves and its ethnic communities present a low level of institutional completeness.[4] As this research also noted, immigrant residents identified the need for greater collaboration between the nonprofit Kamloops Immigrant Society, which delivers services and programs to immigrants, and other relevant organizations, such as ethnic organizations and community initiatives (220). Although groups of immigrants in this city are large enough to organize themselves and to raise funds for their cultural activities, their numbers are not sufficient to create recognizable ethnic business areas or neighbourhoods.

---

4 Kamloops does, however, have a good number of ethnic and religious organizations. The Kamloops Multicultural Society (KMS) alone has twenty-seven such organizations as members. See "Members," Kamloops Multicultural Society, n.d., http://www.kmsociety.ca/members.htm.

The existence of work opportunities is one of the most important reasons for immigrants to choose a city to settle; research on second-tier and smaller cities proposes that access to services, education, and appropriate housing is necessarily linked to access to employment and income (Anucha, Lovell, and Jeyapal 2010; Drolet, Robertson, and Robinson 2010; Sakamoto, Chin, and Young 2010). As an immigrant myself, I ended up settling in Kamloops primarily for reasons of employment. Only six months after I arrived in Canada, I was fortunate to get a job as a sessional instructor at the branch of Thompson Rivers University located in Lillooet, where my husband and I lived for two years. This led to an opportunity to teach at the main Kamloops campus, and, for most of 2006, I commuted between Lillooet and Kamloops, before we finally moved there in January 2007.

I have been able to find work in Canada because my credentials are British, which sets me apart from most immigrants to Canada. As many researchers have noted, the lack of recognition for foreign credentials and experience is a major obstacle for immigrants seeking work in their field, without which they cannot prosper in Canada (see Abu-Laban and Gabriel 2002; Drolet, Robertson, and Robinson 2010; Sakamoto, Chin, and Young 2010; Sethi 2010; Teixeira 2011). This may be the most significant reason for inequality associated with immigration. The lack of recognition for foreign credentials and experience—even the absence of any system for evaluating relative quality and acceptability—is associated with two factors: the fact that professions in Canada are self-regulating and the sweeping assumption that standards are inferior at educational and service-providing agencies in the global south, where most immigrants to Canada now originate. An important structural aspect of immigration in Canada is the points system, established to determine who qualifies as a "skilled worker" (a professional seeking permanent residence and work). Immigrants receive points according to level of education, language proficiency in English or French, work experience, age, and an "adaptability" criterion that includes the language skills of the applicant's spouse, whether the applicant and/or spouse have previously studied or worked in Canada, and whether the applicant has relatives who reside in Canada. To qualify, an applicant must receive a "passing" mark of 67 points (out of a possible total of 100).[5] However, the federal government has been

---

5 "Six Selection Factors: Federal Skilled Workers," *Citizenship and Immigration Canada*, 2017, http://www.cic.gc.ca/english/immigrate/skilled/apply-factors.asp.

looking into reforming this system, realizing that it has not achieved its initial goal of selecting immigrants with broad transferable skills that would secure for them economic success in the long run (McMahon 2013, 41).

The points system guarantees that immigrants who have successfully applied to come to Canada (other than those claiming refugee status) are well-educated people from middle- to upper-class backgrounds in their countries of origin. Newcomers, however, frequently face a drop in their socioeconomic status: because their credentials and experience are not recognized, they are obliged to turn to unskilled jobs to earn an income and start their life in Canada. "These days, university educated newcomers earn an average of 67 per cent of their Canadian-born, university-educated counterparts" and nearly half of immigrants who live in poverty came to Canada as skilled workers (McMahon 2013, 42). In my own research on immigration, and also in socializing with immigrants, I have observed that the lack of recognition of foreign credentials generally comes as a surprise to those who have gained permanent resident status in the category of skilled workers: since their acceptability is measured in terms of education and professional experience, the assumption is that their credentials will be recognized, at least partially. Well-educated immigrants arriving in Canada from countries in the global south are frustrated at having to volunteer to gain some Canadian work experience that will eventually yield them only menial jobs or at having to train all over again to earn Canadian credentials—which is not necessarily possible in their chosen field, since it involves a major investment of time and money. Immigrants to smaller cities are not immune to this problem. However, in spite of this, immigrants to smaller destinations seem to face fewer challenges in finding work, and their average income is higher than those who go to the main gateway cities (Frideres 2006, 6).

Research on immigrants in Kamloops reveals that newcomers identify several advantages to settling in a smaller city: a lower cost of living; greater physical security and less crime; and a more manageable scale, with everything close at hand and easy to find. In addition, immigrants encountered a welcoming host population: as one put it, "Kamloops is friendly" (quoted in Drolet, Robertson, and Robinson 2010, 220). Settling in a small city after living for many years in the huge metropolis of Mexico City, I have had a chance to experience these advantages. To be sure, racism and prejudice against immigrants do exist in smaller communities (see Sethi 2010) as well as in bigger ones, but it is not clear that the stereotypical representation of small cities as small-minded is accurate. However, in view of the standard representation of small cities as xenophobic, what stands out here is the "friendly face" that Kamloops presents to immigrants.

With this in mind, I would like to raise the possibility that a smaller city such as Kamloops could provide an environment in which social diversity, combined with the Canadian multicultural ideology of acceptance, might foster a cosmopolitan openness to human difference that has not yet been explored. Here, I define cosmopolitanism as the attitude that regards people of all colours and origins as deserving of the same level of dignity and respect; this attitude perceives cultural and racial difference as an opportunity for enjoyment and celebration of diversity (see Sánchez-Flores 2010). Kamloops is small enough to be considered a community, in the sense of a place where social organization is founded on personal ties, yet it is big enough to support the lifestyle and infrastructure of an urban centre.

As we have seen, in such communities, the number of immigrants from any one ethnic group is too small to produce institutional completeness, with the result that immigrants must have recourse to the institutions of the host society for services, education, entertainment, and so on—settings in which residents of all origins mingle and interact. This pattern is evident in Kamloops, which enhances its cosmopolitan quality. Even groups of friends who find each other on the basis of ethnicity may adopt an inclusive outlook, welcoming members whose ethnicity differs from that of the majority in the group. For example, I have a circle of friends in Kamloops, which includes people not only from Mexico but also from Costa Rica, Panama, and Colombia, as well as a couple of non-Spanish-speaking Canadians. The local university, which enrols an increasing number of international students and attracts a culturally diverse group of students and staff, has also helped the city to acquire a cosmopolitan hue. However, more research is needed to test the theory that smaller cities promote a cosmopolitan response to human diversity, as well as to investigate the specific social dynamics that may allow for such cosmopolitan possibilities.

Conclusion

Small cities are the latest addition to the social contexts in which the impact of globalization has been felt, and they represent a new, diversified, and exciting field of inquiry into the immigrant experience in Canada. Early immigrants to

Canada arrived to populate the country's vast expanse of territory, but "today's immigrants are mostly urban dwellers. In fact, they are much more likely to live in a metropolitan area than the Canadian-born population" (Chui, Tran, and Maheux 2007, 18). Small cities are a potentially attractive destination for immigrants, as they offer a space where housing is less expensive and the cost of living lower and where employment opportunities may be better. Despite the received wisdom about smaller cities—namely, that their residents tend to be intolerant of difference—how far this remains true is an open question. And yet smaller cities may present challenges that need to be investigated more carefully to find out whether the size of the population and lack of diversity has anything to do with intolerant behaviour. As I have suggested, in such settings, retreat into ethnic enclaves is generally not possible, leaving immigrants little choice but to mingle with the host population. This intermingling may serve to break down barriers created by culturally based assumptions about identity, encourage people to get to know each other as individuals, and foster a cosmopolitan outlook.

Multiculturalism and its policies fail to address the complex experience of settling in communities that are not big enough to cater to specific ethnic groups yet are sufficiently large and diversified to constitute cosmopolitan urban centres where immigrants and host communities mingle and interact. Many questions about immigration to small cities remain: How does settlement occur in these specific social and political environments? To what extent are residents of smaller cities open to diversity, and to what extent do they view immigration as a threat to the Canadian majority? Exploring questions such as these requires finer theoretical tools than the liberal theory of multiculturalism can provide. Multiculturalism preserves a simplistic approach to human identity that is inadequate to understanding the complexity of immigration and settlement. The divisive concept of multiculturalism should be replaced by one of inclusive cosmopolitanism, combined with reflection on the issues of inequality associated with immigration and with the racialization of immigrants as "visible minorities." Acknowledging that small cities are the recipients of racialized immigrants is only a beginning. More research is needed on immigration to small cities to examine their role in fostering in immigrants a sense of belonging, in providing them a welcoming environment, and thus in capturing and retaining newcomers.

References

Abu-Laban, Yasmin, and Christina Gabriel. 2002. *Selling Diversity: Immigration, Multiculturalism, Employment Equity, and Globalization*. Peterborough, ON: Broadview.

Aguiar, Luis L. M., Patricia Tomic, and Ricardo Trumper. 2005. "Work Hard, Play Hard: Selling Kelowna, BC, as Year-Round Playground." *Canadian Geographer* 49 (2): 123–39.

Anucha, Uzo, Alex Lovell, and Daphne Jeyapal. 2010. "The Housing Experiences of Racialized Newcomers in a Second-Tier Canadian City." *Canadian Social Work* 12 (1): 176–83.

Bibby, Reginald W. 1990. *Mosaic Madness: The Poverty and Potential of Life in Canada*. Toronto: Stoddart.

Bissoondath, Neil. 1994. *Selling Illusions: The Cult of Multiculturalism in Canada*. Toronto: Penguin.

Blau, Peter M. 1977. *Inequality and Heterogeneity: A Primitive Theory of Social Structure*. New York: Free Press.

Bonikowska, Aneta, Feng Hou, and Garnett Picot. 2015. *Changes in the Regional Distribution of New Immigrants to Canada*. Analytical Studies Branch Research Paper no. 366. Ottawa: Minister of Industry. http://www.statcan.gc.ca/pub/11f0019m/11f0019m2015366-eng.pdf.

Breton, Raymond. 1964. "Institutional Completeness of Ethnic Communities and the Personal Relations of Immigrants." *American Journal of Sociology* 70 (2): 193–205.

Canada. 1995. Employment Equity Act. SC 1995, c. 44. http://laws-lois.justice.gc.ca/PDF/E-5.401.pdf.

Canada. CIC (Citizenship and Immigration Canada). 2010. *Evaluation of the Welcoming Communities Initiative*. Ottawa: Citizenship and Immigration Canada. http://www.cic.gc.ca/english/pdf/research-stats/ER201103_05E_WCI.pdf.

Chui, Tina, Kelly Tran, and Hélène Maheux. 2007. *Immigration in Canada: A Portrait of the Foreign-Born Population, 2006 Census*. Catalogue No. 97-557-XIE. Ottawa: Statistics Canada.

Cruickshank, Kathy. 2013. "Don't Accept Oppression of Women." Letter to the editor. *Kamloops Daily News*, 28 March.

Di Biase, Sonia, and Harald Bauder. 2005. "Immigrant Settlement in Ontario: Location and Local Labour Markets." *Canadian Ethnic Studies / Études ethniques au Canada* 37 (3): 114–35.

Drolet, Julie, and Jeanette Robertson. 2011. "'In the Smaller City, a Settlement Worker Wears Many Hats': Understanding Settlement Experiences in Kamloops, British Columbia." *Our Diverse Cities* 8: 139–44.

Drolet, Julie, Jeanette Robertson, Picku Multani, Wendy Robinson, and Monika Wroz. 2008. "Settlement Experiences in a Small City: Kamloops, British Columbia." *Small Cities Imprint* 1 (1): 21–30.

Drolet, Julie, Jeanette Robertson, and Wendy Robinson. 2010. "Settlement Experiences in a Small City: Voices of Family-Class Immigrants and of Settlement Workers." *Canadian Social Work* 12 (1): 218–23.

Fong, Eric, and Rima Wilkes. 2003. "Racial and Ethnic Residential Patterns in Canada." *Sociological Forum* 18 (4): 577–602.

Frideres, James S. 2006. "Cities and Immigrant Integration: The Future of Second- and Third-Tier Centres." *Our Diverse Cities* 2: 3–8.

Garland, Jon, and Neil Chakraborti. 2007. "'Protean Times?': Exploring the Relationships Between Policing, Community and 'Race' in Rural England." *Criminology and Criminal Justice* 7 (4): 347–65.

Giménez, Gilberto. 2005. "Cultura, identidad y metropolitanismo global." *Revista mexicana da sociología* 67 (3): 483–512.

Goldenberg, Sheldon, and Valerie A. Haines. 1992. "Social Networks and Institutional Completeness: From Territory to Ties." *Canadian Journal of Sociology / Cahiers canadiens de sociologie* 17 (3): 301–12.

Gwyn, Richard. 1995. *Nationalism Without Walls: The Unbearable Lightness of Being Canadian.* Toronto: McClelland and Stewart.

Knox, Paul L. 2000. "World Cities and the Organization of Global Space." In *Geographies of Global Change: Remapping the World,* edited by R. J. Johnston, Peter J. Taylor, and Michael J. Watts, 232–47. Oxford: Blackwell.

Koopmans, Robert. 2013. "It's Easy to be Racist in Good Ol' Kamloops." *Kamloops Daily News,* 23 March.

Kymlicka, Will. 2010. *The Current State of Multiculturalism in Canada and Research Themes in Canadian Multiculturalism, 2008–2010.* Ottawa: Citizenship and Immigration Canada. http://www.cic.gc.ca/english/pdf/pub/multi-state.pdf.

Lusis, Tom, and Harald Bauder. 2008. "'Provincial' Immigrants: The Social, Economic, and Transnational Experiences of the Filipino Canadian Community in Three Ontario Second-Tier Cities." CERIS Working Paper No. 62. Toronto: CERIS, Ontario Metropolis Centre.

McMahon, Tamsin. 2013. "Land of Misfortune." *Maclean's,* 29 April.

Pandit, Kavita, and Steven R. Holloway. 2005. "New Immigrant Geographies of United States Metropolitan Areas." *Geographical Review* 95 (2): iii–vi.

Phillips, Anne. 2009. *Multiculturalism Without Culture.* Princeton, NJ: Princeton University Press.

Portes, Alejandro, and Julie Sensenbrenner. 1993. "Embeddedness and Immigration: Notes on the Social Determinants of Economic Action." *American Journal of Sociology* 98 (6): 1320–50.

Razin, Eran, and André Langlois. 1996. "Metropolitan Characteristics and Entrepreneurship Among Immigrants and Ethnic Groups in Canada." *International Migration Review* 30 (3): 703–27.

Sakamoto, Izumi, Matthew Chin, and Melina Young. 2010. "'Canadian Experience,' Employment Challenges, and Skilled Immigrants: A Close Look Through 'Tacit Knowledge.'" *Canadian Social Work* 12 (1): 145–51.

Sánchez-Flores, Mónica J. 2010. *Cosmopolitan Liberalism: Expanding the Boundaries of the Individual.* New York: Palgrave Macmillan.

Sethi, Bharati. 2010. "Building Bridges: Exploring New Settlement and Integration Supports in Brantford and the Counties of Brant, Haldimand, and Norfolk Using Community-Based Participatory Research (CBPR)." *Canadian Social Work* 12 (1): 184–91.

Smith, Rogers M. 2007. "Law's Races." In *Identities, Affiliations, and Allegiances,* edited by Seyla Benhabib, Ian Shapiro, and Danilo Petranovic, 362–85. Cambridge, UK: Cambridge University Press.

Statistics Canada. 2013. *Immigration and Ethnocultural Diversity in Canada: National House Survey, 2011.* Catalogue No. 99-010-X2011001. Ottawa: Minister of Industry. http://www12.statcan.gc.ca/nhs-enm/2011/as-sa/99-010-x/99-010-x2011001-eng.pdf.

———. 2017. "Immigration and Ethnocultural Diversity: Key Results from the 2016 Census." *The Daily,* 25 October. https://www.statcan.gc.ca/daily-quotidien/171025/dq171025b-eng.pdf.

Teixeira, Carlos. 2011. "New Canadians in Search of Affordable Rental Housing in Central Okanagan, BC." *Our Diverse Cities* 8: 127–33.

Thobani, Sunera. 2007. *Exalted Subjects: Studies in the Making of Race and Nation in Canada.* Toronto: University of Toronto Press.

TRU (Thompson Rivers University). 2017. *Factbook, Fiscal Year 2016–17.* Kamloops, BC: Thompson Rivers University. https://www.tru.ca/__shared/assets/Factbook_2016-201741020.pdf.

Venture Kamloops. 2018. "Kamloops Community Facts (Residential)." http://www.venturekamloops.com/pdf/DBIK-Community-Facts-Residential-Feb-2018.pdf.

Volpp, Leti. 2001. "Feminism Versus Multiculturalism." *Columbia Law Review* 101 (5): 1181–1218.

Youds, Mike. 2013. "Racist Incident in Shop Shocks Couple." *Kamloops Daily News,* 21 March.

10 Municipal Approaches to Poverty Reduction in British Columbia

A Comparison of New Westminster and Abbotsford

Robert Harding and Paul Jenkinson

How have British Columbia's smaller cities responded to burgeoning poverty rates resulting from neoliberal policies implemented at both the federal and provincial levels? Given that municipalities in Canada have only limited powers of taxation, their ability to generate the revenue required to fund social programs is severely constrained. All the same, cities have tried to address high rates of local poverty by pursuing innovative initiatives in a number of sectors, including housing and child care, sometimes working in partnership with external agencies. By examining the strategies adopted by two small cities in British Columbia, we hope to shed light on both the possibilities and the limitations of municipal responses to poverty and related issues, notably homelessness and addiction.

Alleviating poverty depends in large measure on the availability of affordable housing and the adequacy of income security programs. In 1993, in the face of a growing deficit, the federal government withdrew financial support for new low-cost housing, reinstituting it only in 2001, with the introduction of the Affordable Housing Initiative, and also placed an annual limit of $2 billion on federal contributions to social housing (Irwin 2004, 7). In 1996, the government also ended its commitment to sharing the costs of social programs equally with the provinces when it replaced the Canada Assistance Plan

(CAP), enacted in 1966, with the Canada Health and Social Transfer (CHST). Under CAP, provinces and territories were responsible for welfare assistance and social services, and it was up to them to determine who was eligible and what services would be provided, as well as to calculate how much income an individual or family needed in order to cover basic needs. The federal government would then assume half the cost of providing these payments and services, with no dollar limit placed on the federal contribution. Provinces were, however, responsible for the other half, and they had the power to set welfare income levels—which, by the start of the 1990s, were generally well below the poverty line (National Council of Welfare 1991, 1–2, 3).

As part of an effort to reduce the federal deficit, the CHST instituted a system of block transfer grants from the federal government to the provinces, calculated on a per capita basis, with the funds earmarked for health care, postsecondary education, and social assistance.[1] This new funding formula effectively decreased federal support for the provincial delivery of programs and services in these areas. The result was that, beginning in 1996, total provincial spending per person on social assistance declined yet further, with "Ontario and Alberta leading the way on cuts to welfare rates and tightened eligibility rules" (Bashevkin 2002, 114). By this point, the Canada Mortgage and Housing Corporation (CMHC), which once financed low-cost public housing projects, no longer played a strong direct role in generating a supply of low-cost housing for low-income Canadians.[2]

In 2001, voters in British Columbia elected a Liberal Party government under the leadership of Gordon Campbell, who immediately began

1 Prior to the introduction of the Canada Health and Social Transfer, federal funding for health and postsecondary education had been provided (since 1977) through Established Programs Financing (EPF), which had likewise replaced a system of cost-sharing with block transfer payments to provinces. The CHST thus amalgamated the CAP and EPF programs. In 2004, however, the functions were again reconfigured, with the Canada Social Transfer covering social programs and postsecondary education and the Canada Health Transfer covering health care. For an overview, see "History of Health and Social Transfers," *Department of Finance Canada*, 2014, https://www.fin.gc.ca/fedprov/his-eng.asp.

2 Indeed, for many years, Canada enjoyed the "dubious distinction of being the only Organization for Economic Cooperation and Development (OECD) country without an ongoing national housing program" (Irwin 2004, 7)—a situation that changed only in 2017, when the Trudeau government released its National Housing Strategy (Canada 2017; see also Kading and Walmsley, this volume).

implementing a neoliberal agenda. The economic consequences of cuts to vital programs and services for the province's most vulnerable populations have been particularly harsh. Even though British Columbia is a relatively wealthy province, from 2007 to 2010 it boasted the highest poverty rate of any of the country's ten provinces (Citizens for Public Justice 2012, 5), and the situation has not significantly improved: in 2017, BC stood in second place, with a provincial poverty rate of 13.4 percent as defined by Statistics Canada's low income measure (Klein, Ivanova, and Leyland 2017, 5). From 2002 through 2007, BC also ranked first among the provinces in its level of child poverty (First Call 2010, 4) and, after a brief improvement, was back in first place in 2011, when the rate stood at 18.6 percent, as compared to an average of 13.3 percent for the country as a whole (First Call 2013, 7).[3]

Unsurprisingly, food bank usage has also escalated dramatically. In March 2013, BC food banks assisted 94,002 people, an increase of 27.9 percent over a period of a decade; by 2016, the figure had risen further still, to 103,464 (Food Banks Canada 2013, 24; 2016, 20). To make matters worse, despite the high cost of living in BC, in November 2001 the provincial government froze the minimum hourly wage at $8.00, a freeze that lasted until May 2011. By that time, not only did BC have the lowest minimum wage in the country, but nearly a decade of inflation had dramatically eroded its spending power (see First Call 2010, 8–9). Even after the freeze was lifted and a series of small increases brought the minimum hourly wage up to $10.85 in early 2017, a single person working full time at this wage would earn an annual income of roughly $19,750, "or about $3,500 a year below the poverty line" based on the low income measure (Klein, Ivanova, and Leyland 2017, 6).[4]

---

3 These figures are based on Statistics Canada's before-tax low income cut-offs (LICOs). A low income cut-off is an income threshold, beneath which a family will likely devote a larger share of its income to basic necessities than would an average family. Statistics Canada calculates two sets of LICOs, one based on total income (including government transfers) prior to taxes and the other on after-tax income. In contrast, a low income measure (LIM)—an approach widely used internationally—is defined as 50 percent of the median family income, adjusted for family size, calculated on the basis of annual surveys of family income (Statistics Canada 2009, 7, 11).

4 In fact, as the authors of this report point out, there is no official "poverty line" in Canada. Rather, Statistics Canada uses several different measures of poverty—not only the LICO and the LIM, but also the MBM, or market basket measure. As the authors further note, the LICO has not been rebased since 1992, and while it has been indexed annually for inflation, the actual cost of housing and other basic necessities

British Columbia's smaller cities have thus been forced to respond to provincial policies that emphasize economic growth at the expense of the province's neediest citizens. In what follows, we examine the poverty-reduction strategies employed in two cities in BC's Lower Mainland: Abbotsford, which lies in the Fraser Valley Regional District about 70 kilometres to the southeast of Vancouver, and New Westminster, located in the Greater Vancouver Regional District just 20 kilometres southeast of Vancouver. Despite their proximity, and although the two cities share a number of characteristics, such as rapidly growing populations and a high degree of ethnic diversity, they differ significantly in their approach to social issues, including poverty reduction. Perhaps more than anything, this divergence reflects the sociopolitical character of the two cities, which is itself rooted in their respective histories and community attitudes. In particular, New Westminster's long-standing tradition of progressive politics has enabled that city to implement a living wage policy for civic employees—a proactive measure unprecedented in Canada at the time the policy was adopted. Yet, while both cities have experienced some success in their efforts to alleviate poverty, these efforts have been constrained by a neoliberal fiscal environment that leaves small cities with scant support from higher levels of government.

Close Together and Worlds Apart

New Westminster (originally named Queensborough) was founded in 1859 as the first capital of the newly established Colony of British Columbia, on a site selected by the colony's first lieutenant-governor, Major-General Richard Clement Moody, of the Royal Engineers, who also designed the town plan. The city's early economy was based on forestry and fishing, with numerous lumber mills and canneries located along the Fraser River, but during the twentieth century, the economic base gradually shifted to manufacturing.

---

has been rising faster in many areas than the Consumer Price Index in general. As a result, the LICO is "an increasingly unreliable metric," one that economists at the Canadian Centre for Policy Alternatives no longer use. Moreover, because both the LICO and the LIM calculate poverty rates using the same income thresholds for the entire country, neither can adequately reflect BC's relatively high housing costs. In this respect, the MBM, which is based on the actual cost of a specific "basket" of goods and services in communities of different sizes, is probably the most accurate measure of poverty rates in BC. See Klein, Ivanova, and Leyland (2017, 11–12).

Today, New Westminster has a mixed economy, and although the city retains a large manufacturing base, it, like other municipalities in the region, has witnessed a decline in the industry overall (New Westminster 2008, 9–10). The largest employers in the city are currently the Royal Columbian Hospital, Douglas College, TransLink (Metro Vancouver's public transit provider), and the local school board.[5]

Although New Westminster is transitioning from a working class to a middle class community, the city has a long tradition of grassroots social activism and progressive voting that persists to this day. The high value that residents place on social justice and political activism is reflected in voting patterns in elections at the federal and provincial levels. New Westminster residents have consistently elected candidates from progressive political parties, many of whom have had long records of working for community organizations and advocating for social justice.[6] At city hall, a number of city councillors have worked on developing poverty-reduction strategies during their tenure with city council, in addition to engaging directly in such efforts as part of their professional life. Councillor Jaimie McEvoy, who has served on council since 2008 and has a long history of community involvement, was one of the catalysts for the city's adoption of its Living Wage Policy (McManus 2010). A great deal of poverty-reduction work is also undertaken by voluntary organizations, such as the Olivet Baptist Church, which is home to the New Westminster Food Bank and the Hospitality Project (currently directed by McEvoy), which includes a drop-in centre for children and families. Another prominent nonprofit organization is the Fraserside Community Services Society, which is active in the area of housing initiatives.

---

5 "Business and Economy: Why New West," *City of New Westminster*, 2016, https://www.newwestcity.ca/business-and-economy/economic-development/why-new-west#leading-employers (under "Leading Employers").

6 For example, prior to entering politics, NDP member Peter Julian, one of the two MPs who represent New Westminster (along with neighbouring Burnaby), made his reputation in the community by leading a social action campaign to save St. Mary's, a New Westminster hospital that was eventually closed by the provincial government in spite of a groundswell of public protest. The other federal riding that straddles New Westminster, Port Moody-Coquitlam, is also represented by an NDP MP, Fin Donnelly, who has a background in community work and environmental activism. Provincially, Judy Darcy, the current NDP MLA, has advocated for improvements in child care, public health, programs for the elderly, and education.

Whereas New Westminster is partially defined by its long history of working-class activism, Abbotsford is known for its deep religious roots. In fact, it is regarded as part of the province's "Bible Belt." As in many municipalities, social issues were traditionally viewed as the responsibility primarily of churches and community organizations, rather than local government. Contributions from the faith community in Abbotsford have included the work of Walter Paetkau, founder of Abbotsford Community Services; the varied self-help and employment programs of the Mennonite Central Committee; the sizable supported-housing options created by Communitas Supportive Care Society; and the Cyrus Centre youth emergency housing program. Abbotsford's strong commitment to charitable causes is also borne out by the fact that, as is evident from tax returns, city residents tend to contribute "more to charities, on average, than residents of any other metropolitan area in Canada" (Abbotsford 2006, 3). The same population that supports local responses to poverty and other social issues has, however, voted consistently for candidates at all levels of government who represent conservative parties that support cutting taxes and publicly funded social services.[7]

The Village of Abbotsford was founded in 1891, and the neighbouring districts of Sumas and Matsqui incorporated the following year. The District of Abbotsford was created in 1971, through the amalgamation of the village and the Sumas district, yet the City of Abbotsford, as presently defined, is relatively new: it came to exist only in 1995, when the Matsqui district merged with the District of Abbotsford.[8] Although, historically, Abbotsford's municipal government regarded its mandate as focused primarily on physical infrastructure, the city's involvement in social issues has grown, especially in the wake of the provincial government's Community Charter of 2003 (British Columbia 2003). The charter lays out the principles governing provincial-municipal relations, including the responsibilities and legislative powers of local governments, and Abbotsford has acknowledged that it needs to "plan for and

---

7 At the federal level, Abbotsford's current MP, Conservative Ed Fast, occupies the seat formerly held by far-right icon Randy White. At the provincial level, since the collapse of the conservative Social Credit Party in 1991, Abbotsford MLAs have generally hailed from the BC Liberal Party, a coalition of centre-right forces that effectively replaced Social Credit at a time when the provincial Conservative Party is for all practical purposes defunct.

8 For a detailed account, see "Historic Abbotsford," *City of Abbotsford*, 2017, https://caed.abbotsford.ca/historic-abbotsford/.

respond to issues that impact our social environment" (Abbotsford 2006, v). At the same time, members of Abbotsford's conservative political and religious populations, some of whom sit on city council, exert considerable influence on social planning in this growing city. The municipal government's cautious and conservative nature often runs counter to the more progressive attitudes espoused by the city's extensive network of helping agencies and coalitions such as the Fraser Valley Housing Network, as well as to some of the obligations imposed by the Community Charter. The result has been a vigorous, although sometimes conflicted, social planning experience.

Demographics: Abbotsford and New Westminster Compared

In terms of demographics, Abbotsford and New Westminster, while in some respects similar, exhibit a number of significant differences—differences that have implications for rates of poverty and, to a degree, for the success of measures aimed at alleviating poverty. Tables 10.1 and 10.2 present basic demographic information about the two cities that was collected during the 2016 and 2011 censuses, respectively.[9] This information forms the basis for the observations that follow, which are intended to shed light on the context within which the two cities operate.

---

9 At the time of writing, only some of the data from the 2016 census were available. As a result, Table 10.1 is based on the 2016 census, while Table 10.2 is based on data in the 2011 census. National Household Survey. As is well known, for the purposes of the 2011 census, the federal government, under the leadership of Conservative Stephen Harper, chose to eliminate the mandatory long-form census (LFC), which was replaced by the voluntary National Household Survey (NHS). Although the NHS included questions pertaining to socioeconomic status, critics contend that the data generated by the NHS are weaker than those derived from the LFC. Among other things, at 68.6 percent, the response rate to the NHS was far lower than the response rate of 93.5 percent to the LFC in 2006; response rates were particularly poor among certain segments of the population, including Indigenous communities and low-income earners. Moreover, according to one commentator, when survey data were released to the public in 2013, "information on thousands of smaller communities was withheld because of low response rates" (Ditchburn 2014). In response to such concerns, the Liberal government elected in October 2015 reinstated the LFC for the 2016 census.

Table 10.1 2016 census data for Abbotsford and New Westminster

	Abbotsford	New Westminster
Population	141,397	70,996
Area (km²)	375.5	15.6
Population density (per km²)	376.5	4543.4
Population growth (%) from 2011 to 20116	5.9	7.6
Median age	39.0	41.5
Population aged 14 and under (% of total population)	18.4	12.4
Population aged 65 and over (% of total population)	16.9	15.2
Mother tongue other than English and French (% of total population excluding institutional residents)	32.5	34.7

Source: "Census Profile," Statistics Canada, 2016, for census subdivisions of Abbotsford, British Columbia, and New Westminster, British Columbia, https://www12.statcan.gc.ca/census-recensement/2011/dp-pd/prof/index.cfm?Lang=E..

Table 10.2 2011 National Household Survey data for Abbotsford and New Westminster

	Abbotsford	New Westminster
Demographics		
Visible minority residents (% of total population)	29.6	34.8
Immigrant residents (% of total population)	25.9	33.4
Immigrants arriving between 2006 and 2011	5,425	4,555
Immigrants arriving between 2006 and 2011 (% of total population)	4.1	7.0
Transportation		
Workers using public transit to get to work (% of total labour force)	1.9	28.4
Median commuting duration from home to place of work (in minutes)	15.9	30.2
Workers using private vehicle to get to work, drivers and passengers (% of total labour force)	92.7	63.5

Table 10.2 (cont'd)

	Abbotsford	New Westminster
Education		
Residents aged 25 to 64 with high school diploma or equivalent (%)	30.0	22.8
Residents aged 25 to 64 with postsecondary certificate or diploma below bachelor level (%)	36.8	39.1
Residents aged 25 to 64 with university certificate, diploma, or degree at bachelor level or above (%)	18.2	30.2
Income		
Persons classified as low income in 2010 after tax (% of total population)	14.0	16.9
Median income—persons 15 and over ($)	26,428	31,391
Households spending more than 30% of household income on shelter costs (%)	28.0	34.5

Source: "NHS Profile," Statistics Canada, 2011, for census subdivisions of Abbotsford, British Columbia, and New Westminster, British Columbia, https://www12.statcan.gc.ca/nhs-enm/2011/dp-pd/prof/index.cfm?Lang=E.

Ethnic and Linguistic Diversity

Close to 30 percent of Abbotsford residents belong to visible minority groups. This percentage includes a substantial South Asian community, which, in 2014, accounted for close to a quarter (22.7%) of the population (Abbotsford 2014a, 9). Indeed, the 2006 census revealed that, after metropolitan Toronto and Vancouver, Abbotsford had the highest proportion of visible minorities of any city in the country, the majority of whom (72%) were of South Asian origin (CBC News 2008). New Westminster also has a very heterogeneous population, with nearly 35 percent of its residents coming from visible minority groups. The diverse ethnic makeup of the two cities is reflected by their linguistic pluralism, with approximately one-third of residents of both cities having a mother tongue other than English or French. The immigrant populations of both cities have been steadily increasing, with immigrants adding 7.0 percent to the population of New Westminster between 2006 and 2011 and 4.1 percent to the population of Abbotsford during the same period.

In addition to immigrant groups, both cities are home to Indigenous communities. New Westminster has a fairly diverse population of Indigenous residents, but of particular importance is the Qayqayt First Nation (sometimes called the New Westminster Indian Band)—a nation presently without a land base whose government is headquartered in the city. Abbotsford occupies the traditional unceded territory of two Stó:lō peoples, the Sumas (Sema:th) First Nation, whose Upper Sumas 6 reserve is located in an area of Abbotsford known as Kilgard, and the Matsqui First Nation, whose Sahhacum reserve lies within the city's metropolitan boundaries.

Rural Versus Urban

Despite its growing population, Abbotsford conforms reasonably well to the description of small cities as constituting a cultural "third space," situated as they are "in the shadow of large cosmopolitan cities but still bound by rural history and traditions" (Garrett-Petts 2005, 2). Encompassing an area of about 375 square kilometres, with a population density of 376.5 people per square kilometre, Abbotsford lives up to its self-proclaimed identity as "the City in the Country." In 2016, its population stood at 141,397, making it the province's fifth-largest city. Population projections indicate that rapid urban growth will continue: the city's population is currently projected to increase to 206,000 by 2036.[10] Abbotsford is an agricultural community that boasts the highest gross farm receipts in Canada—an average of $20,441 per hectare, three times more than Ontario's Niagara Regional District (Abbotsford 2011a, 1). In 2011, income from agriculture-related economic activity totalled about $1.8 billion annually, representing about 35 percent of the city's gross domestic product (Abbotsford 2011a, vi).

In contrast to Abbotsford, whose residents are relatively thinly dispersed over several hundred square kilometres, New Westminster is a compact city embedded within a much larger urban conglomeration. With a population in 2016 of 70,996 living in an area of 15.6 square kilometres, the city has a population density of 4,543 residents per square kilometre—twelve times the density of Abbotsford and significantly greater than the density of the

---

10 "Population of Abbotsford 2017," *Canada Population 2017*, 24 January 2017, http://canadapopulation2017.com/population-of-abbotsford-2017.html.

neighbouring cities of Burnaby (2,569) and Coquitlam (1,139).[11] New Westminster's concentrated population means that politicians, residents, and service providers interact on a regular basis and that decision makers are not removed from social problems and local conditions. It is not unusual to encounter political figures, including the mayor, at a local café or restaurant in one of the shopping hubs.

Transportation Issues

In New Westminster, more than one-quarter of the city's labour force relies on public transport to get to work. In part, this is a testament to the world-class public transportation system to which residents, along with other inhabitants of the Greater Vancouver Regional District (GVRD), have access. TransLink, the corporation in charge of Metro Vancouver's regional transportation system, provides New Westminster residents with a comprehensive network of buses. Two SkyTrain lines, encompassing five stations, provide residents with timely access to all services and commercial areas within the city, as well as efficient service to most other cities in the GVRD, such as Coquitlam, Surrey, Burnaby, Richmond, Vancouver, and even North Vancouver (via a sea bus). By SkyTrain, New Westminster is about thirty minutes from downtown Vancouver, while Vancouver International Airport is approximately one hour away. However, for people of limited means, TransLink services are expensive. As of July 1, 2017, during peak hours, the return adult fare for destinations within New Westminster was $5.70, while the return fare for travel to Vancouver was $8.20, about 75 percent of an hour's pay for someone earning minimum wage.

TransLink's transportation projects are supported by the Greater Vancouver Regional Fund, one of three revenue streams generated from the Gas Tax Fund.[12] Because Abbotsford is situated outside the GVRD, it does not benefit from this funding and must therefore choose whether to make the provision of public transport one of its financial priorities. In 2005, Abbotsford's official community plan identified a need for improved transportation choice and efficiency (Abbotsford 2005, 16), as part of its goal to ensure "broad access to community services, social programs, places of worship, high quality health

11 "Census Profiles," *Statistics Canada*, 2016, https://www12.statcan.gc.ca/census-recensement/2016/dp-pd/prof/index.cfm?Lang=E.

12 See "Renewed Gas Tax Agreement," *Union of BC Municipalities*, 2012, http://www.ubcm.ca/EN/main/funding/renewed-gas-tax-agreement.html.

care facilities and public institutions, particularly for people who are economically or socially vulnerable" (3). An agenda for social planning developed by the city in 2006 likewise pointed to transit access as a problem for residents (Abbotsford 2006, 6), specifically people with disabilities (34) and children, youth, and seniors (69, 75). Yet, as of 2009, even though 62 percent of Abbotsford residents were employed within the city limits (Abbotsford 2009, 6), more than 90 percent of the workforce commuted by private car, truck, or van, with only 1.9 percent relying on public transportation to get to work.

An accessible and affordable transit system not only helps to reduce poverty, by enabling low-income residents to access employment and educational opportunities and vital social services, but also enhances the quality of life by facilitating access to activities such as sports, entertainment, and recreation. It is reasonable to assume that, among other things, Abbotsford's lack of efficient and affordable public transportation discourages the pursuit of education and training. Even though Abbotsford is home to a comprehensive regional university, the University of the Fraser Valley, fewer than one in five residents between the ages of twenty-five and sixty-four has an undergraduate certificate, diploma, or degree, as opposed to nearly one in three residents of New Westminster. Unfortunately, Abbotsford's limited public transportation system only exacerbates this situation by making it difficult and time-consuming for some of the city's widely dispersed residents to reach the local university.

Income and Housing

Even though, at the time of the 2011 census, the median income in New Westminster ($31,391) was is approximately 18.8 percent higher than in Abbotsford ($26,428), a larger proportion of New Westminster residents were classified as low-income after taxes—nearly 17 percent, as opposed to 14 percent in Abbotsford. In part, this may be attributable to the significantly higher cost of home ownership and rental in New Westminster as compared to Abbotsford. According to the CMHC, shelter is affordable if its "costs account for less than 30 per cent of before-tax household income."[13] Despite earning higher incomes, over a third (34.5%) of New Westminster residents spend more than 30 percent of their income on housing, in contrast to only 28 percent of

---

13 "About Affordable Housing in Canada," *Canada Mortgage and Housing Corporation*, 2015, http://www.cmhc-schl.gc.ca/en/inpr/afhoce/afhoce_021.cfm.

Abbotsford residents. This situation is not new: both Abbotsford and New Westminster have been facing a shortage of affordable housing since well before the budget cuts of 2002.

Two Small Cities Tackle Poverty Reduction

In Canada (as elsewhere), one of the most visible consequences of neoliberal rule has, of course, been the growth of poverty. In British Columbia, the problem became especially acute in the wake of Gordon Campbell's 2002 provincial budget, which aggravated an already alarming increase in poverty rates, as reflected in the escalating presence of homeless people on city streets. Over the course of the past fifteen years, both Abbotsford and New Westminster have endeavoured to mitigate the impact of poverty, through efforts to increase the supply of low-income housing, for example, and by instituting programs designed to address the needs of vulnerable populations, including those who struggle with mental health issues and/or drug addictions. In addition to pursuing such measures, however, New Westminster has adopted a proactive approach, one that attempts to prevent poverty from happening.

Heading Off Homelessness: New Westminster's Living Wage

The City of New Westminster made its first serious effort to confront the need for affordable housing when it adopted its first housing strategy in 1996. The strategy featured thirty-two recommendations pertaining to rental housing, market housing, low-cost housing, and housing for seniors, as well as to growth management and secondary suites (New Westminster 1996, iv–xii). Over the following decade, the city made some progress towards implementing these recommendations (see CSC 2008, 1). Like many municipalities in BC, however, New Westminster witnessed a steady growth in the number of homeless in the wake of the 2002 budget, from 69 in 2002 to a high of 132 in 2011.

Starting in 2005, the city embarked on a number of initiatives in response to the rise in homelessness, which included the funding of a Homelessness Needs Assessment and Strategy and the creation of a Homelessness Coalition. The city also partnered with BC Housing to develop "28 shelter beds and 84 longer-term transitional and supported housing units," most of which were occupied in 2009 and 2010.[14] By 2011, two emergency shelter units also accommodated children (John Stark, pers. comm., 14 February 2011). In addition, in 2010, the city developed an Affordable Housing Strategy and also set up an Affordable Housing Reserve Fund, which received 30 percent of the revenue from density bonuses. These initiatives were followed by the preparation, in 2011, of a Tenant Displacement Policy, which provided assistance to tenants who were obliged to relocate as the result of redevelopment or rezoning, and, in 2013, of a Secured Market Rental Housing Policy, aimed at both retaining and expanding the supply of rental housing.[15] Evidently, these multiple efforts paid off. In 2014, the City of New Westminster was able to report that it had reduced its total homeless population over three years, from 132 individuals in 2011 to 106 in 2014.[16]

Yet, despite these various efforts, over the three years that followed, the homeless population surged by 25 percent, with the count rising to 133 in 2017. While such an increase is clearly a source of concern, New Westminster Mayor Jonathan Cote noted that it was below the regional average of 30 percent for that period and that the city's unsheltered homeless population had actually decreased by 12 percent since 2014 (McManus 2017b). The city clearly recognizes, however, that it has a long way to go in addressing the needs of the homeless and creating an adequate supply of affordable housing. Its Community Poverty Reduction Strategy, released in 2016, lists a total of seventy actions—ten of them pertaining to housing and shelter—to be implemented over a period of five years. Among other things, the city has resolved to prepare a new Homelessness Strategy, to proceed with the development of two previously designated sites for affordable housing and to explore additional sites, and to investigate the financial feasibility of a rent bank (New Westminster 2016, 18). In October 2017, the city reiterated its commitment to the provision of affordable housing in its community plan (see New Westminster 2017, 95–104).

14 "Report: 2014 Metro Vancouver Homeless Count Results for New Westminster," Beverley Grieve, Director of Development Services, to Mayor and Council, 5 May 2014, https://www.newwestcity.ca/council_minutes/0505_14_CW/11.%20DS%20 2014%20Metro%20Vancouver%20Homeless%20Count.pdf, 3.

15 Ibid., 2.

16 Ibid., 3.

Championed by NDP MLA Judy Darcy, the idea of a rent bank has already come to fruition, thanks in no small measure to donations of loan capital from local credit unions. The program is operated by the Lower Mainland Purpose Society, with the City of New Westminster providing $60,000 over three years to cover administrative costs and with additional funding from the Homelessness Coalition Society (McManus 2017a). As we write, it remains to be seen how successful New Westminster will be in meeting its other commitments—notably to creating housing for people who are homeless or at risk of homelessness and to improving access to affordable housing for low- to moderate-income households (New Westminster 2017, 96). It is nonetheless encouraging that the city is not merely reacting to the housing crisis but is also taking a proactive stance by targeting those at relatively immediate risk of homelessness as well as low-income people who might slip into that category in the future.

Perhaps the most celebrated example of the City of New Westminster's proactive approach to dealing with poverty is its adoption of a Living Wage Policy. While living wage policies had already been implemented in a number of US jurisdictions—such as the state of Maryland and several major cities, including San Francisco, Chicago, and Albuquerque—New Westminster was the first Canadian jurisdiction to implement such a policy. Passed by the city on 26 April 2010 and effective at the start of 2011, New Westminster's policy requires that the city, as well as contractors operating on city property, pay workers a living wage. A living wage policy is the quintessential proactive approach to poverty reduction. The philosophy behind the policy is simple: rather than attempt to lift underpaid workers out of poverty *after the fact*, the approach sets a minimum hourly wage—significantly higher than the regional minimum wage—that is designed to prevent people from falling below the poverty line.

In formulating the policy, the City of New Westminster adopted the definition of a living wage provided in *Working for a Living Wage*, a report released by the Canadian Centre for Policy Alternatives in September 2008:

> The living wage is the hourly rate of pay that enables the wage earners living in a household to:
>
> - Feed, clothe and provide shelter for their family;
> - Promote healthy child development;

- Participate in activities that are an ordinary element of life in the community; and
- Avoid the chronic stress of living in poverty. (Richards et al. 2008, 17)

For the purposes of calculating the wage, the city defines a household as consisting of two parents, both employed full time, and two young children, aged four and seven (New Westminster 2015, 1). The city's living wage level follows the rate set for Metro Vancouver by the Living Wage for Families Campaign, which, as of April 2015, was $20.68 per hour, inclusive of benefits (Ivanova and Klein 2015).

At the time the Living Wage Policy was implemented, predictions were that the impact of the policy would mainly be felt by contractors hired by the city, who had been paying some of their workers less than the living wage. While it was originally assumed that the living wage would also apply to other organizations that operate on city-owned property, in February 2011 the city announced that such organizations would be exempt from the policy (Granger 2011). Ironically, this issue emerged in the context of another progressive city initiative—providing a nonprofit daycare society with a free facility at the city-owned Queensborough Community Centre.[17] Doing so would enable the daycare society to offer parents significantly lower rates, given that the expense of renting space is typically a major component of a daycare's budget. However, as became apparent from the city's announcement, child care workers at Queensborough KIDS (which opened in January 2014) would not be paid the living wage.

The city's clarification of its policy sent an unfortunate message, especially in a city where, as of 2011, 16.9 percent of the population was in a low-income situation after taxes (see table 10.2). Child care workers, who are mostly women, are notoriously underpaid—precisely the type of worker who would benefit most from a living wage policy. Had the city chosen instead to operate the daycare itself, not only would this have ensured that child care workers at the facility were earning a living wage, but it might also have set a precedent that would encourage other daycare operators to follow suit. That said, in

---

17 The City of New Westminster planned to cover the cost of providing this space through the revenue generated by the city's newly instituted Sunday parking fees. Proponents of the daycare initiative had to vie for a share of this new revenue stream along with a number of other interested parties within the city (such as its Engineering Department).

instituting its Living Wage Policy, New Westminster took a pioneering step the effects of which continue to be felt throughout the country.

Mixed Messages: Abbotsford's Housing Initiatives

Although the City of Abbotsford has not implemented a living wage policy, the city has, like New Westminster, taken steps to increase the availability of affordable housing, which the city's Community Planning Division identified in 2006 as one of nine priority areas (Abbotsford 2006, iv). Indeed, the scarcity of affordable housing has posed a major challenge for low-income residents for many years. The city was already facing a critical housing shortage in 2001, when 26 percent of the city's residents were "living in core need" and 2,900 households were estimated to be at risk of homelessness (Abbotsford [2007?], 4). Again, the budget cuts of 2002 only compounded existing problems. In 2004, a one-day homeless count conducted in the Upper Fraser Valley found 226 homeless people in Abbotsford (37 of them youth), while the number of people living in "unaffordable accommodation" and therefore at risk of homelessness was likewise on the rise (Abbotsford 2006, 26).

Abbotsford's Official Community Plan, developed in 2005, represented the city's first major step towards addressing issues of equity, inclusion, and poverty, including the urgent need for affordable housing. Among other things, the plan committed the city to developing "a co-ordinated strategy for increasing housing options for the most vulnerable in the community," which would include the provision of emergency shelters and transition housing (Abbotsford 2005, 33). The city hired a social planner (Abbotsford 2006, 23) and, in 2006, followed through on a recommendation made by its Community Planning Division by creating the Abbotsford Social Development Advisory Committee (ASDAC), which organized an Affordable Housing Working Group (Abbotsford [2007?], 1; see also Abbotsford 2006, 39–42). In the meanwhile, Compassion Park, a small camp for homeless people located in a wooded area adjacent to a subdivision, had come to the attention of local media ("Compassion Park" 2006). Abbotsford Mayor George Ferguson's visited the camp in April 2006 and subsequently expressed a desire to ensure that "no municipality becomes a magnet for transient homeless people" (quoted in "Homeless People on Mayors' Agenda" 2006). The mayor's visit and comments ignited a firestorm of controversy that propelled the issue of homelessness and affordable housing onto the social planning agenda.

In April 2007, in a report to city council, Abbotsford's Community Planning Division brought forward an Affordable Housing Action Plan (AHAP), which included a framework for expanding the city's supply of affordable housing. The action plan outlined in the report consisted of three basic "strategic strands": (1) protecting existing affordable housing stock; (2) encouraging the production of new affordable market housing; and (3) facilitating the production of new affordable nonmarket housing. The report also proposed that the city institute a density bonusing program to generate funds for housing initiatives.[18] Since the mid-1990s, the city had been legalizing secondary suites, with 3,926 formerly illegal suites approved by September 2007.[19] The city also moved to safeguard existing rental properties by implementing a policy that placed strict limitations on the conversion of rental accommodation into strata units when rental availability fell below 2 percent (Abbotsford 2008, 1).

In 2001, the province had ended its regulatory role with respect to supportive recovery homes, and, as a result, unlicensed facilities had proliferated. In 2007, the City of Abbotsford was chosen by the BC Ministry of Health to participate in a pilot registration program, which aimed to reintroduce "some level of accountability and regulation to the supportive recovery house industry." The city subsequently developed a Supportive Recovery House Policy, approved by city council in May 2007, and amended sections of the zoning

18 Report No. DEV 097-2007, "Affordable Housing Action Plan Update," Don Luymes, Manager, Community Planning, to Mayor and Council of the City of Abbotsford, 10 April 2007, https://abbotsford.civicweb.net/filepro/documents/2546?-expanded=8367&preview=8787; see also Abbotsford ([2007?], 2–3); Abbotsford (2011b, 1). Later in the month, the proposals outlined in the report were approved by the city council's Executive Committee. Meeting minutes, Executive Committee, City Council, Abbotsford, 23 April 2007, https://abbotsford.civicweb.net/filepro/documents/19800?preview=8804, item 5.2.3.

19 Report No. ADM 59-2007, "Executive Committee Report: Secondary Suite Enforcement," Grant Acheson, Director, Development Services, and Gordon Ferguson, Manager, Bylaw and Animal Control, https://abbotsford.civicweb.net/document/9090. The legalization of rental suites is a complaints-driven process. When the city receives a complaint about an illegal suite, a bylaw officer is sent to inspect the property. If the suite passes inspection, the owner is offered the opportunity to register it by paying a fee; if it doesn't, the owner is required to remove it.

bylaw accordingly.[20] In September 2008, the City of Abbotsford also signed a memorandum of understanding with the Province of British Columbia, which committed the city to creating one hundred units of social housing. In addition to promising financial support from the province, the agreement outlined procedures for identifying residents at risk of homelessness and selecting nonprofit organizations with which to partner.

Two projects were eventually funded through this arrangement. One of them, the Christine Lamb Residence, which is operated by the Women's Resource Society of the Fraser Valley, provides forty-one units of supportive housing for women and women with children at risk homelessness and/or abuse. The other, the George Schmidt Centre, is a thirty-unit apartment building for men with mental health and/or addictions issues who are at risk of homelessness.[21] The location initially proposed for the facility provoked considerable public hostility, however, and Abbotsford's city council withdrew its support for the site (Baker 2014a). Finally, in 2011, a new location for the centre was found, and the city again partnered with a nonprofit organization, the Kinghaven Peardonville House Society, which agreed to donate land to the city and operate the facility.[22]

In the meanwhile, in 2009, the city embarked on a pilot project, Harmony Flex Housing, in which it partnered instead with a private developer. The project entailed the construction of a cluster of eleven townhouses, each with a two- or three-bedroom main unit and a self-contained secondary rental

---

20 Report No. EDP 298-2010, "Agricultural Land Commission Application at 29183 Fraser Highway," Melissa Pryce, Planner, to Mayor and Council of the City of Abbotsford, 29 November 2010, https://abbotsford.civicweb.net/filepro/documents/12906?preview=20936, 2. A supportive recovery house was defined as a residence that provides "a supportive and structured environment for individuals recovering from drug or alcohol addiction, before they are ready to move into independent housing" (2). See also Report No. DEV 207-2007, "Rezoning Text Amendment to Permit Supportive Recovery Homes," Don Luymes, Manager, Community Planning; Jodi Newnham, Social Planner; and Margaret-Ann Thornton, Senior Planner, to Mayor and Council of the City of Abbotsford, 26 September 2007, https://abbotsford.civicweb.net/filepro/documents/2546?preview=9096.

21 "Affordable Housing," City of Abbotsford, n.d., http://www.abbotsford.ca/community/housing/affordable_housing.htm.

22 "Site Proposed for Transitional Housing for Men in Abbotsford," British Columbia, news release, 8 April 2011, https://news.gov.bc.ca/stories/site-proposed-for-transitional-housing-for-men-in-abbotsford.

suite on the ground floor accessible to seniors or people with disabilities. The townhouses were initially sold at a price 26 percent below their assessed value and only to buyers who could demonstrate a need for affordable housing; if the buyer wished to resell, the new owner had meet to same criteria, and the sale price had to be 20 percent below the assessed value. The inclusion of the rental suite allowed the city to increase its stock of affordable rental housing, while also providing the purchaser with a source of income.[23]

In the fall of 2010, the city established two funds for affordable housing projects, the Affordable Housing Opportunities Reserve Fund and the Affordable Housing Capital Reserve Fund (Abbotsford 2010a, 2010b). The funds—created and sustained by revenue from a combination of sources, including general revenues, property taxes, strata conversion fees, density bonusing, income from the sale of city lands, and donations—have provided support to a number of projects, foremost among them the Extreme Weather Shelter Program and the Elizabeth Fry Firth Residence (a transitional housing facility for women and women with children), as well as to the Lynnhaven Society, which provides furnished rental accommodation for low-income seniors.[24]

In short, between 2005 and 2010, the City of Abbotsford pursued a variety of initiatives in the affordable housing sector. Several subsequent incidents have, however, severely undermined the city's credibility on issues of homelessness. Early in 2009, ASDAC had encouraged the city to enter into a Homeless Encampment on Public Lands Closure Protocol with nonprofit organizations.[25] Although the protocol—which was intended to ensure that the clean-up of homeless camps would be conducted in a respectful manner—was, in theory, adopted, the city neglected to abide by it.[26] On 4 June 2013, in response to complaints from local residents about homeless people in the area, the city dumped chicken manure on a homeless encampment across the

---

23 "Permitting Secondary Suites: Harmony Housing—Abbotsford, British Columbia," *Canada Mortgage and Housing Corporation,* 2017, https://www.cmhc-schl.gc.ca/en/inpr/afhoce/afhoce/afhostcast/afhoid/pore/pesesu/pesesu_006.cfm.

24 "Affordable Housing," *City of Abbotsford,* n.d., http://www.abbotsford.ca/community/housing/affordable_housing.htm.

25 Meeting minutes, Abbotsford Social Development Advisory Committee, 14 January 2009, https://abbotsford.civicweb.net/filepro/documents/19461?preview=10170, item 6.2.

26 Meeting minutes, Abbotsford Social Development Advisory Committee, 12 June 2013, https://abbotsford.civicweb.net/filepro/documents/31331?preview=38155, 1–2.

street from the headquarters of the Salvation Army. Although Abbotsford's city manager claimed that the Salvation Army had "approved" the plan, representatives of the organization indicated otherwise. The action was widely denounced, prompting the mayor to issue a formal apology, and, with the help of a social advocacy lawyer from the Pivot Legal Society, several homeless people planned to file lawsuits concerning the destruction of personal property and violations of human rights (Archer 2013). Among those who condemned the action was the city's own social development advisory committee, with one member of ASDAC calling it "a despicable act"—an act that "belongs in Fascist societies" (quoted in Mills 2013). When asked how such an incident could have occurred in the light of the city's homeless camp closure protocol, Councillor (now Mayor) Henry Braun responded, "My understanding is that this protocol was ignored. I do not know if this was deliberate or if those involved were simply unaware of the protocol" ("Answers from Mayor and Council" 2013).[27]

Only days later, the director of another outreach agency, the 5 and 2 Ministries, reported to ASDAC that, according to residents of Compassion Park, police had destroyed several tents in the encampment and had sprayed several others with bear mace or pepper spray (Bitonti 2013). In the wake of these incidents, the Pivot Legal Society and the BC/Yukon Association of Drug War Survivors filed a lawsuit challenging three city bylaws. The case went to the BC Supreme Court, which, in October 2015, ruled unconstitutional those portions of city bylaws that "prohibit sleeping or being in a park overnight without permits or erecting a temporary shelter" and also denied

---

27 Braun's understanding appears to have been accurate. Two years later, in an examination for discovery conducted on 24 April 2015 in connection with BC/Yukon Association of Drug War Survivors *v.* City of Abbotsford (2014 BCSC 1817), the city manager testified that that the city does not know "what health care or social services are provided to Abbotsford's Homeless after an eviction from a homeless encampment" or "what the meaning of the term 'homeless encampment' is in relation to a city policy document entitled 'Homeless Encampments on Public Lands, Closure, Protocol, Roles and Responsibilities.'" He further indicated that the city does not "maintain a protocol to support homeless people who are evicted from homeless encampments," nor does it "assess the welfare of the occupants of homeless camps in deciding whether to close a camp" or "have any policy established by City Council in relation to homeless encampments." "Opening Statement of the Plaintiff" (New Westminster Registry No. 159480) to the Supreme Court of British Columbia, 6–7, available at http://www.pivotlegal.org/submissions_from_dws_to_the_bc_supreme_court.

the city's request that a temporary injunction banning homeless encampments in Jubilee Park be made permanent.[28] In 2016, the City of Abbotsford duly passed an amended bylaw that permitted homeless people to camp in all but three city parks from 7:00 p.m. until 9:00 a.m. the following day (Abbotsford 2016, sec. 14[b]; see also Baker 2016).

Despite the publicity surrounding these incidents, less than a year later, in February 2014, Abbotsford's mayor and city council voted against rezoning a site in a downtown residential area to make way for a twenty-bed supportive housing unit for homeless men.[29] The project was the work of a local nonprofit organization, Abbotsford Community Services (ACS), which was planning to donate the land in question (valued at a quarter of a million dollars), while BC Housing had committed to providing a capital grant of $2.4 million, as well as annual funding to help cover operating costs. The project had been vigorously opposed by Abbotsford's Downtown Business Association, with the support of the city's Chamber of Commerce, on the grounds that the facility "would return the downtown core to its former derelict state by driving up crime and pushing merchants from the area" (Baker 2014b). Evidently, the association's position was also backed by Mayor Bruce Banman, who cast the deciding vote at the meeting.

Although a follow-up motion, proposing that the city seek funding for a supportive housing facility to be built at a site formerly occupied by a hospital, passed by a vote of 4 to 2, the decision to quash the ACS project constituted a major missed opportunity to take immediate, concrete action to address the needs of homeless men, who represent 60 percent of Abbotsford's homeless population (Fraser Valley Regional District and Mennonite Central Committee, British Columbia 2014, 9). It would be three years before Abbotsford would add to its housing stock for homeless people. On 31 March 2017, Hearthstone Place, a thirty-one unit long-term affordable housing residence operated by ACS, officially opened its doors in downtown Abbotsford to those who are homeless or at risk of becoming homeless. The facility received $5.1 million in capital funding from the provincial government, while the

---

28 Abbotsford (City) *v.* Shantz (2015 BCSC 1909), https://www.canlii.org/en/bc/bcsc/doc/2015/2015bcsc1909/2015bcsc1909.pdf, paras. 6, 5. See also CBC News (2014b, 2015); Omand (2015).

29 Meeting minutes, City Council, Abbotsford, 17 February 2014, https://abbotsford.civicweb.net/filepro/documents/39874?preview=40572, item 4.2.

City of Abbotsford provided the land, worth nearly $600,000, and equity of approximately $350,000.[30]

Orientation to Harm Reduction

In recent years, much has been written about the harm reduction approach to high-risk behaviours, notably habitual drug use, which is designed to minimize the damaging consequences that may accompany those behaviours. While perhaps the most obvious risks pertain to health and personal safety, some of the potential consequences are economic. The high cost of illicit drugs, the transmission of disease, and the loss of a person's employment, housing, and social support network can create considerable economic hardship for the drug user. At the same time, by contributing to increased rates of homelessness, incarceration, and hospitalization, as well as to a loss of economic productivity, drug addiction also represents a cost to society as a whole.

Drawing on models in use in numerous European jurisdictions, in 2001, the City of Vancouver became the first municipality in Canada to embrace harm reduction measures, as part of its Four Pillars approach to the city's drug problems (see MacPherson 2001), and provincial health authorities have generally supported the philosophy (see, for example, BC Ministry of Health 2005). Yet the harm reduction approach has been slow to gain favour in Canada, not the least because of opposition at the federal level. The five-year National Anti-drug Strategy introduced in 2007 by Stephen Harper's Conservative government essentially withdrew support for harm reduction initiatives, and further funding cuts followed in 2012, when the strategy was renewed, despite mounting evidence of the relative ineffectiveness of punitive approaches to drug addiction.[31]

---

30 "Hearthstone Place Now Open: 30 New Supportive Homes in Abbotsford," *Abbotsford Community Services,* 31 March 2017, https://www.abbotsfordcommunityservices.com/news/acs-news/hearthstone-place-now-open-30-new-supportive-homes-abbotsfor.

31 On Harper's policies, see, for example, Nazlee Maghsoudi, "Impeding Access to Healthcare: Harper's Crusade Against Harm Reduction," *The Harper Decade,* 13 October 2015, http://www.theharperdecade.com/blog/2015/10/12/impeding-access-to-healthcare-harpers-crusade-against-harm-reduction. On the failure of punitive approaches, see Valleriani and MacPherson (2015); and Weaver, this volume.

While the City of New Westminster has not formally endorsed a harm reduction approach, neither has it taken a position against it. In fact, according to John Stark, the city offers a number of initiatives that fall within the continuum of harm reduction services. For example, its emergency, transitional, and supportive housing facilities are "minimum barrier" units, in which residents are not prohibited from using illegal drugs on the premises. Furthermore, the city has actively supported harm reduction initiatives offered by community organizations, notably the Lower Mainland Purpose Society, which is based on New Westminster. As part of its wide range of programs (which include the rent bank), the Purpose Society maintains a mobile health van and also offers drop-in services where clients can access a needle exchange and other harm reduction supplies.[32]

In contrast, until January 2014, harm reduction services were not permitted in Abbotsford. In 2005, under the leadership of the mayor, Mary Reeve, the city passed an anti–harm reduction bylaw that banned needle exchanges, supervised injection sites, methadone clinics, and mobile dispensing vans, with Reeve arguing that such services would attract both drugs users from elsewhere and dealers in search of clients. Reeve had the support of Randy White, then Abbotsford's MP, but the bylaw ran counter to the policies adopted by the Fraser Health Authority (FHA) and by other cities belonging to the Lower Mainland Municipal Association (Toth 2010a). Predictably, the city's prohibition of harm reduction measures had direct consequences for the health status of intravenous drug users.

On 19 May 2010, harm reduction advocates held a rally at City Hall. At the time, Abbotsford had the third highest rate of hepatitis C in British Columbia—a province whose hep C rate was already twice the national average (Toth 2010a). Shortly after this widely publicized display of support for harm reduction services, city planning officials, including its social planner, submitted a report to city council recommending that the city reconsider its current policy. The report noted that Abbotsford's approach to harm reduction "is not congruent with FHA harm reduction practices and deflects FHA funding and programming away from Abbotsford that support harm reduction approaches to health care," adding that, in view of the bylaw, "the FHA has not considered

---

32 See "Health Programs," *Purpose Society,* 2017, http://www.purposesociety.org/health-programs/.

funding any expansion of harm reduction services into the Abbotsford area."[33] On 7 June 2010, the city council's Executive Committee considered this report and decided that city staff should undertake a "technical review" of harm reduction, a task that was delegated to ASDAC.[34]

ASDAC proceeded to embark on such a review. In March 2013, after a lengthy process of information gathering and public forums, the city's social planner submitted a report to the Executive Committee, and, in April, the committee directed ASDAC to prepare an amendment to the zoning bylaw.[35] Then, in May, the Pivot Legal Society filed a lawsuit against the city on behalf of three drug users, arguing that the bylaw banning harm reduction services "violates basic human rights" (CBC News 2013). Finally, on 13 January 2014, the city amended the ban on needle exchanges, methadone clinics, and supervised injection sites, paving the way for the Fraser Health Authority to begin implementing its proposed harm-reduction plan (CBC News 2014a).[36]

33 Report No. EDP 147-2010, "Development of a Harm Reduction Policy," Reuben Koole, Social Planner; Carl Johannsen, Manager of Community Planning; and Margaret-Ann Thornton, Director of Planning, to Mayor and Council of the City of Abbotsford, 26 May 2010, https://abbotsford.civicweb.net/filepro/documents/12906?preview=17691. Attached to the report were letters from both the Fraser Health Authority and the Hepatitis C Council of British Columbia asking the city to review the bylaw.

34 Meeting minutes, Executive Committee, City Council, Abbotsford, 7 June 2010, https://abbotsford.civicweb.net/filepro/documents/20059, item 5.1.9, "Development of a Harm Reduction Policy"; meeting minutes, Abbotsford Social Development Advisory Committee, 9 June 2010, https://abbotsford.civicweb.net/filepro/documents/19415?preview=19749, item 3.1.

35 Report No. EDP 36-2013, "Harm Reduction Public Forums Summary," Reuben Koole, Social Planner, to Mayor and Council of the City of Abbotsford, 25 March 2013, https://abbotsford.civicweb.net/filepro/documents/2546?expanded=30608&preview=31343; meeting minutes, Executive Committee, City Council, Abbotsford, 22 April 2013, https://abbotsford.civicweb.net/filepro/documents/30654?preview=31786, item 4.2, "Harm Reduction Public Forums Summary." The amendment to the bylaw was submitted to the Executive Council in November: see Report No. EDP 154-2013, "Harm Reduction Zoning Bylaw Amendment and Related Regulatory Documents," Reuben Koole, Social Planner, to Mayor and Council of the City of Abbotsford, 25 November 2013, https://abbotsford.civicweb.net/document/39488.

36 See also meeting minutes, City Council, Abbotsford, 13 January 2014, https://abbotsford.civicweb.net/filepro/documents/19391?expanded=39874&preview=40173, item 4.11, "Bylaw No. 2268-2013."

Underserved Populations

In New Westminster, a number of population groups fall between the cracks. For example, while a significant supply of nonmarket housing is available for traditionally targeted populations such as families, people with disabilities, and seniors, there is a dearth of such housing for single adults (John Stark, pers. comm., 11 May 2011). Yet single, unattached individuals are highly vulnerable to poverty—much more so than individuals who are part of family units.[37] Also, as we have seen, New Westminster's Living Wage Policy is not enough to protect people who work in child care and other low-paying jobs predominantly occupied by women. Other groups who may lack access to services include immigrants who speak neither English nor French and people whose literacy skills are very limited (Jaimie McEvoy, pers. comm., 10 May 2011). In addition, of all the communities within the GVRD, New Westminster has one of the highest percentages of seniors (those over the age of sixty-five) living alone—a group whose needs often go unmet (John Stark, pers. comm., 11 May 2011).

Although Abbotsford's 2006 social planning agenda likewise identified "seniors' issues" as one of its nine priority areas, two others were "children's issues" and "youth issues" (Abbotsford 2006, iv–v). In response to these concerns, ASDAC created the Abbotsford Child and Youth Friendly Working Group, which subsequently produced *Child and Youth Friendly Abbotsford: Community Strategy* (Honey-Ray and Enns 2009). The city's endorsement of this strategy, in November 2009, created a planning framework within which children's needs were considered in all planning decisions. One significant outcome of the working group's recommendations was the Abbotsford Youth Health Centre, founded through a partnership among ACS, the Abbotsford Division of Family Practice, Impact Youth and Family Substance Use Service, and the BC Ministry of Children and Family Development (Gross 2014, 4).

Yet, despite the attention the city has paid to the needs of youth, homelessness among young people is a source of serious concern. As of 2014, youth between the ages of fifteen and nineteen represented 7 percent of the city's population, yet they constituted 12 percent of its total homeless population

---

37 In 2011, more than one out of four unattached Canadians qualified as low income after taxes—27.2 percent of men and 28.3 percent of women. "Persons in Low Income After Tax (in Percent, 2007–2011)," *Statistics Canada*, 2013, http://www.statcan.gc.ca/tables-tableaux/sum-som/l01/cst01/famil19a-eng.htm.

(Fraser Valley Regional District and Mennonite Central Committee, British Columbia 2014, 8).

Another key priority area identified in 2006 was "diversity and inclusion" (Abbotsford 2006, iv). Although, in its planning, Abbotsford has recognized the ethnic diversity of its population, a number of marginalized groups continue to lack a voice in the city's social planning processes. Gustavo Gutiérrez (1983, 65) contends that no "great leap forward" can occur "until the marginalized and exploited have begun to become the artisans of their own liberation—until their voice makes itself heard directly, without mediations, without interpreters." At least four populations seem generally to be denied the opportunity to participate in civic affairs: immigrant and migrant farm workers, who experience high rates of poverty, an issue that is not addressed in the city's Agricultural Plan; high-risk populations, such as intravenous drug users, whose access to health services was for many years impeded by Abbotsford's anti–harm reduction bylaw; people recently released from penal institutions, who lack adequate access to reintegrative housing; and lesbian, gay, bisexual, transgender, queer (LGBTQ) communities.

In 2006, the City of Abbotsford acknowledged that it had "work to do if it is to be a tolerant and accepting community of all community members" (Abbotsford 2006, 34). Just to take one example, tolerance is not always extended towards LGBTQ people in Abbotsford. In the fall of 2008, in response to complaints from parents, the Abbotsford School District decided to withdraw a provincially sponsored course, Social Justice 12, from the city's secondary schools. Offered as an elective to Grade 12 students, the course, which included modules on sexual orientation and gender discrimination, had been instituted as a pilot program the previous year, in response to a legal challenge (CBC 2009).[38] LGBTQ students responded by attempting to organize, via Facebook, a Pride parade but had to scuttle their plans in the face of online protests from "hundreds" of city residents (Rolfsen 2008). It was only five years later, in May 2013, that the first such

---

38 The implementation of the course was part of the settlement of a legal challenge brought by a gay couple, who argued that the exclusion of gays from Abbotsford school curricula amounted to systemic discrimination. In response to the school board's decision to pull the course, the same couple mounted a second challenge, with the result that the course was reinstituted in the fall of 2009, with the provision that students could enrol in it only with their parents' written permission (CBC 2009).

parade took place in Abbotsford, with more than five hundred people participating (Huffington Post BC 2013).

On the ground, however, community organizations such as the Fraser Valley Youth Society, TransFamily Services BC, and the Positive Living Fraser Valley Society have been active in providing services to LGBTQ communities and promoting their inclusion in social programming. For example, in 2011, Abbotsford Community Services submitted a proposal to the federal government's New Horizons for Seniors Program with the goal of setting up a support group for LGBTQ seniors. The result was Over the Rainbow, a peer-led group, formed in 2012, that met monthly to explore issues surrounding healthy aging for older members of the LGBTQ community.[39] Unfortunately, though, the group failed to gain enough traction to survive.

The city's commitment to LGBTQ equity remains somewhat equivocal. On 13 July 2015, a rainbow flag was raised outside city hall, in response to a request that the city fly the flag for a week to coincide with Fraser Valley Pride Celebration. City council had consented to the request at its 15 June meeting, but, at the same time, it directed staff to draw up a "flag policy." The resulting report, submitted on 3 July, recommended that the city fly only the flag of the United Nations and the flags of other countries or of Abbotsford's sister cities, in honour of visiting dignitaries. At its meeting on 13 July—the same day that the rainbow flag was raised—the council's Executive Committee approved the new flag protocol, thereby ensuring that a first would be a last.[40]

Distinct Community Visions

Since the early 2000s, both New Westminster and Abbotsford have sought to incorporate poverty-related issues into their respective planning agendas. Yet, although separated by a mere twenty-five minutes on the TransCanada

---

39 "Over the Rainbow," *BC211*, 19 June 2014, http://redbookonline.bc211.ca/service/11771093_11771093/over_the_rainbow.

40 Meeting minutes, City Council, Abbotsford, 15 June 2015, https://abbotsford.civicweb.net/filepro/documents/43665, item 8.2; Report No. COR 055-2015, "Draft Council Policy No. 100-3-02 (Flag Protocol)," Bill Flitton, Director, Legislative Services, and George Murray, City Manager, to Mayor and Council of the City of Abbotsford, 3 July 2015, https://abbotsford.civicweb.net/document/45675; meeting minutes, Executive Committee, City Council, Abbotsford, 13 July 2015, https://abbotsford.civicweb.net/filepro/documents/43684?preview=45925.

Highway, the two cities have developed quite different approaches to poverty reduction. New Westminster has tended to adopt a holistic perspective, endeavouring to integrate poverty reduction into various aspects of its planning, and has also recognized the need for proactive measures. In contrast, Abbotsford has been slow to embrace a comprehensive approach to poverty reduction. In 2005, the city signalled its intention to enter the social planning arena by making issues such as "quality of life," "social well-being," and "cultural diversity" a priority in its Official Community Plan (Abbotsford 2005, i). In the years that followed, however, its efforts to address such issues tended to be somewhat haphazard, often undertaken in reaction to competing interests, with the focus falling chiefly on the shortage of affordable housing, notably for seniors and low-income families.

In particular, despite some notable achievements in the area of housing, and despite the city's recognition that "it is less expensive to address homelessness and housing issues through prevention than after the fact" (Abbotsford 2006, 25), Abbotsford has shown itself reluctant to take decisive action to reduce homelessness. Rather, the city initially adopted an antagonistic approach to its most vulnerable residents, using the full weight of the law to swiftly remove their encampments while simultaneously blocking housing initiatives that would reduce the need for such camps. Indeed, in reviewing this history, one senses a tension between representatives of Abbotsford's conservative "Bible Belt" population and more progressive voices within the community—including the city's own social development advisory committee, whose advice city council was prone to ignore. In 2013, the chair of ASDAC commented, "So many things we recommend disappear into a void. We don't know where they go and we don't know why they are ignored" (John Sutherland, quoted in Mills 2013).[41]

Between 2011 and 2014, Abbotsford's homeless population increased by 29 percent, from 117 to 151, the largest increase of any community within

41 In 2014, following the election of Henry Braun as mayor, the newly constituted city council disbanded ASDAC, as part of a structural overhaul intended to streamline council's operations that saw twenty advisory committees reduced to eight (Butler 2014). Affordable housing now falls under the purview of the new Development Advisory Committee, while the Homelessness Action Advisory Committee (also new) assumes responsibility for the welfare of city's homeless population. "Council Committees," City of Abbotsford, 2018, https://www.abbotsford.ca/city_hall/mayor_and_council/city_council_committees.htm.

the Fraser Valley Regional District (Fraser Valley Regional District and Mennonite Central Committee, British Columbia 2014, 5). In March of that year—only a month after putting an end to the ACS proposal for a low-barrier housing facility for homeless men—Abbotsford's city council set up a Task Force on Homelessness, which was mandated to collaborate with community members to develop a coordinated plan of action. Perhaps unsurprisingly, news of the task force's creation was greeted with a measure of skepticism. As Ward Draper, a pastor with 5 and 2 Ministries, commented, "To me, it's just another committee. It doesn't even have the main community service providers represented" (quoted in Sasagawa 2014).

The task force's report, *Homelessness in Abbotsford: Action Plan* (Abbotsford 2014b), appeared seven months later, in October. The plan outlined five strategic directions:

1. Facilitate a Housing First approach, rather than housing only
2. Advocate for housing and wrap-around support
3. Initiate a prevention program
4. Create a culture of awareness, inclusiveness, and respect
5. Foster collaboration between agencies, community, and government.

The plan stipulated a three-year time frame for implementation. Unfortunately, it appears that the initial skepticism was justified. By early 2017, Abbotsford's homeless population stood at 271—a 79.5 percent increase over the 2014 figure of 151 (Fraser Valley Regional District and MCC Community Enterprises 2017, 4).

Like Abbotsford, in the wake of provincial budget cuts, the City of New Westminster witnessed a steady growth in the number of homeless, from 69 in 2002 to 132 in 2011. As noted earlier, between 2011 and 2014, the total number of homeless dropped by 19.7 percent, from 132 to 106. Moreover, better than two-thirds of that population—72 out of 106, or 68 percent—was sheltered, that is, living in homeless shelters, transition housing, or safe houses. Indeed, between 2008 and 2014, the city achieved a 52.8 percent drop in the number of unsheltered homeless, from a high of 72 in 2008 to 34 six years later (Greater Vancouver Regional Steering Committee on Homelessness 2014, 57). While New Westminster has thus made significant progress in addressing the needs of homeless people, the city's director of Development Services warned in 2014 that further gains "could be jeopardized by funding reductions targeting people who are homeless or at risk of being homeless," pointing to the city's failure to renew contracts with the Lookout Emergency Aid Society and the Hospitality Project, which together offer outreach, advocacy, and referral services, as well as with the Senior Services Society, which provides temporary housing services for seniors.[42]

New Westminster's crowning achievement has been the implementation of its Living Wage Policy. A number of organizations in BC, such as the Hospital Employee's Union and the Metro Vancouver Living Wage for Families Campaign, have promoted the living wage as an effective way to reduce poverty among the working poor. While this policy applies only to employees of and contractors to the city and obviously does nothing to address the situation of people who lack paid employment, the city has set a good example for other employers in the city and for other municipalities. Indeed, the city's bold action created a ripple effect. Within a year of New Westminster implementing its Living Wage Policy, the City of Esquimalt followed suit, and, in May 2011, the country's largest credit union, Vancity, announced that it would implement a living wage for its workers (Paley 2011). Numerous other Canadian municipalities, among them Kamloops, Calgary, Saskatoon, and Kingston, are engaged in living wage discussions as well (Cooper and Johnstone 2013).

Living Wage Fraser Valley—a campaign organized by Vibrant Abbotsford, a community action group dedicated to poverty reduction—sets a living wage for the Fraser Valley, which local employers can voluntarily implement.[43] In addition to Vancity, living wage employers in Abbotsford include the Mission Community Skills Centre, the Mount Lehman Credit Union, the Pacific Community Resources Society, and SARA for Women (Hopes 2016; "SARA for Women" 2017). They do not, however, include the City of Abbotsford. In

---

42 "Report: 2014 Metro Vancouver Homeless Count Results for New Westminster," Beverley Grieve, Director of Development Services, to Mayor and Council, 5 May 2014, https://www.newwestcity.ca/council_minutes/0505_14_CW/11.%20DS%20 2014%20Metro%20Vancouver%20Homeless%20Count.pdf, 4.

43 The Fraser Valley living wage is calculated annually. In 2015, it stood at $17.27 an hour, but it dropped in 2016 to $16.28 and again in 2017 to $15.90, a decrease that reflected federal government income transfers from the Canada Child Benefit, which began in July 2016. It rose significantly in 2018, however, to $17.40, largely in response to the soaring price of housing. For further information, see "Resources," *Vibrant Abbotsford*, 2018, http://vibrantabbotsford.ca/resources, as well as the website of the Living Wage for Families Campaign, http://www.livingwageforfamilies.ca/.

June 2017, not long after Vancouver announced its adoption of a living wage policy, Abbotsford city councillor Ross Siemens indicated that, while the issue had been raised at council, the city was not prepared to make a "snap decision" about whether to pay city workers a living wage (quoted in Olsen 2017). While the trend towards combatting poverty through the implementation of living wage policies seems to be gathering momentum, the City of Abbotsford is in no danger of setting an example for others.

Dreaming a Better Future

In recent years, British Columbia has experienced high poverty rates, increasing homelessness, and a demand for basic foodstuffs so great that the province's growing number of food banks can barely keep up. Small cities, such as Abbotsford and New Westminster, have had their resources stretched to the limit in attempting to respond to shortages of affordable housing and the need to provide shelter for the homeless, many of whom struggle with mental health issues and/or addictions, as well as numerous other issues associated with economic deprivation. While many of the services and programs that have emerged in response to these social problems have been well intentioned, they are often piecemeal, disjointed, limited in scope and uneven in application, and contingent on funding partnerships. Clearly, a more comprehensive approach is required, one that addresses the full range of basic human needs over the course of a lifetime, including income security, housing, food security, child care, transportation, education and training, and health care. Such an approach should also incorporate measures aimed at preventing poverty, in part by identifying at-risk individuals and families, many of whom belong to marginalized populations. Such a sweeping program would strike to the heart of the structural inequalities that underlie poverty in this fundamentally wealthy country, but without a shift in political will, it will remain a dream.

Small cities such as New Westminster and Abbotsford have shown a willingness to engage in social issues and have demonstrated resolve and creativity in funding and delivering programs and services, sometimes in partnership with community organizations as well as with federal and provincial agencies. These locally driven strategies are consistent with the Vibrant Communities initiative of the Tamarack Institute, an approach that puts poverty reduction on the agenda of the Canadian public and has the potential to bring about modest reductions in poverty rates.[44] However, the Vibrant Communities initiative ultimately favours adapting to—rather than challenging—the vast structural inequalities in Canada society. In fact, as Dennis Raphael (2011, 419, 422) argues, Vibrant Communities has a tendency "to downplay the importance of influencing public policy at the provincial and federal levels and a reluctance to put forward critical analyses of the economic and social forces that drive policy-making that creates poverty."

The problem remains, however, that the level of stable, secure baseline funding required to dramatically reduce poverty (much less to eliminate it) far outstrips the limited revenue-generating capacity that municipal governments have under the constitution. Addressing this shortfall would require serious commitment on the part of both senior levels of government, especially the federal. While cities are limited to "property tax and parking," and provinces to direct taxation, the federal government has the ability to levy both direct and indirect taxes. Since the federal government has, by far, the greatest powers of revenue generation of the three levels of government, the onus is on it to take the initiative. It could start with an overhaul of the Canada Social Transfer, one that would replace block transfers calculated on a per capita basis for each province with an across-the-board cost-sharing formula designed to ensure that, even in lean economic times, provinces would receive the support they need from Canada's central government. With respect to social assistance, the federal government could require provinces to index income security rates to the living wage in specific municipalities so that those who depend on such assistance are not forced below the poverty line, on the understanding that the federal government would assume a share of the cost. It would also be helpful if the provincial minimum wage could be indexed to the rate of inflation so that its value would not erode over time. As analysts at the Caledon Institute of Social Policy so aptly put it, not indexing benefits is like "closing a door slightly more every year and allowing fewer and fewer people to pass through" (Battle, Torjman, and Mendelson 2016).

Finally, even though, in June 2017, the federal government made a commitment to the creation of 40,000 subsidized child care spaces over the next three years (Scotti 2017), Canadians are still a long way from having access to a free universal child care program, such as is available in many European

---

44 See "Vibrant Communities: Cities Reducing Poverty," *Tamarack Institute,* 2018, http://www.tamarackcommunity.ca/citiesreducingpoverty.

countries. Such programs remove a significant obstacle from the path of caregivers, mostly women, who either wish or need to join the workforce or would like to pursue further education or develop new skills, and the country's failure to implement such a program amounts to a denial of equity.

If the federal government were to enact such reforms, the BC government would no longer have an excuse not to reinstate funding for services and programs that it has been steadily gutting since the early 2000s. It is no surprise that these cuts have correlated with burgeoning food bank use and a dramatic upsurge in provincial poverty rates and in homelessness. Lack of access to efficient and affordable public transportation also plays a role in keeping poverty rates high. The province could recognize that the need for such transportation is not confined to Metro Vancouver and make a significant investment in the province's smaller cities by contributing to the cost of public transportation infrastructure and service. Such investment would help to level the playing field when it comes to poverty reduction.

Municipal governments can contribute to poverty reduction by creating a supportive local atmosphere. They can set a good example by implementing proactive poverty reduction policies, such as a living wage for civic employees, and by rewarding local employers who voluntarily adopt such a policy. Municipalities can also counter punitive approaches to drug addiction by promoting harm reduction measures. In a country that prides itself on its multiculturalism and its reputation as a fair and just society, it is essential that social policies target marginalized and at-risk populations and that local services are inclusive and welcoming to all people regardless of gender, age, colour, culture, religious affiliation (if any), and sexual orientation.

Small cities cannot do all this on their own, however, nor can provinces: Canada's federal government needs to make good on its responsibility for the social and economic well-being of the country's citizens, regardless of the region in which they live. In that regard, there are signs that things may be changing for the better. In 2017, the federal government began consultations with businesses, community organizations, academic experts, and members of the public about the creation of a national poverty reduction strategy. While such a strategy would certainly be a step in the right direction, imagine if the government committed itself to actually eliminating poverty altogether. That is precisely what a private member's bill (Bill C-545) introduced into Parliament in June 2010 sought to do. Titled "An Act to Eliminate Poverty in Canada," the bill would have imposed "on the federal government the obligation to eliminate poverty and promote social inclusion" (Canada 2010, sec. 2). The bill never got beyond its first reading. A similar private member's bill was introduced in October 2013, which likewise foundered.[45] Perhaps the federal government could begin by revisiting such proposed legislation, with a view to passing it into law.

Acknowledgements

The authors would like to thank the planning professionals and community advocates who directed us to key resources and provided the context for poverty reduction issues in Abbotsford and New Westminster, including John Stark, Tristan Johnson, Jaimie McEvoy, Christina Ragneborg, Sue Federspiel, Reuben Koole, Don Luymes, Jodi Newnham, Cherie Enns, Ron van Wyk, Stacey Corriveau, Gail Franklin, Kathy Doerksen, and Barry Shantz. Paul would also like to extend a special thanks to his wife, Lydia, for keeping the rest of the world at bay while he spent copious hours writing and researching, and to Bernadette Jenkinson Le for her expertise on urban planning and her practical assistance with referencing and research questions.

References

Abbotsford. 2005. *Official Community Plan, 2005*. Chilliwack, BC: Fraser Valley Regional District.

———. 2006. *Abbotsford Cares: Agenda for Social Planning in the City of Abbotsford*. Abbotsford, BC: City of Abbotsford, Development Services, Community Planning Division.

———. [2007?]. *Affordable Housing Opportunity Fund Backgrounder*. Abbotsford, BC: City of Abbotsford. http://www.abbotsford.ca/AssetFactory.aspx?did=9426.

———. 2008. *Policy Manual: Strata Conversion*. 18 December. Abbotsford, BC: City of Abbotsford, Economic Development and Planning Services. https://abbotsford.civicweb.net/document/47461.

45 Bill C-545 was introduced by Tony Martin, NDP MP from Sault Ste. Marie, Ontario, and Bill C-233 by Jean Crowder, NPD MP from Nanaimo-Cowichan. BC. See "Private Member's Bill: C-545, An Act to Eliminate Poverty in Canada," *Parliament of Canada*, 2011, http://www.parl.ca/LegisInfo/BillDetails.aspx?Bill=C545&Language=E&Mode=1&Parl=40&Ses=3; and "Bill C-233 (Historical): Poverty Elimination Act," *OpenParliament.ca*, n.d. [2015?], https://openparliament.ca/bills/41-2/C-233/.

———. 2009. *Commuting and Places of Work in the Fraser Valley Regional District*. Regional Snapshot Series: Transportation and Transit. Chilliwack, BC: Fraser Valley Regional District, Regional Planning Division.

———. 2010a. *Policy Manual, No. C003-05: Affordable Housing Opportunities Reserve Fund*. Abbotsford, BC: City of Abbotsford. https://abbotsford.civicweb.net/document/47513.

———. 2010b. *Affordable Housing Capital Reserve Fund Establishment Bylaw, 2010 (Bylaw 1996-2010)*. Abbotsford, BC: City of Abbotsford. https://abbotsford.civicweb.net/document/19837.

———. 2011a. *City of Abbotsford Agriculture Strategy*. Abbotsford, BC: City of Abbotsford.

———. 2011b. *Affordable Housing Strategy*. Abbotsford, BC: City of Abbotsford.

———. 2014a. *City of Abbotsford: 2014 Demographic Profiles*. Abbotsford, BC: City of Abbotsford, Planning and Development Services.

———. 2014b. *Homelessness in Abbotsford: Action Plan*. Abbotsford, BC: City of Abbotsford.

———. 2016. *Consolidated Parks Bylaw, 2016 (Bylaw 2456-2015)*. Abbotsford, BC: City of Abbotsford. https://abbotsford.civicweb.net/document/47737.

"Answers from Mayor and Council." 2013. *Abbotsford Today*, 19 August.

Archer, Mike. 2013. "Salvation Army Was 'in Agreement' with Manure-Dump at Abbotsford Homeless Camp." *Vancouver Sun*, 25 July.

Baker, Rochelle. 2014a. "Abbotsford's Street Fight." *The Tyee*, 31 January. https://thetyee.ca/News/2014/01/31/Abbotsford-Homeless-Crisis/.

———. 2014b. "Abbotsford Quashes Housing Project for Homeless Men." *The Tyee*, 18 February. https://thetyee.ca/News/2014/02/18/ACS-Project-Quashed/.

———. 2016. "Abbotsford City Council Updates Bylaw Allowing Homeless People to Sleep in Parks." *Global News*, 1 February.

Bashevkin, Sylvia. 2002. *Welfare Hot Buttons: Women, Work, and Social Policy Reform*. Toronto: University of Toronto Press.

Battle, Ken, Sherri Torjman, and Michael Mendelson. 2016. "The Canada Child Benefit Needs to Be Fully Indexed to Inflation." *Globe and Mail*, 14 April.

BC Ministry of Health. 2005. *Harm Reduction: A British Columbia Community Guide*. Victoria, BC: Ministry of Health.

Bitonti, Daniel. 2013. "Police-Homeless Tensions on the Rise in Abbotsford." *Globe and Mail*, 18 June.

British Columbia. 2003. Community Charter. SBC 2003, c. 26. http://www.bclaws.ca/Recon/document/ID/freeside/03026_10.

Butler, Alex. 2014. "Changes Coming to Council Meetings, Committees." *Abbotsford News*, 25 December.

Canada. 2010. Bill C-545: "An Act to Eliminate Poverty in Canada." 1st reading, 16 June 2010. 40th Parl., 3rd Sess. Ottawa: Public Works and Government Services Canada. http://www.parl.gc.ca/HousePublications/Publication. aspx?DocId=4633657.

———. 2017. *Canada's National Housing Strategy: A Place to Call Home*. Ottawa: Government of Canada.

CBC News. 2008. "BC Is Nation's Most Ethnically Diverse Province: StatsCan." *CBC News*, 2 April. http://www.cbc.ca/news/canada/british-columbia/b-c-is-nation-s-most-ethnically-diverse-province-statscan-1.759993.

CBC News. 2009. "Abbotsford School Board Permits Controversial Social Justice Elective." *CBC News*, 10 February. http://www.cbc.ca/news/canada/british-columbia/abbotsford-school-board-permits-controversial-social-justice-elective-1.819865.

———. 2013. "Drug Users Sue Abbotsford over Anti–Harm Reduction Bylaw." *CBC News*, 21 May. http://www.cbc.ca/news/canada/british-columbia/drug-users-sue-abbotsford-over-anti-harm-reduction-bylaw-1.1322179.

———. 2014a. "Abbotsford Strikes Down Ban on Harm Reduction Programs." *CBC News*, 14 January. http://www.cbc.ca/news/canada/british-columbia/abbotsford-strikes-down-ban-on-harm-reduction-programs-1.2495991.

———. 2014b. "Abbotsford Homeless Crackdown Goes to B.C. Supreme Court. *CBC News*, 4 July. http://www.cbc.ca/news/canada/british-columbia/abbotsford-homeless-crackdown-goes-to-b-c-supreme-court-1.2695974.

———. 2015. "Abbotsford Homeless Win in B.C. Supreme Court. *CBC News*, 21 October. http://www.cbc.ca/news/canada/british-columbia/abbotsford-homeless-court-ruling-1.3281875.

Citizens for Public Justice. 2012. *Poverty Trends Scorecard: Canada 2012*. Ottawa: Citizens for Public Justice. http://www.cpj.ca/files/docs/poverty-trends-scorecard.pdf.

"'Compassion Park': A Growing Home for Homeless." 2006. *Vancouver Sun*, 10 May.

Cooper, Tom, and Alex Johnstone. 2013. "It Pays to Pay a Living Wage." *The Monitor*, 1 May. Canadian Centre for Policy Alternatives. https://www.policyalternatives.ca/publications/monitor/it-pays-pay-living-wage.

CSC (CitySpaces Consulting). 2008. *Affordable Housing Strategy: Backgrounder 1*. Prepared for the City of New Westminster. http://www.newwestcity.ca/database/rte/AHS%20Backgrounder1.pdf.

Ditchburn, Jennifer. 2014. "StatsCan Asks for Social Insurance Numbers in Test Runs for 2016 Census." *Huffington Post*, 8 July. http://www.huffingtonpost.ca/2014/07/08/statscan-sin-social-insurance-number_n_5568066.html?view=screen.

First Call. 2010. *2010 Child Poverty Report Card*. Vancouver: First Call: BC Child and Youth Advocacy Coalition, with the support of SPARC BC.

———. 2013. *2013 Child Poverty Report Card*. Vancouver: First Call: BC Child and Youth Advocacy Coalition, with the support of SPARC BC.

Food Banks Canada. 2013. *Hunger Count 2013*. Mississauga, ON: Food Banks Canada.

———. 2016. *Hunger Count 2016*. Mississauga, ON: Food Banks Canada.

Fraser Valley Regional District and Mennonite Central Committee, British Columbia. 2014. "Homelessness in the Fraser Valley: The Continuing Challenge." Slide presentation, 13 May.

Fraser Valley Regional District and MCC Community Enterprises. 2017. *Preliminary Findings: 2017 FRVD Homeless Count*. 22 March.

Garrett-Petts, W. F., ed. 2005. *The Small Cities Book: On the Cultural Future of Small Cities*. Vancouver: New Star Books.

Granger, Grant. 2011. "City of New Westminster Interprets Living Wage Policy." *New Westminster News Leader*, 9 February.

Greater Vancouver Regional Steering Committee on Homelessness. 2014. *Results of the 2014 Homeless Count in the Metro Vancouver Region*. Vancouver: RSCH.

Gross, Brian. 2014. *Abbotsford's Youth Health Centre: Background, Operational, Outcome and Budgetary Report (2010–2014)*. Abbotsford, BC: Abbotsford Youth Health Centre Leadership Team.

Gutiérrez, Gustavo. 1983. *The Power of the Poor in History*. Translated by Robert R. Barr. New York: Orbis Books.

"Homeless People on Mayors' Agenda." 2006. *The Province*, 25 April.

Honey-Ray, Lucie, and Cherie Enns. 2009. *Child and Youth Friendly Abbotsford: Community Strategy*. Abbotsford, BC: City of Abbotsford.

Hopes. Vikki. 2016. "New Living Wage Employer." *Abbotsford News*, 26 December.

Huffington Post BC. 2013. "Abbotsford Pride Parade a First for 'Bible Belt' Region." *Huffington Post*, 26 May. http://www.huffingtonpost.ca/2013/05/26/abbotsford-pride-parade_n_3338033.html.

Irwin, John. 2004. *Home Insecurity: The State of Social Housing Funding in BC*. Vancouver: Canadian Centre for Policy Alternatives, BC Office, and Tenants Rights Action Coalition.

Ivanova, Iglika, and Seth Klein. 2015. *Working for a Living Wage: Making Paid Work Meet Basic Family Needs in Metro Vancouver—2015 Update*. Vancouver: Living Wage for Families Campaign, First Call, and Canadian Centre for Policy Alternatives.

Klein, Seth, Iglika Ivanova, and Andrew Leyland. 2017. *Long Overdue: Why BC Needs a Poverty Reduction Plan*. Vancouver: Canadian Centre for Policy Alternatives, BC Office.

MacPherson, Donald. 2001. *A Framework for Action: A Four-Pillar Approach to Drug Problems in Vancouver*. Vancouver: City of Vancouver.

McManus, Theresa. 2010. "Living Wage Draws Kudos from Across the Nation." *The Record* (New Westminster), 1 March.

———. 2017a. "New Westminster Set to Launch Rent Bank Program." *The Record* (New Westminster), 4 April.

———. 2017b. "Homelessness Grows by 25 Per Cent in New West." *The Record* (New Westminster), 12 April.

Mills, Kevin. 2013. "Committee Condemns Manure Incident, Searches for Homeless Solutions." *Abbotsford News*, 12 June.

National Council of Welfare. 1991. *The Canada Assistance Plan: No Time for Cuts*. Ottawa: Minister of Supply and Services. http://publications.gc.ca/collections/collection_2012/cnb-ncw/H68-28-1991-eng.pdf.

New Westminster. 1996. *New Westminster Housing Strategy*. New Westminster, BC: City of New Westminster.

———. 2008. *Livable City Strategy: An Economic Development Plan for New Westminster*. New Westminster, BC: City of New Westminster.

———. 2015. *Living Wage Policy*. Issued January 2011, revised January 2015. New Westminster, BC: City of New Westminster, Human Resources.

———. 2016. *Community Poverty Reduction Strategy*. New Westminster, BC: City of New Westminster.

———. 2017. *Our City 2041: New Westminster Official Community Plan*. New Westminster, BC: City of New Westminster.

Omand, Geordon. 2015. "Homeless in Abbotsford, B.C., Win Right to Camp Outside." *Globe and Mail*, 21 October.

Olsen, Tyler. 2017. "Living Wage on City Radar, But Officials Wary of 'Snap Decision.'" *Abbotsford News*, 28 June.

Paley, Dawn. 2011. "Canada's Largest Credit Union Adopts a Living Wage." *The Tyee*, 2 June. http://thetyee.ca/Blogs/TheHook/Rights-Justice/2011/06/02/VancityLivingWage/.

Raphael, Dennis. 2011. *Poverty in Canada: Implications for Health and Quality of Life*. 2nd ed. Toronto: Canadian Scholar's Press.

Richards, Tim, Marcy Cohen, Seth Klein, and Deborah Littman. 2008. *Working for a Living Wage: Making Paid Work Meet Basic Family Needs in Metro Vancouver*. Vancouver: Canadian Centre for Policy Alternatives, First Call: BC Child and Youth Advocacy Coalition, and the Community Social Planning Council of Greater Victoria.

Rolfsen, Catherine. 2008. "Abbotsford Pride Parade Quashed by Online Protesters." *Vancouver Sun*, 24 November.

"SARA for Women Named Living Wage Employer." 2017. *Abbotsford News*, 16 April.

Sasagawa, Emi. 2014. "Homeless Population Spikes in Abbotsford." *The Tyee,* 13 May. http://thetyee.ca/News/2014/05/13/Abbotsford-Homeless-Spike/.

Scotti, Monique. 2017. "Liberals Announce New Child-Care Agreement, but Who Will It Help?" *Global News,* 12 June. https://globalnews.ca/news/3520212/liberals-announce-new-child-care-agreement-but-who-will-it-help/.

Statistics Canada. 2009. *Low Income Cut-Offs for 2008 and Low Income Measures for 2007.* Ottawa: Minister of Industry. http://www.statcan.gc.ca/pub/75f0002m/75f0002m2009002-eng.pdf.

Toth, Christina. 2010a. "More Harm Than Good: Mobile Needle Truck Could Beat City Bylaw." *Abbotsford Times,* 18 May.

———. 2010b. "Another Look at Harm Reduction." *Abbotsford Times,* 11 June.

Valleriani, Jenna, and Donald MacPherson. 2015. "Why Canada Is No Longer a Leader in Global Drug Policy." *Globe and Mail,* 27 October.

11 Integrated Action and Community Empowerment

Building Relationships of Solidarity in Magog, Québec

Jacques Caillouette

In this chapter, I explore the question of how small cities develop into genuine communities. Drawing on examples from a municipality in Québec, I argue that a greater degree of cohesion among local actors will enhance the capacity of small cities to take charge of their future. In practice, then, a crucial challenge for such cities is to succeed in developing a sense of community that will allow these various actors to engage in collective action. My argument does not assume that small cities inherently constitute communities. On the contrary, as in the case of larger centres, small cities can experience several forms of breakdown. Social fragmentation can undermine cohesive action, as can the marginalization of certain social groups. Similarly, tensions among groups of actors who hold competing interests or visions can discourage the development of collaborative projects. This lack of cohesion is especially apparent in top-down, bureaucratic approaches, founded on a business model, that leave no scope for citizen participation and pay no attention to local communities, thereby undermining their vitality.

For a municipality to become a community, however, more than simply a process of integration is needed: a process of inclusion must occur as well. In many cases, certain groups are marginalized, and these marginalized populations, as well as organizations working in close contact with them, need to be included in the community. In the context of their model of integrated community development, Frank Moulaert and Jacques Nussbaumer (2008, 103, 109) refer to the need to build local relationships of integration through "actions in support" ("actions en faveur") of the active participation of marginalized populations. Aside from efforts to improve government assistance programs, what matters is to move beyond the fragmentation of local spheres of activity caused by the presence of multiple organizations and by management procedures designed with specific sectors in mind. I agree with Jean-Eudes Beuret and Anne Cadoret (2010, 153), who argue, with regard to France, that an urgent need exists for the "defragmentation" of local areas, with the goal of moving beyond a "mosaic-like" approach to management.[1] In short, the challenge is to arrive at an experience of community as a "shared social reality" (Day 2006, 154) constructed through the actions of all those who reside in a given area.

To illustrate my comments, I turn in what follows to the small city of Magog, which is located in the regional county municipality (RCM), of Memphrémagog, one of six RCMs in Québec's administrative region of Estrie. I focus specifically on two examples: first, the cross-sectoral interventions developed by the city and its RCM in response to massive job losses in the community in the early 2000s and, second, the more recent adoption by Memphrémagog's Centre de santé et de services sociaux (CSSS; Centre for Health and Social Services) of an internal policy pertaining to the role of the CSSS in the development of the communities it serves.[2] These illustrations will then enable me to tackle community cohesion as an issue central to the vitality of small cities, both in the province of Québec and elsewhere.

1 Beuret and Cadoret (2010, 153) argue that "the demands of local defragmentation give rise to critically important demands for collaboration among the actors called upon to move beyond a mosaic-like management of the area" (« les besoins de défragmentation du territoire engendrent des besoins de concertation très importants entre des acteurs appelés à dépasser une gestion en mosaïque du territoire »). Here, as elsewhere, translations are my own.

2 These examples, and others like them, are described in greater detail in Caillouette, Garon et al. (2009), Étude de pratiques innovantes en développement des communautés dans les sept Centre de services de santé et de services sociaux de l'Estrie.

Integrated Action in Response to Job Losses in Magog

The RCM of Memphrémagog is located at the western end of the administrative region of Estrie, which encompasses most of the area formerly known as the Eastern Townships. In addition to the city of Magog, the RCM includes the town of Stanstead and eight municipalities, among them Eastman and North Hatley (see figure 11.1). Covering more than 1,300 square kilometres, Memphrémagog is noted for its numerous lakes and mountains. At the time of the 2011 census (when this research was completed), roughly 48,500 people lived in the RCM, more than half of them (25,358) in Magog, a city that serves as the economic, commercial, and industrial hub of the region.

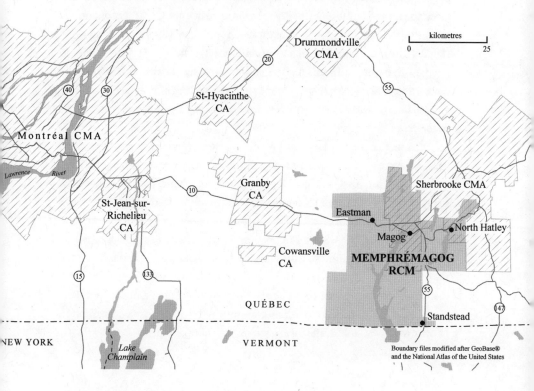

Figure 11.1. The Memphrémagog RCM and environs

Since the early 2000s, Magog's industrial sector has largely been dismantled. In May 2005, the Olymel plant, specializing in the processing of deli meats, announced that it would permanently cease operations by the end of the year, and over the following months the company laid off more than five hundred employees. These layoffs came on top of other job losses, with a total of 1,746 manufacturing jobs vanishing between 2003 and the end of 2005 (Caron 2010). Given Magog's total population of about 23,000 at the time, this meant that a large proportion of its population was affected by the layoffs. Other massive job losses occurred between 2007 and 2009, following the Olymel shutdown, the most noteworthy being the permanent closing of a textiles manufacturer, CS Brooks (500 jobs), GDX Automotive (400 jobs), and the Québecor printing plant (400 jobs) (Caron 2010).

News of the layoffs sent a shock wave throughout the entire Memphréma-gog RCM. The implications were especially grave for the city of Magog, which faced the loss of numerous quality jobs for its residents. Commenting on the magnitude of the situation, a spokesperson from the Memphrémagog CSSS stated: "The loss of more than a thousand jobs in a city of a little over 20,000 people—that's huge. There's a risk that our working class, which is basically our middle class, will fall apart."[3] Spurred by a feeling of urgency, economic and social, the various stakeholders in the region joined forces in response to the crisis.

Even before the Olymel plant officially ceased operations, cross-sectoral links were created, in this case between the employment and social services sectors. The Human Resources Department of the Olymel plant contacted the manager of the Community Services Program at the Memphrémagog CSSS to request that support be provided within the plant prior to its shutdown, thereby affording the CSSS an opportunity to develop an approach based on locating services within the workplace itself. A social worker was assigned to the Olymel plant, articles were produced for the local newspaper dealing with the various problems that could be experienced as a result of job loss, workers were provided with directories of community resources, and information booths were available at mealtimes on all shifts.

---

3 « Plus de 1000 pertes d'emplois pour une ville qui compte à peine plus de 20 000 habitants, c'est énorme. C'est notre classe ouvrière, qui est quand même de la classe moyenne, qui risque de s'effriter. » Quotations, here and throughout this chapter, are drawn from interviews conducted in Magog in late 2005 and early 2006 with members of Memphrémagog's Comité de soutien au milieu.

The Comité de soutien au milieu

Immediately following news of the impending layoffs at Olymel, the mayor of Magog called upon various community stakeholders to establish an economic recovery committee for the region—the Comité de relance économique. Apart from the representative from the Memphrémagog CSSS that was quoted above, most of those mobilized were drawn from the economic sector, including the Centre local d'emploi and the Centre local de développement, as well as Développement économique Québec and the Economic Development Agency of Canada. The roughly twenty members of the committee also included representatives from the school board and the municipal government, as well as a number of elected officials (municipal, provincial, and federal). The committee began by establishing a plan of action that gave priority to the creation of new employment opportunities, to compensate for the jobs lost.

In June, another committee—the Comité de soutien au milieu (Community Support Committee)—was created. This committee, which was coordinated by a community organizer from the Memphrémagog CSSS, set three objectives for itself (CSSSM 2005, 1). The first was to develop an understanding of the psychosocial needs of those who had been laid off in order to identify collaborative strategies that would help these workers cope with the stress of job loss. The willingness to engage in collaborative action was integral to this first objective, and the other two objectives reaffirmed this direction. The committee's second aim was to ensure that all those involved viewed the current situation from a holistic perspective, economic as well as social, and its third was to establish links between partners from the social services sector and those working in other areas, such as the Comité de relance (Recovery Committee) and the subcommittee the Comité d'aide au reclassement (Employment Transition Committee). As these objectives illustrate, in its efforts to provide support for unemployed workers, the Comité de soutien au milieu embraced an integrated vision that was global in nature as opposed to narrowly sectoral.

The makeup of the Comité de soutien au milieu was likewise strongly cross-sectoral. In addition to the mayor of Magog, it included representatives from the Memphrémagog CSSS, the local MP's office, the municipal housing office, the education sector, and several community organizations, including the Corporation de développement communautaire (Community Development Corporation). According to members of the Comité de soutien au milieu, interaction among the various participants was conducive to mutual understanding and to learning how to work collectively from a broad perspective, rather than in isolation. As one member observed:

> As members of this committee, the various participants have an opportunity to talk to each other, to learn about their respective missions and about what they do. They might say: "Ah! So that's what you do. I could refer people to you . . ." And that's extremely important because one of the major challenges in developing partnerships involves knowing what's in place and what all is being done.[4]

Although the Comité de soutien au milieu focused on social needs, it was closely linked to the Comité de relance économique, whose mission was essentially economic. This linkage enabled actors from the social services sector to demonstrate the relevance of their own field of action to economic matters.

As members of the Comité de soutien au milieu, those from the field of social services had the opportunity to demonstrate their knowledge and practical skills and were thus able to enter more effectively into dialogue with those from the economic field, a process that served to validate both their expertise and their way of approaching problems. As one member of the committee, someone, not from CSSS, who represented a coalition of community organizations, put it:

> I am a firm believer in partnership, especially socioeconomic partnerships. If people from the social and economic fields don't come together, no real solution will ever be found. [. . .] I think it's very important that stakeholders from these two fields learn to interact and discover that, in many ways, they are very much alike. [. . .] The very fact that the Comité de soutien au milieu existed meant that discussions didn't just focus on an economic recovery plan; social concerns were addressed as well, and social stakeholders also had a role to play.[5]

---

4 « En étant sur ce comité-là, tous les intervenants, provenant de divers milieux, se parlent et apprennent sur les missions des autres et sur ce qu'ils font. Ils se disent : *Ah oui, tu fais ça. Je pourrais t'envoyer des gens...* Et ça, c'est super important parce qu'un des gros défis, pour bâtir des liens de partenariat, c'est de connaître tout ce qui existe et tout ce qui se fait. »

5 « Moi, je crois énormément au partenariat et à un partenariat au niveau socio-économique. Si les acteurs sociaux et les acteurs économiques ne s'assoient pas ensemble, on ne trouve jamais de véritable solution. [...] Je trouve que c'est bien

These crossovers between the social and economic spheres helped to foster relationships that, in the medium term, were integral to the development of coordinated interventions on the part of multiple actors, that were more holistic in nature and comprehensive in scope.

All in all, the job losses in Magog seem to have driven local agencies and organizations to develop new structures and innovative ways to deal with the crisis. The result was an approach that, through the partnerships it fostered and upon which it also drew, contributed to the consolidation of a community capable of mounting an integrated response.

The *Guide de l'aidant*

One of the initiatives of the Comité de soutien au milieu was to develop a guide for the families and friends of those who had been laid off. Titled *Guide de l'aidant: Comment soutenir une personne qui vit des difficultés reliées à une perte d'emploi* (MRC Memphrémagog 2006; *A Guide for Those Who Care: How to Support Someone Who Is Experiencing Difficulties as a Result of Job Loss*), the guide outlines the basic principles of a helping relationship, as well as offering advice about how to react appropriately and safely to potentially aggressive behaviour. In the description of a Memphrémagog CSSS staff member, the guide "provides basic ideas about how to listen to a distressed person for those who are not members of a helping profession but are rather a neighbour, a brother, or a colleague who used to work on the same assembly line."[6]

The *Guide de l'aidant* well illustrates the power of the process of network construction made possible through the work of the Comité de soutien au milieu. The guide is addressed not to individuals who have lost their job but rather to members of their support networks. In other words, the guide is not aimed directly at people in their role as the beneficiaries or consumers of social services but rather as active players in community affairs. Its

---

important que les acteurs de ces deux secteurs apprennent à se parler et à découvrir que quelque part, ils se ressemblent beaucoup. [...] Le fait qu'il y avait le Comité de soutien, ça a permis qu'on ne parle pas uniquement d'un plan de relance seulement économique, mais qu'on parle aussi de toute l'autre partie sociale, que les acteurs sociaux soient aussi greffés. »

6 « [C'est un guide qui] donne des notions de base quand on écoute quelqu'un qui vit une situation de détresse mais qu'on n'est pas un professionnel de la relation d'aide, alors on est plutôt le voisin, le frère, le collègue qui a travaillé sur la même chaîne de montage. »

fundamental goal is to provide people with the tools they need to engage actively and collaboratively with their fellow citizens and to reinforce and empower the networks that support persons who have lost their job. As a member of the Memphrémagog CSSS staff put it:

> What was innovative about this project is that it allowed us to reach out to all those in the community who were personally affected by the problem—affected not because they had lost their job but because they knew a neighbour or friends who had. In that sense, while the guide helped to enable all community members to support those who had lost their jobs, it also enabled organizations to make a contribution over and above their involvement in the Comité de soutien au milieu.[7]

As a result, the *Guide de l'aidant* allowed community members to transition from the *user* mode, in which an individual is viewed as a client who consumes services, to one of *engagement,* in which individuals become citizens capable of acting together in solidarity. Both through what it proposes and where—people helping people, in the ordinary settings of daily life—the guide aims to strengthen community cohesion and to nurture relationships that will enable these communities to become spaces within which their members can find support and grow. Speaking about the guide's impact, a member of the Memphrémagog CSSS's managerial staff commented:

> I am thinking of my hairdresser, who told me how much she appreciated having such a tool, since she didn't know how to react when people started discussing their problems. Now people are able to make a response. In that sense, it empowers all those many people who want to help others, even if, at times, they're still not quite sure what to do.[8]

---

7 « Ce qu'il y avait d'innovateur avec ce projet, c'est qu'il nous permettait d'aller trouver toutes les personnes dans la communauté qui se sentaient touchées par le problème; pas touchées au sens qu'elles perdaient leur emploi, mais touchées parce qu'elles connaissaient un voisin ou des amis qui avaient perdu leur emploi. Alors dans ce sens-là, autant on a donné plus de pouvoir à tous les citoyens pour aider les gens qui perdaient leur emploi, autant on a donné plus de pouvoir aux organisations pour contribuer, par le Guide, d'une part, mais aussi par leur participation au sein du comité de soutien. »

8 « Je pense à ma coiffeuse qui m'a dit qu'elle était vraiment contente d'avoir un outil comme ça parce qu'elle ne savait pas quoi faire lorsque les gens lui parlaient de leurs difficultés. Là, les gens peuvent donc donner une réponse... Dans ce sens-là, ça donne

All in all, the *Guide de l'aidant*—in the way that it was produced, circulated, and used—encouraged the formation of social bonds. Not only did it contribute to the forging of relationships among actors from various sectors, as well as between residents and the resources locally available to them, but it also created bonds of solidarity among community members themselves.

The *Guide de l'aidant* is but one illustration. The Comité de soutien au milieu designed other interventions as well, which, if space allowed, could likewise be used to demonstrate how certain strategies work to promote integration among the various actors within a community. But let us turn instead to another example, one that reveals how, in a small city such as Magog, a public agency can strengthen local cohesion by revising its mode of operation.

A Policy of Support for Local Self-Direction

Any public agency or institution has the potential to help build the capacity of local communities to assume control over their own affairs. In April 2011, the Memphrémagog CSSS adopted an internal policy (CSSSM 2011) pertaining to its role within the communities it serves, one founded on an emerging perception of itself as an agency rooted in local territory and fundamentally cross-sectoral in nature. In accordance with this policy, in its work within these communities the CSSS presents itself as one among many local actors who interact with one another. In positioning itself in this way, the CSSS seeks to ensure that its actions will contribute to the empowerment of the communities that fall within its jurisdiction.

The approach adopted by the Memphrémagog CSSS rests on what might be described as a "territorial" vision. In Québec, a "regional county municipality" (RCM) is generally home to a number of specific municipalities, each of which in turn contains multiple communities. Moreover, because the term *community* is applied at a variety of territorial scales, a "community" can in fact encompass a great many local communities. This understanding informs the policy developed by the Memphrémagog CSSS, which defines the organization's "territory" as consisting of numerous communities with which it is brought into association in the course of its work. As the policy recognizes, the planning process can occur either at the local level (a municipality or even a

---

du pouvoir à beaucoup de monde qui ont cette volonté-là d'aider d'autre monde, mais qui, parfois, ne sait pas quoi faire. »

specific neighbourhood) or at the supralocal level of the RCM itself. In other words, stakeholders act and interact at various territorial scales. By reframing the populations it serves as its territorial affiliates, the Memphrémagog CSSS positions itself as an agent capable of enhancing the power of those communities to take action on their own behalf.

The policy adopted by the Memphrémagog CSSS identifies three modes of action, one *structural,* one *cross-sectoral,* and one relating to *reinforcement.* In its structural activities, the Memphrémagog CSSS assumes a dynamic role in the life of the territory it serves, seeking to contribute to its overall vitality. This is particularly the case in the area of economic growth, where the CSSS views itself as a partner in the creation of jobs and economic opportunities for local residents and businesses. By developing home-based services, social housing projects, and specialized clinics, for example, the CSSS aims to help "shape the local environment and increase its appeal, while at the same time creating jobs" ("à structurer le milieu de vie et à le rendre plus attrayant tout en créant de nombreux emplois": CSSSM 2011, 3).

In its cross-sectoral activities, the Memphrémagog CSSS works to foster new partnerships among the various stakeholders within its territory. The CSSS seeks to play a proactive role in planning by remaining on the lookout for approaches that contribute to the development of communities as a whole—approaches that involve citizen participation and that "call upon all the sectors of activity within a given milieu (economic, educational, community-based, and so on)" ("interpellent l'ensemble des secteurs d'activités du milieu [économique, éducatif, communautaire, etc.]": CSSSM 2011, 4). In addition, in establishing a network of health and social services within its territory, the CSSS aims for a more local understanding of existing needs, one in keeping with a cross-sectoral orientation and that also provides scope for community participation. Its goal is to forge cross-sectoral partnerships and to remain responsive to the needs of the community members who use its services.

In its reinforcing role, the Memphrémagog CSSS seeks to adopt a non-bureaucratic approach that will serve to strengthen existing community networks. By engaging in actions that more closely resemble the way that people naturally operate within local networks, the CSSS hopes to reinforce the power of these networks. As the policy indicates, in its interactions with families, schools, daycare centres, seniors' residences, medical clinics, community organizations, and the like, the CSSS aims to conduct itself in a more spontaneous manner, a way that allows for "more spontaneous actions (at the very moment when needs become apparent and an intervention is first undertaken), while at the same time working to decrease the cumbersomeness of bureaucratic response mechanisms" (CSSSM 2011, 5: "des actions plus spontanées (au moment où le besoin et la mobilisation se manifestent) tout en diminuant la lourdeur des mécanismes bureaucratiques de liaison/référence"). The goal is to increase the capacity of those whom it serves "to cope with problem situations on their own and take charge of their own direction" (4: "de prise en charge endogène des situations problèmes et du développement"). The CSSS thus seeks to develop supportive interventions that, from both the emotional and the functional perspective, will strengthen the bonds between people and their loved ones, their networks, and the community as a whole.

In adopting this policy, the Memphrémagog CSSS deliberately situates itself as an active member of the local communities in which it is involved. Its aim is not simply to provide services to these communities but to enhance their capacity for autonomous action. By recognizing its embeddedness in the territory within which it operates, this public agency is able to join with other local actors to form a community.

Acting in Concert: The Collective Construction of Community

Graham Day's (2006) conception of "community" can help us grasp the difficulties faced by small cities as they strive to develop into true communities. According to Day, a group of people who reside in the same area do not necessarily constitute a community. A community results when people succeed in coming together despite their diverse backgrounds and differing interests. A community is not a static location or an enduring state of affairs but instead emerges from "the accumulated decision-making processes of many social actors" (2006, 115). A community is thus more aptly understood as an ongoing process—a socially constructed, lived reality the creation of which rests on the ability of its members to join together to engage in concrete actions. This definition of the concept demands that linkages be established among various interests, groups, and civic institutions, with a community developing from a constantly evolving combination of diverse elements. As Day observes, such a definition "resonates better with contemporary concerns to do with cohesion, 'development,' and regeneration, rather than maintenance and preservation of an existing state of affairs" (117). Building on analyses by Zygmunt Bauman (2001), Day points out that "rather than being taken for granted, community becomes increasingly fought over, and subject to choice and intention" (122).

My own analyses of the evolution of communities align with this perspective. In terms of lived experience, a community is much more a matter of social cohesion than an objective reality frozen in time. Moreover, I suggest that, by virtue of their interventions, public service agencies number among the actors who together create the social reality of community. In fact, as we have seen, by viewing themselves as locally embedded, government service agencies can enhance the capacity for collaborative action within a given area.

To complement this dynamic understanding of community, it is useful to link the concept to the notion of "territoriality," in the sense of belonging to a specific place. The term *territory* generally has legal connotations: it refers to an area of land over which a specific group of people claim ownership and thus exercise formal jurisdiction. As a result, *territoriality* tends to connote an attitude of possessiveness, a desire to maintain control over one's territory and prevent the incursion of outsiders. However, the term can be understood more inclusively, as referring to an awareness of place as the locus of common bonds—to "a collectively experienced sense of commitment to a given territory" (Caillouette, Dallaire et al. 2009, 14: "le rapport engagé et collectivement vécu à ce territoire"). If community is a process, then one could argue that territoriality is what makes it possible for people to engage in that process: it is what allows a territory to come alive as a community. Acting to foster the development of true community thus means working to create a space within which people, even in the face of their diversity, feel a shared sense of investment. Through their concrete actions, they are able to forge ties based on a sense of belonging, mutual appreciation, and the spirit of collaboration.

Beuret and Cadoret's understanding of local territories as sites of *concertation* seems to tally quite well with this perspective. As they define the term, *concertation* is "the collective construction of visions, objectives, and common projects with a view to joint action or decision making" (Beuret and Cadoret 2010, 18).[9] Such a process, they argue, requires that synergies be created among three categories of stakeholders: government organizations, local elected officials, and community members who come forward

---

9 « [La concertation désigne un processus de] construction collective de visions, d'objectifs, de projets communs, en vue d'agir ou de décider ensemble. »

with projects. The examples presented above—the integrated response to job losses in Magog and the policy adopted by the Memphrémagog CSSS—both demonstrate how such synergies can serve as the basis for the building of community relationships.

Local Roots and Extraterritorial Resources

Too often, public institutions and agencies regard the people they serve as their "clients," without recognizing that these supposedly passive consumers have a vested interest in the area in which they live. As Denis Bourque and René Lachapelle (2010, 49–50) point out, services are typically delivered in a rigid, top-down manner that leaves little room for community initiative. In contrast, public agencies should work to foster relationships that encourage community participation and a sense of solidarity, as well as an atmosphere of sociability and mutual respect. In fact, the vertical configuration of public services, which relates to the delivery of programs by agencies that target specific sectors, needs to dovetail smoothly with their horizontal configuration, which encompasses community participation and cross-sectoral action founded on a sense of shared territory.

As I see it, by encouraging social participation across a given territory, public agencies, such as Centres de santé et de services sociaux, will in fact be able to carry out their public duties more effectively. Contrary to a fragmented vision, in which problems are viewed in terms of specific populations who are then keyed to specific programs, approaches that are grounded in a sense of shared territory support the coming together of a genuine community. As I and my colleagues argue elsewhere,

> It is a shared sense of territorial identity that enables those involved in specific projects to move beyond their institutional, sectoral, or purely professional identities and to explore the practical realities of partnership. . . . Partnerships allow their members to emerge from their isolation, perhaps even their self-centredness, and acknowledge one another as parts of a ensemble that lies at the heart of the experience of both community and territory. (Caillouette, Garon et al. 2009, 19)[10]

10 « C'est cette participation à une identité territoriale qui permet aux acteurs, dans des projets spécifiques, de sortir de leur identité institutionnelle, sectorielle ou strictement professionnelle et d'expérimenter de réelles pratiques de partenariat. [...] Les

The response to job losses in Magog in the early 2000s and the policy adopted in 2011 by the Memphrémagog CSSS fostered the emergence and consolidation of a true sense of community in the region. In both cases, the strategies that were designed enabled a diverse array of actors to build the practical capacity to work in concert, which facilitated the emergence of collective actions at the local level. As a result, both the city of Magog and the Memphrémagog RCM became more than abstract spaces within which action can occur: they came to constitute spaces within which people joined together to build a community.

Beyond the immediate benefits they bring, collaborative actions make it possible for both specific stakeholders and the public at large to see themselves as involved in a common cause, namely, that of the community to which they belong. This recognition helps to build the foundation for a collective sense of self-confidence, which in turn supports social relationships, the ability to take action, and the creative pursuit of new projects. However, even though these community activities are grounded in the local, it would be a mistake to think of them as a form of withdrawal. While endogenous, local enterprises are necessarily linked to the outside world—that is, to broader systems of action. Denying this relationship to external realities only impedes the capacity of people to innovate at the local level. Rather, it is by turning to these broader sources of support and successfully mobilizing them that local communities are able to expand their capacity for collective action and thus reinforce their internal cohesion.

A neighbourhood, a village, a city, and an RCM are territories that people, with the support of their public agencies and institutions, must claim as their own in order to take action. But if such communities are to fully realize their own capacities, they must embrace broader associations and forms of solidarity. In order to identify effective avenues for action at the local level, for example, an RCM needs to draw on its entire network of connections at the regional level—and, beyond that, at the national level. Indeed, especially in conditions of crisis, a government must mobilize all the means at its disposal to come to the support of local action.

---

partenariats permettent aux acteurs de sortir de leur isolement, voire de leur repli sur eux-mêmes, pour se reconnaître mutuellement comme partie d'un ensemble commun au fondement d'une réalité de communauté et de territoire. »

At the same time, these external sources of support must be prepared to rise to the challenge of working at the local level. Claude Jacquier and Dominique Mansanti (2005) call attention to the issue of competing frames of reference specifically in connection with approaches to community development. "It is particularly difficult," they write, "to build partnerships between stakeholders and professionals who operate within sectoral policy frameworks that are unrelated to one another, even if, in many cases, the purposes of these policies and the populations to which they apply happen to be the same" (22).[11] Partnerships between outside organizations or agencies and local community actors may likewise be complicated by differing frames of reference, which may in part reflect differences in territorial scale.

In emphasizing a sense of rootedness in territory as a key factor in defining one's identity, I do not, of course, mean to suggest that it is the sole dimension of identity, whether for individuals or for organizations, institutions, and public agencies. Rather, territory constitutes but one point of reference among many others, all of them interrelated and sometimes in tension. Organizations and public agencies whose identity rests in part on their territorial affiliation can legitimately reinterpret or find ways to rationalize their sectoral mandate, but they cannot entirely set it aside. It is therefore not a matter of designating territory as the sole anchor of institutional identity but rather of viewing that territory as a significant point of reference relative to belonging, meaning, understanding, and the production of self. Like that of individuals, a public agency's identity derives from various sources and may even shift somewhat depending on the projects undertaken. Yet, in defining their identity, public agencies typically ignore their embeddedness in territory. As a result, they come to function like branches of a service delivery operation, with no ties to the specific dynamics of the communities they serve.

Conclusion

Beginning in the 1980s, public policy in Québec gradually grew more decentralized, with the province recognizing, if at times hesitantly, that citizen

---

11 « Il est particulièrement délicat de construire des collaborations entre des acteurs et des professionnels inscrits dans des champs de politiques sectorielles étrangers les uns aux autres même si, le plus souvent, les objets et les populations dont ils traitent sont les mêmes. »

participation constitutes a driving force for local and regional development. This trend accelerated in the early 2000s, with reforms that reflected a desire to move beyond sectoral approaches and to enhance the capacity of local areas to engage in self-determination. One thinks, for example, of the creation, in 2003, of the Conférences régionales des élus (CRÉs), regional bodies made up of elected representatives who were involved in municipal planning and functioned as liaisons with the provincial government, and of the consolidation (also in 2003) of existing health and social service agencies into local CSSSs, which became the central agents in the provision of health and social services.[12] One thinks as well of Québec's Politique nationale de la ruralité (National Policy for Rural Affairs), which has unfolded in three phases (inaugurated in 2001, 2007, and 2014) and has done much to promote the vitality of local communities. The same pattern could be observed in the education sector, in the field of child care, and among organizations that provide social services and economic aid, all of which demonstrated a willingness to put down roots in local territories. These various reconfigurations of power provided us with a glimpse of the potential for new relationships among local actors, relationships that would enable communities to see themselves as agents able to exercise a measure of control over their own development.

In the wake of the provincial elections of 2014, however, health and social services policies in Québec, including those that bear on local development, have undergone a major change of direction under the influence of the neoliberal discourse of austerity (see Bourque 2017). Reforms enacted by the new government have either abolished or diverted from their original mission numerous elements of the participatory model put in place in Québec over the preceding decades (Klein 2016, 1). These reforms have included the elimination of CRÉs and an overhaul of the structure of Québec's health and social services network that has abolished CSSSs as autonomous entities by merging them with other institutions, particularly the hospitals in their region.[13] In the

---

12 CRÉs were created by Bill 34, Loi sur le Ministère du Développement économique et régional et de la Recherche, and CSSSs by Bill 25, Loi sur les agences de développement de réseaux locaux de services de santé et de services sociaux. Both bills received final assent on 18 December 2003.

13 The elimination of CSSSs was accomplished by the passage, in February 2015, of Bill 10, An Act to Modify the Organization and Governance of the Health and Social Services Network, in Particular by Abolishing the Regional Agencies, which came into effect on 1 April 2015: see http://www.assnat.qc.ca/

area of rural policy, the government has reconfigured its relationship to RCMs by eliminating Rural Pacts, as well as cutting funding to Solidarité rurale du Québec.[14] In short, the Québec government appears to have abandoned its commitment to consultation with civil society organizations and to the co-construction of public policies.

One recognizes, of course, that the shift to local action does not necessarily mean that newly emerging solidarities will result in the inclusion of marginalized populations. Nor does decentralization guarantee more robust state assistance to local communities in trouble. On the contrary, celebrating local capacities for action may mean that communities facing difficulties will be left to fend for themselves. Far from encouraging broader and more inclusive forms of solidarity that promote community cohesion, granting greater authority to the local level could in fact tighten the hold of traditional local elites, thereby serving to weaken inclusive principles of governance. However, while we must be alert to the possible reentrenchment of local powers, such an outcome was not seen in my analysis. As I have tried to show, from both a theoretical and a practical perspective, small cities can enhance their capacity to guide their own development by investing in local spaces as sites of cohesion and collective self-affirmation.

In closing, I would like to come back to the integrated response to the massive job losses suffered by the small city of Magog in the early 2000s. What impact do such collaborative strategies have in the context of a small city? While, in the case of Magog, it would be difficult to argue that the strategy contributed significantly to the creation of new jobs, the work of the Comité de soutien au milieu, with its emphasis on cross-sectoral partnerships, served to consolidate a sense of community solidarity. We can thus infer that such

---

en/travaux-parlementaires/projets-loi/projet-loi-10-41-1.html. On the decision (effective 31 March 2016) to abolish the CRÉs, see « Foire aux questions – Dissolution des conférences régionales des élus (CRÉ) », *Québec, Affaires municipales et Occupation du territoire*, 2018, https://www.mamot.gouv.qc.ca/developpement-territorial/gouvernance-municipale-en-developpement-local-et-regional/pour-plus-de-precisions/foire-aux-questions-dissolution-des-conference s-regionales-des-elus-cre/.

14 Bruno Jean and Bill Reimer, *Québec's Approach to Regional Development: An Historical Analysis*, 23 February 2015 [text of webinar], Rural Policy Learning Commons / Communauté d'apprentissage des politiques rurales, http://billreimer.net/research/files/JeanReimerRPLCWebinarReQuebecPolicy20150223V06.pdf, 13.

integrated approaches, if adopted consistently over time in connection with various issues and projects, will help to build and sustain a local democracy that allows much greater scope for community engagement, while at the same time contributing to the development of administrative models that support projects of the sort that emerge from local collaboration.

In order to build community, a small city needs to foster feelings of belonging and mutual respect among local residents and provide them with opportunities to express their solidarity with other members of the community, thereby empowering them to assume an active role in the economic and social development of the territory in which they live. In other words, the process of community building serves to increase the confidence and sense of cohesion felt by local residents, as well as their capacity for action, both individually and collectively. The forging of concrete links founded on cooperation, both among residents themselves and between residents and locally based agencies and organizations, is fundamental to the development of projects that, in the longer term, will contribute to the creation of a more democratic society, one capable of overcoming the challenges it faces. This, in short, is the most important consequence of the integrated strategy employed in response to the crisis in Magog—the capacity to build, through concrete actions, forms of solidarity that not only liberate the powers of expression, action, cohesion, and creativity that community members already possess but also enable them to exercise those powers in collaboration with those who live and work beside them.

References

Bauman, Zygmunt. 2001. *Community: Seeking Safety in an Insecure World.* Cambridge, UK: Polity Press.

Beuret, Jean-Eudes, and Anne Cadoret. 2010. *Gérer ensemble les territoires : vers une démocratie coopérative.* Paris: Éditions Charles Léopold Mayer.

Bourque, Denis. 2017. "À qui appartient le développement des communautés?" *Le Devoir,* 24 June.

Bourque, Denis, and René Lachapelle. 2010. *L'organisation communautaire en CSSS.* Québec: Presses de l'Université du Québec.

Caron, Richard. 2010. "Mobilisation contre les pertes d'emplois à Magog." Paper presented at the Colloque du Réseau québécois des intervenantes et intervenants en action communautaire (RQIIAC), Ottawa, 3–5 June.

Caillouette, Jacques, Nicole Dallaire, Ginette Boyer, and Suzanne Garon. 2009. "Territorialité, action publique et développement des communautés." *Économie et solidarités* 38 (1) (special issue: *Solidarité, économie sociale et développement local,* edited by Jacques L. Boucher and Pierre-André Tremblay): 8–23. http://www.ciriec.uqam.ca/pdf/numeros_parus_articles/3801/ES-3801-02.pdf.

Caillouette, Jacques, Suzanne Garon, Nicole Dallaire, Ginette Boyer, and Alex Ellyson. 2009. Étude de pratiques innovantes en développement des communautés dans les sept Centre de services de santé et de services sociaux de l'*Estrie : analyse transversale de sept études de cas.* Montréal: Cahier du Centre de recherche sur les innovations sociales (CRISES), no. ET0903. http://crises.uqam.ca/upload/files/publications/etudes-theoriques/ET0903.pdf.

CSSSM (Centre de santé et de services sociaux de Memphrémagog). 2005. *Présentation du comité des partenaires en support au milieu face aux pertes d'emplois annoncées à Magog.*

———. 2011. *Politique concernant le rôle du CSSSM en développement des communautés.* 26 April.

Day, Graham. 2006. *Community and Everyday Life.* London: Routledge.

Jacquier, Claude, and Dominique Mansanti. 2005. *Le développement social local,* vol. 2: *Les acteurs, les outils, les métiers.* Dossiers d'études no. 70. CERAT—Pôle villes et solidarités, Institut d'études politiques de Grenoble.

Klein, Juan-Luis. 2016. "Le territoire dans la construction d'une vision alternative de développement." *Revue vie économique* 8 (1): 1–9.

Moulaert, Frank, and Jacques Nussbaumer. 2008. *La logique sociale du développement territorial.* Québec: Presses de l'Université du Québec.

MRC Memphrémagog. 2006. *Guide de l'aidant : comment soutenir une personne qui vit des difficultés reliées à une perte d'emploi.* Magog, QC: Centre de santé et de services sociaux de Memphrémagog.

12 Small City, Large Town?

Reflections on Neoliberalism in the United Kingdom

Graham Day

As the introduction to this volume points out, deciding what exactly constitutes a "small city" is somewhat problematic. In terms of population, definitions have ranged from as few as 5,000 residents to more than 250,000, with an upper limit sometimes set at 50,000. Some conceptualizations embrace the whole of urban life "beyond the metropolis" (Bell and Jayne 2006), while others seek to anchor small cities more closely to a rural environment. In Britain, the term *city* retains something of its older connotations of relative prestige and social importance; the designation "city" is a badge of social status, for which towns can compete. But there is also a more modern presumption, namely, that, to count as a city, a place must be large and must exert a commanding influence over a much wider area. This chapter aims to position the small city in the British context, to examine the thesis that smallness correlates in some way with positive social outcomes (such as a sense of "community"), and to outline some of the main themes of recent academic and governmental urban discourse. I seek, in particular, to indicate the current "direction of travel" of British towns and cities and to illustrate with examples the wide variety of contemporary urban experiences. I will argue that diversity and division are a reality in British communities, no matter what their scale, and that a major effect of recent policies has been to weaken the power of local government, whilst increasing the complexity and fragmentation of the urban scene, often in the name of "localism" and community empowerment.

Locating the Small City

Officially, there are currently sixty-nine cities in the United Kingdom, of which fifty-one are in England. Until 1888, the title "city" was conferred only on places that possessed a cathedral. This meant that cities could range in size from absurdly small (St. David's, in Wales, which, as of the 2011 census, had fewer than 2,000 residents) to very large. A number of cathedral cities today still have populations of 30,000 or less, among them Bangor, Ely, Ripon, Truro, and Wells. Conversely, some of the largest urban centres in Britain, without cathedrals, were not designated as cities until the ecclesiastical link was broken, after which recognition based on a combination of size and function, as well as effective lobbying, meant that most of the main urban centres qualified for the title. To celebrate the millennium, a competition was held, and three new cities—Brighton and Hove, Inverness, and Wolverhampton— were created from a list of thirty-nine applicants. Three more gained city status for the Queen's Diamond Jubilee in 2012: Chelmsford, Perth, and St. Asaph. However, there is still a group of very large towns, mainly in the old industrial north of England, that have never been granted official city status. Thus, for example, Barnsley, Bolton, Doncaster, Gateshead, Luton, Northampton, Rotherham, Walsall, Wigan, and Warrington are still "towns."

Looked at in terms of scale alone, Britain currently has five urban centres—London, Birmingham, Glasgow, Leeds, and Sheffield—with more than half a million inhabitants, and another forty or so with populations close to or over 200,000 (see figure 12.1). Together, these larger agglomerations account for well over a third of the British population. From a United Kingdom perspective, therefore, most of the best-known urban centres far exceed the scale of the small city. These include the chief cities of Scotland (Edinburgh and Glasgow), Wales (Cardiff and Swansea), and Northern Ireland (Belfast), as well as those of England. An extensive government report, titled *State of the English Cities* (Parkinson et al. 2006), took as its cut-off point a 2001 population exceeding 125,000, and on this basis identified fifty-six English cities, or "primary urban areas." These were defined in physical terms, as consisting of continuous built-up areas, rather than in terms of any local authority or administrative boundaries. A set of associated thematic publications provided detailed analyses of these cities in relation to key aspects of demography, employment, ethnic composition, and social cohesion. The "major cities" examined accounted for 58 percent of the English population

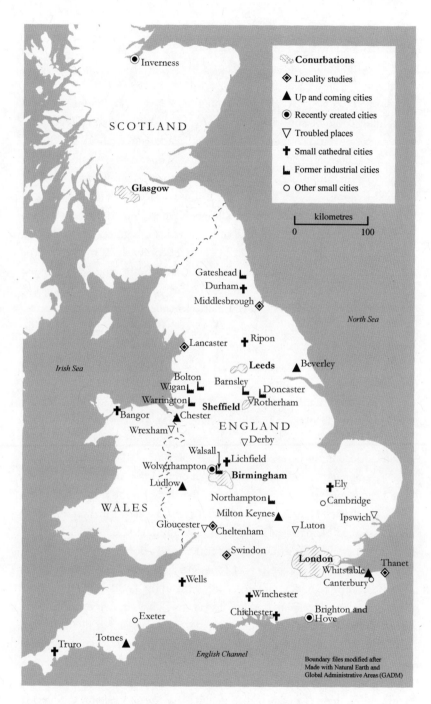

Figure 12.1. Small cities in England, Wales, and Scotland

and 63 percent of its employment. This pattern reflects the early, and thorough, urbanization of Britain, especially England.

According to the *State of the English Cities* report, in the British context, "small cities" could be defined as those with resident populations between 125,000 and 275,000. Urban areas containing between 50,000 and 125,000 inhabitants could be considered "large towns," while those with populations under 50,000 would count as "small towns" (Parkinson et al. 2006, 25). The small cities considered by Canadian colleagues in this volume would therefore equate to a mixture of large and small British towns, all of which would be referred to commonly as "towns." This still leaves a considerable range and variation in their shape and function, however. Apart from the cathedral cities already mentioned, many of which continue to act as significant county and district centres, these towns could be classified variously as market towns, seaside resorts, ex-industrial centres, and administrative and service hubs, which usually have a subregional rather than regional importance. Alongside a mass of fairly indistinguishable commercial, residential, and service centres, these towns would include a number of places that have international significance, like Stratford, Cambridge, and Canterbury. Since Wales, Scotland, and Northern Ireland are notably more rural than England, nearly all large towns and small cities in the United Kingdom are in fact English.

There is some truth in the claim that these towns are relatively underresearched. Sallie Westwood and John Williams (1997, 4) comment that "current theorising about the city tends to celebrate the quixotic and the flux of the urban world, and the diversity of the cityscape. But, as with the earlier theorists, the emphasis . . . has consistently been on the cities of the metropolitan core." The greater part of writing about "the city" and the urban, including most case studies, focuses on the very large centres—above all, London—and the pressing problems of the inner city, multiculturalism, and social divisions and differences (see, for instance, Buck et al. 2002; Pacione 1997; Taylor, Evans, and Fraser 1996). The experience of major urban riots during the summer of 2011 in some of England's largest cities, including London, Birmingham, Manchester, and Liverpool (see Lewis et al. 2011), has strengthened this tendency. Trying to gain a clear impression of what is going on in smaller places is frustrating, given that, even when the processes under examination are very general and widespread in their impact, the detailed data and illustrations almost always refer to big city contexts. In the absence of more precise information, there is a danger that analyses that are accurate for the biggest cities will be applied willy-nilly to other places where they are not wholly appropriate, with a resultant loss of specificity.

The main thrust of strategic attention to urban policy and governance is also directed at the "core" cities, which are regarded as the key drivers of economic and social change. Indeed, there has been something of a recent revival of enthusiasm for big cities and their dynamic influence, in Britain and across Europe (British Chambers of Commerce 2007; Buck et al. 2005; Power, Plöger, and Winkler 2007). According to the *State of the English Cities* report, so far as cities in England are concerned, "the process of urban renaissance, especially in city centres, is well entrenched" (Parkinson et al. 2006, 11). As the report goes on to say, "The years of decline and decay have been overcome. There is now an opportunity to create centres of economic and social progress that will shape the country for a generation" (13).

The UK government has responded to this challenge by promoting a series of "city deals," in which city authorities, working in partnership with other local agencies such as enterprise boards, are given greater decision-making powers and additional funding, in exchange for assuming more responsibility to stimulate economic growth and development in their areas. Between 2010 and 2014, deals were struck in England with the eight largest cities outside of London, known as the Core Cities, followed by the twenty next largest and/ or fastest-growing English cities. By 2016, the strategy had been extended to embrace Glasgow, Aberdeen, and Inverness, in Scotland, and Cardiff, in Wales (Ward 2016). Further impetus towards consolidating the dominance of the big cities is provided by efforts to bring all the great cities of north England together into a so-called "northern powerhouse," a project that merited the creation of a dedicated ministerial post.[1] By comparison, there has been a relative neglect of the part played by smaller urban centres, inspired perhaps by the conviction that they are somehow free of both the excitements and the problems of big city life, as is suggested in the implied contrast between the "flux" and diversity typical of the city and the sameness and calm to be found elsewhere. Big cities are regarded as the leading edge of social, cultural, and political development, whereas "lesser" places must trail along behind, subject to metropolitan influence but rarely themselves sources of leadership

---

1 For more information on the government's Northern Powerhouse vision and the nearly £17 billion investment in "skills, innovation, transport, and culture" to boost local economic growth, see https://northernpowerhouse.gov.uk.

and innovation. The smaller the place, it would seem, the greater the dangers of provincialism and insularity.

This is a sentiment to which many social scientists subscribe, as is apparent in their choice of residential locations and topics of study. Their preference for the intellectual stimulations of the larger conurbations may explain the relative lack of detailed descriptions of life in the smaller towns and suburbs. In Britain, some early examples do exist of attempts to paint a rounded picture of small-town life, such as the repeat study of Banbury (Stacey 1960; Stacey et al. 1975) and research conducted in Glossop (Birch 1959) and in Peterhead (Moore 1982). One argument for focusing on smaller towns was that they represented more "manageable" social spaces, with greater potential for a "knowable community" (Williams 1973, 203), than did larger places, which made it feasible to examine them holistically. It could also be said that smaller places enabled their inhabitants to form a complete impression of local society and to know where they belonged within it in a way not possible in larger, more amorphous social surroundings. Such historically embedded systems of "local social status" (Plowman, Minchinton, and Stacey 1961) enabled places to be imagined as a single, functioning "community."

However, in both the later investigations in Banbury and the study of Peterhead, the conclusion was drawn that it was becoming impossible to sustain this position. Stacey (1975) wrote of the "kaleidoscopic" nature of modern Banbury, while Moore (1982) confessed that he was unable to get a theoretical grip on the complexity of social organization in Peterhead, despite its small size. Those anthropologists and geographers who were keen to maintain the holistic approach retreated to the still smaller scale of the "village" or very small town, with populations of no more than a few thousand (Bell 1994; Cohen 1982; Rapport 1993). Consequently, a gap, or grey area, opened up between knowledge of city life and of the intimacies of the small, usually rural, "community." A wave of "locality" studies (Cooke 1989; Harloe, Pickvance, and Urry 1989; Day and Murdoch 1993) did turn attention again to several of the larger towns (Cheltenham, Lancaster, Middlesbrough, Swindon, and Thanet), but this time with the explicit intention of locating them within a broader explanatory framework, so as to uncover how general economic and social processes of "restructuring" (Lovering 1997) produce local effects in particular places. This meant that these towns tended to be seen as on the receiving end of external pressures and forces. Nevertheless, the research attracted criticism for treating places as "hermetically sealed" and so failing to escape the impression that the world was composed of a series of "static and bounded" units (Charlesworth and Cochrane 1997, 219).

Such an impression is important for the expectation, if not the reality, that the town is different from the city: self-containment, a coherent and readable structure, and at least a relatively "human" scale, could be thought to provide the conditions for a safe, stable, and potentially "idyllic," social milieu. Although there is not such a strong tradition of admiration for the town in Britain as in the United States, such a view does have many supporters, who uphold the model of the town as a peculiarly satisfactory social environment. A 2011 BBC television series (*Town, with Nicholas Crane*) explored the theme that, by virtue of their scale and depths of connection, towns could offer the perfect recipe for living.[2] Arguably, even in the larger cities, many of the worst threats of anonymization, disorder, and social alienation feared by urban theorists are staved off by breaking up the urban mass into smaller, more controllable districts, neighbourhoods, and "urban villages"—rendering them more like a set of adjacent towns than a single gigantic sprawl. To many of its residents, even London resembles an amalgam of distinctive town-sized locations rather than a single entity. People live in and identify with their borough rather than (or as well as) with London as a whole. In some instances, they hardly ever leave the local area (O'Byrne 1997).

A good example of the way in which geographical boundaries fail to match up with social perceptions is the planned "new town" of Milton Keynes, which has been among the fastest growing British towns in recent years and, with a population now standing at over 265,000, is firmly entering the "city" dimension. Its founders were influenced intellectually by North American visions of the city of the future as a car-centred, low-density, postindustrial "non-place urban realm" (Webber 1964), but these ideas were subverted by its residents' desire to envision the place instead as a set of interconnected villages. Although this "bucolically English retreat into a simulacrum of village life" is attributed to a fit of "collective nostalgia" (Charlesworth and Cochrane 1997, 224), it suggests the power exercised over people's imaginations by images of desirable, historically grounded versions

---

2 In the BBC's description of the series, Crane "celebrates the forgotten world of the town, smaller than a city, more intimate, more surprising." (http://www.bbc.co.uk/programmes/b020t88m). For additional discussion, see "Insight into Towns," *OpenLearn*, 2011, http://www.open.edu/openlearn/body-mind/insight-towns.

of urban life, in which a moderate-sized town will provide the best sort of setting for comfortable everyday social interaction. However, it has to be recognized that these symbolic constructions are vulnerable to disconfirmation by empirical reality: towns do not always work as well as expected. In fact, towns are extremely varied, generalization is fraught with danger, and smallness alone will not guarantee order and social harmony.

Differentiating Towns

There is no reason at all to expect all towns to be alike, since they develop under different circumstances and for different reasons and follow their own routes to growth and change. In most cases, they grow up around a specialization in some key activity, usually a particular trade or industry—or a function like a market town, spa, or leisure resort—to which their fortunes then become tied. At the same time, there are economic and social forces so powerful that they leave few places unchanged. A number of key influences have affected the position of British towns, large and small, over recent decades, to which towns have responded in differing ways. Depending on the outcomes of this interplay between external and internal factors, as well as on the balance between the pressures for everywhere to become more alike and the struggle to maintain some distinctiveness, their fortunes have diverged considerably.

A great swathe of former industrial towns have had to struggle with the consequences of deindustrialization. Writing in the early 1990s, one author commented that large parts of Britain contained towns and cities that had lost their purpose: "Built in an ugly age, hewn out of red brick and smoke, such places have little to recommend them beyond their grainy accents and a certain stoical resignation" (Burns 1991, 63). Many, but by no means all, of these ex-industrial centres were in the North and the Midlands, and one consequence of their decline has been the disappearance of "the world of the proud, resolutely *local* Midland or northern English industrial city" (Wilson 1997, 131) that was once the epitome of provincialism. However, a crude north-south division would be overly simplistic, since there are also towns in the south and southwest that have suffered from a similar collapse of a previously dominant kind of work, and with it, their *raison d'être*; the Medway towns in Kent would be a case in point. Wherever there is industrial decline or a sharp change of economic direction, towns can be left high and dry, with all the concomitant problems of unemployment, poverty, poor skills, and lowered motivation. (See Charlesworth [2000] on Rotherham, for a graphic example.) For many, these struggling towns have become unattractive places to live, and they have produced more than their share of social problems. Their persistent malaise has led some to argue that many are now "not only in the wrong place, but are also of the wrong size" (Leunig and Swaffield 2007, 17); since they have outlived their usefulness, their populations should be encouraged or persuaded to decant elsewhere, probably to the larger, more dynamic cities (Webber and Swinney 2010). As well as being highly controversial politically, such a migration would require a reversal of recent population trends whereby people have tended instead to move out of the larger British cities towards more desirable suburbs, the countryside, and, in many cases, the towns. Of course, the towns that attract them are different from those that are decaying socially and economically.

For every "failing" town or small city, there are as many examples of success. Towns of similar size and configuration feature among both the ten best and the ten worst performing British places (Webber and Swinney 2010), and there are some strong performances in places outside of London and the South East. Towns that have managed to diversify their economic base, to attract significant service or financial activity, or to plug into the knowledge economy have done well, and it is these towns that often seem to hold out the greatest contemporary appeal for their quality of life and social desirability. A list of towns notable for their "affordable affluence" drawn up in 2007 by a British bank named, among others, Beverley, Chester, Perth, and Salford—all towns in northern Britain. The list was compiled on the basis of availability of upscale places to eat and drink, museums and galleries, good schools, and prestige car dealerships (Hooper 2007). The connection between these attributes and social class is obvious: these are (or are on the way to being) middle-class or "gentrified" towns. In an era of place marketing, the possession of such prestigious cultural "lifestyle" facilities has become a key consideration in determining how well a town does in comparison to others. Towns compete with one another to sell themselves as safe and prosperous places in which to live, work, and have one's children educated. The most successful are those that manage to discover a distinctive and enviable niche, which gives them a purpose and draws people to them.

It was no accident that the BBC *Towns* series included episodes on both Ludlow and Totnes. Located in the West Midlands county of Shropshire,

Ludlow (population 11,000) has gained a reputation as a centre for high-quality food and eating, built initially around its possession of Michelin-starred restaurants. Material accompanying the BBC series refers to Ludlow as "the loveliest town in England."[3] Totnes (population 9,000) is an environment-friendly "transition town," located in Devon, that is home to alternative middle-class or "new age" lifestyles.[4] Both could be said to generate exceptional levels of social and cultural capital, helping to keep alive the notion that it is still possible to find a twenty-first-century urban idyll. Both, however, are also very small market towns in rural surroundings. A similar case would be Hay-on-Wye, which, through a process of clustering like that undergone in emerging industrial districts, became known as the "town of books" for its multiple bookshops and then its prominent literary festival. By mimicking the entrepreneurialism of some of the larger cities through strong discourses of local success, distinctiveness, and community-mindedness, these towns are currently the kind of places that are probably best able to perpetuate the mythology of the homogeneous, trouble-free, rewarding social environment. They are as attractive to comfortably off, well-educated, mobile professionals as the more salubrious, "posher" city districts. Many, however, would consider them to be little more than country villages, whose contribution to overall national well-being is strictly limited. It may be that smallness is crucial here in facilitating a single-mindedness of purpose that would be hard to achieve elsewhere without intervention by a very determined and powerful central authority.

Obviously, extreme caution should be exercised before accepting these versions of small town life at anything like face value. In an ethnographic

---

3 Graham Nielson, "Ludlow: The Loveliest Town in England?" *OpenLearn,* 2011, http://www.open.edu/openlearn/society/politics-policy-people/sociology/ ludlow-the-loveliest-town-england?in_menu=19028. Nielson is quoting John Betjeman, who wrote in 1943 that Ludlow "is probably the loveliest town in England, with its hill of Georgian houses ascending from the river Terne to the great tower of the cross-shaped church" (*English Cities and Small Towns* [London: William Collins, 1943], 24).

4 The transition town movement seeks to develop more self-sufficient and low-carbon ways of living, to combat the threats posed by climate change and fossil-fuel consumption. See, for example, the website of Transition Town Totnes, https://www. transitiontowntotnes.org/, a community-based organization that seeks to "strengthen the local economy, reduce our environmental impact, and build our resilience for a future with less cheap energy and a changing climate."

account of his hometown, Todmorden (population 16,000), Steve Hanson (2014) describes some of the local practices that not only make the town distinctive but also capture considerable media attention. In his description of the community's food-growing scheme, known as "Incredible Edible Todmorden," Hanson notes how these activities create the sense that the town "is constructed and reconstructed by benign, holistic localists" (44), obscuring the extent to which life there is just as open to contemporary flows of migration, capital, and technology as it is in larger places. Ideas of friendliness, intimacy, and community are mobilized on behalf of what he terms "deracinated localism." Hanson excoriates the degree to which "small towns have been understood in the past as discretely bounded, framed by methodological nationalism, viewed through the lenses of a provincialism which has produced much that is negative in sociology as a whole, not just community research" (24).

Trouble in Eden?

From time to time, dramatic events remind people that smaller and less well-known towns and cities are not at all immune from the problems and crises of larger urban centres: serial killings of young women in Gloucester (1992) and prostitutes in Ipswich (2006), grooming and sexual exploitation of young people in Derby (2011), Rochdale (2012), and Oxford (2013), racial and ethnic violence in Burnley (2001) and Wrexham (2003), even acts of terror with origins traceable to Oldham (2012) or Luton (2005). Like instances of gun crime in the very small towns of Hungerford (1987) and Dunblane (1996), such events frequently evoke a shocked response: these are not places where such things should happen. But this reaction merely shows an ignorance of the darker side of communities. There is ample evidence that nowhere is "ordinary" enough to be immune from social division, deprivation, violence, and abuse.

The presumption that smaller places may function better as communities relies heavily on deductions made from their assumed homogeneity: "smallness" is supposed to signify an absence of splits along the key socially divisive lines of class, ethnicity, and religious affiliation. If towns are assumed to be undifferentiated spaces, then their populations may be thought not to vary starkly enough, or in sufficiently large numbers, to create strong lines of demarcation. However, as Norbert Elias and John Scotson (1965) showed so brilliantly, localized differences and local social constructions of difference, like small-scale divisions between neighbourhoods and estates, mean that even towns and villages are far from impervious to social cleavage, including the extraordinarily fierce antagonisms that can be generated by what Freud (1930) termed "the narcissism of small differences." Furthermore (and as preceding chapters have shown so clearly), small numbers and social rarity can make people vulnerable to being marginalized and ostracized as "deviant" cases, with their behaviour scrutinized more closely than it might be in a more anonymous setting. When probed by ethnographic research, the denial of difference and division is invariably revealed to have more to do with subjective frameworks of "community in the mind" than any objective reality. Moreover, there is good reason to believe that under the pressures of contemporary change, towns have not only been compelled to distinguish themselves as much as possible from one another; they have also been pulled apart internally.

Urban Policy: Modernization and Regeneration, Inclusion and Exclusion

For the past thirty years, British politics has been dominated by neoliberal thinking (Hall 2011). Despite changes of government and ruling party, the underlying tenets have remained consistent throughout the period: the primacy of the market, the gradual narrowing and/or withdrawal of state intervention, and its replacement by a mixture of private enterprise, voluntary action, and individual self-provision, often in the form of local "partnerships." Theodore, Peck, and Brenner (2011, 15) summarize the goal to which neoliberals aspire as "open, competitive and unregulated markets, liberated from state intervention and the actions of social collectivities." The implementation of this philosophy has had profound spatial effects, with consequences for the social geography of Britain, including the organization of towns, their interconnections, and internal structures. Some of the early effects were explored in the "localities" research referred to previously (see also Pacione 1997), which dealt with the urban repercussions of deindustrialization and deregulation of labour markets.

Subsequently, the central concern of urban policy has been "regeneration," primarily or exclusively understood as an economic matter. This has involved the remaking of urban spaces to accommodate new industries, centres of consumption, and upscale residential properties. Success is measured by the development of business parks, shopping centres, and office blocks. Towns have been encouraged to become more competitive with one another, including as recipients of public funding. In 1994, twenty urban initiatives were rolled up into a Single Regeneration Budget (SRB), for which local authorities had to bid. After 1997, the "New Labour" government of Tony Blair continued in the direction of reducing the role of the public sector and enhancing that of private enterprise. The powers and resources of local authority were curtailed, and "many local services were privatised or opened up to competitive tendering" (Parkinson et al. 2006, 15). A number of new quangos (quasi-autonomous nongovernment organizations), such as Development Corporations and Regional Development Agencies, assumed responsibility for strategic planning and delivery, weakening the role of local government and diluting its democratic accountability. Usually, these bodies were headed by business and commercial interests, especially property developers, who have been active wherever possible in clearing out "redundant" urban facilities and replacing them with new, more economically "vibrant" activities.

Concentration on economic revitalization and "modernization" of the urban fabric and governance often came at the expense of widening social division. In particular, there was growing evidence of significant spatial concentrations of deprivation, social isolation, and exclusion. Areas and neighbourhoods left out of the regeneration process were likely to suffer from poor and deteriorating physical environments and associated social stigmatization. Although these problems were more visible in the big cities (Lovering 1997, 66), they were also reflected elsewhere: growing inequality and polarization were general features of British society. Indeed, the team documenting the condition of English cities in the mid-2000s noted that, while overall levels of deprivation and concentrations of poverty were greatest in the largest cities, cities were not necessarily more polarized than the rest of the country because they also had fewer areas that were especially prosperous. In fact, on the basis of comparisons of the incidence of the most and least deprived 10 percent of neighbourhoods, it was apparent that deprivation was almost as marked in the towns of the north and west and was an equally prominent feature of some southern towns (Turok et al. 2006, 9–11).

In 1997, the incoming prime minister, Tony Blair, referred to the growth in Britain of "an underclass of people cut off from society's mainstream" (quoted in Buck et al. 2002, 7). This was an acknowledgement that the distance between different social groupings within the society was expanding, a development to which the changes taking place in urban space had made a significant contribution. Gordon Hughes (2007, 180–83) describes how patterns of social inclusion and exclusion had been rearranged as urban regeneration and development projects produced outcomes of simultaneous "gentrification" and "ghettoisation." Certain groups were being denied access to particular areas and facilities, leading to struggles over the control of public and private spaces. The divisions that resulted were heavily inscribed by class, race, and ethnicity but also reflected distinctions of age, generation, gender, and sexual orientation. It was the vulnerable and marginal who were being penalized—those who were homeless, poor, very elderly or very young, or in any way considered to be socially disruptive and out of step with the main currents of behaviour and lifestyle.

These processes of separation and exclusion, thoroughly documented for the metropolitan centres, had their counterparts in the smaller places. One example that has attracted much comment is the decline of the urban "high street." The development of out-of-town shopping centres in almost every place of any size has brought about a desertion of the traditional retail and commercial streets that were once the main focus of everyday urban activity. A typical account describes how the nation's high streets are "being taken over by identikit chain stores and supermarkets. Guilty of destroying the identity of our towns, this cloning of our town centres also increases their vulnerability to economic shocks" (NEF 2010, 6). Economic recession and austerity since the financial crash of 2008 has indeed aggravated the situation, with large numbers of closures of independent stores and retrenchment by some of the larger chains, leaving gaping holes in many high streets and emptying the town centres. Increasingly, these areas are used, by day, mainly by the urban poor and the relatively immobile (older people, young mothers) engaged in low-price and "charity" (thrift) shopping. By night, they are occupied predominantly by the younger generation, whose behaviour, fuelled by alcohol, often intimidates others into staying at home. Fear of crime and antisocial behaviour results in widespread avoidance of town centres after dark.

According to the 2010 New Economics Foundation "clone town" report, despite their other attractions as university towns, Cambridge and Exeter were found to be among the places with the least diverse, blandest retail offerings. The greatest variety of independent stores was found in Whitstable, a town of 30,000, whose residents were said to be joining together to ensure that any future development "celebrates local distinctiveness, and supports the development of a local culture that is sustainable" (NEF 2010, 3). Other towns are doing likewise, especially by battling against the continuing encroachment of the giant supermarket chains (Harris 2011). In Britain, four supermarket groups dominate the retail grocery market, together commanding roughly a 70 percent share of sales.[5] The town of Crediton, not far from Exeter and hailed as enabling "a near-idyllic lifestyle" featuring "good community spirit, glorious Devon countryside and great shopping" (NEF 2010, 21), saw the opening in 2009 of a new Tesco superstore, covering 5,500 square metres of land just outside the town—the eighth supermarket to appear within a fifteen-mile radius. In more populous regions, the construction of giant shopping malls located close to the main population concentrations has sucked much of the spending power out of vast numbers of towns around them. These consumer "paradises" are patrolled by private security guards and are easily accessible only by car; they are targeted primarily at families and young people with ample disposable income. Meanwhile, struggling local economies are forced back towards reliance upon the money spent by "failed consumers" and the welfare dependent (Hughes 2007, 182), together with those excluded on other grounds from sharing in the new retail opportunities. As has frequently been noted, for example, young black men attract especially close attention from security staff.

The physical separation of different types of urban spaces does much to exert control over people's behaviour, but it is supplemented by other more direct measures. By 1994, it was said that 95 percent of local councils were considering installing CCTV schemes, and Britain already had more such systems in operation than any other nation. Much of the actual surveillance was carried out by private for-profit organizations, bringing a whole new set of enforcement agents into operation alongside the police (Gerrard and Thompson 2011; Lewis 2011). This brought "the spectre of social control and growing segregation to previously-public spaces where people used to mix more or less freely" (Graham, Brooks, and Heery 1995, 17). It exposed to sanction those who were felt not to "belong" or whose behaviour was frowned upon; in King's Lynn, for instance, CCTV was employed to monitor offences like drunkenness, evading parking meters, littering, and underage smoking

---

5 "Market Share of Grocery Stores in Great Britain from January 2015 to March 2017," *Statista: The Statistics Portal,* 2017, https://www.statista.com/statistics/280208/grocery-market-share-in-the-united-kingdom-uk/.

(18). Following the 1998 Crime and Disorder Act, reinforced in 2003 with the Anti-social Behaviour Act, offending individuals could be subjected to "antisocial behaviour orders" (ASBOs), and places could also be restricted by blanket bans on groups congregating together or on actions such as consuming alcohol. There were also experiments with imposing curfews on repeat offenders and teenagers. The first place to attempt to enforce such a measure was Wigton, Cumbria, with a population of 6,000 (Lusher 2004).

Cohesion and Empowerment: Mobilizing "the Community"

Serious disturbances in some of the largest English northern towns in 2001 prompted a number of government reports examining their causes and policy implications, including a national level review commissioned by the UK Home Office and known as the Cantle Report, which introduced into public policy the concept of "community cohesion" (Cantle 2001). In many ways, cohesion could be seen as a suggested remedy, intended to repair some of the damage being inflicted by regeneration and renewal, although the report's findings added a further important dimension to the growing impression that all was not well in British communities:

> The team was particularly struck by the depth of polarisation of our towns and cities. The extent to which these physical divisions were compounded by so many other aspects of our daily lives was very evident. Separate educational arrangements, community and voluntary bodies, employment, places of worship, language, social and cultural networks mean that many communities operate on the basis of a series of parallel lives. These lives often do not seem to touch at any point, let alone overlap and promote any meaningful interchanges. . . .
>
> There is little wonder that the ignorance about each other's communities can easily grow into fear, especially where this is exploited by extremist groups determined to undermine community harmony and foster divisions. (Cantle 2001, 9)

The unstated premise behind this passage is that the key dividing lines now are those that arise between different ethnic and religious groupings: between the white majority and ethnic minorities, but also among the ethnic minorities themselves. The potential for such divisions is an element that has been added to British towns during the decades following the Second World War, as a result of substantial immigration from the former British Empire, which brought in new workers to fill jobs at the lower levels of the labour market, mostly in old industrial centres. When the emphasis shifted away from traditional industries, especially textiles and clothing, these workers suffered particularly badly.

Ethnic minority populations add a further element of variability to urban locations. Although they are concentrated mainly in the Midlands and, especially, London and the South East, they represent a significant percentage of the population in most regions of England (ONS 2012, 6–7). The *State of the English Cities* report noted that their overall share in the population decreased steadily in line with the size of places, in a clear urban-rural (and hence city-town-village) gradient (Parkinson et al. 2006, 52). At that time, the proportion of "non-white" residents in the cities varied from 27.4 percent in Bradford to 0.9 percent in Barnsley. The distribution of specific ethnic groups was also found to vary considerably, with one or two groups predominating in some cities whereas others had a more varied ethnic composition (53). Over time, minority individuals and families have spread out from their original areas of residence, so that some minority presence is now standard in most places.

Between 2006 and 2014, around 1.5 million EU nationals moved to Britain, the majority from the accession countries of Eastern Europe, with Poles surpassing Indians as the largest foreign-born community in Britain (ONS 2016, 7; see also Hawkins 2018). Many of these new migrants moved to places in which ethnic minority populations had not previously figured strongly, to work, for example, in food production and processing centres in relatively rural areas. According to an index of integration constructed by the think tank Policy Exchange (Goodhart and Norrie 2016), the least integrated places in Britain are either the old mill towns of Yorkshire and Lancashire, with large minorities of people of Pakistani heritage, or towns in eastern England that have experienced an influx from the European Union. Out of 160 towns and cities with a population of at least 20,000, Boston, in Lincolnshire, which has a particular concentration of Portuguese and eastern European residents, was ranked at the bottom, closely followed by nearby Wisbech and Spalding. Oldham, which lies in Greater Manchester, and Bradford, in West Yorkshire, were the other worst-performing towns (4–5). In 2016, anti-immigrant sentiment proved to be one of the strongest factors behind the British decision to leave the EU, and it was places like these that voted most enthusiastically for Brexit.

The disturbances that occurred in 2001 had a strong ethnic dimension, involving young South Asian (mostly Pakistani) men in confrontation with local white youths and the police. Understandably, then, the Cantle Report focused on issues related to the separation of ethnic "communities." It concluded that area-based regeneration initiatives often reinforced this separation, as well as fuelling resentment when it appeared that certain groups were receiving disproportionate support or that "funding was being provided to minority ethnic groups for what some white political leaders saw as being trivial or unnecessary purposes" (Cantle 2001, 17). Racism and Islamophobia were also seen as playing a part in bringing about social exclusion. "Community cohesion" was thus about helping such divided communities to develop "common goals and a shared vision" and thereby "mesh into an integrated whole" (70). Acting on the Cantle Report, the central government determined that each area should prepare a local community cohesion plan, to promote "cross-cultural contact between different communities at all levels, foster understanding and respect, and break down barriers" (Cantle 2001, 11). In 2006, the government convened the Commission on Integration and Cohesion (CIC), which amended the initial "one size fits all" national strategy to permit greater emphasis on particular places, neighbourhoods, and communities, thus enabling "a distinctively local focus" (McGhee 2008, 51).

In developing their plans, many local authorities broadened the range of cohesion to embrace differences of age, gender, and interest. A typical example was the town of Wrexham, in Wales, which had its own brush with intercommunal violence in "riots" between locals and Iraqi Kurd refugees in 2003. According to its Community Cohesion Strategy, Wrexham contains "a significant number of geographical communities and communities of interest" knitted together in a "complex array of community relationships" (Wrexham County Borough Council 2011, 1). The strategy seeks to foster community cohesion by providing "a measure of how well different communities develop and relate to each other":

> Our definition of cohesion describes the ability of all communities to
> function and grow in harmony together. It aims to build commun-
> ities where people feel confident that they belong and are comfortable
> mixing and interacting with others. . . . The process of integration
> is about helping positive relationships to develop between differ-
> ent groups and communities, towards a shared understanding and
> common values. (1)

As this quotation suggests, the development of the cohesion agenda involved a step forward in recognizing the reality of division and diversity in most modern British communities, regardless of their scale. McGhee (2008, 51) cites statements made by government ministers and officials responsible for the work of the CIC acknowledging the need to tackle "new elements" associated with "new and complex pictures of diversity in our local communities, reflecting globalisation and economic change" and to adapt policies that reflect the circumstances of local communities that are "each experiencing changes in a different way."[6] Nevertheless, an implicit sense lingers that with the right policy corrections and an appropriate local steer, it will be possible to return to something like the traditional version of a cohesive, integrated, and active local community. As members of the 2006 *State of the English Cities* research team conceded, however, the prospects for the successful implementation of such an agenda seem limited, owing to the "many ambiguities and differences in the way the terms social and community cohesion are interpreted and acted upon by different organisations. Although these concepts seem useful for involving diverse stakeholders in consensus building, there is a danger of glossing over dilemmas, differences and divisions with fairly meaningless generalities and innocuous objectives" (Turok et al. 2006, 281). Peter Somerville (2011) similarly warns that the notion of a "strong, cohesive, active community" that undergirds the community cohesion agenda "assumes the absence of an analysis of the problems and value conflicts that beset communities in Britain today: it alludes to those problems, but in such a way as to depoliticise them and turn them into problems of municipal management" (213).

Accentuating the Local

Despite very strong contemporary pressures conducive to making places more alike, often subsumed theoretically under the term *globalization,* many of the developments sketched above have had quite opposite effects: they introduce heightened possibilities for local variation, which works its way through the entire urban system. Thus, when discussing the small towns of rural Wales (of which there are more than eighty, with populations ranging between 1,000

6 "Ruth Kelly's Speech on Integration and Cohesion," *The Guardian,* 24 August 2006. Kelly delivered her remarks at the launch of the CIC.

and 17,000) Woods (2011, 162) comments that, like towns anywhere else, they are "dynamic places that have evolved over time and are continuing to develop according to the particular configurations of social, economic, political and environmental forces and resources found in each town." He adds that, as the rural population has become more mobile and more fluid in lifestyle and consumer choices, an ordering of functions has emerged that is not necessarily determined by population size or accessibility. Corinna Patterson (2011) illustrates this with a comparison between two Welsh market towns, seemingly alike in size and historic roles and both comparatively remote from large population centres. Despite their similarities, they appear to have become locked into greatly contrasting trajectories, one stagnating, if not in actual decline, and the other showing a capacity to innovate and develop, earning a reputation for forward-looking social and environmental change. The differences are due to a complex combination of the attitudes of local authorities, evolving social composition, and variations in cultural ethos and values, channelled by some key local actors. In the case of the more successful town, for instance, considerable leadership has been exercised by a group of incomers closely associated with a local centre for alternative technology. The other town appears to lack any equivalent dynamic focus.

In the past, governments might have considered it a priority to assist local authorities in levelling out these differences. Now, however, with a change in prevailing political ideologies and in the face of severe and growing fiscal pressures, the state has gradually been withdrawing its readiness and ability to do so. Under New Labour, this withdrawal involved a reduction in the level of central state support and a smaller role in people's lives for local government. There was, within the national government, a deep suspicion of the power of elected local members and, perhaps even more so, of appointed local officials, who were viewed as potentially obstructive, bureaucratic, and not sufficiently "on message" with the modernization agenda. According to Hazel Blears, who served as Secretary of State for Communities and Local Government from 2007 to 2009,

> we brought into government quite big prejudices against local author-
> ities across the field of policy. And in some ways quite rightly. Because
> some of them were rubbish. And you wouldn't have trusted them
> to wash the pots, let alone run a community. . . . What the Labour
> government did was, in its early days, create a series of parallel tracks
> almost to get round local authorities . . . whether that was in further

education, or housing, or the NHS foundation trusts—all that kind of thing. (Quoted in Jones 2011, 208)

On the one hand, New Labour continued the process of hollowing out the local state that Margaret Thatcher had begun. On the other hand, there was a rhetorical commitment to engage with and "empower" communities to take a more active role in shaping their own futures. This was exemplified in programs like the New Deal for Communities (and its Welsh parallel, Communities First) and the National Neighbourhood Renewal Strategy, both targeted at the most deprived neighbourhoods. After 2006, Local Strategic Partnerships were given a key role in formulating Local Area Agreements, which aimed at "joined up" working across different public services; the partnerships acted as forums in which key interests, including hard-to-reach groups and voluntary organizations, could be brought together (Hughes 2007, 17). As already noted, these developments ensured a substantially increased role in local decision making for business and the organized voluntary sector, but real participation that reached beyond this into the lives of "ordinary" citizens was often limited. The transfer of funding from the public sector towards support for private enterprise and voluntary effort made welfare for individuals and families increasingly conditional upon the effectiveness of the local economy (Eisenschitz 1997, 131): the provision of both public and private services tended to mirror local growth and affluence. Popularly, this is known as "the postcode lottery"—where you happen to live becomes decisive for opportunities and rewards—and, as Aram Eisenschitz notes, it enhances local discretion while undermining universal rights.

Despite the avowed ideological distance between the main political parties, there is a marked continuity between these tendencies and the "Big Society" strategy advocated by the former Conservative leader, David Cameron. The strategy, adopted by the (Conservative–Liberal) Coalition Government formed in 2010, was underpinned by core themes of localism, a diminishing role for the state, increased accountability, and greater individual responsibility (Lawless 2011). Stuart Hall (2011, 718) described the coalition as "saturated in neo-liberal ideas," a neoliberal machine working at full throttle. Among its core tenets was what Hall calls "the lure of 'localism'" (720). The 2011 Localism Act was intended to "replace the old, top-down systems of targets and central micromanagement" and to "turn government on its head, taking power away from Whitehall and putting it into the hands of people and communities" (United Kingdom, DCLG 2010a, 1). Allegedly, a smaller, rebalanced state would "improve people's lives, encourage innovation to flourish and draw people together in civic pride." Rewards and incentives will be deployed to "nudge people in the right direction" (2).

In this process, large sectors have been taken out of the sphere of local government control. There have been significant political battles around health, previously reorganized away from democratic local authority control into unelected local NHS trusts, and now operating through direct commissioning of services by medical practitioners themselves, with a steadily growing role for private sector providers (Matthews 2017), and education, with the creation of so-called academies and "free"—that is, deregulated but publicly funded—schools, both independent from local government supervision. Social housing, formerly a key local responsibility, had already been taken away by Conservative "right-to-buy" legislation in 1980. Now the planning system has been relaxed, with an imposed predisposition to approve new developments (qualified only by a vague test of "sustainability"), which favour developers and the construction industry. The new approach has been justified by claims that the planning process had allowed local government and "special interests" (like environmentalists and countryside campaigners) to act as a brake on necessary growth. Changes in the provision of social care and welfare have gone in the same direction, with a war waged on "benefit dependency." Some spectacular failures of social care have led to fierce political and media attacks on the capacity of local government to take responsibility for, and to administer, social programs, while the delivery of services and benefits is increasingly entrusted to an ever-expanding assortment of private providers and "social entrepreneurs," with the recipients cast as "customers" and "clients."

In the name of empowerment and community involvement, these developments shift power away from the authority of elected representatives and public officialdom towards particular sectional groups and interests, such as parents, faith communities, and (largely self-selected) voluntary associations. Those groups, or "communities," that are able to mobilize the loudest voices and command the greatest resources are privileged, while the weak and vulnerable are left out. A dreadful confirmation of this conclusion was provided by the Grenfell Tower disaster in June 2017, in which a twenty-four-storey housing unit was destroyed by fire and scores of poor people lost their lives. Residents of the public housing block had been warning of serious safety hazards for years, but their voices had been ignored. The ensuing public controversy laid bare the gross disparities of wealth and power and the severe spatial inequalities existing within one of the richest of London boroughs, Kensington and Chelsea.

Reflecting on the earlier New Deal for Communities program, Lawless (2011, 60) notes a predictable finding: an overrepresentation of the views of older, white, employed, more "middle-class," and better educated sections of the community. Furthermore, and more fundamentally, the program raised questions as to whether, in a society so thoroughly divided by differences of occupation, interest, and social stratification, it was actually possible to define "communities of place"—that is, to make any assumptions about how local opinion would coalesce around a shared location. He suggests that, if it is possible to define them at all, then such communities would not exist even at the modest scale of 10,000 people: a consistent message emerged from the program that such a number was "simply too big" to make sense to residents themselves (58).

Conclusion

In justifying its "localism" strategy, the UK Coalition government contended that it was keen to disperse power away from the centre and eager to see communities take charge of their own fates. Rather than resulting in an unfair "postcode" lottery,

> decentralisation will allow different communities to do different things in different ways to meet their different needs. This will certainly increase variety in service provision. But far from being random—as the word "lottery" implies—such variation will reflect the conscious choices made by local people. The real lottery is what we have now, where one-size-fits-all policies are imposed by the centre whether or not they work locally. (United Kingdom, DCLG 2010b, 5)

This shift of responsibility to the local level has been speeded up significantly by pressures to cut the public deficit and make major reductions in the costs of the public sector—the "austerity" imperative brought about by the financial crash of 2008, which has bitten deeply into local authority budgets. The end result has been further fragmentation and complication in the provision of services and resources, as well as an additional loss of coherence in the framework of urban governance, as an increasingly mixed bag of agents and interests are brought into the process. This fragmentation continues a pattern of urban disintegration that has been going on in the United Kingdom for decades. The changes assist some local people (and many others who are not at all local) to secure the ascendancy of their views over those of others, and help to perpetuate the relationships of inclusion, marginalization, and exclusion which ensure that few places, no matter what their size, can truly be represented as homogeneous or "cohesive" communities.

As we have seen, the evidence base in relation to Britain's large towns and small cities tends to be lacking; they form something of a "missing middle" between the very large metropolitan centres and the more "homely" small towns and villages. They are subjected to many, if not all, of the same pressures that affect the core urban centres—albeit, with respect to policy decisions and interventions, more often as an afterthought to intentions and purposes directed elsewhere. However, despite the encroachment of cultural and material sameness, often characterised simply as "globalization," there are many continuing social and economic processes which serve to encourage differentiation and diversity among smaller urban centres, enough to guarantee that they will continue to react in their own distinct and interesting ways.

References

Bell, David, and Mark Jayne, eds. 2006. *Small Cities: Urban Experience Beyond the Metropolis*. London and New York: Routledge.

Bell, Michael Mayerfeld. 1994. *Childerley: Nature and Morality in a Country Village*. London: University of Chicago Press.

Birch, Anthony. 1959. *Small-Town Politics: A Study of Political Life in Glossop*. Oxford: Oxford University Press.

British Chambers of Commerce. 2007. *A Tale of the Cities: The Best of Times?* London: British Chambers of Commerce.

Buck, Nick, Ian Gordon, Peter Hall, Michael Harloe, and Mark Kleinman. 2002. *Working Capital: Life and Labour in Contemporary London*. London and New York: Routledge.

Buck, Nick, Ian Gordon, Alan Harding, and Ivan Turok, eds. 2005. *Changing Cities: Rethinking Urban Competitiveness, Cohesion, and Governance*. London: Palgrave Macmillan.

Burns, Richard. 1991. "The City as Not London." In *Whose Cities?* edited by Mark Fisher and Ursula Owen, 62–70. London: Penguin.

Cantle, Ted. 2001. *Community Cohesion: A Report of the Independent Review Team.* London: Government of the UK, Home Office.

Charlesworth, Julie, and Allan Cochrane. 1997. "Anglicising the American Dream: Tragedy, Farce, and the 'Postmodern' City." In Westwood and Williams, *Imagining Cities*, 219–32.

Charlesworth, Simon J. 2000. *A Phenomenology of Working Class Experience.* Cambridge, UK: Cambridge University Press.

CIC (Commission on Integration and Cohesion). 2007. *Our Interim Statement.* Wetherby, UK: Commission on Integration and Cohesion.

Cohen, Anthony P., ed. 1982. *Belonging: Identity and Social Organisation in British Rural Cultures.* Manchester: Manchester University Press.

Cooke, Philip, ed. 1989. *Localities: The Changing Face of Urban Britain.* London: Unwin Hyman.

Day, Graham, and Jonathan Murdoch. 1993. "Locality and Community: Coming to Terms with Place." *Sociological Review* 41 (1): 82–111.

Eisenschitz, Aram. 1997. "The View from the Grassroots." In Pacione, *Britain's Cities*, 150–76.

Elias, Norbert, and John L. Scotson. 1965. *The Established and the Outsiders.* London: Frank Cass.

Freud, Sigmund. 1930. *Civilization and Its Discontents.* London: Hogarth Press.

Gerrard, Graeme, and Richard Thompson. 2011. "Two Million Cameras in the UK." *CCTV Image* 42 (Winter): 10–12. http://www.securitynewsdesk.com/wp-content/uploads/2011/03/CCTV-Image-42-How-many-cameras-are-there-in-the-UK.pdf.

Goodhart, David, and Richard Norrie. 2016. *Integration Index.* London: Policy Exchange. https://policyexchange.org.uk/wp-content/uploads/2016/09/integration-index.pdf.

Graham Stephen, John Brooks, and Dan Heery. 1995. "Towns on Television: Closed Circuit TV Surveillance in British Towns and Cities." Electronic Working Paper no. 17. Centre for Urban Technology, University of Newcastle upon Tyne.

Hall, Stuart. 2011. "The Neo-liberal Revolution." *Cultural Studies* 25: 705–28.

Hanson, Steve. 2014. *Small Towns, Austere Times: The Dialectics of Deracinated Localism.* Winchester, UK: Zero Books.

Harloe, Michael, Chris Pickvance, and John Urry, eds. 1989. *Place, Policy, and Politics: Do Localities Matter?* London: Unwin Hyman.

Harris, John. 2011. "Supermarket Sweep." *Guardian Weekend,* 6 August.

Hawkins, Oliver. 2018. *Migration Statistics.* Briefing Paper no. SN06077. London: House of Commons Library.

Hooper, Duncan. 2007. "Top 10 British Towns for 'Affordable Affluence.'" *The Telegraph,* 3 September.

Hughes, Gordon. 2007. *The Politics of Crime and Community.* Basingstoke, UK: Palgrave Macmillan.

Jones, Owen. 2011. *Chavs: The Demonization of the Working Class.* London: Verso.

Lawless, Paul. 2011. "Big Society and Community: Lessons from the 1998–2011 New Deal for Communities Programme in England." *People, Place and Policy Online* 5 (2): 55–64.

Leunig, Tim, and James Swaffield. 2007. *Cities Limited.* London: Policy Exchange.

Lewis, Paul. 2011. "You're Being Watched: There's One CCTV Camera for Every 32 People in UK." *The Guardian,* 2 March.

Lewis, Paul, Tim Newburn, Matthew Taylor, Catriona Mcgillivray, Aster Greenhill, Harold Frayman, and Rob Proctor. 2011. *Reading the Riots: Investigating England's Summer of Disorder.* London: London School of Economics and Political Science and *The Guardian.*

Lovering, John. 1997. "Global Restructuring and Local Impact." In Pacione, *Britain's Cities,* 63–87.

Lusher, Adam. 2004. "The Clock Struck 9pm, the Curfew Started But Still the Teenagers Taunted the Police." *The Telegraph,* 4 April.

Matthews, David. 2017. "The Battle for the National Health Service: England, Wales, and the Socialist Vision." *Monthly Review* 68 (10): 25–35.

McGhee, Derek. 2008. "A Past Built on Difference, a Future Which Is Shared: A Critical Examination of the Recommendations Made by the Commission on Integration and Community Cohesion." *People, Place and Policy Online* 2 (2): 48–64.

Moore, Robert. 1982. *The Social Impact of Oil: The Case of Peterhead.* London: Routledge and Kegan Paul.

NEF (New Economics Foundation). 2010. *Re-imagining the High Street: Escape from Clone Town Britain.* London: New Economics Foundation.

O'Byrne, Darren. 1997. "Working-Class Culture: Local Community and Global Conditions." In *Living the Global City: Globalization as a Local Process,* edited by John Eade, 73–89. London and New York: Routledge.

ONS (Office of National Statistics). 2012. *Ethnicity and National Identity in England and Wales: 2011.* Release date: 11 December 2012. London: Office of National Statistics.

———. 2016. *Population of the UK by Country of Birth and Nationality: 2015.* Release date: 25 August 2016. London: Office of National Statistics.

Pacione, Michael, ed. 1997. *Britain's Cities: Geographies of Division in Urban Britain.* London and New York: Routledge.

Parkinson, Michael, Tony Champion, Richard Evans, James Simmie, Ivan Turok, Martin Crookston, Bruce Katz, Alison Park, Alan Berube, Mike Coombes et al.

2006. *State of the English Cities: A Research Study*. London: Government of the UK, Office of the Deputy Prime Minister.

Patterson, Corinna. 2011. "Wales in a Global Neighbourhood: The Impact of Globalization on Two Welsh Market Towns." *Contemporary Wales* 24 (1): 86–112.

Plowman D. E. G., W. E. Minchinton, and Margaret Stacey. 1961. "Local Social Status in England and Wales." *Sociological Review* 10 (2): 161–202.

Power, Anne, Jörg Plöger, and Astrid Winkler. 2007. *Transforming Cities Across Europe: An Interim Report on Problems and Progress*. CASE Report 49. London: London School of Economics, Centre for Analysis of Social Exclusion.

Rapport, Nigel. 1993. *Diverse World-Views in an English Village*. Edinburgh: Edinburgh University Press.

Somerville, Peter. 2011. *Understanding Community: Politics, Policy, and Practice*. Bristol: Policy Press.

Stacey, Margaret. 1960. *Tradition and Change: A Study of Banbury*. Oxford: Oxford University Press.

Stacey, Margaret, Eric Batstone, Colin Bell, and Anne Murcott. 1975. *Power, Persistence, and Change: A Second Study of Banbury*. London: Routledge and Kegan Paul.

Taylor, Ian, Karen Evans, and Penny Fraser. 1996. *A Tale of Two Cities: A Study in Manchester and Sheffield*. London and New York: Routledge.

Theodore, Nik, Jamie Peck, and Neil Brenner. 2011. "Neoliberal Urbanism: Cities and the Rule of Markets." In *The New Blackwell Companion to the City*, edited by Gary Bridge and Sophie Watson, 15–25. Oxford: Wiley-Blackwell.

Turok, Ivan, Ade Kearns, Dave Fitch, John Flint, Carol McKenzie, and Joanne Abbotts. 2006. *State of the English Cities: Social Cohesion*. London: Government of the UK, Department for Communities and Local Governance.

United Kingdom. DCLG (Department for Communities and Local Government). 2010a. *Draft Structural Reform Plan*. London: Government of the UK, Department for Communities and Local Government.

———. 2010b. *Decentralisation and the Localism Bill: An Essential Guide*. London: Government of the UK, Department for Communities and Local Government.

Webber, Chris, and Paul Swinney. 2010. *Private Sector Cities: A New Geography of Opportunity*. London: Centre for Cities.

Webber, Melvin M. 1964. "The Urban Place and the Nonplace Urban Realm." In *Explorations into Urban Structure*, edited by Melvin M. Webber, 79–153. Philadelphia: University of Pennsylvania Press.

Westwood, Sallie, and John Williams, eds. 1997. *Imagining Cities: Scripts, Signs, Memory*. London and New York: Routledge.

Williams, Raymond. 1973. *The Country and the City*. London: Chatto and Windus.

Wilson, Elizabeth. 1997. "Nostalgia and the City." In Westward and Williams, *Imagining Cities*, 127–39.

Woods, Michael. 2011. "Market Towns in Rural Wales: A Differentiated Geography." In *Rural Wales in the Twenty-First Century: Society, Economy and Environment*, edited by Paul Milbourne, 149–68. Cardiff: University of Wales Press.

Wrexham County Borough Council. 2011. *One Wrexham: Community Cohesion Strategy, 2011–14*. Wrexham, Wales: Wrexham County Borough Council. http://www.wrexham.gov.uk/assets/pdfs/community_cohesion/strategy_2011_2014.pdf.

Conclusion
The Way Forward

Far from constituting the idyllic imagined communities of yesteryear, today's small city is the site of serious inequities and social tensions. While these problems have been fuelled by various factors, including the decline of traditional industries and racist responses to an increasingly multiethnic environment, they are the consequence, most fundamentally, of the globalization of capital and the application of neoliberal principles of economic and social governance. Not only have these forces generated growing poverty and homelessness, they have also created an atmosphere of competition for increasingly scarce resources, circumstances that foster mutual suspicion and, at times, xenophobia. The result has been a process of social fragmentation, in which the phenomenon of othering is amply evident. In this collection, we have sought to describe the experience of the small city from the perspective of those constructed as outsiders by dominant groups—groups whose understanding of community tends to be unforgiving of difference. At the same time, we have discussed ideas and practical approaches that emphasize inclusion and equity.

As the discussions in the first part of this book reveal, certain residents of small cities are routinely forced to endure expressions of hostility directed at them by other residents. This hostility is manifest not only in individual actions but also in the willingness on the part of both local government and more privileged groups to brand the less fortunate as a threat to their own safety and prosperity. The spatial layout of the small city—in which well-established residential areas often lie in close proximity to contested urban spaces—contributes to the virulence of the backlash against those deemed to be disruptive of social harmony. When those who feel a sense of ownership of public space daily collide with panhandlers, sex workers, and drug users or simply with homeless people pushing shopping carts, intense expressions of anger and moral outrage typically result. This public outrage can lead to vigilantism, but it also prompts civic policies aimed at "cleaning up" downtown cores and relatively upscale neighbourhoods. Such policies are especially appealing to municipal government when, as is often the case, the small city is seeking to market its uniqueness, attract new investments, and perhaps promote itself as a tourist destination.

These perceived challenges to the social order generate the most visible exercise of local power. Local responses to the presence of "undesirables" generally consist of more aggressive policing, coupled with new legislation. Whether implemented by police, bylaw officers, or other civic officials, these policies generally rest on the three Ds: denial, discomfort, and dispersal. The first is principally a response of neglect, one that involves the refusal to recognize the rights and needs of the socially marginalized. The second and third comprise practices such as the imposition of curfews in parks; prohibitions against camping; the aggressive enforcement of laws prohibiting panhandling and squeegee activity; charges of theft for the appropriation of shopping carts; the physical removal of sex workers, addicts, and other unwanted elements from public spaces now defined as "red zones"; and the rigorous patrolling of parks and alleyways to keep "suspect" residents on the move. Because they are founded on exclusion, these practices intensify the fault lines between the city's dominant social classes, who implicitly claim the right to shape the community in their own image, and those relegated to the position of outsiders.

Perhaps the most egregious strategy of exclusion employed by local governments is "red zoning," a tactic that originally targeted sex workers. The creation of "no-go" zones is fundamentally a strategy of dispersal, aimed at the physical removal of such workers—who, in smaller cities, are overwhelmingly female—from specified public spaces. This tactic of dispersal is generally accompanied by a widespread denial that women engaged in the sex trade are at risk, with respect to both their physical safety and their psychological and social well-being, and are therefore deserving of protection. This attack on sex workers reflects the strong gender bias that exists in connection with social supports. Men predominate among the visibly homeless, and their situation is often linked to a lack of adequate mental health care and/or to substance abuse. As a result, men have been the recipients of many social programs. In contrast, women without children are more often found among the hidden homeless, and significantly fewer front-line resources exist to address their health and safety needs—whether these be emergency shelters or second-stage transitional housing. Although the situation is changing, traditional gender attitudes and inequities have a tenacious presence in small cities.

This tendency towards social conservatism is also evident in attitudes towards ethnicity and race. Canada officially embraces a philosophy of multiculturalism, and Canadians often pride themselves on what they perceive as the absence of racism in this country. We are quick to point out that, for the most part, major Canadian cities do not feature the racialized enclaves that exist in many large cities in Britain and the United States, nor have they generally been home to race riots. But, to exist, racism need not take on such overt forms as police shootings or lynchings; it can also be "polite, denied, and accepted" (Brown 1989, 25) and hence much more insidious. Quite apart from the appalling treatment meted out to Indigenous peoples in the past, we need only to look at the present-day situation of First Nations, many of whom now reside on reserves adjacent to our small cities. The ongoing exclusion of the Indigenous population from the Canadian community is reflected in the parallel existence of local governments—band councils and municipal councils—that have vastly different resource opportunities, taxation mechanisms, and powers. "Separate but unequal" thereby becomes the hallmark of Indigenous and non-Indigenous communities living side by side—whether the issue is water treatment, housing, schools, or public transit. The division of jurisdictional responsibilities between federal and provincial governments contributes to this estrangement, in part by creating legal and administrative obstacles to developing common goals within a common region. Regardless of constitutional arrangements, an urgent need exists for more equitable and collaborative planning processes.

The process of othering so fundamental to racism extends, of course, to visible minorities, including newly arrived Canadians who choose to settle in small cities, and are not necessarily warmly received. But othering is also evident with regard to "invisible" minorities. To protect themselves from stereotyping, stigmatization, and discrimination, LGBTQ people living in small cities have often found it necessary to hide their sexual orientation. Experience has taught them that it is not safe to reveal themselves in certain settings. Parolees are in a similar position. Not only is their history of incarceration a huge liability with regard to possibilities for employment, but it also severely limits their hopes for social acceptance. The intensity of the pressure felt by individuals to conceal certain aspects of their identity is a barometer of the strength of a community's investment in othering as the basis for self-definition and as a mechanism for maintaining social dominance. Put conversely, the intensity of this pressure is a measure of the community's willingness to tolerate diversity. Younger people, who have been raised in a global world, seem on the whole to be more accustomed to, and thus more accepting of, differences in race and culture. Small cities that deliberately embrace diversity may thus find they easily attract a youthful demographic.

The social issues confronting small cities today are, in short, numerous, complex, and difficult to resolve, inasmuch as they are rooted in deeper and more pervasive problems: systemic poverty, unemployment and precarious employment, racism and other discriminatory attitudes, and gendered forms of oppression that flow from a patriarchal and heteronormative world view. In attempting to formulate equitable solutions, local governments must contend with constraints imposed from within the community, including the prevalence of NIMBYism, reactionary community values that uphold a narrow definition of acceptable and unacceptable behaviour, and support for punitive approaches founded on legal sanctions and stricter law enforcement. Local governments are, moreover, often engaging with social issues for the first time. Their resources are limited, and they may lack the bureaucratic structures and personnel required to cope with these new challenges. In addition, they must operate in the face of senior levels of government that not only continue to offload responsibilities onto them but also circumscribe, both legally and financially, the possibilities for civic action and reform.

The question thus remains of how, in the face of the economic and social consequences of neoliberalism, small cities can succeed in building a sense of community based on the ideals of acceptance, accommodation, and inclusion. In spite of the above constraints, new voices are proposing alternative ways to manage this social complexity, with an emphasis on non-punitive methods. Increased collaboration exists among local health care and social work professionals, nonprofit organizations, and local government, which has resulted in more inclusive and participatory approaches to community planning. These collaborative efforts build upon "small town" qualities of cooperation and community solidarity that now coexist with the increased institutional and occupational diversity of the small city. Through the participation of a wide spectrum of community members, the ongoing negotiation of differences in the planning process, and the building of complex partnerships, the small city can encourage mutual understanding and work towards building community cohesion.

At the heart of this process is a local government that accepts a social agenda as part of its responsibilities. One concrete expression of this acceptance is the existence of a civic social plan. Another is the creation of a formal position of social planner or community developer within local government, with a mandate to implement inclusive approaches to civic planning. Both suggest that local government is not only recognizing and assuming responsibility for a broader range of citizen needs than before but is also incrementally extending its authority in order to promote the development of healthier and more supportive communities. From a practical political perspective, these initiatives increase the likelihood of leveraging financial resources from higher levels of government while at the same time strengthening the work of many local community groups.

In order to build community, local governments will need to take an activist stance with respect both to their own citizens and to senior levels of government. Moving citizens from a state of denial to one in which they recognize the needs of others demands awareness building and education. The pursuit of a social agenda also obliges local government to become involved in planning and programming in areas where it may lack experience, capacity, and adequate resources. Most significant, then, is the need for a more active form of leadership than in the past, one characterized by visible and vocal advocacy on the part of the mayor, city council, and senior civic employees. Building inclusive local communities demands leaders who are able to gain buy-in from citizens who might otherwise resist progressive initiatives. But it also requires substantial financial commitments from both the federal and provincial governments. Funding is needed to provide housing, income supports, mental health and addiction services, and resources for child care, as well as anti-racist, anti-sexist, and anti-homophobic education programs, and securing such funding again presupposes active civic leadership.

In Canada, as in Britain, official government concern exists for the "health of communities," and yet small cities have often found themselves left to the vagaries of the global economy, with its winners and losers. Those fortunate enough to have highly marketable resources do well, while others go into decline. In the Canadian tradition, they end life as ghost towns. In addition, as small-city governments begin to advocate more insistently for assistance from higher levels of government, senior government may be apt to respond inconsistently, adopting a sort of "squeaky wheel gets the grease" approach and thereby allowing disparities to develop in the distribution of funding and services among equally deserving communities. Ruling out this possibility will demand a commitment to egalitarianism on the part of senior levels of government, whose duty it is to ensure the fair and equitable distribution of resources.

Although the future of small cities is by no means guaranteed, our collection suggests that their full potential has yet to be realized. Municipal efforts to retain and attract investment are now widespread, but civic efforts must go beyond "rebranding" and offering incentives to new businesses. Local governments must also find ways to address the needs of those citizens who have been disadvantaged by broader economic restructuring. In our view, cross-sectoral initiatives and engagement with a broad array of community groups offer the best means to respond to unemployment and other local effects of economic dislocation. This approach seems to us better suited to the concerns of small cities than the focus on "creative clusters" inspired by the research of Richard Florida. By establishing links among local government, businesses, and universities, clusters seek to attract and retain young, educated entrepreneurs and foster a local "creative class," which has been touted as the new engine of economic growth. With its focus on securing new business investments, however, this model can end up leaving many citizens behind.

Instead, we favour a model of cross-sectoral collaboration founded on the active participation of citizens from all walks of life. This approach goes beyond the notion of a "creative class" to encompass a broad cross-section of individuals, institutions, and community groups who collaborate to address the economic insecurities of the region, which then become the basis for the creation of local economic opportunities. Entrepreneurialism is broadened to include social enterprises developed with the cooperation of nonprofit groups, businesses, universities, and government to open the door to stable employment and a living wage for the community's marginalized citizens. Forging a community depends in part on creating new avenues to employment in the face of national and global economic change.

If smaller cities are able to offer employment opportunities and lower costs of living, they will draw new residents. For the small city to become a destination for recently arrived immigrants, however, the element of truth in the perception that small-city communities are predominantly white, exclusionary, and unaccommodating to newcomers needs to be challenged through education, policy, and, above all, practice. Whereas larger cities are known for their pattern of ghettoization, a much deeper engagement between well-established Canadians and recent immigrants is, in theory, possible in the context of a small city. Realizing this potential for a richer quality of cosmopolitanism than is generally available in our largest urban centres will require a commitment on the part of civic leaders to dispelling the ignorance and fear that fuel prejudice. Small cities seeking to become more economically secure and resilient must make good on their claim to be safe and welcoming places for all to live.

In short, local governments need to be socially engaged. Such engagement generates community awareness and opens opportunities not only to solicit additional funding from higher levels of government but also to advocate for legislative change. In the meanwhile, local governments can work quite inexpensively to promote a stronger, more concrete sense of community simply by engaging in an inclusive and participatory approach to civic planning. Small cities need to recognize the diversity that exists within their boundaries, and local government can lead the way by allowing the voices of the Other—addicts, sex workers, parolees, First Nations, the homeless, and so on—to be heard at city hall. But the marginalized also need to sit at the planning table. Community attitudes towards homelessness and addiction have changed as a result of participatory planning, and this success can be extended to other marginalized groups in the city.

Citizens have long looked to local government for concrete material benefits, but with small cities now facing serious pressures, progressive councillors and civic staff have the opportunity to start a dialogue about the social dimension of community life. Marginalized and unrepresented citizens cannot simply be left out in the cold, subject to the shifting winds of the local political will. The capacity for local social innovation and the equitable treatment of all citizens are, after all, foundational principles of Canadian community life. Canada's small cities have been dealt a hard blow by the combination of neo-liberalism and the global economy. But it need not be a crippling blow. With the return of the Liberals to power in October 2015, are we finally emerging from the lengthy period in which senior levels of government abandoned the sense of compassion and fairness so long associated with Canada? If so, we would do well to seize the moment. Local governments and concerned citizens need to deliver a clear message to Ottawa that it is time to restore a measure of truth to the country's self-image. Perhaps this, in turn, will prompt those in Ottawa to develop national benchmarks for the "healthy community" and to provide the support necessary to create such communities.

Reference

Brown, Rosemary. 1989. *Being Brown: A Very Public Life*. Toronto: Random House.

Contributors

Lorry-Ann Austin is a sessional lecturer at Thompson Rivers University, where she teaches courses in social welfare, social work practice, and human development, as well as a clinical social worker with the Interior Health Authority. Prior to earning her MSW from the University of British Columbia, she worked for a decade as a television and radio news reporter based in Kamloops.

Jacques Caillouette is a professor in the School of Social Work at the Université de Sherbrooke, where his teaching focuses on community organization and social movements. His research interests include collaborative research methodologies, community development, interculturalism, and the political construction of an unified sense of regional identity. As a long-standing member of the Centre for Research on Social Innovations (Centre de recherche sur les innovations sociales, CRISES), he is closely involved with the work of its Policy and Social Practices section, in particular.

Graham Day is emeritus reader in sociology at Bangor University, in Wales. A specialist in the sociology of Wales and in community and rural sociology, he is the author of *Making Sense of Wales* (2002), *Theorizing Nationalism* (with Andrew Thompson) (2004), and *Community and Everyday Life* (2006), among other publications. In addition to his academic research and writing, Day has been extensively involved with projects in rural development and participatory democracy. Along with colleagues at Bangor, he has been a participating member of EuroIdentities, a multinational EU research project that employs biographical narratives to study the evolution of European identity.

Robert Harding is an associate professor in the School of Social Work and Human Services at the University of the Fraser Valley, in British Columbia. After working in child welfare in Manitoba and Québec, he relocated to

Aotearoa in 1989, where he served as a community development consultant and policy advisor in the public health system. Upon returning to Canada, he guided the University of the Fraser Valley in partnering with the Stó:lō Nation to develop an Indigenous social services diploma program based on traditional principles of healing and helping. His research, which has appeared in numerous publications, focuses on discourse about social policy, poverty, and Indigenous self-governance issues.

Wendy Hulko is an associate professor in the Faculty of Education and Social Work at Thompson Rivers University in Kamloops, BC. She holds degrees in sociology and Spanish (BA), social work (MSW), and sociology and social policy (PhD) and has worked in the field of aging for over twenty years, in areas such as residential care nursing, hospital social work, and government policy. She conducts research on aging and health in collaboration with equity-seeking groups, including First Nation Elders, older women, queer youth, and rural residents, and has published widely. In 2016, Hulko was awarded the TRU Excellence in Scholarship Award in recognition of her research accomplishments.

Paul Jenkinson is a social worker and activist with extensive experience in the area of child welfare in British Columbia. His interest in systemic solutions to poverty issues in small-city contexts has been informed by the lived struggles of families, single mothers, the elderly, and those with addictions and mental health challenges. A registered social worker, he holds an MSW from the University of British Columbia and has been invited to lecture in social work programs throughout the province. He has also served on the board of the British Columbia Association of Social Workers and was for five years the chair of its Child Welfare and Family Committee.

Terry Kading is an associate professor of political science at Thompson Rivers University, where he teaches courses in Canadian politics, comparative politics, and local government. The editor of *No Straight Lines: Local Leadership and the Path from Government to Governance in Small Cites* (2018), he is also involved in several community-based research projects with a focus on social and economic challenges in the small city.

Sharnelle Matthew is the mental health clinician for six Secwepemc communities. She has worked as a counsellor in Secwepemc territory since 2001, serving Aboriginal people both on and off reserve. A registered social worker and a registered clinical counsellor, she holds an MSW from the University of British Columbia and was a sessional instructor at Thompson Rivers University from 2010 to 2013. She is from the Simpcw First Nation, where she has lived her whole life, and enjoys being connected with her family and community.

Kathie McKinnon has been the supervisor of the Wellness Team at Secwepemc Child and Family Services in Kamloops, BC, since 2008 and has taught social work as a sessional instructor at Thompson Rivers University since 2010, in addition to maintaining a private practice. A registered social worker and a registered clinical counsellor, she has an MSW from Memorial University and a PhD in psychology from the Vrije Universiteit Brussel. Her dissertation, "Intertwining Hope, Strengths, and Resistance as Transformative: Women's Verbal and Visual Narratives," focuses on the stories and art created by nine co-inquirers and on how their conversations, deeply experiential and rich in meaning, illuminate the importance of storytelling in therapeutic practice and suggest new ways of relationally being-with in therapeutic space.

Jennifer Murphy is the former chair of the School of Social Work and Human Service at Thompson Rivers University in Kamloops, BC. Her research interests include critical criminology, narrative analysis, and critical social work pedagogy. Her social work practice was mainly in the field of mediation, as a family justice counsellor, helping separated families to develop a parenting plan for their children. In her research, she employs qualitative methods to explore the reintegration of former prisoners into the community upon release from federal penitentiaries. Both her master's and doctoral work involved interviewing men and women on parole to gain an understanding of the challenges they faced and how they navigated through a myriad of barriers towards reintegration, with her dissertation concerned, in particular, with desistance rather than recidivism.

Diane Purvey is dean of the Faculty of Arts at Kwantlen Polytechnic University, in Surrey, BC. Her research focuses on alternatives to prescriptive norms, particularly in the context of institutions, including restorative justice practices in elementary schools and the history of deinstitutionalization of mental health clients in British Columbia. She is the co-author (with John Belshaw) of *Vancouver Noir, 1930–1960* (2011) and of *Private Grief, Public Mourning: The Rise of the Roadside Shrine in British Columbia* (2009), as well as the co-editor (with Christopher Walmsley) of *Child and Family Welfare in British Columbia: A History* (2005). A longtime resident of Vancouver's Downtown Eastside, Purvey has worked at the Carnegie Community Centre, has volunteered with food banks, and has collaborated with residents' associations to create more inclusive communities.

Mónica J. Sánchez-Flores is an assistant professor in the Department of Sociology and Anthropology at Thompson Rivers University, Kamloops, BC. She holds a PhD in sociology and a master's degree in social and political theory, both from the University of Edinburgh. Her research focuses on the social construction of the concept of race, the role of mindfulness and complex identities in equity, diversity, and inclusion training, the settlement experience of immigrants, as well as on sociological theory, multiculturalism, and cosmopolitanism. She has taught in a variety of disciplines (politics, sociology and social theory, literature, history) in Mexico, India, and Canada since 2000 and is the author of *Political Philosophy for the Global Age* (2005) and *Cosmopolitan Liberalism: Expanding the Boundaries of the Individual* (2010).

Christopher Walmsley is professor emeritus at Thompson Rivers University. He taught social work for over twenty-five years at Thompson Rivers University, the University of Manitoba, and the University of British Columbia. He is the author of *Protecting Aboriginal Children* (2005) and the co-editor (with Diane Purvey) of *Child and Family Welfare in British Columbia: A History* (2005). He has also published numerous articles and reports on fathers and child welfare. He lives in New Westminster, BC.

Sydney Weaver holds an MSW and a PhD in social work from the University of British Columbia and has worked in child welfare and addictions services for many years, in clinical practice as well as in policy analysis, research, and teaching. Her research focuses on the critical analysis of health and social services and policy in relation to substance-using marginalized peoples, with a view to improving outcomes for families. On the premise that social work should be transformative, she adopts an intersectional, decolonizing approach that aims to further social justice and has developed and conducted training for social workers in best practices with substance-using parents. She currently works with the Heatley Community Health Centre, in Vancouver's Downtown Eastside, as well as in private practice.